Abnormal Psychology in Context

The Australian and New Zealand Handbook

Abnormal Psychology in Context is a practical and contemporary handbook for both students of abnormal psychology and allied mental health practitioners. This text is one of the first of its kind, providing a specific focus on abnormal psychology from Australian and New Zealand – rather than US – perspectives. Nadine Pelling and Lorelle Burton have crafted a highly relevant resource, showcasing the most recent Australasian research in a clear format designed for ease of use.

Written by leading researchers from Australia and New Zealand, each chapter examines a particular psychological disorder, details symptoms and responses, and includes relevant statistics, case studies, further reading, and links to community resources. The chapters give equal weight to Australian and New Zealand experiences in abnormal psychology matters.

Succinctly written yet richly detailed, *Abnormal Psychology in Context* is an essential resource that students can carry from the classroom into the workplace.

Additional resources for instructors are available online at www.cambridge.edu.au/academic/abnormalpsychanz.

Nadine J Pelling is a Fellow of the Australian Counselling Association and Senior Lecturer in Clinical Psychology and Counselling in the School of Psychology, Social Work and Social Policy at the University of South Australia.

Lorelle J Burton is Professor of Psychology in the School of Psychology and Counselling at the University of Southern Queensland.

ABNORMAL PSYCHOLOGY IN CONTEXT

THE AUSTRALIAN AND NEW ZEALAND HANDBOOK

Edited by

Nadine Pelling and
Lorelle Burton

CAMBRIDGE
UNIVERSITY PRESS

University Printing House, Cambridge CB2 8BS, United Kingdom

One Liberty Plaza, 20th Floor, New York, NY 10006, USA

477 Williamstown Road, Port Melbourne, VIC 3207, Australia

314-321, 3rd Floor, Plot 3, Splendor Forum, Jasola District Centre, New Delhi - 110025, India

103 Penang Road, #05-06/07, Visioncrest Commercial, Singapore 238467

Cambridge University Press is part of the University of Cambridge.

It furthers the University's mission by disseminating knowledge in the pursuit of education, learning and research at the highest international levels of excellence.

www.cambridge.org
Information on this title: www.cambridge.org/9781107499775

© Cambridge University Press 2017

This publication is in copyright. Subject to statutory exception and to the provisions of relevant collective licensing agreements, no reproduction of any part may take place without the written permission of Cambridge University Press.

First published 2017

Cover designed by eggplant communications

A Cataloguing-in-Publication entry is available from the catalogue of the National Library of Australia at www.nla.gov.au

ISBN 978-1-107-49977-5 Paperback

Additional resources for this publication at www.cambridge.edu.au/academic/abnormalpsychanz.

Reproduction and communication for educational purposes
The Australian *Copyright Act 1968* (the Act) allows a maximum of one chapter or 10% of the pages of this work, whichever is the greater, to be reproduced and/or communicated by any educational institution for its educational purposes provided that the educational institution (or the body that administers it) has given a remuneration notice to Copyright Agency Limited (CAL) under the Act.

For details of the CAL licence for educational institutions contact:

Copyright Agency Limited
Level 15, 233 Castlereagh Street
Sydney NSW 2000
Telephone: (02) 9394 7600
Facsimile: (02) 9394 7601
E-mail: info@copyright.com.au

Reproduction and communication for other purposes
Except as permitted under the Act (for example a fair dealing for the purposes of study, research, criticism or review) no part of this publication may be reproduced, stored in a retrieval system, communicated or transmitted in any form or by any means without prior written permission. All inquiries should be made to the publisher at the address above.

Cambridge University Press has no responsibility for the persistence or accuracy of URLs for external or third-party internet websites referred to in this publication, and does not guarantee that any content on such websites is, or will remain, accurate or appropriate.

Please be aware that this publication may contain several variations of Aboriginal and Torres Strait Islander terms and spellings; no disrespect is intended. Please note that the terms 'Indigenous Australians' and 'Aboriginal and Torres Strait Islander peoples' may be used interchangeably in this publication.

I wish to dedicate this book to those whose deaths affected me during the writing and editing of the manuscript. Specifically, I dedicate this work to my mum Maureen Toth, my stepmother Raquel Pelling, my friend Lance Forster, and mentor Robert Tribe. Additionally, I dedicate this work to DH who also passed away during this time. Your lives had impact and you are, and will continue to be, missed.

Nadine Pelling

Contents

About the editors ix
Acknowledgements x
Contributors xi

Section I **Rationale, structure, and overview** 1

1 **Introduction** 2
Nadine Pelling

2 **Handbook structure** 4
Nadine Pelling

3 **Abnormal psychology overview** 6
Nadine Pelling

Section II **Cultural diversity and resources** 9

4 **Diversity in Australia** 10
Natalie Jackson

5 **Diversity in New Zealand** 34
Natalie Jackson

6 **Indigenous and bicultural resources** 54
Nadine Pelling

7 **Clinical practice with Indigenous Australians** 57
Joseph Randolph Bowers and Dwayne Kennedy

Section III **Disorders and psychological practice related items** 63

8 **Neurodevelopmental disorders** 64
Robyn Young and Anna Moffat

9 **Schizophrenia and related psychotic disorders** 76
Vaughan Carr, Melissa J Green, and Elliot M Bell

10 **Depressive disorders** 94
Gavin Beccaria

11 **Bipolar disorders** 106
Tanya Hanstock and Samson Tse

12 **Anxiety disorders** 116
Amanda Hutchinson

| 13 | Obsessive-compulsive and related disorders | 129 |

Rebecca Anderson and David Garratt-Reed

| 14 | Trauma- and stressor-related disorders | 143 |

William Hough

| 15 | Dissociative disorders and somatic symptoms and related disorders | 154 |

Martin Dorahy and Indra Mohan

| 16 | Feeding and eating disorders | 175 |

Leah Brennan, Sarah Mitchell, and Jake Linardon

| 17 | Elimination disorders | 189 |

Christine Grove and Chris Hardwick

| 18 | Sleep-wake disorders | 202 |

Kurt Lushington and Silvia Pignata

| 19 | Disruptive, impulse-control, and conduct disorders | 216 |

Vicki McKenzie and Kelly Allen

| 20 | Substance-related and addictive disorders | 229 |

Nicki Dowling, Kate Hall, and Petra K Staiger

| 21 | Neurocognitive disorders | 243 |

Karen A Sullivan and Alice Theadom

| 22 | Personality disorders | 258 |

Phillip S Kavanagh

| 23 | Paraphilic disorders | 266 |

Michael Proeve and Peter Chamberlain

| 24 | Other conditions that may be a focus of clinical attention | 276 |

Susana Gavidia-Payne and Bianca Denny

Section IV Special foci relevant to abnormal psychology   289

| 25 | Suicide and self-harm | 290 |

Kenneth Kirkby and Sunny Collings

| 26 | Compulsory treatment | 301 |

Christopher Ryan, Cristina Cavezza, Gregg Shinkfield, and Sascha Callaghan

Index   *310*

About the editors

Nadine Pelling is a Fellow of the Australian Counselling Association, clinical psychologist, and member of the Australian Psychological Society. She is employed full-time as a senior lecturer in Clinical Psychology and Counselling at the University of South Australia and maintains a small private practice in the southern suburbs of Adelaide.

Lorelle Burton is a member of the Australian Psychological Society and Professor of Psychology at the University of Southern Queensland. Lorelle has been an invited assessor for national teaching excellence awards and grants and has led numerous national collaborative research projects on student transition. She is an internationally recognised psychology educator and her current research focus involves leading cross-community collaborations to promote community capacity building and wellbeing.

Acknowledgements

We wish to acknowledge Natalie Jackson for her work on the Suicide and Self-harm chapter included in Section IV of this handbook. Specifically, Natalie assisted with the statistical referencing presented in the chapter.

Nadine Pelling and Lorelle Burton

Contributors

Dr Kelly Allen is a sessional academic, an educational and development psychologist in private practice, and a school psychologist. Kelly is an honorary fellow at the Melbourne Graduate School of Education and a full member of the Australian Psychological Society (APS), where she works with the national executive of the APS College of Educational and Developmental Psychologists in the position of Treasurer. She also represents Australia and New Zealand on the committee on the Status of International Affairs with the American Psychological Society's Division 15 (Educational Psychology).

Dr Rebecca A Anderson is a lecturer and Deputy Director of the Clinical Psychology Program at Curtin University. Dr Anderson has published book chapters and international peer-reviewed journal articles in the area of anxiety disorders, and has authored self-help treatments for obsessive compulsive disorder (OCD), generalised anxiety disorder, body dysmorphic disorder, and health anxiety. Dr Anderson is a chief co-investigator on a large federally funded grant examining online treatments for adolescents with OCD. Dr Anderson is also currently on the board of directors for the Australian Association for Cognitive and Behaviour Therapy.

Associate Professor Gavin Beccaria is the Program Coordinator of the Clinical Psychology program at the University of Southern Queensland (USQ). Gavin has worked at USQ since 2007. Prior to joining academia, Gavin worked at Queensland Health for 13 years. His most recent position was Director of Psychology Toowoomba Health Service District. Gavin also has a small part-time private practice. When not working, Gavin enjoys spending time with his wife, Lisa and children, Alicia and Benjamin.

Elliot M Bell is a lecturer and clinical psychologist in the Rehabilitation Teaching and Research Unit of the Department of Psychological Medicine and Rehabilitation at the University of Otago. He conducts research in social cognition and neurocognition in schizophrenia and other severe mental disorders. His clinical expertise is in rehabilitation and cognitive behavioural therapy for major mental illness.

Dr Joseph Randolph Bowers is a counselling psychotherapist, clinical supervisor, mental health and disability specialist, teacher, mentor, trainer, scholar, and community advocate. He maintains a private practice with www.abilitytherapyspecialists.org. Dr Bowers is an honorary member of the Australian Counselling Association; founding editor of the international research journal *Counselling, Psychotherapy, and Health*; founding member of the Psychotherapy and Counselling Federation of Australia; associate scholar with the Centre for World Indigenous Studies (US); invited scholar of the Dr Bowers Perpetual Special Collection at the Mi'kmaq Resource Centre at Cape Breton University in Canada; and honorary recipient of the Eagle Feather from Elders in Sacred Council of the Mi'kmaq First Nation.

Leah Brennan is an associate professor of clinical psychology at Australian Catholic University where she leads the Body Image, Eating, and Weight Clinical Research Team and the Clinic for Healthy Eating and Weight. She is an endorsed clinical, health, and educational and developmental psychologist. Her research focuses on the role of psychology in understanding and treating feeding, eating, weight, and body image disorders and their biopsychosocial comorbidities. She has worked as a clinical and health psychologist in a range of community and hospital settings, providing assessment and treatment for individuals with these conditions.

Sascha Callaghan is a lawyer and lecturer in health law and ethics at the University of Sydney. Her research focus is in mental health law, capacity, and consent to medical treatment. She is currently a lead researcher in the Sydney Neuroscience Network on intersections between neuroscience, law, and ethics.

Vaughan Carr is Professor of Psychiatry and Chair of Schizophrenia Epidemiology at the University of New South Wales, Adjunct Professor of Psychiatry at Monash University, and a senior consultant psychiatrist in Monash Health. His research includes genetic, neurobiological, cognitive, clinical, and psychosocial investigations of schizophrenia and other disorders.

Cristina Cavezza is a clinical and forensic psychologist at the Victorian Institute of Forensic Mental Health (Forensicare) in Melbourne. She holds honorary appointments as clinical lecturer at the University of Melbourne and as clinical associate at Swinburne University of Technology. Originally from Canada, she has lived and worked in Melbourne for the past 10 years. While she holds a predominantly clinical position assessing and treating remand prisoners and offenders with mental illnesses, she is engaged in scholarly writing, teaching, and academic research.

Dr Peter Chamberlain is an assistant professor in the Centre for Applied Psychology at the University of Canberra and a visiting research fellow at the University of Adelaide. He has forensic experience as a clinical psychologist in the South Australian Health Department, working within the Forensic Mental Health Network providing assessment and treatment services for sexual offenders. Peter has also assisted in the training of child protection officers within a variety of services such as police, family services, and corrections.

Sunny Collings is Professor of Psychiatry and Director of the Social Psychiatry and Population Mental Health Research Unit at the University of Otago, Wellington. She works with people at high risk of suicide and the clinicians caring for them. She also focuses on suicide in her research, policy, and coronial advisory work. She has a particular interest in the social context of suicides.

Dr Bianca Denny is a clinical psychologist, lecturer, and researcher affiliated with the Division of Psychology at RMIT University. Her clinical and research interests broadly encompass health and clinical psychology, training of health professionals, student wellbeing, and resilience of children and families.

Martin Dorahy is a clinical psychologist and professor in the Department of Psychology, University of Canterbury, Christchurch. He has published over 80 peer-reviewed journal articles and co-edited three books in the area of psychotraumatology. He is on the board of directors of the International Society for the Study of Trauma and Dissociation (ISSTD). He maintains a clinical practice focused primarily on the adult sequelae of childhood relational trauma.

Associate Professor Nicki Dowling is currently an associate professor of psychology in the School of Psychology at Deakin University, with honorary positions at the University of Melbourne and the Australian National University. She is a registered clinical psychologist, has significant experience as a problem gambling counsellor, and is currently the Victorian State Representative for the National Association of Gambling Studies. She is a clinical researcher with expertise in investigating the prevalence and aetiology of problem gambling and the development and evaluation of prevention and intervention programs for problem gambling.

Dr David Garratt-Reed is a lecturer in undergraduate psychology at Curtin University, specialising in teaching theory and practice relating to psychological disorders. He is also a clinical psychologist registrar in private practice. His research interests are in the area of risk avoidance in OCD and anxiety.

Associate Professor Susana Gavidia-Payne works at RMIT University, where she has forged extensive clinical and research expertise. Susana's current focus is on researching resilience processes and outcomes in children and families who experience socio-economic disadvantage and disability.

Melissa J Green is Associate Professor and National Health and Medical Research Council RD Wright Biomedical Research Fellow in the School of Psychiatry at the University of New South Wales. She conducts research in the cognitive neuroscience and genetics of schizophrenia and bipolar disorder, as well as in the epidemiology of childhood risk factors for psychosis.

Christine Grove is currently a practising child and adolescent psychologist and lecturer at Monash University. Christine is passionate about topics of equality, young people's experiences, and mental health. Her experience includes working with young people and their families in various supporting roles, in particular supporting families with children who may be experiencing developmental concerns such as encopresis or enuresis. View Christine's research and practice interests at http://monash.academia.edu/ChristineGrove.

Dr Kate Hall is a senior lecturer in addiction and mental health at Deakin University, holds a joint appointment between Deakin University and Victoria's Youth Support and Advocacy Service, and is a visiting lecturer in the postgraduate programs at Monash and Swinburne universities. Her research in the area of translation science has focused on disseminating evidence-based treatments in real world settings.

Dr Tanya L Hanstock is a senior clinical psychologist and convenor of the clinical psychology program at the University of Newcastle. She specialises in the area of bipolar disorder. Dr Hanstock helped establish the first specific child and adolescent bipolar disorder clinic in Newcastle and is passionate about ensuring the best assessment and treatment for people with mental illness and the best training for mental health practitioners. She is currently completing a PhD in the area of life logging, healthy lifestyles and predictors, and prevention of relapse in people with bipolar disorder. Dr Hanstock has completed a Doctorate of Clinical and Health Psychology.

Chris Hardwick is a clinical psychologist who has worked for 7 years with the specialist multidisciplinary team at the Enuresis Clinic at the Children's Hospital at Westmead, Sydney. He uses mainstream psychological rationales to inform a pragmatic approach when helping Australian families maximise the potential of paediatric treatment of incontinence. He has worked extensively with other specialist paediatric medical teams and also has a strong interest in training allied health and nursing professionals working in the field of paediatric continence in Australia.

William Hough is currently a clinical psychologist in private practice who specialises in the treatment of mental disorders, in particular posttraumatic stress disorder (PTSD). He has had a long history of employment in acute hospital settings thus bringing a great deal of clinical experience to his practice. William has published in the field, worked as an adjunct lecturer and his PhD thesis was concerned with the aetiology of PTSD and the bidirectional relationship between trauma and sensitisation.

Dr Amanda Hutchinson is a clinical psychologist and senior lecturer at the University of South Australia. She also works in private practice in Adelaide with a particular emphasis on the treatment of anxiety, depression, and stress-related issues in adults. Her research interests include health psychology, cancer prevention, cognition and cancer, and mindfulness.

Dr Natalie Jackson is an adjunct professor (demography) in the School of People, Planning and Environment at Massey University (Albany, New Zealand). She is also Director of Natalie Jackson Demographics Ltd. Her primary expertise is on the subnational ending of population growth, the underlying demographic drivers of these trends and their consequences for all levels of government, labour market, welfare state, education and healthcare policy, and business in general. She leads a Royal NZ Society Marsden project "The subnational mechanisms of the ending of population growth – towards a theory of depopulation" (Maori translation: "Tai Timu Tangata. Taihoa e? – The ebbing of the human tide. What does it mean for the people?").

Dr Phillip S Kavanagh lectures in both clinical and personality psychology at the University of South Australia. His research interests intersect the areas of social, personality, evolutionary, and clinical psychology. Dr Kavanagh also works privately as a clinical psychologist and is registered as a clinical psychologist in both Australia and New Zealand.

Dr Dwayne Kennedy is a counsellor, mental health worker, consultant, life coach, and teacher. Dr Kennedy has been working with people and studying minority issues for the last 31 years.

Kenneth Kirkby is Professor of Psychiatry at the University of Tasmania. His research interests included internet-delivered cognitive behaviour theory (CBT), epidemiology, psychoimmunology, history of psychiatry, and drug-induced amnesia. Professor Kirkby is a past director of beyondblue and a past president of the Royal Australian and New Zealand College of Psychiatrists (RANZCP). He has worked with some patients with long-term suicidal preoccupations for a quarter of a century and is respectful of both their anguish and their fortitude.

Jake Linardon is a PhD candidate in the Body Image, Eating, and Weight Clinical Research Team in the School of Psychology at Australian Catholic University, Melbourne. His research interests lie in understanding, preventing, and treating eating disorders. His research aims at identifying the mechanisms of action for psychological interventions for disordered eating as well as identifying theoretically based variables associated with treatment outcome.

Professor Kurt Lushington is Head of the School of Psychology, Social Work, and Social Policy at the University of South Australia. He is a member of the Sleep Research Society, Australian Psychological Society, and Australasian Sleep Association. Kurt is a clinical psychologist and has written extensively on all aspects to do with sleep and its disorders. He is the current chair of the Australasian Sleep Association subcommittee for Behavioural Management of Sleep Disorders. His other research interests include work and stress, as well as the impact of digital technologies on teaching, with publications in both areas.

Dr Vicki McKenzie is a senior lecturer in educational psychology at the University of Melbourne. Dr McKenzie has presented at national and international conferences on building coping skills and resilience in young people. Training psychologists for professional practice in schools has been a central component of Dr McKenzie's professional career, and she has also supervised many psychologists in gaining endorsed status. She is currently Deputy Chair of the APS College of Educational and Developmental Psychologists, and is a fellow of the Australian Psychological Society.

Dr Sarah Mitchell is a clinical research fellow at the Australian Catholic University and a member of the Body Image, Eating, and Weight Clinical Research Team. Her research interests centre on the assessment and treatment of feeding and eating disorders. She is particularly interested in psychosocial predictors of the emergence of feeding and eating disorders and predictors of treatment outcomes. Sarah has also worked as a clinical psychologist at several Victoria-based eating disorders speciality services.

Anna Moffat completed her PhD at Flinders University in South Australia. To date, her research has focused on imitation ability in children with autism and the associated oscillatory activity in the brain. She is currently the manager of the Flinders Early Intervention Research Program, which provides early intensive behavioural intervention to young children with autism. In addition, she is working on a nationwide project investigating child wellbeing in the middle years.

Dr Indra Mohan is a consultation liaison psychiatrist for Northern Area Mental Health Services based at the Northern Hospital, Epping, Victoria. He has an interest in mood disorders, somatic symptom disorder, anxiety disorders, and electroconvulsive therapy (ECT). He has published peer-reviewed journal articles and been involved in training and teaching of medical students and registrars.

Dr Silvia Pignata is a lecturer within the School of Engineering at the University of South Australia. She is a work and organisational psychology researcher and has expertise in organisational stress interventions with a focus on strategies that incorporate wellbeing and morale building activities, particularly their potential to reduce psychological strain. Her other research interests include sleep research in children and adolescents; the psychosocial aspects of occupational health and safety; and the interaction of people and socio-technical systems within the work environment.

Dr Michael Proeve is a senior lecturer in the School of Psychology at the University of Adelaide. He has published journal articles in national and international journals, and book chapters regarding assessment and treatment of sexual offenders. He has also conducted nationally competitive research concerning risk assessment of sexual offenders. For over 20 years, Michael has worked as a clinical and forensic psychologist in correctional, mental health, and private practice settings. He has been a member of government and non-government committees and has consulted nationally concerning child sexual abuse issues.

Christopher Ryan is a clinical associate professor in psychiatry at Sydney's Westmead Hospital and the Centre for Values, Ethics, and the Law in Medicine at the University of Sydney. He is regularly invited to speak both in Australia and internationally, and in over a hundred publications he has investigated areas such as delirium, body integrity identity disorder, deliberate self-harm, risk categorisation, patient–therapist sexual contact, mental health legislation, advance directives, physician-assisted dying, and euthanasia.

Gregg Shinkfield is a senior clinical psychologist at the Victorian Institute of Forensic Mental Health (Forensicare) in Melbourne. He holds an honorary appointment of clinical associate at Swinburne University of Technology. Having completed his postgraduate clinical training at Massey University (New Zealand), he has lived and worked in Melbourne since 2007. His specialist areas of practice include the assessment and treatment of forensic mental health clients, with a predominant focus on provision of services to women presenting with severe mental illness and complex personality dysfunction.

Associate Professor Petra K Staiger is a senior academic and a clinical psychologist within the School of Psychology at Deakin University. Her research primarily targeting treatment of addiction is cross-discipline and cross-institutional and has a translational focus. Her research expertise is in investigating the aetiology and treatment of individuals with addictive behaviour problems, with a particular focus on those with complex needs (i.e., polydrug users and those with comorbid mental health problems).

Karen A Sullivan is Professor in the School of Psychology and Counselling at the Queensland University of Technology, Brisbane. Professor Sullivan is a clinical neuropsychologist. Her clinical and research work deals with neurocognitive disorders.

Alice Theadom is a senior research fellow and registered psychologist at the Auckland University of Technology. Dr Theadom specialises in the epidemiology and psychological adjustment of neurological conditions.

Professor Samson Tse is the Associate Dean at the Faculty of Social Sciences and Director of the Master of Social Science in Counselling Programme at the Department of Social Work and Social Administration, the University of Hong Kong. Prior to his relocation to Hong Kong, Samson worked in New Zealand for more than 20 years. Between 1998 and 2002, Samson was appointed by the Mental Health Commission of New Zealand as member of the Practitioners Reference Group. Samson is a founding member of the Collaborative Research Team for the Study of Bipolar Disorder (CREST.BD) consortium at the University of British Columbia, Canada.

Robyn Young first developed an interest in autism while studying savants as part of her PhD in savant syndrome. This work became the subject of an ABC documentary titled *Uncommon Genius*. She went on to develop a screening tool for autistic disorder, known as the Autism Detection in Early Childhood (ADEC). Together with colleagues at Flinders University, she has developed an intervention program called SPECTRA. Her work has now turned to older persons with autism spectrum disorder. She has published more than 30 papers on autism spectrum disorder and has presented at national and international conferences.

Section

Rationale, structure, and overview

1

Introduction

Nadine Pelling

Abnormal psychology is often a core course in both undergraduate and postgraduate psychology programs across North America, Europe, and Australasia. The vast majority of abnormal psychology textbooks come from the United States of America (US). This academic focus on US abnormal psychology is not surprising given the relatively large number of people living in the US, that it is ranked third in terms of country population in the world, and is the most populous country in which English is the primary language spoken (Statistics Times, 2016; United Nations Department of Economic and Social Affairs/Population Division, 2015). Additionally, the *Diagnostic and Statistical Manual of Mental Disorders* (5th ed.; *DSM-5*; American Psychiatric Association, 2013) originates from the US. The available US resources are, understandably, US-centric and contain mostly US statistics and applied examples. Furthermore, if reference to community resources is made these are likely to be US-based and not accessible, or of low relevance, to Australasian populations.

There are few abnormal psychology resources that present Australian and New Zealand (NZ) materials including statistics, case studies, and community resources. Recent Australian-focused resources include a special issue published by Pelling (2015) in the *International Journal of Mental Health*. Further, there are both Australian- and NZ-based authors publishing practice- and education-relevant abnormal psychology resources. However, up until now no resource has existed detailing the Australian and NZ experience and response to abnormal psychology matters in a succinct and applied manner. This handbook on abnormal psychology in the Australian and NZ context is designed specifically to make such academic and applied abnormal psychology resources available.

This handbook has been compiled to include material by lead researchers and applied practitioners from Australia and NZ. Consequently, the resulting resource is valuable to both students of abnormal psychology and also applied mental health practitioners across Australia and NZ. We hope you enjoy reading and making use of this handbook which purposefully highlights and showcases our Australasian research and practice relating to abnormal psychology.

References

American Psychiatric Association. (2013). *Diagnostic and statistical manual of mental disorders* (5th ed.). Arlington, VA: Author.

Pelling, N. (2015). Special issue: Mental health in Australia. *International Journal of Mental Health. 44*(1–2), 1–3.

Statistics Times. (2016). *List of North American countries by population 2015.* Available: http://statisticstimes.com/population/north-american-countries-by-population.php

United Nations Department of Economic and Social Affairs, Population Division. (2015). *World population prospects: The 2015 revision, key findings and advance tables.* Working Paper No. ESA/P/WP.241. Available: http://esa.un.org/unpd/wpp/publications/files/key_findings_wpp_2015.pdf

2

Handbook structure

Nadine Pelling

This handbook has been purposefully created to focus on Australian and New Zealand (NZ) abnormal psychology research, statistics, and applied practice. This handbook has thus been designed with a specific structure for ease of use. Specifically, after general handbook rationale and structure information is offered, some basic information regarding abnormal psychology and applied practice is provided. This presentation is followed by a brief examination of the cultural and demographic compositions of Australia and NZ and related resources. The bulk of this handbook then examines various psychological disorders. Finally, the handbook concludes with an examination of two psychological practice-related items relevant to abnormal psychology: suicide and non-suicidal self-harm and then mandated or involuntary treatment.

As noted previously, the bulk of this handbook focuses on various psychological disorders. The disorders examined are those presented in the American Psychiatric Association's *Diagnostic and Statistical Manual of Mental Disorders* (5th ed.; *DSM-5*; American Psychiatric Association, 2013), and are in the same order as in the *DSM-5*. The exceptions to this presentation are those disorders for which there was limited Australian- and NZ-based information to justify inclusion in this handbook. Therefore, this handbook examines 17 specific disorders (or areas of treatment foci) whereas the DSM-5 presents a greater number of diagnostic categories.

For each disorder (or area of treatment focus) examined, a standard organisation has been maintained for presentation. Explicitly, contributing authors have been asked to begin with an introduction to each disorder (or area of treatment focus) including an examination of **signs** and **symptoms**, followed by an examination of the presentation of same in Australia and then NZ including **incidence** and **prevalence**, and then to present a case example. Cases have been chosen to focus on either an Australian or NZ example, and to comply with ethical standards relating to the presentation of client information for educational purposes (specifically, either a created or composite example is presented). Specific de-identified client material has only been used with the written permission of said client (Australian Psychological Society, 2007). Authors have identified research and practice support information specific to both Australia and NZ. References are provided for readers who wish to explore the topics examined in context in greater detail.

Key terms

- **Sign.** Objective evidence of a disorder. A sign can be recognised by others.
- **Symptom.** Subjective evidence of a disorder. Others know about a symptom if they are told about it.
- **Incidence.** The rate of newly diagnosed disorders. An incidence rate can be relatively high but a prevalence rate relatively low if the disorder in question resolves quickly.
- **Prevalence.** The actual number of diagnosed disorders. A prevalence rate can be relatively high but an incidence rate can be relatively low if the disorder in question does not resolve quickly.

To purposefully limit the size of this handbook authors have provided additional case examples and short-answer questions with answers relating to their specific focus area separately for inclusion on this handbook's companion website instead of in the main handbook. These supplementary materials will be made available exclusively to instructors using this handbook to facilitate the use of the book in an educational setting.

References

American Psychiatric Association. (2013). *Diagnostic and statistical manual of mental disorders* (5th ed.). Arlington, VA: Author.

Australian Psychological Society. (2007). *Code of ethics*. Melbourne, Vic: Author.

3

Abnormal psychology overview

Nadine Pelling

Defining abnormality

Abnormality can be defined in a number of ways. However, in terms of psychological difficulties the term "abnormality," or "psychopathology," generally refers to a problematic pattern of thought, feeling, and/or behaviour that disrupts one's sense of wellness or functioning either socially or occupationally. A mental or psychological disorder involves a recognisable set of symptoms and signs that cause distress to the individual involved and impair their functioning (Burton, Westen, & Kowalski, 2015). The psychopathological signs and symptoms presented by an individual are "recognisable" when compared with various classification systems and thus are used to make a diagnosis.

There are two main classifications systems used to make mental health related diagnoses: the fifth edition of the *Diagnostic and Statistical Manual of Mental Disorders* published by the American Psychiatric Association (5th ed.; *DSM-5*; 2013) and the *International Statistical Classification of Diseases and Related Health Problems 2010 Edition (ICD-10)* (World Health Organisation, 2011). An examination of the pros and cons of both classifications is beyond the scope of this handbook. Therefore, the *DSM-5* will simply be described in terms of structure and use as this is the classification system that was focused on when structuring this handbook.

DSM-5 overview

The *DSM-5* is the current edition of the *Diagnostic and Statistical Manual of Mental Disorders* in use and outlines recognisable sets of symptoms and signs that distress individuals and impair their functioning, most often focused on for treatment and support. The *DSM-5* itself presents material in sections, including background regarding the development of the *DSM-5*, with the bulk of material being related to the diagnostic criteria for the various disorders.

The *DSM-5* provides applied clinicians with an organising framework as well as a common language regarding signs and symptoms and thus diagnoses that can assist communication and assist and guide research and treatment. The information presented in the *DSM-5* includes how various cognitive, emotional, and/or behavioural signs and symptoms cluster together in the diagnoses described. The use of a diagnosis thus creates a shared understanding with other practitioners familiar with the diagnostic classification system used. Therefore, communication between practitioners is made more efficient. There are, of course, drawbacks as well as benefits to the use of diagnostic labels and interested readers are referred to Beccaria (2013) for a detailed yet concise review of the *DSM-5* and discussion of such topics.

The *DSM-5* groups clinical disorders into 22 main areas from neurodevelopmental disorders to substance-related and addictive disorders through to other conditions that may be the focus of clinical attention. This handbook explores most of these within the Australian and New Zealand (NZ) context.

Applied professions

A number of professions work with those impacted by mental illness. The main professional areas in Australia and NZ to work with mental illness include psychology, counselling, social work, and psychiatry.

In Australia applied psychological practice is legally regulated by the Psychology Board of Australia with support from the Australian Health Practitioner Regulation Agency. Similarly, in NZ psychology is regulated by the New Zealand Psychologists Board. The main association that provides support to psychological practitioners in Australia, and the one that provides the ethical code that must be used by psychologists, is the Australian Psychological Society. The New Zealand Psychological Society supports psychologists in NZ.

Counselling is voluntarily regulated in Australia with two main associations mainly involved in the promotion of counselling services and support of counselling practitioners: the Australian Counselling Association and the Psychotherapy and Counselling Federation of Australia. These two associations have a joint register called the Australian Register of Counsellors and Psychotherapists. In NZ the New Zealand Association of Counsellors voluntarily regulates and supports counselling and counselling practitioners.

Social work is voluntarily regulated in Australia by the Australian Association of Social Workers. In NZ, the New Zealand Association of Social Workers operates in a similar capacity.

Psychiatry is a branch of medicine. Psychiatrists, unlike psychologists, are thus medical practitioners. The Royal Australian and New Zealand College of Psychiatrists (RANZCP) is responsible for training, educating, and representing psychiatrists in both Australia and NZ (www.ranzcp.org).

New Zealand – psychology, counselling, and social work regulation and associations

- Psychology:
  - New Zealand Psychologists Board (psychologistsboard.org.nz)
  - The New Zealand Psychological Society (http://psychology.org.nz)
- Counselling:
  - New Zealand Association of Counsellors (http://nzac.org.nz)
- Social work:
  - Aotearoa New Zealand Association of Social Workers (http://anzasw.nz)

Australia – psychology, counselling, and social work regulation and associations

- Psychology:
  - Psychology Board of Australia (www.psychologyboard.gov.au)
  - Australian Psychological Society (http://psychology.org.au)
- Counselling:
  - Australian Counselling Association (http://theaca.net.au)
  - Psychotherapy and Counselling Federation of Australian (www.pacfa.org.au)
  - Australian Register of Counsellors and Psychotherapists (www.arcapregister.com.au)
- Social work:
  - Australian Association of Social Workers (www.aasw.asn.au)

References

American Psychiatric Association. (2013). *Diagnostic and statistical manual of mental disorders* (5th ed.). Arlington, VA: Author.

Beccaria, G. (2013). *A student's guide to the DSM-5*. Milton, Australia: John Wiley & Sons.

Burton, L., Westen, D., & Kowalski, R. (2015). *Psychology: An Australian and New Zealand edition* (4th ed.). Milton, Australia: John Wiley & Sons.

World Health Organisation. (2011). *International statistical classification of diseases and related health problems 2010 edition (ICD-10)*. Geneva: Author. Available: www.who.int/classifications/icd/en/

Section **II**

Cultural diversity and resources

4

Diversity in Australia

Natalie Jackson

Introduction

Notwithstanding the overarching distinction between Indigenous and non-Indigenous Australians, diversity in Australia is for the most part synonymous with country of birth, migrant generation, and the more esoteric expression of these data in what we term "culture". And with almost half of the population either first or second generation immigrant, Australia is home to one of the world's most ethnically diverse populations. Socio-economic diversity is of course intimately connected to these demographic characteristics, but for the most part appears in Australian data collections disaggregated either by geographic area or overseas born/Australian born rather than broad ethnic group because of the way in which Australian statistics are presented. This is in contrast with the approach in New Zealand (NZ) which disaggregates most publicly available data by ethnicity (see Chapter 5 describing NZ's population). In other words, there are many ways of measuring, interpreting, collecting, and presenting *diversity* data. Australia tends to present diversity data in groups related to geographic area and nation of origin whereas NZ presents diversity in collections relating to ethnicity first and foremost.

Australia – what is diversity?

There are many aspects of diversity. These include items often focused upon in therapeutic contexts and psychological studies: age, family background, gender, race, religion, sexual orientation, socio-economic status, ability/disability, and nation of origin.

An examination or analysis of diversity (diversity analysis) in populations can focus on two broad types of diversity: inherent diversity (traits people are born with) and acquired diversity (aspects gained from experience).

Examples of inherent diversity would be one's country of birth and sex. Acquired diversity characteristics are increasingly attributed to personal, social, and economic success.

Community Profiles and related data collections developed by the Australian Bureau of Statistics (ABS) provide a wide variety of diversity-related data, and are drawn on in this chapter. At the same time this chapter is not a substantive analysis of that diversity. It is a descriptive presentation for reference by users of this text book. When asked to write this description of diversity in Australia (and the following description of diversity in NZ) my brief was to paint a broad picture of who Australians are including collective and individual aspects of diversity so as to place the information on abnormal psychology and related matters forming the bulk of the book into context. Because there are not only many ways in which diversity is measured and interpreted, but there are also immeasurable ways that diversity data are collected and presented, the following description of the Australian population is simply one way of presenting the data available.

Accordingly, this chapter (and its analogue for NZ, Chapter 5) presents just a selection of data that reflect Australia's diversity. Most data are drawn directly from the ABS, which is Australia's primary source of demographic, social, and economic data. Those interested in a more complex analysis of the Australian population can delve further into the data available. For additional data, readers should pursue the many ABS data collections sourced.[1]

The chapter begins with an overview of Australia's spatial diversity, then presents a selection of socio-demographic and socio-economic data. Where available, data are discussed for three broad groups: the total population, migrant (or overseas-born) populations, and the Aboriginal and Torres Strait Islander population (or Indigenous/non-Indigenous populations). The chapter concludes with a targeted examination of some diversity-related characteristics present in Australia's psychological workforce.

Spatial distribution

With the majority of its population living in five cities and around its coastline, Australia has one of the developed world's most urbanised and coastally resident populations (ABS, 2011a). As sung in the national anthem, Australia is "girt by sea", drawn from the originally controversial work "The Song of Australia" by Caroline Carleton: "a land … floating free, [F]rom mountain-top to girdling sea". As such, Australia is a relatively secure continent. This relative security is thought to contribute to the relaxed attitude of many Australians, both "new" and Australian born, although there are equally very remote areas with sizeable populations which seldom, if ever, see the ocean.

Relative state and territory size may also play a role in the community identity of Australians, partly because each state has its own government and administrative apparatus, and partly because of constitutionally predetermined financial subsidies

---

[1] Where data have been drawn directly from the ABS and there has been no added analysis, the reference is given as ABS. Where analysis has been applied (e.g., raw data have been converted to percentages for easier comparison), the reference is given as Author/ABS. This is to protect ABS from any computational errors made by the author, and not to claim ownership of the data.

flowing from the larger to the smaller states, some irrespective of changes in population share. The nature of financial subsidies often results in heated state-to-state debate in the media, resulting in people taking on a certain degree of "state identity". Added to that is the differential impact in each state and territory of, on the one hand, the proportion of Aboriginal and Torres Strait Islander peoples, and on the other, overseas migration resulting in some being somewhat more ethnically diverse and having younger or older age structures than others.

Population share and role of migration

Over the past three decades, four states have lost population share while two – Queensland and Western Australia – have gained, along with small gains for both territories (ABS, 2014a, Table 4). These state-level shifts are primarily the result of different levels of interstate and overseas migration (Figure 4.1, ABS, 2011b, which shows the annual average net gain or loss across the past three decades). Queensland (Qld.), Western Australia (WA), and the Australian Capital Territory (ACT) typically gain both interstate and overseas migrants, although numbers are very small for the latter. By contrast, New South Wales (NSW) and Victoria (Vic.) gain the majority of the balance of overseas migrants (37.0% and 26.0% respectively across these three decades), but typically lose interstate migrants. South Australia (SA), Tasmania (Tas.), and the Northern Territory (NT) also experience this pattern – again with very low numbers. There have also been some changing fortunes over the period. Since the early 2000s, Queensland, Victoria, and Western Australia have each increased their share of overseas migrants while NSW's dominant share has decreased; Queensland's dominant share of interstate migrants has decreased; and NSW's losses have reduced (see Table 4.1 for summary data).

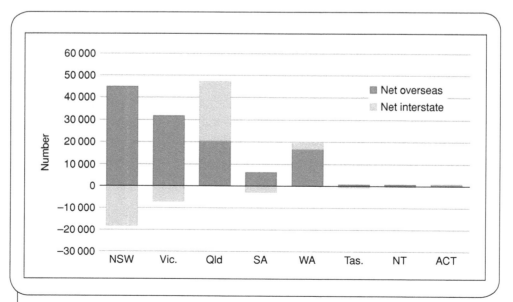

Figure 4.1 Annual average net interstate and net overseas migration by state and territory, 1981–2011
Source: Author/ABS (2011b, Table 2)

Table 4.1 Summary demographic information, Australia's states and territories, selected years

	New South Wales	Victoria	Queensland	South Australia	Western Australia	Tasmania	Northern Territory	Australian Capital Territory	Australia
Population									
Population (2014)	7518472	5841667	4722447	1685714	2573389	514762	245079	385996	23490736
Population share (% 2014)	32.0	24.9	20.1	7.2	11.0	2.2	1.0	1.6	100.0
Share Aboriginal and Torres Strait Islander peoples (% 2012)	2.9	0.9	4.2	2.3	3.8	4.7	29.8	1.7	3.0
Sex ratio (males: females, 2014)	98.6	97.9	99.3	98.3	102.4	99.3	112.2	98.8	99.1
Broad age group (years, 2014)									
0–14 years	18.8	18.3	19.8	17.7	19.1	18.4	22.0	18.8	18.8
15–24 years	13.0	13.3	13.7	13.0	13.5	12.7	14.6	14.2	13.3
25–54 years	41.1	42.3	41.3	40.0	43.8	37.5	47.0	44.7	41.7
55–64 years	11.7	11.3	11.3	12.4	11.0	13.7	9.8	10.5	11.5
65+ years	15.4	14.9	14.0	17.0	12.9	17.7	6.6	11.8	14.7
Total	**100.0**	**100.0**	**100.0**	**100.0**	**100.0**	**100.0**	**100.0**	**100.0**	**100.0**
Median age (years, 2014)	37.9	37.3	36.8	39.9	35.8	41.6	31.8	34.9	37.3

(*cont.*)

Table 4.1 (*cont.*)

	New South Wales	Victoria	Queensland	South Australia	Western Australia	Tasmania	Northern Territory	Australian Capital Territory	Australia
Migration									
Net overseas migration (1981–2011 annual average)	44722	31696	20366	6180	16902	738	855	842	122301
Net interstate migration (1981–2011 annual average)	(18568)	(7123)	26781	(2642)	2441	(736)	(429)	290	–
Net overseas migration share (%)									
1981–1982	38.7	23.9	14.2	6.5	14.3	0.8	1.0	0.7	100.0
2010–2011	29.9	27.3	18.4	5.9	16.4	0.6	0.4	1.1	100.0
Geography (2011)									
Urban centre and locality	90.2	89.4	91.6	87.2	86.4	81.6	79.3	29.4	88.0
Section of state ranges	2.2	3.0	1.3	5.1	5.3	8.8	10.4	29.4	4.3
Section of state	1.0	1.5	2.9	3.1	2.9	4.8	6.9	29.4	2.5
Significant urban area	6.6	6.1	4.2	4.6	5.4	4.8	3.4	11.8	5.3
Total	**100.0**	**100.0**	**100.0**	**100.0**	**100.0**	**100.0**	**100.0**	**100.0**	**100.0**
Geographic units	599	395	453	195	206	125	87	17	2090

Source: population data – Author/ABS (2015a) (note: data for 2014 is subject to revision); migration data – Author/ABS (2011b, Table 2); geographic data – Author/ABS (2012a)

Urban/rural distinction

Within these state and territory boundaries, urbanisation has also contributed to greater or lesser growth in the cities and major urban areas, while the rate of urbanisation is now slowing, plausibly because the proportion living in an area designated urban is in most cases approaching maximum levels (see ABS, 2005, 2012a for geographical boundaries). In 2013, just 10.5% of Australia's population was considered as living in a rural area. However, because the definition of what constitutes "urban" (and the balance, "rural") in Australia is based on urban centres containing just 1000 persons, it is important to note that areas commonly combined to define "rural Australia" (that is, "localities and remainder of state") "contain considerable areas of urban style development, peri-urban development and substantial infrastructure" (ABS, 2012a, p. 18). Such definitions should be kept in mind when considering the possible role of residence in the analysis of contemporary pathologies. Judd et al. (2002), for example, found that socio-demographic factors were more powerful predictors of difference in prevalence than the location of residence.

Spatial diversity and age structure

Complicating the rural/urban story, however, is that states, territories, and even local government areas within states and territories are quite differentiated demographically. As explained further later in this chapter, underlying differences in birth and death rates are impacted upon (and driven) by the differing levels and types of migration outlined above. The resulting age–sex structures of Australia's two oldest states (Tasmania and SA) and two youngest territories (ACT and NT) differ markedly to each other, and also to their "middle-aged" counterparts: NSW, Victoria, Queensland and WA (see Table 4.1). These age structures play a role in state- and territory-level socioeconomic diversity, such as educational qualifications and income, because "middle-aged" populations typically have greater proportions in the higher educated and higher income-earning age groups, while older and younger populations each have proportionately fewer, for different reasons. Structurally younger populations have proportionately more individuals at the ages at which higher qualifications and higher incomes are still being gained; older populations have proportionately more in the age groups which completed their schooling many years ago, when fewer went on to higher qualifications – and are also likely to have more retired individuals. While *individuals* certainly gain qualifications as they age, fewer are gained at older than younger ages, so all else remaining equal, qualifications (and income) distribution gaps at state/territory level are difficult to close (as is also the case for subpopulations with markedly differing age structures, such as Indigenous and non-Indigenous Australians; see Jackson, 2008).

However, there are important exceptions to the rule. Migrants typically bring skills and qualifications with them, so those states/territories/local government areas which gain a disproportionate share, as discussed earlier, also tend to see their qualifications distributions enhanced. The ACT and WA are two such examples, attracting people with very specific types of skills, where higher than average incomes are related to the specific type of industry. The proportion of people at older, and younger, ages changes in various population groupings over time. Thus, an examination of structural ageing (defined as an increasing proportion at older ages) can tell us if a population is getting older or becoming more youthful over time. The rate of structural ageing is another phenomenon with implications for understanding and tracing change in social behaviour at group level, over time. As populations age, the proportions exposed to the risk of certain behaviours change; proportions at younger ages reduce, as those at older ages increase. As a result, while younger populations have been shown to have, for example, higher overall crime rates than older populations, the crude crime rate reduces as the proportion in the highest risk age groups – typically 15–24 years – falls (e.g., Rosevear, 2012). By contrast, older populations are exposed to the risk of increasing dependency, loss of second-language skills, failing health – but also to the "risk" of holding greater wealth.

As can be seen from the summary data in Table 4.1, the NT's population is Australia's youngest because it has somewhat greater proportions of people aged 0–64 years and somewhat lower proportions aged 65+ years than the other states and territories. This is in part a reflection of the territory's significantly higher than average proportion of Aboriginal and Torres Strait Islander people (30% compared with 3.0% nationally), who are on average very much younger than that of the total population – discussed later – and in part because of substantial net migration gain over the prime working ages, responding to employment demand. Tasmania, by contrast, has the lowest proportion aged 15–64 years and the highest proportion aged 65+ years (17.7%) resulting in the oldest median age (41.6 years), primarily the result of many years of net migration loss at young adult ages. The situation for the second oldest state, SA, is similar to that of Tasmania, while the second youngest jurisdiction, the ACT, has relatively high proportions at 15–24 and 25–64 years due on the one hand to the presence of three universities and on the other to its large public service sector (Author/ ABS, 2015a).

Spatial diversity and income distribution

One overarching spatial characteristic that underpins and interacts with most other population composition variables is socio-economic diversity. Average weekly ordinary full-time earnings for employed adults (15+ years) in November 2014, by state and territory, show that the ACT ($1702.10), WA ($1673.10) and NSW ($1492.30) had average weekly earnings above the national average ($1477), although NSW clearly lies closer to its lower-than-average-earning counterparts (ABS, 2015b). Tasmanian incomes are lowest at $1266.80. Contributing to this disparity, the ACT has a high proportion of public sector workers who on average earn more than those in the private sector, while WA has recently experienced a resource sector boom which has influenced wages in the mining sector and allied industries.

Among the many other factors affected by age and sex structure are unemployment, rates of home ownership, satisfaction with life, even social class. The analysis of social data at group level thus requires methodological engagement with this demographic diversity, so that "apples are compared with apples." A conventional approach to controlling for age structural differences, for example, holds the age structure of a comparator population constant and applies it to the age-specific rates for a particular variable (e.g., unemployment) to the population(s) of interest (Jackson, 2013). This technique "weights" the age-specific rates of the variable for the population of interest to the same "standard" age distribution as the comparator population. When the resulting rates by age are summed, the now *age-standardised* average is directly comparable. It says that this would be the average unemployment rate (or any other summary rate) for population X *if it had the same age distribution* as population Y. The results are very telling. For example, around 27% of the difference in the crude unemployment rate between NZ's European and Māori populations in 2013 is accounted for by the differences in age structure (see Chapter 5).

The importance of taking account of differences in population composition when undertaking social analysis cannot be over-emphasised. The proposition pertains to many other compositional variables that a student of psychology might look at. Both suicide and happiness (life satisfaction) rates, for example, are correlated not only with age, but also marital status. To compare the suicide or life-satisfaction rates of populations differentiated by marital status would first require standardising the data to the marital status of the chosen standard (comparator) population – and plausibly to *both* the marital status and age structure of that population. So too would analyses undertaken at subnational spatial level, such as a comparison of life-satisfaction rates (or rates of marriage, divorce, unemployment, and so on) by region or territorial authority area, when those spatial units are highly differentiated by age or any other compositional variable.

Indigenous composition

In 2011, Australia's Aboriginal and Torres Strait Islander population numbered approximately 669 900 persons and, as indicated earlier, accounted for just on 3% of the total population, although the proportion differs markedly by state and territory (Table 4.2). The largest populations of Aboriginal and Torres Strait Islander peoples lived in NSW (208 500 people, 2.9%) and Queensland (189 000 people, 4.2%), and the smallest in the ACT (6200 people, 1.7%). However, the highest proportion of any state or territory occurs in the NT, where Aboriginal and Torres Strait Islander peoples number 68 850 but comprise just on 30% (ABS, 2013a).

Table 4.2 also gives the median age of the Aboriginal and Torres Strait Islander and the non-Indigenous populations. Although there is some variance by state and territory, the greatest variance is by Indigenous status, with half the Aboriginal and Torres Strait

Section II Cultural diversity and resources

Table 4.2 Estimated resident population by Indigenous status, 30 June 2011

	Population			Median age (years)	
	Aboriginal/ Torres Strait Islander (number)	%	Non-Indigenous (number)	Aboriginal/ Torres Strait Islander	Non-Indigenous
New South Wales	208476	2.9	7010053	21.4	38.0
Victoria	47333	0.9	5490484	21.7	37.3
Queensland	188954	4.2	4287824	21.0	37.2
South Australia	37408	2.3	1602206	22.3	39.8
Western Australia	88270	3.8	2265139	22.4	36.8
Tasmania	24165	4.7	487318	21.7	41.3
Northern Territory	68850	29.8	162442	23.8	34.8
Australian Capital Territory	6160	1.7	361825	22.1	34.7
Australia	669881	3.0	21670143	21.8	37.6

Source: ABS (2013a)

Islander population nationally aged less than 22 years, compared with 37.6 years for the non-Indigenous population.

These data must, however, be understood as "best estimates" with, for example, numbers for 2011 representing a very large increase in the Aboriginal and Torres Strait Islander population from the June 2006 estimate of 517000. Based on both descent from an Aboriginal or Torres Strait Islander and acceptance of that descent by other Aboriginal and Torres Strait Island peoples, rigorous assessment of Aboriginal and Torres Strait Island numbers is challenging (ABS, 2001, 2014b), with factors to be taken into account such as inconsistency of the official definition of an Indigenous person with what can be collected in the census; the propensity to identify as Indigenous differing over time and between collections; the existence of people who do not know their Indigenous status; under-reporting of infants and male youth, and the measurement of net census undercount in remote areas. Especially pertinent is "lost" identity due to past (stolen generation) policies which sought to assimilate Aboriginal and Torres Strait Islander children into the white population (Australian Human Rights Commission, 1997; Walter & Andersen, 2013, pp. 33–9). ABS (2001) included an enduring caution for analysts of Indigenous issues, noting that "it is important that there be an awareness of the assumptions involved in estimation. If an analyst does not take account of the uncertainty involved, for example not acknowledging the variation in population that could exist, then the conclusion from that analysis could well be flawed."

Australia – disparate impact

Spatial, demographic and/or compositional diversity can have far-reaching implications, such as the potential for policies to have a 'disparate impact' on one or other population – and its individual members – as a result of that diversity.

Jackson (2002), for example, looked at the impact of a 2001 policy change in NZ under which the age of eligibility for the adult rate of unemployment benefit was suddenly raised from age 20 to age 25. The Māori population was disproportionately exposed to the risk of that policy by virtue of its relatively youthful age structure, just fractionally older than that of Australia's Aboriginal and Torres Strait Islander population. Irrespective of the difference in unemployment rate, in 2001 there were proportionately more than two Māori aged 15–19 years for every European at that age.

Applying similar arguments to Australia elicited that an increase in disparity between Indigenous and non-Indigenous Australians in gaining a bachelor degree or higher between 1981 and 2006 directly coincided with the introduction of Australia's Higher Educational Contribution Scheme (HECS) in 1989, and between 1998 and 2000 in the mainstreaming of an Indigenous-specific student income support scheme, ABSTUDY (Jackson, 2008, p. 18). While the growing gap cannot be conclusively attributed to either the policy developments or differential age structures, the correlation means that age structure should be taken into account when developing policy.

Socio-demographic characteristics

Country of birth

With almost half of the Australian population either a first or second generation immigrant and, with the sole exception of the 3% who are Aboriginal and Torres Strait Islander peoples, all other Australians also by definition descended from a migrant, the nation is home to one of the world's most ethnically diverse populations. The concept of generation is used to describe these population waves, defined by the ABS (2012b) as follows.

First generation Australians are people living in Australia who were born overseas. This is a diverse group of people incl uding Australian citizens, permanent residents, and long-term temporary residents. In 2011, there were 5.3 million first-generation Australians (27% of the population which stated country of birth).

Second generation Australians are Australian-born people living in Australia, with at least one overseas-born parent. In 2011, there were 4.1 million second generation Australians (20% of the population stating country of birth).

*Third-plus generation Australians are Australian-born people whose parents were both born in Australia, but one or more of their grandparents may have been born overseas, or they may have several generations of ancestors born in Australia. **This group also includes most Aboriginal and Torres Strait Islander people.** In 2011, there were 10.6 million third-plus generation Australians (53% of the population stating country of birth).*

Overseas migrant destination

Spatially, the majority of Australia's overseas-born population live in a capital city (82% in 2011, compared with 66% of all Australians) (ABS, 2012b). This greater propensity to live in a capital city largely reflects the location of family members and/or people with the same ethnic background, the point of entry into the country, employment opportunities, and certain visa conditions (ABS, 2012b). Propensity to live in a capital city also differs by generation, with third generation Australians less likely to do so than second or first generation. Relatedly, country of birth differs somewhat by state and territory. Tasmania has the lowest proportion of overseas born at just 12.3% (ABS, 2015c).

Birthplace

A particularly important point about Australia's ethnic diversity is the marked change over time in the main countries of migrant origin. In the immediate period after the Second World War, Australia's immigrants typically came from the United Kingdom and Ireland. This wave was shortly followed by immigrants from Southern and Eastern Europe. During the 1970s, a wave of migrants arrived from South-East Asia, while since the 1980s there has been an increase from other Asian and Middle Eastern countries (ABS, 2012b). These changes have resulted in the proportion of the overseas-born population of European-origin decline substantially, from almost 90% in 1947 to 40% in 2011, while the proportion from the Middle East and Asia has increased from 3% to 37% (ABS, 2014c). However, within those broader aggregations, the United Kingdom remains the dominant individual country of birth, in 2011 accounting for 21% of Australia's overseas-born population, followed by NZ (9.1%), China (6.0%), India (5.6%), and Italy 3.5% (ABS, 2012b, 2014c).

Birthplace and age

The above shifts are even more profound when viewed by age, and illustrate what the late Graeme Hugo regularly described as "multiculturalism in Australia being a highly age-specific phenomenon." The successive population waves arriving from the United Kingdom, Ireland, and other European countries in the 1940s and 1950s today disproportionately comprise the older age groups, while the younger age groups are disproportionately of Middle Eastern and Asian origin (Author/ABS, 2015c, Table 6.1).

Examining birthplace by age also identifies an element of Australia's diversity that is seldom noted and may challenge popular perceptions: the oldest age groups in fact contain the highest proportions of overseas born. The highest proportion occurs at 70–74 years of age, where just on 39% is overseas born, compared with less than 15% for all age groups below 19 years. The disproportionate number of older overseas-born Anglo-Celts in the Australian population is also not because they are "recent" arrivals (ABS, 2012b). Despite the fact that most migrants are relatively young on arrival, those who gain citizenship age along with everyone else, resulting in Australia's overseas-born population being substantially older, and its Australian-born population substantially younger, than the median age of 37.1 years for all Australians would suggest.

Ancestry

In Australia, the concept of ancestry essentially equates to "cultural group" being "an indication of the cultural group that [those filling in their census form] most closely identify with," and usually, but not always, reflects the country of origin of parents and grandparents (ABS, 2012b). While this may seem a straightforward proposition, it introduces a number of methodological issues for the analyst, not least that because people may state more than one ancestry (the 2011 Australian census permitted two), the summed number of responses exceeds the population head count.

Over 300 ancestries were identified at the 2011 census, with English, Australian, Irish, Scottish, Italian, and German the top six (ABS, 2012b). Greek and Dutch ancestries appeared at positions 9 and 10, which meant that among the top 10 ancestries only Chinese and Indian were included. As already indicated, this reflects not only the relative size of each population, but also year of arrival.

Just under one-third of all census respondents identified with more than one ancestry, while second generation migrants were the most likely to do so (46%) followed by third generation migrants at 36% (ABS, 2012b). First generation migrants were least likely (just 14%) to report a second ancestry, plausibly because of lower levels of inter-country marriage among their (non-Australian) parents and grandparents. There also

Table 4.3 Generations by selected ancestries, Australia, 2011

Generations in Australia						
Ancestry	Persons*	Proportion of total population	First generation	Second generation	Third-plus generation	Also stated another ancestry
	'000	%	%	%	%	%
English	7238.5	36.1	18.5	20.1	61.4	53.5
Australian	7098.5	35.4	2.0	18.3	79.6	38.5
Irish	2087.8	10.4	12.9	13.9	73.2	80.4
Scottish	1792.6	8.9	17.1	19.1	63.8	78.3
Italian	916.1	4.6	24.1	41.0	34.9	44.3
German	898.7	4.5	17.3	19.8	62.9	75.4
Chinese	866.2	4.3	74.3	21.3	4.4	16.2
Indian	390.9	2.0	79.8	18.6	1.6	12.9
Greek	378.3	1.9	30.9	44.8	24.3	26.2
Dutch	335.5	1.7	32.5	43.3	24.2	55.1

* Table presents collective responses to ancestry question. As some people stated two ancestries, the total persons for all ancestries exceed Australia's total population.
Source: ABS (2012b)

appears an intuitively correct gradient on Table 4.3, with third generation respondents (those born in Australia with both parents also born in Australia) more likely than either second or first generation migrants to identify with one of the top six "long-standing" ancestries.

Language

Closely connected to country of birth and ancestry is language spoken at home. In 2011, English remained the dominant language spoken at home (81.0%), followed distantly by Mandarin, Italian, Arabic, Cantonese, Greek, Vietnamese, Spanish, Hindi, and Tagalog (ABS, 2012b, 2012c, Table T10). However, there has been a small decline in the proportion speaking only English, and a consequent increase in the proportion speaking another language. Both the number and proportion of those speaking an Australian Indigenous language has also seen a small increase. At the same time, there has been a decline in the proportion (and in some cases, number) speaking several of the longer-standing European languages, such as Croatian, Dutch, German, Greek, Italian, and Polish, plausibly related to the older age structures and thus greater numbers of deaths (relatively speaking) among these communities. Equally notable increases are evident in both proportions and numbers speaking the "newer" Hindi, Korean, Mandarin, Persian, Punjabi, Sinhalese, Tamil, and Thai languages. The aggregate "Other" languages has also seen a sizeable increase.

While over 80% of the Australian population thus speak "only English" at home, non-English languages are playing an increasing role for both Aboriginal and Torres Strait Islander peoples and many migrant communities. And while there are some "shift-share" changes occurring between the older and newer migrant language groups, it should be noted that many older female migrants from Europe never entered the formal workforce, and by contrast with their spouse and children were less exposed to the need to learn English. For such people, as they age, dependence on mother-tongue for communication increases.

Religious affiliation

Australia's diverse ethnic/ancestry/country of birth composition is reflected in an equally diverse religious structure, although it should be kept in mind that for many, religious affiliation is notional as opposed to actual attendance, engagement with, or level of religiosity.

Christianity remains Australia's most common religion. In 2011 it was claimed by almost 90% of those stating a religion, a little lower than in 2001 (note: the denominator *excludes* those stating "no religion") (Author/ABS, 2012c, Tables T12a, 12b, 12c). The decline in proportional share affected 8 of the 19 main Christian religions defined in ABS data, while numbers also declined in absolute terms for 5 (Anglican, Churches of Christ, Presbyterian and Reformed, Salvation Army, and Uniting Church). By contrast, numbers increased by over 437 000 for the Catholic religion (in 2011 accounting for 37% of all religions) but because of its size the percentage increase was one of the smallest. There were more notable percentage increases in numbers for Assyrian Apostolic, Oriental Orthodox, and "Christian not further defined."

All non-Christian religions saw both increased numbers and increased percentage share, with numbers increasing most substantially for Buddhism, Hinduism, Islam, and "Other Religious Groups." At the same time, the number of Australians stating "no religion" increased by 1.9 million and in 2011 accounted for 24% of those stating their religion, whether a specific religion or no religion. As with all other social variables, there is substantial underlying diversity by age, but this cannot be examined here (see ABS, 2012c).

Birth rates and family formation

Overall, Australia's overseas-born women have a lower total fertility rate (in 2011, an average 1.8 births per woman) and a higher median age at childbearing (the age above and below which half of all births occur) than Australian-born women (1.9 births per woman), a fact that often surprises people (ABS, 2013b, Table 1). Within this picture, Australia's youngest childbearing ages are for women from North Africa and the Middle East, and this is reflected in their having the highest average number of births per woman (3.0). Childbearing rates at 15–19 and 20–24 years are also relatively high for NZ-born women, reflecting the pattern in NZ, although the resulting total fertility rates for NZ and Australian-born women do not differ greatly (2.1 and 1.9 births per woman respectively), and their median ages at childbearing in 2011 were almost identical, 30.6 and 30.3 years respectively. By contrast, childbearing at younger ages is lowest for women born in North-East Asia, with the total fertility rate of 1.4 births per woman similar to the low rates observed in their countries of origin. Even for women born in high-fertility countries and migrating to Australia, birth rates tend to adapt quite quickly to Australian levels and patterns (Abbasi-Shavazi & McDonald, 2000, pp. 234–5).

Fertility and family formation patterns also differ by Indigenous/non-Indigenous status (ABS, 2014d, Table 11.8). Both groups have experienced overall declines in total fertility rates (to 1.9 and 2.3 births per woman in 2013), and increases in median age at childbearing. However, childbearing continues to takes place at much younger ages for Aboriginal and Torres Strait Islander women, currently peaking at 20–24 years compared with 30–34 years for non-Indigenous women – a characteristic that may reflect an Indigenous pattern of childbearing and may not necessarily move to the older ages of non-Indigenous people as indicated in "second demographic transition" theory (Johnstone, 2011).[2] Earlier caveats regarding the approximate nature of Indigenous enumeration should be recalled (Walter & Andersen, 2013, pp. 33–9), as both the numerators and denominators for these rates are subject to a number of data collection limitations (ABS, 2014e).

---

[2] Second demographic transition theory holds that social change related to partnering and family formation patterns causes overall fertility levels to first decline to replacement level (2.1 births per woman), then age at childbearing to increase (Lesthaeghe and van de Kaa 1986). See www.eaps.nl/scientific-activities/working-groups/second-demographic-transition-europe-completed

Mortality

Australia's mortality (death) rates and patterns similarly differ by region/country of birth/Indigenous status; however, these rates are not as straightforward to interpret. Median age at death (the age above and below which half of all deaths occur) is lowest for NZ-born males and females (69.0 and 77.6 years respectively) and highest for males born in Southern and Eastern Europe (81.2 years) and females born in North-West Europe (85.3 years) (ABS, 2013c, Table 1). However, the low median age at death for the NZ-born population reflects its relative youthfulness in Australia, while the high median ages for southern, eastern, and north-west Europe reflect their older age structures.

A more robust indicator of mortality differences is "life expectancy": the average number of years of life remaining at a given age. However, even this indicator is difficult to use for comparison in relation to migrant country of birth, because the average age of arrival in Australia is around 27 years. Accordingly, an ABS analysis used life expectancy at age 30 years as the base (ABS, 2002). It showed that around 1997–1999, Australian-born residents generally had lower life expectancy at 30 years (men 47.4 years, women 52.5 years) than the first generation overseas-born population (men 48.9 years, women 53.6 years), suggesting that migrants may have more favourable health than the Australian-born population. As noted for the fertility differentials, the mortality differential has also been broadly attributed to migrant selectivity (i.e., the characteristics of migrants).

Recent data indicate that life expectancy at birth 2010–2012 was around 69.1 years for Aboriginal and Torres Strait Islander males and 73.7 years for females (ABS, 2013d), compared with 79.7 and 83.1 years for all Australian males and females respectively (ABS, 2014e, 2014f). These estimates, along with a few studies (e.g., Wilson, Condon, & Barnes, 2007) indicate some improvement over time, although measurement of life expectancy for Aboriginal and Torres Strait Islanders remains subject to many data limitations. Either way it is clear that rates remain well below those of all Australians (around 12 and 11 years respectively for males and females). These differences, by and large, have their antecedents in Australia's colonial past, as opposed to having "cultural" explanations (Walter & Andersen, 2013).

Household and family composition

The category "family households" has comprised just over two-thirds of Australian households at each of the last three censuses (ABS, 2012c, Table 14). While numbers for all household types have increased, couple families without children have increased slightly as a proportion, accounting for one-quarter of all households in 2011, while couples with children have declined slightly, from one-third in 2001 to just on 31% in 2011. One-parent families have remained fairly static, at 10.5% to 10.6%, while "other" family types have declined slightly, in 2011 accounting for just over 1%.

Among non-family households, lone person households have increased minutely, in 2011 accounting for almost one-quarter of all households, while there have been slightly greater percentage increases in the numerically much smaller "group" and "other" household types.

The trend of an increasing proportion of couple without children families and a concomitantly decreasing proportion of couples with children is likely to continue, as it reflects several discrete trends by age, among them declining birth rates, an increase in the number of those in their mid-to-late 20s and early 30s who have not yet had (and may never have) children, and a substantially greater increase at age 50 and above of those who may have had children, but are now "empty-nesters". Lone person households are also expected to increase, as population ageing results in a greater proportion widowed.

Data on the social marital status of families with children indicate that in 2011 just over three-quarters of Australia's families with children had parents who were either married or in a de facto relationship. This proportion had declined fractionally between 2001 and 2011, and just over 22% were headed by a single parent, again the proportion altering only minutely since 2001 (ABS, 2012c, Table 27).

The 2011 census enumerated 33 714 same-sex couples, 32% more than in 2006 (ABS, 2012d). As in previous censuses, male couples outnumbered female couples at a ratio of 109 male couples per 100 female couples; however, the gap has narrowed since 1996 (when data on same-sex couples were first collected) and there were 137 male couples for every 100 female couples. In 2011, same-sex couples accounted for 0.7% of all couple families, up from 0.6% in 2006, and more than twice the proportion in 1996 (0.3%) although this differs greatly by age. According to the ABS, these are similar rates to those for NZ (see Chapter 5).

The very youthful age structure of the Indigenous Australian population noted earlier results in this group having a slightly greater proportion living in family households (81% compared with 71% for non-Indigenous households) (ABS, 2012e, Table I12). Within the family household category, one-parent families account for somewhat greater proportion of Indigenous than non-Indigenous households (27% compared with 10%), as do multiple family households (5.5% compared with 1.5%). Conventionally reflecting a younger age structure, one-person households are, on the other hand, relatively low for Indigenous people (14% compared with 25%).

Comparison between migrant and non-migrant families shows that migrant families have higher proportions in couple families both with and without children, and lower proportions in one-parent families (ABS, 2011c, Table 2). Migrants born in a main English-speaking country have higher proportions of couple families without children than their counterparts born in other than a main English-speaking country and lower proportions of both couple families with children and one-parent families. Migrants arriving between 2005 and 2010 had the overall highest proportions of couple without children families (almost 50%), and overall lowest proportions of both couple with children and one-parent families, attesting to the younger age and lifecycle stage of recent migrants. Those arriving before 2005 had relatively high proportions of couple with children and one-parent families, suggesting that time since arrival allows for family formation.

As with all other social characteristics, family and household composition is cross-cutting by age, sex, individual country of birth (see also ABS, 2013e), subnational region, and socio-economic status. The diversity is too great to expand upon further in this chapter, but a search on the ABS website in addition to references given will quickly identify relevant material.

Socio-economic characteristics

Qualification levels

Australia's modal qualification is Certificate III and IV, in 2011 accounting for 34% of those stating a qualification (ABS, 2012c, Table 30c). Notably, this proportion has declined since 2001, as has the proportion holding certificate I and II qualifications, in both cases reflecting the general ascendance to a higher qualification. That is, for many people qualifications are a fluid situation, with lower levels superseded as higher qualifications are gained. This "shift-share" effect can also be seen in the small decline in proportions holding a graduate diploma and graduate certificate alongside increases in other tertiary level qualifications, especially postgraduate degree. However, the importing of qualifications along with migrants is also involved. Before moving on to discuss that situation, it should also be noted that there have been significant changes in qualification levels by sex over the past two decades, with females increasingly more likely than males to hold all but postgraduate degree and certificate III and IV qualifications. For example, in 2011 females were 1.3 times as likely as males to hold a Bachelor degree, up from 1.2 times as likely in 2001, and 1.73 times as likely to hold a graduate diploma or graduate certificate, up from 1.66 times as likely in 2001. In 2011, females were also 0.9 times as likely as males to hold a postgraduate degree, up from 0.6 times as likely in 2001.

Qualifications by Indigenous Australian status

In 2011, the modal qualification for the Aboriginal and Torres Strait Islander population was similarly certificate III and IV, held by almost 52% of Indigenous people stating a non-school qualification (ABS, 2012e, Table 115c). This rate is somewhat higher than for the non-Indigenous population (33.8% of whom hold such a qualification), while non-Indigenous people are 2.8 times as likely to hold a postgraduate level qualification, 2.2 times as likely to hold a bachelor degree and 1.2 times as likely to hold an advanced diploma. These differentials are also greater at younger ages, with non-Indigenous people aged 20–24 and 25–29 years being respectively 4.8 and 4.6 times more likely than their Indigenous counterparts to hold a postgraduate qualification, 4.1 and 2.8 times more likely to hold a bachelor degree and 2.2 and 1.3 times more likely to hold an advanced diploma. Indigenous females are, however, more likely than non-Indigenous females to hold higher levels of postgraduate, graduate, and diploma level qualifications than their male counterparts (ABS, 2012e, Tables 115a and 115b).

Migrant qualifications

The qualification levels of Australia's migrants are typically higher than the non-migrant population, in part reflecting entry visa requirements. In 2010, males and females born overseas were respectively 10% and 8% more likely than Australian-born people to hold a non-school qualification. This was true for all age groups with the sole exception of 15–19 years (ABS, 2011d, Table 9). More recent survey data indicate that around 72% of migrants arriving in the last 10 years had obtained a non-school qualification before their arrival in Australia (ABS, 2014e, Table 3). Of these, 72% had obtained a bachelor degree or higher, 15% an advanced diploma or diploma, and 12% a certificate level qualification. However, having a qualification does not necessarily translate into using it or having it recognised. Only one-third of recent migrants who had obtained a non-school qualification before arrival had those qualifications recognised in Australia, in many cases because they did not seek, or have not yet sought, to have their qualification recognised (ABS, 2014f, Tables 3 and 16).

Qualifications and employment

Those born overseas and holding a non-school qualification were more likely to be employed either full-time or part-time than their Australian-born equivalents, while the opposite was true for those without a non-school qualification (with Australian born having higher employment rates) (ABS, 2011d, Table 9).

Further differentials exist by whether those born overseas were born in a main English-speaking country or elsewhere (ABS, 2011d, Table 9). Those born in a country other than a main English-speaking country and aged less than 45 years in 2010 were more likely to hold a non-school qualification than their counterparts born in a main English-speaking country; this was also the case for all males and all females. Those born overseas in a country other than a main English-speaking country and holding a non-school qualification had equal proportions employed full-time (50.3%) but were more likely to be employed part-time than their counterparts born in a main English-speaking country.

Differences also exist by industry and occupation of employment (ABS, 2011d, Table 9) as well as migrant visa and residence status (ABS, 2014f, Table 2). Overall, however, the data paint a picture of Australia's overseas born being more highly qualified than the Australian born and more likely to work in a skilled occupation or industry, with these margins being generally greater for those born in other than a main English-speaking country and for those arriving since 2006. These characteristics are likely to mirror the changing entry requirements for migrant visas and should not be interpreted as reflecting the general aptitude or intellectual capacities of either population (Lee & Bean, 2010). Indeed, the exceptions also show that being overseas born and holding a non-school qualification is equally associated with higher proportions in lower skilled occupations and industries, suggesting that the qualifications of some overseas born may not translate to the same type of employment as for the Australian born.

Reflecting their lower qualification levels, the Aboriginal and Torres Strait Islander population has substantially lower labour force participation and employment rates and higher unemployment rates than the non-Indigenous population (ABS, 2012e, Table I14). However, as discussed earlier, in addition to data collection issues the marked age structural disparities between these populations should be kept in mind when considering these economic differentials, as younger and older populations are differently exposed to the risk of unemployment (see Jackson, 2013 Chapter 7 for age standardisation methodology).

Sex differentials suggest that while females have lower labour force participation rates than males irrespective of Indigenous status, Indigenous females within the labour force have higher employment rates than males and lower unemployment rates. For non-Indigenous males and females, both employment and unemployment rates (within the labour force) are the same. Sector differences show less variance by Indigenous status, with the majority of both groups employed in the private sector, and this being similar by sex (ABS, 2012e, Table I14).

Diversity and the Australian psychological workforce

Finally, this chapter briefly turns to the age–sex structure of Australia's psychologist workforce. The data indicate an increasingly feminised and rapidly ageing occupational group (Australian and New Zealand Standard Classification of Occupations [ANZSCO] code 27323 comprised of clinical psychologists, educational psychologists, organisational psychologists, psychotherapists, and psychologists not further defined). Between 2006 and 2011, the number of psychologists employed in Australia grew by 7.9% (+5165 positions) (Table 4.4). Just over one-third of this growth occurred at

Table 4.4 Selected indices, psychologists, Australia, 2006 and 2011

	2006		2011		Change 2006–2011	
	N	%	N	%	N	%
Males	3307	(22.1)	4109	(24.6)	+802	(+24.3)
Females	10131	(77.9)	14494	(75.4)	+4363	(+43.1)
Total	13438	(100.0)	18603	(100.0)	+5165	(+67.4)
Sex ratio (M:F)	0.33		0.28		–	(–13.2)
Average age	43.7		44.5		–	(+2.0)
% 55+ years	20.6		24.3		–	(+18.0)
Employment entry: exit ratio 15–29: 55+ years	0.76		0.58		–	(–23.3)

Source: Author/ABS (2006, 2011e)

55+ years of age, although the ageing of the baby boomer cohorts (officially born 1946–65) and plausibly remaining employed in the occupation across the period accounts for some of that growth. In 2001 the baby boomers were aged 41–60 years, and in 2006 were aged 46–65 years; the growth in numbers at 60–64 years in Figure 4.2 suggests a cohort effect among the leading-edge baby boomers. That said, there has also been a significant increase in numbers employed in this occupational group at 35–39 years (predominantly females) which is not a cohort effect. Reflecting this trend, Table 4.4 identifies a continuing feminisation of the occupation, with the sex ratio (males per female) falling from 0.33 in 2006 to 0.28 in 2011.

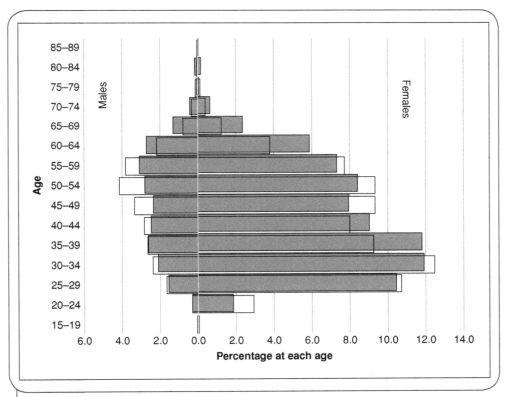

Figure 4.2 Age–sex structure, psychologists, Australia, 2006 and 2011
Source: Author/ABS (2006, 2011e)

But it is the ratio of people at labour market "entry" to "exit" age which epitomises the ageing of this occupation (among many). In 2006, there had been almost 8 psychologists employed at 20–29 years for every 10 at 55+ years, at which time 20.6% was aged 55+ years; by 2011 that ratio had fallen to 0.58 (less than 6 per 10), with 24.3% aged 55+ years. This occupation is somewhat older than the total Australian workforce, which in 2011 had approximately 17.6% aged 55+ years. Irrespective of the likelihood of a longer work life, Figure 4.2 indicates that most people have retired from this occupation by age 75, and that retirement starts in earnest from age 65.

Those interested in descriptions of the Australian counselling workforce vs. psychological are referred to Pelling, Brear and Lau (2006), Pelling (2005), Armstrong (2006), Schofield (2008), Schofield et al. (2006), and Lack and Pelling (2009).

References

Abbasi-Shavazi, M. J., & McDonald, P. (2000). Fertility and multiculturalism: Immigrant fertility in Australia, 1977–1991. *International Migration Review, 34*(1), 215–242.

Armstrong, P. (2006). The Australian Counselling Association: Meeting the needs of Australian counsellors. *International Journal of Psychology* [Special issue "Counselling in Australia"], *41*(3), 153–155.

Australian Bureau of Statistics (2001). *Demography working paper 2001/4—Issues in estimating the Indigenous population.* Cat. no. 3126.0. Canberra: Author.

Australian Bureau of Statistics (2002). *Australian demographic statistics, Sep 2001.* Cat. no. 3101.0. Canberra: Author.

Australian Bureau of Statistics (2005). *Information paper. Regional policy and research in Australia – the statistical dimension information development plan for rural and regional statistics.* Cat. No 1362.0. Canberra: Author.

Australian Bureau of Statistics (2006). *Age 5 year age groups (AGEP) by occupation 06 (ANZSCO) (OCC06P) and sex male/female (SEXP) counting: Persons, place of usual residence (TableBuilder).* Canberra: Author.

Australian Bureau of Statistics (2011a). *Australian population grid, 2011.* Cat. no. 1270.0.55.007. Canberra: Author.

Australian Bureau of Statistics (2011b). *Australian demographic statistics.* Cat. no. 3101.0. Canberra: Author.

Australian Bureau of Statistics (2011c). *Migrants, family characteristics Australia, 2009–10.* Cat. no. 34150DS0059, Table 2. Canberra: Author.

Australian Bureau of Statistics (2011d). *Migrants, education and work, Australia, May 2010.* Cat. no. 34150DS0051, Table 9. Canberra: Author.

Australian Bureau of Statistics (2011e). *Census of population and dwellings, persons by place of usual residence, AGE5P—Age in five year groups by OCCP—4 digit level and SEXP (TableBuilder).* Canberra: Author.

Australian Bureau of Statistics (2012a). *Australian statistical geography standard (ASGS): Volume 4—Significant urban areas, urban centres and localities, section of state, July 2011.* Cat. no. 1270.0.55.004. Canberra: Author.

Australian Bureau of Statistics (2012b). *Cultural diversity in Australia. Reflecting a nation: Stories from the 2011 Census – 2012–2013.* Cat. no. 2071.0. Canberra: Author. Available: www.abs.gov.au/ausstats/abs@.nsf/Lookup/2071.0main+featu res902012–2013

Australian Bureau of Statistics (2012c). *Time series profile. Australia.* Cat. no. 2003.0. Canberra: Author.

Australian Bureau of Statistics (2012d). *Same-sex couple families. Reflecting a nation: Stories from the 2011 Census, 2012–2013.* Cat. no. 2071.0. Canberra: Author.

Available: www.abs.gov.au/ausstats/abs@.nsf/Latestproducts/2071.0Main%20Feature s852012%E2%80%932013?opendocument&tabname=Summary&prodno=2071.0&iss ue=2012%E2%80%932013&num=&view=

Australian Bureau of Statistics (2012e). *Aboriginal and Torres Strait Islander peoples (Indigenous) profile, 2011*. Cat. no. 2002.0. Canberra: Author.

Australian Bureau of Statistics (2013a). *Estimates of Aboriginal and Torres Strait Islander Australians, June 2011*. Cat. no. 3238.0.55.001. Canberra: Author. Available: www.abs. gov.au/ausstats/abs@.nsf/PrimaryMainFeatures/3238.0.55.001?OpenDocument

Australian Bureau of Statistics (2013b). *Migrants, births, Australia, 2011*. Cat. no. 34150DS0077. Canberra: Author.

Australian Bureau of Statistics (2013c). *Migrants, deaths, Australia, 2011*. Cat. no. 34150DS0078. Canberra: Author.

Australian Bureau of Statistics (2013d). *Life tables for Aboriginal and Torres Strait Islander Australians, 2010–2012*. Cat. no. 3302055003DO001_20102012. Canberra: Author.

Australian Bureau of Statistics (2013e). *Migrant families in Australia – Perspectives on migrants, March 2013*. Cat. no. 3416.0. Canberra: Author. Available: www.abs.gov.au/ ausstats/abs@.nsf/Latestproducts/3416.0Main+Features2Mar+2013

Australian Bureau of Statistics (2014a). *3101.0 Australian demographic statistics (June years)*. Canberra: Author.

Australian Bureau of Statistics (2014b). *Estimates and projections, Aboriginal and Torres Strait Islander Australians, 2001 to 2026*. Cat. no. 3238.0. Canberra: Author.

Australian Bureau of Statistics (2014c). *Australian historical population statistics, 2014*. Cat. no. 3105.0.65.001. Canberra: Author.

Australian Bureau of Statistics (2014d). *Births, Australia, 2013*. Table 11.8. Cat. no. 3301.0. Canberra: Author.

Australian Bureau of Statistics (2014e). *Deaths, Australia, 2013*. Cat. no. 33020DO020. Canberra: Author.

Australian Bureau of Statistics (2014f). *Characteristics of recent migrants, Australia, November 2013*. Cat. no. 62500DO001_201311. Canberra: Author.

Australian Bureau of Statistics (2015a). *Australian demographic statistics, September 2014*. Cat. no. 31010DO002_201409. Canberra: Author.

Australian Bureau of Statistics (2015b). *Average weekly earnings, Australia, November 2014*. Cat. no. 6302.0. Canberra: Author.

Australian Bureau of Statistics (2015c). *Migration, Australia, 2013–14*. Cat. no. 34120DO006_201314. Canberra: Author.

Australian Human Rights Commission. (1997). *Bringing them home: The stolen children report*. Available: https://www.humanrights.gov.au/our-work/aboriginal-and-torres- strait-islander-social-justice/publications/bringing-them-home-stolen

Jackson, N. O. (2002). The doubly-structural nature of Indigenous disadvantage. Indigenous age structures and the notion of disparate impact. *New Zealand Population Review, 28*(1), 55–68.

Jackson, N. O. (2008). Educational attainment and the (growing) importance of age structure: Indigenous and non-Indigenous Australians. *Journal of Population Research, 25*(2), 223–244.

Jackson, N. O. (2013). Population-level analysis. In M. Walter (Ed.), *Social research methods: An Australian perspective* (3rd ed., pp. 147–173). Melbourne: Oxford University Press.

Johnstone, K. (2011). Indigenous fertility transitions in developed countries. *New Zealand Population Review, 37*: 105–123.

Judd, F. K., Jackson, H. J., Komiti, A., Murray, G., Hodgins, G., & Fraser, C. (2002). High prevalence disorders in urban and rural communities. *Australian and New Zealand Journal of Psychiatry, 36*, 104–113.

Lack, C. W., & Pelling, N. (2009). Who are Australian counsellors and how do they attend to their professional development? In N. Pelling, J. Barletta, & P. Armstrong (Eds.), *The practice of clinical supervision* (pp. 212–221). Bowen Hills, Qld: Australian Academic Press.

Lee, J., & Bean, F. (2010). *The diversity paradox. Immigration and the color line in twenty-first century America.* New York: Russell Sage Foundation Press.

Lesthaeghe, R., & van de Kaa, D. (1986). Twee demografische transities? In: D. J. van de Kaa, & R. Lesthaeghe (eds), *Bevolking: Krimpen groet*, Deventer: Van LoghumSlaterus.

Pelling, N. (2005). Summary of the survey on the membership of the Australian Counselling Association. *Counselling Australia, 5*(4), 115–118.

Pelling, N., Brear, P., & Lau, M. (2006). A survey of advertised Australian counsellors. *International Journal of Psychology, 41*(3), 204–215.

Rosevear, L. (2012). The impact of structural ageing on crime trends: A South Australian case study. *Trends and Issues in Crime and Criminal Justice*, No. 431. Canberra: Australian Institute of Criminology.

Schofield, M. (2008). Australian counsellors and psychotherapists: A profile of the profession. *Australian Counselling and Psychotherapy Research* [Special issue "Counselling & Psychotherapy Research"], *8*(1), 4–11.

Schofield, M., Grant, J., Holmes, S., & Barletta, J. (2006). The Psychotherapy and Counselling Federation of Australia: How the federation model contributes to the field. *International Journal of Psychology* [Special issue "Counselling in Australia"], *41*(3), 194–203.

Walter, M., & Andersen, C. (2013). *Indigenous statistics. A quantitative research methodology.* Walnut Creek, CA: Left Coast Press Inc.

Wilson, T., Condon, J. R., & Barnes, T. (2007). Northern Territory Indigenous life expectancy improvements, 1967–2004. *Australia and New Zealand Journal of Public Health, 31*(2), 184–188.

Recommendations for further reading/resources

General

Easterlin, R. (1987). *Birth and fortune* (2nd ed.). Chicago: University of Chicago Press.

Epstein, G. S., & Heizler (Cohen), O. (2015). Ethnic identity: A theoretical framework. *IZA Journal of Migration, 4*(9), 1–11. http://dx.doi.org/10.1186/s40176-015-0033-z

Glen, N. (1976) *Cohort analysis.* London: Sage Publications.

Hewlett, S., Marshall, M., & Sherbin, P. (2013). How diversity can drive innovation. *Harvard Business Review*, *Dec.* Available: https://hbr.org/2013/12/how-diversity-can-drive-innovation

Mannheim, K. (1929/1952/1993). The problem of generations. In L. K. Wolff (Ed.), *From Karl Mannheim* (2nd ed., pp. 351–398). New Brunswick, NJ: Transaction Publishers.

Nijkamp, P., & Poot, J. (2015). Cultural diversity – a matter of measurement. In P. Nijkamp, J. Poot, & J. Bakens. (Eds.), *The economics of cultural diversity.* (pp. 17–51) Cheltenham, UK: Edward Elgar.

Ryder, N. (1965). The cohort as a concept in the study of social change. *American Sociological Review*, *30*, 843–861.

Australian

ABS (2013f). *Measures of Australia's progress, 2013.* Cat. no. 1370.0. Canberra: Australian Bureau of Statistics.

Kukutai, T., & Taylor, J. (2012). Postcolonial profiling of Indigenous populations: Limitations and responses in Australia and Aotearoa New Zealand. *Special issue on Indigenous Demography, Space, Populations, Societies*.

Perera, S., Seal, G., & Summers, S. (Eds.). (2010). *Enter at own risk: Australia's population questions for the 21st Century.* Perth: Black Swan Press.

5

Diversity in New Zealand

Natalie Jackson

Introduction

Mirroring Chapter 4 on Australia, this chapter outlines the equally diverse nature of New Zealand's population. As will be shown, different historical issues have led to diversity being measured somewhat differently in New Zealand (NZ) – such as a focus on ethnicity as opposed to country of birth – while paradoxically, in NZ the description of people defined by particular countries of birth as "ethnics," as is often the case in Australia, is never heard. Reflecting a host of underlying definitional problems, the chapter also covers related measurement issues and their methodological implications. Where important to further analysis, these issues are briefly explained. As in the chapter on Australia, this chapter provides background demographic and socio-economic data for use by students, rather than substantive analysis of diversity.[1]

New Zealand – what is diversity?

Interest in diversity differs by country. In NZ, diversity typically makes people think of "ethnic group," that is, whether people are (broadly) Māori, European, Pacific Island, or Asian in origin, while in Australia diversity tends to be thought of in terms of country of birth and generation of migrant. Like age and sex, these are examples of "inherent diversity" (traits people are born with).

By contrast, diversity gained from experience, such as one's personal, social, and economic characteristics, is termed "acquired diversity." Acquired characteristics also tend to differ at group level, such as by ethnic group or spatially (e.g., by region), and require methodological consideration when making sub-population comparisons.

---

[1] Where data have been drawn directly from Statistics New Zealand and there has been no added analysis, the reference is given as Statistics NZ. Where analysis has been applied (e.g., raw data have been converted to percentages for easier comparison), the reference is given as Author/Statistics NZ. This is to protect Statistics NZ from any computational errors made by the author, and not to claim ownership of the data.

Spatial distribution

With over 85% of its population living in an urban area NZ, like Australia, has one of the developed world's most urbanised populations. In 2013, two-thirds of NZ's population lived in its 13 cities (one-third in Auckland alone), up from 62% in 1996. Between 1996 and 2013, 90% of population growth was accounted for by just five cities and eight urban districts, while one-third of the overall 67 territorial authority areas declined in size, primarily because of net migration loss at young adult ages. NZ's urbanisation is, however, now slowing – plausibly because the proportion living in an urban area is approaching its maximum.

At the same time, urban and "rural" living differs greatly by one of the central characteristics of this chapter – ethnicity. At the 2013 Census, NZ's Asian, Pacific Island, and Middle Eastern/Latin American/African populations were disproportionately likely to be living in Auckland (66.0%, 65.0%, and 53.0% respectively), while only 27.0% of those of European origin and 25.0% of Māori did so (Author/Statistics NZ, 2014a). A related issue for Māori is that of "place." Many Māori make a distinction between where they "live" and where they "stay." Where one "lives" tends to relate to one's *turangawaewae* or *rohe* (where one's feet belong/ancestral land), while where one "stays" refers to where one currently resides. Being either *mana whenua* (residing in one's own *rohe*) or *mataawaka* (residing away from one's *rohe*) can have wellbeing implications. This would appear somewhat different to the role of "neighbourhood" in wellbeing (Ivory et al., 2012).

Thus, the populations of NZ's regions and local government areas, like those of Australia (Chapter 4), differ and, in addition to ethnicity and country of birth, do so markedly in terms of age and sex structure, industry and occupation, labour force status, income, education, and so on. Each of these variables is also, of course, cross-cutting. It is not possible to deal with such detail in this chapter, but it should be kept in mind when undertaking related analyses.

One overarching feature, however, is the level of socio-economic diversity. This factor underpins and interacts with most other characteristics, so is provided here by way of setting the scene for NZ. Figure 5.1 shows median household income for each of NZ's 16 regional council areas by comparison with the national average (in 2013, $63 800). Three regions have median household income above the national average: Auckland, Wellington, and Canterbury. The remaining regions are all below the national average, ranging between $59 600 (Waikato) and $46 900 (Northland), with the total variance between the relatively wealthy Auckland and its relatively poor northern neighbour, Northland, almost $30 000.

Before moving on from this brief overview, one other important spatial factor in contemporary NZ is the aftermath of the Christchurch earthquakes of 2010 and 2011, the latter of which killed 185 people and destroyed large swathes of the central business district and surrounding suburbs and homes. The disaster resulted

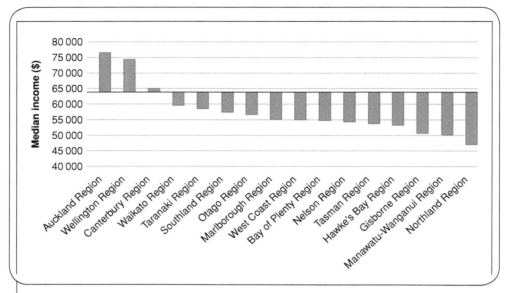

Figure 5.1 Median household income for the usually resident population living in a private dwelling, by regional council area and comparison with the NZ average, 2013 census
Source: Author/Statistics NZ (2014b, Table 12). This work is based on/includes Statistics New Zealand's data which are licensed by Statistics New Zealand for re-use under the Creative Commons Attribution 4.0 International licence.

in the displacement of over 20 000 people from the city, with many areas across the country (and in Australia) gaining earthquake "refugee" inflows. Population growth is now returning to the city as the rebuild begins, but it is yet unknown how many of those displaced by the traumatic events will return, or how many internal migrants and/or overseas-born among those rebuilding the city will eventually remain.

Socio-demographic characteristics

Unlike Australia, where diversity is primarily measured in terms of country of birth and generation since migration (i.e., first, second, third), diversity in NZ is primarily measured in terms of ethnic group. This is because, until the 1990s, NZ had relatively few people who were not of either Māori or European origin – less than 8% in 1991 (Pool et al., 2005, p. 47), a vastly different situation just two decades later when 20% of the 2013 census population identified as neither Māori nor European (Author/Statistics NZ, 2014a). However, NZ's measurement of ethnicity, and thus analysis by ethnicity, is *analytically* problematic due to the "multiple count" method of enumeration via which people identifying as more than one ethnic group are counted more than once (see also Kukutai 2011, 2012, and Walter & Andersen 2013 on the political aspects of constructing ethnic boundaries).

New Zealand – measuring ethnic diversity

Since 1986, ethnicity in NZ has been measured according to the ethnic group or groups that people specify they belong to, the underlying concept being "self-identified ethnic affiliation." This is a substantially different and thankfully more contemporary approach to the measurement of ethnicity by comparison with the "race" and "blood fraction" indices used in NZ until 1971 and 1981 respectively.

The "multiple count" approach means that people can be counted in more than one ethnic group. In 2013, over half of the 692 300 people identifying as Māori specified more than one ethnic group, and when considered against the total population head count (4.442 million), accounted for 15.6%. However, when all ethnic group responses are summed in this way, the population head count is exceeded by 11.3%; that is, the resulting proportions sum to 111.3%. This makes description of the data very difficult, because people automatically question if percentages appear to sum to more than 100.

Panel A of Table 5.1 shows that the NZ population headcount in 2013 was 4 442 100 persons, while Panel B shows that numbers when summed totalled 4 943 200 persons, giving an "ethnic over-count" of 501 100 persons (11.3%). This ethnic over-count has also increased since 1996, when it was 9.6%, as there has not only been an increase in the propensity of people of Māori origin to identify both themselves and their children as Māori (a trend referred to in census data as "inter-ethnic mobility"), but the increasing numbers of overseas-born in the population is also increasing the number identifying with more than one ethnic group.

My own preferred approach – for descriptive clarity – is to sum the responses and calculate the proportions so that they total 100% (the approach taken for Panel B). However, when the responses are summed, the proportion of Māori drops to 14%, that is, 14.0% of all *responses* to the ethnic group question in the 2013 census were Māori. In NZ, where financial reparation for historical injustices is still being pursued and settled, this methodological conundrum could have significant financial implications for tribal groups (*iwi*). Similarly, it can have implications when various socio-economic factors are being analysed by ethnicity, and/or policy is being conceptualised or developed. It is thus very important to be clear about the statistic to which one is referring: the head count proportion or the response count proportion.

Two related measurement issues require brief mention. The first is that the proportion specifying Māori ethnicity increases as age decreases, in part because of an ongoing increase in the propensity of young adults and children to identify (or be identified in the census by their parents) as Māori. The second is that NZ's ethnic groups differ markedly by age structure, due to underlying demographic differences

Table 5.1 NZ usually resident population by major ethnic group* based on head count (Panel A) and summed responses (Panel B), 1996, 2001, 2006, 2013

	1996	2001	2006	2013
Panel A: Headcount percentages*				
European or Other ethnicity (incl. "New Zealander")	82.4	79.2	76.8	74.6
Māori	15.4	15.1	14.9	15.6
Pacific peoples	6.1	6.7	7.2	7.8
Asian	5.2	7.0	9.7	12.2
Middle Eastern/Latin American/ African	0.5	0.7	0.9	1.2
Total (headcount)	109.6	108.8	109.5	111.3
Number – total headcount	3 732 000	3 880 500	4 184 600	4 442 100
Panel B: Response count percentages*				
European or Other ethnicity (incl. "New Zealander")	75.2	72.8	70.1	67.0
Māori	14.0	13.9	13.6	14.0
Pacific peoples	5.6	6.2	6.6	7.0
Asian	4.8	6.5	8.8	11.0
Middle Eastern/Latin American/ African	0.5	0.7	0.8	1.1
Total (ethnic groups summed*)	100.0	100.0	100.0	100.0
Number – ethnic groups summed	4 090 350	4 221 800	4 582 200	4 943 200

* Multiple ethnic origin count means that people may be counted in more than one ethnic group
Source: Author/Statistics NZ (2014a). This work is based on/includes Statistics New Zealand's data which are licensed by Statistics New Zealand for re-use under the Creative Commons Attribution 4.0 International licence.

in fertility, mortality and migration – and their historical antecedents (Pool 1991, 2015). Today the European-origin population is relatively old, with a median age of 41 years, and the Māori and Pacific Island populations relatively young, with median ages of 24 and 22 years respectively. NZ's rapidly growing Asian population, and somewhat smaller but also rapidly growing Middle Eastern/Latin American/ African (MELAA) population, have median ages in the middle of the distribution, at 31 and 29 years respectively. Thus the proportions of each ethnic group *by age* differ dramatically to those indicated for each *total* group in Tables 5.1 and 5.2 and must be taken into account when making any group level comparisons regarding social indicators.

Irrespective of the measure used, it is, however, important to record that even at 14.0% Māori comprise the largest Indigenous population of their four "settler" country counterparts (NZ, Australia, Canada, United States), with the next largest group being Australia's Aboriginal and Torres Strait Islander population at just below 3.0%. For Māori, the situation contributes to a strong sense of common identity vis-à-vis the numerically dominant European-origin population. However, it must also be cautioned that the Māori "population" is not a single unit; it is comprised of many tribal subgroups (*iwi*, *hapu*, *whanau*) which have always identified strongly as independent entities.

Looking ahead, the speed with which NZ's ethnic composition is changing, and that this will plausibly see the Asian ethnic group draw level with Māori numbers within a decade (Statistics NZ, 2009), is a related factor requiring acknowledgement. Asian people aged 25–34 years now outnumber Māori at that age (in 2013, 95 000 compared with 85 000), a significant change since just 2001 when young Māori outnumbered young Asians by more than two to one (Statistics NZ, 2014a, Table 6).

Country of birth

Accompanying these trends, country of birth data provide an additional and extremely important perspective on NZ's changing ethnic and cultural diversity (Figure 5.2, see also Statistics NZ, 2014c, Table 5). In 1936, 19% of NZ's usually resident population had been born overseas, the vast majority (77%) from the United Kingdom (UK) and Ireland. By the mid-1980s, the proportion of overseas-born had dropped to 15–16%, due at first to the birth of NZ's baby boomers (in NZ officially 1946–65) and then to the leading-edge baby boomers reaching reproductive age and having their own children. As Figure 5.2 shows, the trend was accompanied by substantial decline in the proportion of overseas born with a UK, Irish, or Continental birthplace and an increase in the proportion from the Pacific Islands, Asia, and "Other" country – largely the Middle East, Latin America, and Africa. The NZ-born proportion then began to fall and the overseas-born to increase, by 2013 accounting for one-quarter of the population (this excludes the generally 4% to 6% who either do not specify or specify inadequately their country of birth). While the UK/Ireland remains a dominant birthplace of NZ's overseas-born, those with an Asian birthplace are now on equal footing.

The shift in the composition of the overseas-born population from predominantly Anglo-Celtic in the mid-20th century to Pacific Island peoples and Asians by the end of the 20th century is quite remarkable. However, as was noted also for Australia in Chapter 4, the shift is even more remarkable when examined by age. In 2013, the successive waves of migrants from each country of birth show an intuitively correct pattern, with Asian, Pacific Island, and Middle Eastern/African migrants dominant across the young adult and parental age groups, and Anglo-Celtic post-war migrants disproportionately comprising the older overseas-born age groups (Statistics NZ, 2014c, Table 5). These differences mean that younger and older cohorts grow up alongside very different "peer populations," which may play a role in the development of differing generational attitudes.

Section II Cultural diversity and resources

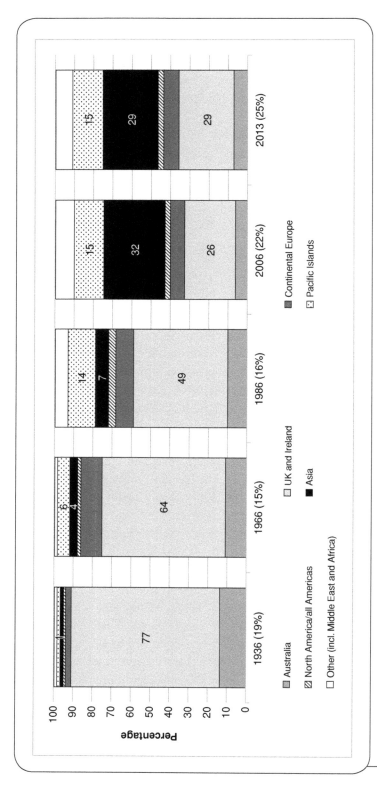

Figure 5.2 Country of birth for the overseas-born usually resident population of NZ, selected years 1936–2013
Source: Author/Statistics NZ (various years), New Zealand population by birthplace. This work is based on/includes Statistics New Zealand's data which are licensed by Statistics New Zealand for re-use under the Creative Commons Attribution 4.0 International licence.

The related importance of cohort size (the relative size of each birth cohort), the historical period it is born into, and the age at which it is passing through particular historical (period) effects, was outlined in Chapter 4. Here we focus only on its ethnic diversity aspects. For NZ's currently older cohorts, born between the 1920s and 1940s, life has thus been lived alongside a relatively large proportion of Anglo-Celtic contemporaries, a relatively small proportion of Māori, and very few other ethnic groups or nationalities. By contrast, NZ's youngest cohorts, born this century and currently aged 0–16 years, have substantially lower proportions of European than their parents and grandparents" cohorts (when at the same age), and relatively high proportions of Māori, Pacific peoples, and Asian. For cohorts currently around age 25–34, European "dominance" is also greatly reduced, with (as noted earlier) Asian outnumbering Māori, a sizeable Pacific peoples component, and the presence of a visible Middle Eastern/Latin/American /African minority (Statistics NZ, 2014c, Table 5).

The extent to which these differences may result in the development of "Mannheimian" entelechies or generational styles (Mannheim, 1929) would be interesting to investigate. In the interim, what can be observed from these data is that young Māori and Pacific peoples currently account for almost one-third of NZ's children. The implication is that they will account for a similar proportion of future labour market entrants, and thus there is likely to be (and as indicated later in this chapter, will need to be) increased attention to their education, training, and health needs. The slightly higher proportions of young Asian people currently in the early labour market entry ages (20–34 years) by comparison with both the Māori and Pacific peoples populations is more a reflection of migration for educational purposes than it is of permanent citizenship – although this may change in the future.

Language

Attesting to NZ's growing ethnic diversity is an ongoing increase in the number of languages spoken. Of those who stated their language ability in the past three censuses (and who were old enough to speak these languages), 96% speak English and this has remained unchanged since 2001 (Author/Statistics NZ, 2014c, Table 7). By contrast, a relatively small proportion speak Māori, and this declined across the period. Underlying data by age show that this decline is concentrated among younger Māori, particularly at primary school age and at 25–39 years; by contrast, above age 45 the proportion speaking Māori has increased, significantly so at 75+ years. Other languages to see a decline across the period were French (minor decline) and NZ sign language (greater decline). All other languages saw an increase, with the greatest for Hindi (numbers trebling since 2001), Northern Chinese (doubling since 2001), Other Sinitic (+87%), Tagalog (numbers quadrupling), Afrikaans (more than doubling), and Spanish and Korean (increasing by 84% and 66% respectively). The number speaking more than one language has increased from 16% in 2001 to 20% in 2013.

Religious affiliation

NZ's changing ethnic composition is reflected in an equally diverse religious structure, although it should be noted that affiliation is notional as opposed to attendance or religiosity. Christianity remains the most common religion, in 2013 acknowledged by just under half of New Zealanders; however, between 2006 and 2013 there was a decline in numbers for all mainstream Christian religions and all Māori Christian religions (Statistics NZ, 2014c, Table 2). By contrast, numbers affiliated with the Sikh religion doubled, alongside smaller percentage growth but larger numerical increases for Buddhism, Hinduism, and Islam. These increases partially offset the overall decline in the number of people acknowledging at least one religion. As with all other social variables, there is substantial underlying diversity by age, ethnicity, and region. Regional numbers with at least one religious affiliation, for example, are both highest and increased fractionally for Auckland (by 1.2%) while at the other end of the scale, they declined by 21.0% for Gisborne – albeit Gisborne continuing to have a relatively high rate of acknowledged religion (Author/Statistics NZ, 2014b, Table 2).

Birth rates and family formation

Accompanying, and in some cases underpinning, the foregoing socio-demographic differences are quite disparate demographic patterns and trends by ethnic group. Māori and Pacific Island women, for example, have their children on average 4–5 years younger than their European and Asian counterparts (Statistics NZ, 2015). For Māori and Pacific Island women, the combination of relatively youthful population age structures (meaning that proportionately more women are at reproductive age) and relatively young ages at childbearing combine to keep these populations young. This is not to suggest that overall fertility rates are not trending downward, as indeed they are, but rather that the pattern of relatively youthful childbearing has not yet changed. Demographic transition theory suggests that this situation most likely reflects underlying differences in educational attainment and employment opportunities, total fertility rates falling in the first stage of demographic transition but childbearing not shifting to older ages until conditions characterising the second demographic transition are met, such as high levels of higher education and an increase in the opportunity costs associated with early childbearing. Reflecting those conditions, NZ's Asian women have the highest overall median age at childbearing (30.8 years in 2013), followed closely by European (30.7 years) (Statistics NZ, 2015). By comparison, the median age at childbearing for Pacific Island and Māori women is 27.2 and 25.8 years respectively. There are, however, other theories that propose an "Indigenous" model of childbearing whereby youthful childbearing is highly valued and supported, and may not succumb to western ideals (Johnstone, 2011).

Mortality differentials

Also playing a role in keeping the age structures of the Māori and Pacific Island populations younger than those of the European and Asian populations are ethnic differences in life expectancy and survivorship that, for Māori and European at least, reach well back into NZ's colonial past (Pool 1991, 2015). Proportionately more deaths at younger ages for the Māori and Pacific Island populations mean that fewer reach old age. The data indicate an improving situation over time, with the gap in life expectancy at birth between Māori and non-Māori in 2013 around half its 1950s levels, for both males and females (Statistics NZ Period Life Tables). For males the gap since 1996 has narrowed somewhat less than for females, from 8.8 to 7.3 years for males and from 9.3 to 6.8 years for females (–17.0% and –26.9% respectively). Life expectancy at birth for NZ's Pacific peoples has only been published for the two most recent observations, 2006 and 2013. These data also show a small improvement across that period, while notably life expectancy at birth is slightly greater for NZ's Pacific peoples than for Māori, for both males and females (note: data are not available for other ethnic groups).

Family and household composition

As might be expected, ethnic (and regional) differences in family formation, fertility, and mortality, along with social change, are, as in Australia, reflected in changes in family and household composition, and differences between subpopulation groups.

In 2013, just below half (48.1%) of NZ's population was currently married/not separated, with this proportion declining fractionally since 2006 (Author/Statistics NZ, 2014b, Table 3). Those previously married but either separated, divorced, or widowed (in total 17.0% in 2013) also declined fractionally as a proportion, while those never married or in a civil union (35% in 2013) saw a minor increase.

As with all other social characteristics, these proportions and trends differ by ethnic group and across the country, but the variance is relatively small. Typically, the differences reflect the underlying age structure, ethnic groups, and regions with the youngest populations tending to have slightly higher than average proportions either never married or currently married, and slightly lower proportions separated/divorced or widowed, while ethnic groups and regions with the oldest populations tend to have the lowest proportions never married and overall highest proportions both married and separated/divorced or widowed (Author/Statistics NZ, 2014b, Table 3). However, this general rule does not hold true in all cases and suggests – as indicated later – the role of other factors such as socio-economic status.

The social arrangements underlying registered relationship status in NZ indicate minor growth in the proportions living in a de facto relationship (from 12.9% to 13.0% between 2006 and 2013), divorced (4.6% to 4.9%), or never married/never partnered

(23.5% to 24.0%), and minor decline in the proportions with a spouse, separated, or widowed (in 2013 respectively 45.6%, 2.5%, and 4.7%) (Statistics NZ, 2014b, Table 4). Again, there is diversity across the country, but also with relatively little variance tending to reflect underlying differences in age structure, ethnic composition, and socio-economic status.

As in Australia, the proportion of NZ families living as a couple without children has increased steadily over the past 13 years (from 39.0% to 40.9%), while both couples with children and one-parent families have declined (in 2013 accounting for respectively 41.3% and 17.8%) (Author/Statistics NZ, 2014d, Table 1). Couples with children thus remain NZ's dominant family type, but they exceed couples without children by barely half a percentage point, down from a three percentage point difference in 2001. The trend towards more couple without children families is likely to continue, as it reflects two discrete trends by age: an increase in those in their mid-to-late 20s and early 30s who have not yet had (and may never have) children, and a substantially greater increase at age 50 and above of those who may have had children, but are now "empty nesters."

According to Statistics NZ (2014d, Table 20), of the 469 290 couple with children families in 2013, 1476 were same-sex couples, the majority of whom were female (79.3%). Of the 465 306 couples without children in 2013, same-sex couples accounted for 6852. Of these, 3486 were female couples and 3366 were male couples.

NZ's most common household type, accounting for more than two-thirds of all household arrangements, remains that of one family living alone (Statistics NZ, 2014b, Table 14). While numbers have increased, primarily because of underlying increase in population size, this household type has seen a fractional decline in its share of all household types across the past 13 years. Conversely, all but multi-person households have seen a minor increase in percentage share.

There has, however, been a sizeable numerical increase in the number of households with either two families or three or more families. Multiple family household types are most common for Pacific peoples, followed by Asian and Māori (the order depending on specific household type), and least common for European (Statistics NZ, 2014e). Māori and Pacific peoples are also more likely than their European and Asian counterparts to be in a one-parent family household, while Europeans are somewhat more likely than all others to be living in a one-person household. Some of these differences reflect underlying differences in age structure, with the Māori and Pacific peoples populations having greater proportions at young family formation ages, the Asian population having significant proportions attending tertiary education (and thus more likely to live in multi-family/person households), and the European population having a greater proportion at older ages, where there is greater chance of being widowed and living alone. However, they may also reflect differing familial value systems, and/or differing social-economic status resulting in different levels of housing affordability.

Demographic diversity and its methodological implications

As outlined earlier, differences in the size and ethnic composition of each birth cohort, due to differences in fertility, mortality, and migration rates, result in markedly different age structures by ancestry/ethnic group and state/territory/region. Among the many factors affected by age structure are unemployment, average income levels, rates of home ownership, satisfaction with life, even social class. Younger populations have greater proportions "at risk" of still being at school, experiencing unemployment, family formation, low incomes, and so on, while older populations have greater proportions "at risk" of holding higher qualifications, more senior occupational positions – and wealth. The analysis of social and socio-economic data thus requires methodological engagement with this demographic diversity, so that "apples are compared with apples."

A conventional approach, outlined in Chapter 4 but repeated here because of its importance to robust analysis, holds the age/sex structure of a comparator population constant and applies it to the age-specific rates for a particular variable (e.g., unemployment) for all populations with which it is being compared (Jackson, 2013). This "weights" the age-specific rates for each population to the same "standard" age distribution. When the resulting rates by age are summed, the now "age-standardised" average is directly comparable. It says that this would be the average unemployment rate (or any other rate) for population X *if it had the same age distribution* as population Y. The results are very telling. For example, around 27% of the difference in the crude unemployment rate between NZ's European and Māori populations in 2013 is accounted for by the differences in age structure. The importance of taking account of differences in age structure, especially when formulating policy interventions to reduce "gaps" between populations, cannot be over-emphasised. The proposition pertains to many other social or socio-economic variables that a student of psychology might examine.

Disparate impact

One example of such an analysis is the application of the "legal" concept of disparate impact – essentially meaning "disproportionate impact." As indicated throughout this chapter, spatial, socio-demographic, and socio-economic diversity can have far-reaching implications, such as the potential for policies to have a disparate impact on one or other subpopulation – and its individual members – as a result of that diversity. Jackson (2002), for example, looked at the impact of a 2001 policy change under which the age of eligibility for the adult rate of unemployment benefit was suddenly raised from age 20 to age 25. She showed that the Māori population was disproportionately exposed to the risk of that policy by virtue of its relatively youthful age structure. Irrespective of the difference in unemployment rate, in 2001 there were *proportionately* more than two Māori aged 15–19 years for every European at that age. Not yet examined by region, it is plausible to expect that regions with higher proportions of Māori would have experienced somewhat greater negative impacts, while positive impacts from differences in age structure are also now presenting opportunities (Jackson, 2008, 2012). These methodological issues should be kept in mind when reading the following section on socio-economic diversity.

Socio-economic characteristics

Qualification levels

In 2013, NZ's Asian population had the overall highest proportions with a university qualification (31.0%), followed closely by the Middle Eastern/Latin American/African (30.0%), "Other ethnicity" (19.9%), and European-origin populations (18.6%) (Author/Statistics NZ, 2014f). "Other ethnicity" and European each have relatively high proportions with a vocational qualification (11.0% and 9.4% respectively), while Pacific Island, Other ethnicity, European then Māori have the highest proportions with a school qualification (50.2%, 49.9%, 47.6%, and 45.7% respectively). Notably, there is very little difference in the latter category between each ethnic group, a "fluid" situational status reflecting that this is in many senses a "holding" category into which people move (from having no qualifications), and then move on. In part reflecting their relative youth, Māori and Pacific peoples have the highest proportions with no qualifications.

A problem with analyses such as this is that certain qualifications are more prevalent by age. Both "no qualifications" and "school qualifications" are strongly bi-modal by age, with the highest proportions of those with no qualifications at the youngest and oldest age groups, and the highest proportions with a school qualification at the youngest and middle age groups. There is also the equally important "shift-share" effect, whereby as people get older they pass through the different qualification categories, leaving "no qualifications" and then "school qualifications" behind as they move on to "vocational" and then higher qualifications.

Applying the technique of "standardisation" outlined earlier (which controls for the effects of different age structures) shows that the "no qualification" rates would be even higher for the Māori and Pacific Island populations vis-à-vis European if they did not have their relatively youthful age structures, which are currently advantageous for the gaining of qualifications – a very important point for policy development. The opposite is the case for those with a "school qualification," where standardisation to the European age structure causes the proportions (of Māori and Pacific peoples with these qualifications) to *decrease*. That is, if the Māori and Pacific peoples' populations had the older age structure of the European-origin population, their proportions with a school qualification would decrease because more would be at the ages at which people begin to move on to higher qualifications, and leave "school qualifications only" behind.

The exercise is far from academic, as policy is often developed to try to reduce these "gaps," and/or they are used to explain other social and psycho-social outcomes. The age-structural, fluidity and shift-share effects of data therefore need to be kept in mind when linking them with different pathologies (positive and negative) by ethnicity.

Labour force status

Although qualifications – or lack thereof – have a direct effect on labour force status, similar age-related impacts need to be kept in mind when analysing the latter. At the 2013 census the Māori, MELAA, and Pacific peoples' populations had the lowest proportions employed full-time (43.4%, 42.1%, and 42.0% respectively) and the highest proportions unemployed, with unemployment highest for Māori and Pacific peoples (10.4% and 10.0% respectively) (Author/Statistics NZ, 2014g). In each case, these proportions would be *lower* if they had the older age structure of the European population. This is because on the one hand the modal age of full-time employment in NZ is 40–54 years, where there are proportionately fewer Māori, Pacific Island, Asian, and MELAA people (than there are European), and on the other, the modal age of unemployment is 15–24 years, where there are proportionately more Māori, Pacific Island, Asian, and MELAA.

There is somewhat less variance by ethnicity in terms of part-time unemployment, partly because part-time employment is bi-modal by age – both the highest numbers and age-specific rates occurring at 15–24 years when people are also studying, and at 40–44 years where people are caring for children, beginning to reduce full-time employment (whether by choice or involuntarily), and/or, especially for women, re-entering the workforce after childrearing. Similar comments apply to those "not in the labour force," which is even more strongly bi-modal by age, highest at 15–19 years, where labour force entry is just beginning, with a second peak at 65 years and above, when retirement enters the picture. The lowest rates of not being in the labour force occur at 45–49 years, when childrearing activities are lowest, and – as indicated earlier – qualification levels are highest.

Income

The two final socio-economic variables outlined here are income level and income source. Although these variables typically become dependent variables when considered alongside qualifications and labour force status, they also assist in providing additional "qualitative" background information about each group, as parental income is closely associated with the a-priori propensity of their children to study and gain higher qualifications.

In 2013, the total median personal income in NZ was $28 500. It was highest at 45–49 years ($42 300), followed closely by 40–44, 55–59, and 35–39 years ($41 800, $41 700, and $40 700 respectively) (Statistics NZ, 2014h). The "Other ethnicity" and European ethnic groups had by far the highest median personal incomes ($37 100 and $30 900 respectively), followed by Māori, Asian, MELAA, and Pacific peoples ($22 500, $20 100, $19 800, and $19 700 respectively). The interacting nature of age structure, qualifications, and labour force status are of course involved, with disproportionately more European in the highest qualification, highest full-time labour force status, and highest income-earning age groups, and disproportionately more of the other ethnic groups at the ages at which study is still being undertaken, qualifications being gained, labour market entry being negotiated, and childbearing and childrearing undertaken, complexities which cannot be further examined here.

Personal income source data for the NZ usually resident census population in 2013 show that "wages, salary, commissions, and bonuses" were the dominant source of income for all ethnic groups (note that more than one source may be given), with this source ranging from 51.7% for the MELAA population to 63.6% for those of "Other ethnicity" (Statistics NZ, 2014i). The European and "Other ethnicity" groups had the greatest number of income sources per capita, 1.5 in each case, with interest, dividends, rent and/or other investments the second most common source, followed by self-employment or business for those of "Other ethnicity," and NZ Superannuation or Veterans Pension for European. (Note: With few exceptions, NZ superannuation is universally available to all NZ citizens from age 65; it is not means-tested.) In part reflecting their much younger age structures – and thus much smaller proportions at older age – these sources were much less prevalent for Māori and Pacific peoples, who had somewhat higher proportions with no source of income, or receiving either a domestic purposes benefit or an unemployment benefit. Similarly reflecting their younger age structures, but also higher proportions engaged in study, the Asian and MELAA ethnic groups also had high proportions with no source of income. However, both latter groups also had notable proportions gaining income from self-employment and business, and the Asian population, also from interest, dividends, rent, and/or other investments – suggesting underlying differences by age.

The New Zealand psychological and psychiatric workforces

Finally, and briefly, this chapter turns to the age-sex structure of the psychologist and psychiatric nurse workforces. The data indicate two increasingly feminised and rapidly ageing occupations. Between 1996 and 2013 the number of psychologists employed in NZ grew by 67.1% (+840 positions). Over half of these positions were added at 50–64 years of age, although the ageing of the baby boomer cohorts (born 1946–65) remaining employed across the period account for much of that growth (Figure 5.3 and Table 5.2). This ageing can be traced via the shaded bars located at 35–39 years in 1996, when the largest baby boomer cohort, born in 1961, was aged 35 years and at 50–54 years in 2013, when that cohort was aged 52 years. In 1996 there had been eight psychologists employed at 15–29 years for every 10 at 55+ years, at which time 43.5% was aged 55+ years; by 2013 that ratio had fallen to 0.3 (3 per 10), with 47.3% aged 55+ years. This occupation is somewhat older than the total NZ workforce, but it has aged at a similar rate. Table 5.2 also identifies a significant feminisation of the occupation, with the sex ratio (males per female) falling from 0.49 to 0.43.

Table 5.2 Age–sex structure, psychologists (NZSC099 24441), New Zealand, 1996 and 2013

	1996		2001		2006		2013		Change 1996–2013	
	N	%	N	%	N	%	N	%	N	%
Males	414	(33 1)	402	(30.5)	486	(28.7)	519	(24.8)	+105	(+25.4)
Females	837	(66.9)	915	(69.5)	1206	(71.3)	1572	(75.2)	+735	(+87.8)
Total	1251	(100.0)	1.317	(100.0)	1692	(100.0)	2091	(100.0)	+840	(+67.1)
Sex Ratio (M: F)	0.49		0.44		0.40		0.33		–	(–33.3)
Average Age	43.5		42.6		44.5		47.3		–	(+8.8)
% 55+ years	13.2		12.5		20.4		28.7		–	(+117.6)
Employment Entry: Exit Ratio 15–29: 55+ years	0.8		1.1		0.5		0.3		–	(–63.1)

Source: Author/Statistics NZ (2014i). This work is based on/includes Statistics New Zealand's data which are licensed by Statistics New Zealand for re-use under the Creative Commons Attribution 4.0 International licence.

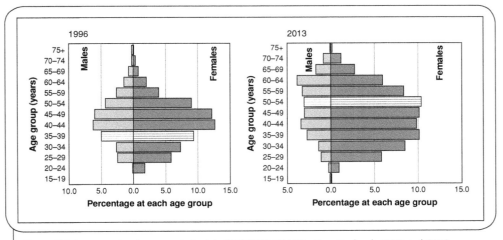

Figure 5.3 Age–sex structure, psychologists (NZSC099 24441), New Zealand, 1996 and 2013
Source: Author/Statistics NZ (2014). This work is based on/includes Statistics New Zealand's data which are licensed by Statistics New Zealand for re-use under the Creative Commons Attribution 4.0 International licence.

Table 5.3 and Figure 5.4 repeat the exercise for psychiatric nurses. Between 1996 and 2013, the number of psychiatric nurses employed in NZ fell slightly (–6.1%; –66 positions), accompanied by significant ageing of the workforce. In 1996 there had been 14 psychiatric nurses employed at 15–29 years for every 10 at 55+ years, at which time 40.5% was aged 55+ years; by 2013 that ratio had fallen to 0.2 (2 per 10), with 48.6%

Table 5.3 Age–sex structure, Psychiatric Nurses (NZSC099 22313), New Zealand, 1996 and 2013

	1996		2001		2008		2013		Change 1996–2013	
	N	%	N	%	N	%	N	%	N	%
Males	393	(35.8)	463	(35.3)	552	(31.8)	309	(29.9)	−84	(−21.4)
Females	705	(64 2)	858	(64.7)	1182	(68.2)	723	(70.1)	+18	(+2.6)
Total	1098	(100.0)	1326	(100.0)	1734	(100.0)	1032	(100.0)	−66	(−6.0)
Sex Ratio (M: F)	0.56		0.55		0.47		0.43			(−23.3)
Average Age	40.5		42.9		45.5		48.6			(+20.0)
% 55+ years	7.7		10.6		18.3		31.4			(+310.4)
Employment Entry: Exit Ratio 15–29: 55+ years	1.4		0.9		0.5		0.2			(−84.3)

Source: Author/Statistics New Zealand (2014i). This work is based on/includes Statistics New Zealand's data which are licensed by Statistics New Zealand for re-use under the Creative Commons Attribution 4.0 International licence.

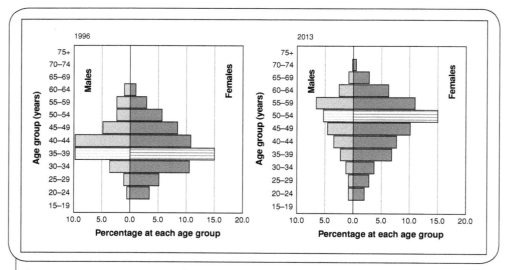

Figure 5.4 Age–sex structure, Psychiatric Nurses (NZSC099 22313), New Zealand, 1996 and 2013
Source: Author/Statistics NZ (2014). This work is based on/includes Statistics New Zealand's data which are licensed by Statistics New Zealand for re-use under the Creative Commons Attribution 4.0 International licence.

aged 55+ years. This occupation is both substantially older than the total NZ workforce and has aged at a much faster rate. As for NZ's psychiatric nurses, Table 5.3 also identifies significant feminisation of the psychiatric nurse occupation, with the sex ratio falling from 0.56 to 0.43 (males per female).

Bibliography

Friesen, W. (2015). *Asian Auckland: The multiple meanings of diversity*. Auckland. Asia New Zealand Foundation.

Hewlett, S., Marshall, M., & Sherbin, P. (2013). How diversity can drive innovation. *Harvard Business Review*, December Issue. Available: https://hbr.org/2013/12/how-diversity-can-drive-innovation

Nijkamp, P., & Poot, J. (2015). Cultural diversity – a matter of measurement. In P. Nijkamp, J. Poot, & J. Bakens (Eds.), *The economics of cultural diversity* (pp. 17–51) Cheltenham, UK: Edward Elgar.

References

Ivory, V., Witten, K., Salmond, C., En-Yi Lin, R. Q. U., & Blakely, T. (2012). The New Zealand index of neighbourhood social fragmentation: Integrating theory and data. *Environment and Planning A*: *44*, 972–988. http://dx.doi.org/10.1068/a44303

Jackson, N. O. (2002). The doubly-structural nature of Indigenous disadvantage. Indigenous age structures and the notion of disparate impact. *New Zealand Population Review*, *28*(1), 55–68.

Jackson, N. O. (2008). Educational attainment and the (growing) importance of age structure: Indigenous and non-Indigenous Australians. *Journal of Population Research*, *25*(2), 223–244.

Jackson, N. O. (2012). Māori and the [potential] demographic dividend. *New Zealand Population Review, 37*, 65–88.

Jackson, N. O. (2013). Population-level analysis. In Maggie Walter (Ed.), *Social research methods: An Australian perspective* (3rd ed., pp. 147–173). Melbourne: Oxford University Press.

Johnstone, K. (2011). Indigenous fertility transitions in developed countries. *New Zealand Population Review, 37*, 105–123.

Kukutai, T. (2011). Building ethnic boundaries in New Zealand: Representations of Māori identity in the census. In P. Axelsson & P. Skold (Eds.), *Indigenous peoples and demography: The complex relation between identity and statistics* (pp. 33–54). Berghahn.

Kukutai, T. (2012). Quantum Māori, Māori quantum: State constructions of Māori identities in the Census, 1857/8–2006. In R. McClean, B. Patterson, & D. Swain (Eds.), *Counting, stories, moving ethnicities: Studies from Aotearoa New Zealand*. Hamilton: University of Waikato.

Mannheim, K. (1929/1952/1993). The problem of generations. In K. Wolff (Ed.), *From Karl Mannheim* (2nd ed., pp. 351–398). New Brunswick, NJ: Transaction Publishers.

Pool, I. (1991). *Te Iwi Māori. A New Zealand population: Past, present and projected*. Auckland: Auckland University Press.

Pool, I. (2015). *Colonization and development in New Zealand between 1769 and 1900: The seeds of Rangiatea*. Springer.

Pool, I., Baxendine, S., Cochrane, W., & Lindop, J. (2005). *New Zealand regions, 1986– 2001: Population structures*. Discussion Paper No. 53. Hamilton: Population Studies Centre, University of Waikato. October.

Statistics New Zealand. (2009). *Subnational ethnic population projections (2006 Base – 2009 Update) Tables 4e, 4m, 4p, 4a*. (Excel Spreadsheets). Wellington, NZ: Author.

Statistics New Zealand (2014a). *ERP – Estimated resident subnational population by ethnic group, age, and sex, at 30 June 1996, 2001, 2006 and 2013*. (Excel Spreadsheets). Wellington, NZ: Author.

Statistics New Zealand (2014b). *2013 Census regional summary tables, part 2*. (Excel Spreadsheets). Wellington, NZ: Author.

Statistics New Zealand (2014c). *2013 Census quick stats about national highlights*. (Excel Spreadsheets). Wellington, NZ: Author.

Statistics New Zealand (2014d). *2013 Census quick stats about families and households*. (Excel Spreadsheets). Wellington, NZ: Author.

Statistics New Zealand (2014e). *Customised Excel database, ethnic group (total responses) and household composition by age groups and sex for usual residents in households in private occupied dwellings*. Wellington, NZ: Author.

Statistics New Zealand (2014f). *Customised Excel database, ethnic group (total responses), highest qualification and birthplace by age groups and sex for the census usually resident population count aged 15 years and over, 2013 census*. Wellington, NZ: Author.

Statistics New Zealand (2014g). *Customised Excel database, ethnic group (total responses), labour force status by age groups and sex for the census usually resident population count aged 15 years and over, 2013 census*. Wellington, NZ: Author.

Statistics New Zealand (2014h). *Customised Excel database, ethnic group (total responses), age groups and sex by median income for the census usually resident population count aged 15 years and over, 2013*. Wellington, NZ: Author.

Statistics New Zealand (2014i). *Customised Excel database, area of usual residence and occupation (NZSCO99 v1.0) by age groups and sex for the employed census usually resident population count aged 15 years and over, 1996, 2001, 2006, 2013*. Wellington, NZ: Author.

Statistics New Zealand (2015). *Customised Excel database, age-specific fertility rates by single year of age and ethnicity, 2001, 2006, 2013*. Wellington, NZ: Author.

Statistics New Zealand (various years). *New Zealand period life tables*. (Excel Spreadsheets). Wellington, NZ: Author.

Statistics New Zealand (various years). *New Zealand population by birthplace. Census of population and dwellings*. (Excel Spreadsheets). Wellington, NZ: Author.

Walter, M., & Andersen, C. (2013). *Indigenous statistics. A quantitative research methodology*. Walnut Creek, CA: Left Coast Press Inc.

Recommendations for further reading/resources

General

Series: *Ethnic and Racial Studies*, Routledge.

Epstein, G. S., & Heizler (Cohen), O. (2015). Ethnic identity: A theoretical framework. *IZA Journal of Migration, 4*(9), 1–11. http://dx.doi.org/10.1186/s40176-015-0033-z

Lee, J., & Bean, F. (2010). *The diversity paradox*: *Immigration and the color line in twenty-first century America*. New York: Russell Sage Foundation Press.

Australia

Kukutai, T., & Taylor, J. (2012). Postcolonial profiling of Indigenous populations: Limitations and responses in Australia and Aotearoa New Zealand. *Special issue on Indigenous demography, space, populations, societies.*

New Zealand

Kukutai, T. (2011). Māori demography in Aotearoa New Zealand: Fifty years on. *Special Issue of New Zealand Population Review, 37*, 45–64. (released in 2012)

Kukutai, T. (2013). The structure of urban Māori identities. In E. Peters & C. Andersen (Eds.), *Indigenous in the city: Contemporary identities and cultural innovation* (pp. 311–331). Canada: UBC Press.

Kukutai, T., & Didham, R. (2011). Re-making the majority? Ethnic New Zealanders in the 2006 census. *Ethnic and Racial Studies*, 1–20.

Kukutai, T., & Rarere, M. (2013). Tracking patterns of tribal identification in the New Zealand census, 1991 to 2006. *New Zealand Population Review, 39*, 1–23.

Maré, D. C., Pinkerton, R. M., Poot, J., & Coleman, A. (2012). Residential sorting across Auckland neighbourhoods. *New Zealand Population Review, 38*, 23–54.

McIntosh, T., & Mulholland, M. (2011). *Māori and social issues*. Auckland: Ngā Pae o te Māramatanga Huia Publishers.

Pool, I. (2011). Population change. *Te Ara – the Encyclopedia of New Zealand*. Wellington: Ministry for Culture and Heritage. Available: www.TeAra.govt.nz/en/population-change

Spoonley, P., & Bedford, R. D. (2012). *Welcome to our world? Immigration and the reshaping of New Zealand*. Auckland: Dunmore Publishing.

Statistics New Zealand (2014j). *Customised Excel database, area of usual residence (2013), ethnic group (total responses), age groups and sex by sources of personal income (total responses) for the census usually resident population count aged 15 years and over, 2013*. Wellington, NZ: Author.

6

Indigenous and bicultural resources

Nadine Pelling

In 2007 I guest edited a special issue on Indigenous counselling for the journal *Counselling, Psychotherapy and Health* published by the Australian Counselling Association. This followed the publication of a scholarly review I conducted on Indigenous mental health and substance abuse in 2006 (Pelling, 2006a, 2007). I am, nonetheless, not an expert on Indigenous Australian psychology and recognise my limitations in this area. If competence in any applied area relates to knowledge, self and other awareness, and skill, then I must admit that I am lacking in competence in these important Australian psychological foci (Pelling, 2006b) and similarly am lacking in terms of bicultural New Zealand (NZ) competence.

However, I have worked with Dwayne Kennedy and Joseph Randolph Bowers to ensure that the current edition of this handbook provides a framework for relating to Australian Indigenous psychology and counselling. Additionally, there are international sources of published information on both Indigenous and bicultural issues relevant to abnormal psychology. Indigenous issues are a focus of the Inter-Agency Support Group (IASG) of the United Nations (UN) and information can be found through the UN main page for those interested in supporting and promoting the mandate of the UN Permanent Forum on Indigenous Issues within the UN forum (UN, 2016).

Related to Australian psychology, the Australian Psychological Society (APS) has an interest group focusing on Aboriginal and Torres Strait Islander Peoples and Psychology (2016). This APS interest group makes available resources and publications as well as online training. Similarly, the Australian Indigenous Psychologists Association (AIPA) has published various papers including a discussion paper relating to the determinants of Indigenous social and emotional wellbeing (Kelly et al., 2010). Another author in the area of Indigenous psychology is Victoria Hovane (2015). The AIPA provides leadership on issues related to the social and emotional wellbeing and mental health of Aboriginal and Torres Strait Islander peoples in Australia and offers cultural competence workshops (AIPA, 2015, 2016).

Bicultural NZ psychological information can be found through the New Zealand Psychological Society (NZPsS). The NZPsS has bicultural articles published by year in the *New Zealand Journal of Psychology*, thus highlighting the importance of bicultural psychology in NZ. The NZPsS has a National Standing Committee on Bicultural Issues (NSCBI) that advises on appropriate cultural development (NZPsS, 2016). In NZ, a number of related presentations and publications on bicultural psychology are available (Waitoki et al., 2015; Dudgeon et al., 2016; Macfarlane, Blampied, & Macfarlane, 2011).

Australia – resources

- Australian Psychological Society (http://groups.psychology.org.au/atsipp/)
- Australian Indigenous Psychologists Association (www.indigenouspsychology.com.au)
- Indigenous Allied Health Australia (www.indigenousalliedhealth.com.au)
- National Aboriginal Community Controlled Health Organisation (www.naccho.org.au)
- Australian Indigenous HealthInfoNet (www.healthinfonet.ecu.edu.au)

New Zealand – resources

- New Zealand Psychological Society (www.psychology.org.nz/nga-kete/nzpss-bicultural-resources/)

References

Australian Indigenous Psychologists Association. (2015). *Working together: The journey towards cultural competence with Aboriginal and Torres Strait Islander Peoples for non-Indigenous mental health practitioners*. Available: www.culturalcompetence.net.au

Australian Indigenous Psychologists Association. (2016). *The AIPA: About us*. Available via www.indigenouspsychology.com.au

Australian Psychological Society. (2016). *Aboriginal and Torres Strait Islander peoples and psychology*. Melbourne: Author. Available: https://groups.psychology.org.au/atsipp/

Dudgeon, P., Waitoki, W. W., LeMay, R., & Nikora, L. (Eds.) (2016). Social inclusion and Indigenous peoples. *Social inclusion*. 4(1), 101 pages. Available: www.cogitatiopress.com/ojs/index.php/socialinclusion/issue/view/36

Hovane, V. (2015). Improving outcomes through a shared understanding of family violence in Aboriginal communities: Towards an Aboriginal theory of family violence. *InPsych*. 37(5). Available: https://www.psychology.org.au/inpsych/2015/october/hovane/

Kelly, K., Dudgeon, P., Gee, G., & Glaskin, B. (2010) Living on the edge: Social and emotional wellbeing and risk and protective factors for serious psychological distress among Aboriginal and Torres Strait Islander people. *Discussion Paper No. 10*. Darwin: Cooperative Research Centre for Aboriginal Health.

Macfarlane, A. H., Blampied, N. M., & Macfarlane, S. H. (2011). Blending the clinical and the cultural: A framework for conducting formal psychological assessment in bicultural settings. *New Zealand Journal of Psychology, 40*(2), 5–15.

New Zealand Psychological Society. (2016). National Standing Committee on Bicultural Issues (NSCBI). Available: www.psychology.org.nz/about-nzpss/nscbi

Pelling, N. (2006a). Indigenous mental health and substance use. In N. Pelling, R. Bowers, & P. Armstrong (Eds.), *The practice of counselling* (pp. 208–223). Melbourne: Thomson Publishers.

Pelling, N. (2006b). Counsellor competence. In N. Pelling, R. Bowers, & P. Armstrong (Eds.), *The practice of counselling* (pp. 36–45). Melbourne: Thomson Publishers.

Pelling, N. (2007). Special issue: Indigenous counselling, psychotherapy, and health. Guest N. Pelling. (Ed.), *Counselling, Psychotherapy, and Health, 3*(2).

United Nations (2016). *Inter-Agency Support Group: Indigenous issues*. Available www.un.org/development/desa/indigenouspeoples

Waitoki, W., Masters, B., Nikora, L. W., Black, R., & Nairn, R. (2015). Psychology's relationship with Indigenous peoples in a global space: Perspectives from Aotearoa/New Zealand. *Australian Psychological Society Annual Conference*. Conference held at Gold Coast, Australia.

7

Clinical practice with Indigenous Australians

Joseph Randolph Bowers and Dwayne Kennedy

Joseph Randolph Bowers

As an area of enquiry, abnormal psychology tends to focus on mental and emotional disorders and their consequent diagnosis and treatment. Relating to Indigenous Australians, it is important to challenge the conceptual focus on a diagnostic model and the consequent focus on mental disorder treatment. Instead, Aboriginal and Torres Strait Islander peoples tend to focus on the cultural and spiritual aspects of human experience.

Cultural and spiritual phenomena, including great focus on family and tribal relationships, are essential in the culture of Aboriginal and Torres Strait Islander peoples. If we remember mainstream family norms at the turn of the 19th century, extended families were much more common. Children were raised by their uncles, aunts, and grandparents. The nuclear family of couple and children alone is a recent development. Indigenous culture, by comparison, maintains the centrality of familial bonds that integrates with a "national" identity. In Australia, I have found this is expressed by the sacredness of "country" as both a geophysical place and also as a spiritual space that is connected to Dreamtime within family and blood relations.

When psychologists – or for that matter, any other helping professional – approach issues of mental health and other phenomena, we need to first take note of our biased and prejudicial positions. You may say, I am not prejudiced! I don't have bias! This is a natural reaction. But when we decode the meaning of bias and prejudice, we begin to realise that our family upbringing, parental influences, sibling relationships, school experiences, learning opportunities or challenges, familial genealogy, cultural, and linguistic background all have a great part to play.

Many then ask, how are these factors important to my work today? From an Aboriginal and Torres Strait Islander perspective, we say that my identity is not my own. I am my family, tribe, and nation. In other words, I am the sum total of all my experiences – but more than this, my Indigenous social being is of higher value than my identity as a person. In another way of speaking, my identity is my people and my country. Like the Australian song, "We are one, though we are many."

These cultural, value-based, and belief system layers must be front and centre. A greater openness and suspension of bias and prejudice must occur. This includes our education and training in therapy! Most especially! Why is this? Because often book knowledge and training experience interferes with actually being present to another person in a therapeutic way. How much more is this true with Indigenous Australians who can look through someone very quickly and who turn off when we are being inauthentic and using jargon? Relationship is key. Indigenous Australian work comes more from integrating heart and mind in a soulful approach that is real and down to earth.

This type of approach works alongside the person, in collaboration with Aboriginal and Torres Strait Islander peoples. Like in family therapy, the process must be slowed down and paced. The therapist must "sit back," truly "shut up" and actually listen – in a way that is outside our normal Western sense of listening. We mean a much more contemplative state of being with another and attending to the ecology of the world around us. At the same time, all our skill and knowledge can be brought to bear on practical and down-to-earth interventions.

Interventions need to make sense to the client, not so much to us. In other words, the meaning of my communication is the response I get. My meaning as a therapist is not in my head, but in how the other person takes things in, processes them, and then comes to an understanding. A good psychologist will be looking with a curious, open mind and heart, in a soulful manner, seeking to comprehend the felt sense of the client. Even more so with an Indigenous client or with people of other cultures or linguistic or religious backgrounds.

Lastly, before we enter into an exercise for reflection, allow me to offer an Indigenous perspective on the science of abnormal psychology. Aboriginal and Torres Strait Islander peoples' science is interested in ecological relationships within a complex web of nature, environment, and human interactions. At its base, the science is observational. Built on this base is experimental learning. Indigenous Australian approaches tend to rely heavily on learning through experience and action, and then feedback. The reflective process is also action oriented; in some ways, it is a lot like strength-based experiential and psychodynamic psychotherapy. In Indigenous methods, the context is shifted into an ecology and meaning system based in generally Aboriginal and Torres Strait Islander beliefs, values, and attitudes.

Take a step back from this handbook. Consider all you have learned so far. Much of psychology seeks naturally to pass on a wealth of factual knowledge. Much of what you are learning is vital clinical information, from one point of view. But from an Aboriginal and Torres Strait Islander perspective, take a new and fresh look at this field of inquiry and practice and know that some concepts linked to abnormal psychology need to be culturally challenged.

Exercise for reflection

Imagine for a moment that none of this huge body of abnormal psychology information was available. Science was young and psychology was a new field of practice.

Now take this environment into a curious mindset and look at your work from an ecological perspective. You are aware of interconnections, with your near and far geo-environments, family system, nearby community systems, wider social and cultural systems, and macro-cultural movements and social psychologies. Consider you are related to your country and hemisphere on the planet. You have a relationship with the desert, the oceans, the islands to the north, the pole to the south. Now extend this awareness outward to the whole earth. Feel the earth as more than a mere physical presence but indeed as a living organism and an entity, a being pulsing with life and with a living flesh that we glibly call soil or dirt. Science is even now discovering how the soil and organisms within transmit information between plants and across distances. Everything is in some way interconnected.

From this "heart and head" space, what changes in your views of abnormal psychology? Are things as "black and white" as you first imagined or assumed? Is there more genuine inquiry and hard work to be done in exploring the nature of reality? Or are you happy with receiving the knowledge of others and not bothering to do any real growth and work yourself?

Take these questions and write yourself a short essay, perhaps 400 words or so. The focus of your writing might be your strongest reaction, question, or feeling while reading this reflection. Be curious about your internal world, and attend to your beliefs, values, and attitudes. How do you view Aboriginal and Torres Strait Islander peoples' concerns in psychology and in abnormal psychology in particular? What ways does the field need to change and grow to work effectively in Aboriginal contexts? What skills and methods do Aboriginal people have that can enlighten and inform a more holistic approach to abnormal psychology? Explore the literature and take a very curious, open mind and heart to these issues.

Indigenous Australian identity: A personal reflection

Dwayne Kennedy

Aboriginal and Torres Strait Islander peoples tend to identify with both their cultural identity and ego identity. "Cultural identity" involves the larger community, of which we are each a part, whereas "ego identity" involves the individual measure of the whole "cultural identity." Such a complex sense of identity, in cases where it exists, will inevitably result in various challenges and choices that differ to those faced by "mainstream" Australians, and may need to be taken into consideration when applying mainstream psychology and ideologies in the Aboriginal and Torres Strait Islander context.

In gaining a greater understanding of Aboriginal and Torres Strait Islander cultural identity, one must first realise that Indigenous Australian culture has centuries of oral tradition, of passing down knowledge, understanding, and skills verbally. When working with Aboriginal and Torres Strait Islander peoples, it may be helpful to operate within the context of narrative therapy to assist in the "telling of their story." This supports Indigenous Australians' oral traditions and creates a professional space in which self-disclosure and discovery can happen; the skills of the practitioner/ psychologist will assist the client to build and apply meaning and understanding to their life and lived experiences. This process of integration can bring people together in a space in which they feel comfortable sharing their ideas and stories.

To be effective, the professional practioner/psychologist needs to be a flexible thinker, providing the tools that best match the particular needs of the client, and providing a learning environment that best matches the client's learning style. In the case of Indigenous Australians, this may involve providing a cultural learning environment that is conducive to specific cultural needs. For example, it may be that some Indigenous clients feel more comfortable expressing themselves through creative, artistic means, so the tools necessary to faciliate this form of expression should be made available. Through such methods, "dominant cultural structures and ideologies" can be resisted and a space created for transpersonal restructuring of personal identity through the processes of learning, unlearning, and becoming free from dominant ways of thinking.

Recommendations for further reading/resources

Arthur, N., Collins S. (Eds.). (2010). *Culture-infused counselling: A theoretical framework and practical guide for infusing culture into all aspects of professional practice.* Calgary: CounsellingConcepts.

Atkinson, J. (2002). *Trauma trails, recreating song lines: The transgenerational effects of trauma in Indigenous Australia.* Melbourne: SpinifexPress.

Atkinson, J., Kennedy D., & Bowers R. (2006). Aboriginal and First Nations approaches to counselling. In Pelling N., Bowers R., & Armstrong P. (Eds.), *The practice of counselling.* Melbourne: Thomson Publishers.

Bowers, R. (2005). Our stories, our medicine – exploring holistic therapy integrating body-wellness, mindfulness, and spirituality: An Indigenous perspective on healing, change, and counselling, and the social and political contexts of an emerging discipline. *Counselling Australia, 4*(4), 114–117.

Bowers, R. (2007a). A bibliography on Aboriginal and minority concerns: Identity, prejudice, marginalisation, and healing in relation to race, gender, sexuality, and the ecology of place. *Counselling, Psychotherapy, and Health, 3*(2), Indigenous Special Issue, 29–71.

Bowers, R. (2007b). Clinical suggestions for honouring Indigenous identity for helpers, counsellors, and healers: the case of "Marsha". *Counselling, Psychotherapy, and Health, 3*(2), Indigenous Special Issue, 13–28.

Bowers, R. (2007c). Diversity in creation: Identity, race, sexuality and Indigenous creativity. *International Journal of Diversity in Organisations, Communities and Nations, 7*(1), 3–7.

Bowers, R. (2008). Counsellor education as humanist colonialism: Seeking post-colonial approaches to educating counsellors by exploring pathways to an Indigenous aesthetic. *Australian Journal of Indigenous Education, 37,* 71–79.

Bowers, R. (2010a). Identity, prejudice, and healing in Aboriginal circles: Models of identity, embodiment, and ecology of place as traditional medicine for education and counselling – A Mi'kmaq First Nation perspective. *AlterNative – International Journal of Indigenous Studies, 6*(3), 203–221.

Bowers, R. (2010b). A Mi'kmaq First Nation cosmology: Investigating the practice of contemporary Aboriginal traditional medicine in dialogue with counselling – toward An Indigenous therapeutics. *Asian Journal of Counselling and Psychotherapy, 1*(2), 111–124.

Bowers, R. (2012). From little things big things grow, from big things little things manifest: An Indigenous human ecology discussing issues of conflict, peace, and relational sustainability. *AlterNative – International Journal of Indigenous Studies, 8*(3), 290–304.

Carson, B., Dunbar, T., Chenhall, R., & Bailie R. (Eds.). (2007). *Social determinants of Indigenous health*. Crows Nest: Allen & Unwin.

Duran, E. (2006). Healing the soul wound: Counseling with American Indians and other native peoples. In Ivey, A., & Wing, Sue D., (Eds.). *Multicultural foundations of psychology and counseling series*. New York: Teachers College Press.

Eckermann, A., Dowd, T., Chong, E., Nixon, L., Gray, R., & Johnson, S. (2006). *Binan Goonj, bridging cultures in aboriginal health* (2nd ed.). Sydney: Churchill Livingstone.

Kennedy, D. (2006). *Indigenous awakenings: Facing the challenges of education, culture, and healing in Aboriginal Australia*. A thesis submitted for the degree of Master of Education with Honours, School of Professional Development and Leadership University of New England. October.

Kennedy, D. (2011). *Dreaming emu: Indigenous cultural empowerment through art as therapy – Men & healing from the violence of colonisation*. Australia: University of New England.

Paul, D., (2006). *First nations history: We were not the savages: Collision between European and Native American civilizations* (3rd ed.). Halifax: FernwoodPublishing.

Purdie, N., Dudgeon, P., Walker, R., & Calma, T. (Eds). (2010). *Working together: Aboriginal and Torres Strait Islander mental health and wellbeing principles and practice*. Canberra: Office of Aboriginal and Torres Strait Islander Health, Department of Ageing.

Section **III**

Disorders and psychological practice related items

8

Neurodevelopmental disorders

Robyn Young and Anna Moffat

Introduction

Neurodevelopmental disorders are a group of disorders characterised by impairments of social, academic, or occupational functioning. By definition, the onset of all disorders listed under this category must be in early development, usually prior to school age. Grouped broadly, neurodevelopmental disorders are classified in the American Psychiatric Association's *Diagnostic and Statistical Manual of Mental Disorders* (5th ed.; *DSM-5*; American Psychiatric Association, 2013) under the following six categories:

- intellectual disability
- neurodevelopmental communication disorders
- autism spectrum disorder (ASD)[1]
- attention deficit hyperactivity disorder
- neurodevelopmental motor disorders
- specific learning disorder.

Intellectual disability has many causes and is heterogeneous in presentation. Neurodevelopmental intellectual disabilities include intellectual developmental disorder, which is characterised by deficits in intellectual and adaptive functioning (when compared to an individual's peers). The DSM-5 and *International Statistical Classification of Diseases and Related Health Problems 2010 Edition (ICD-10;* WHO, 2011) codes, respectively, for intellectual development disorder are 319 and F70–F73. Clinical assessment in addition to standardised intelligence testing is required to confirm deficit, and severity is rated on a four-point scale defined by differences in conceptual, social, and practical domains. Global developmental delay (GDD; 315.8 [F88]) is the diagnosis

---

[1] Until 2013 the 4th edition of *Diagnostic and Statistical Manual of Mental Disorders* (*DSM-IV-TR*; American Psychiatric Association, 1994) listed autism spectrum disorder as a number of different disorders (e.g., autistic disorder, Asperger's disorder) grouped into the category "Pervasive developmental disorders". From the release of the *DSM-5* (American Psychiatric Association, 2013) these disorders have been grouped into one diagnosis of autism spectrum disorder (ASD). This chapter will refer to all pervasive developmental disorders as ASD.

provided for children under the age of 5 years where assessment of functioning is unreliable and standardised testing is difficult. Nevertheless, development is considered delayed across all aforementioned areas and overall adaptive functioning is poor. Reassessment after a period of time to confirm diagnosis is required. Children who have sensory or physical impairments (such as vision or hearing loss, or a concurrent mental disorder) that render assessment of intelligence difficult may be diagnosed with unspecified intellectual disability (intellectual development disorder; 319 [F79]). However, this diagnosis is used only rarely and would also be in addition to poor adaptive functioning skills relative to similarly impaired peers. Due to the varying predictive validity of current assessments for children, particularly those under the age of 5, reassessment is required.

Neurodevelopmental communication disorders comprise deficits in speech (expressive means of communication), language (a structured system of communication including spoken and written words, sign language, pictures, or symbols) and communication (a method of having impact on another individual via verbal or non-verbal methods). Five classifications are included in this group: language disorder (315.39 [F80.9]), speech sound disorder (315.39 [F80.0]), childhood-onset fluency disorder (stuttering; 315.35 [F80.81]), social (pragmatic) communication disorder (315.39, [F80.89]) and unspecified communication disorder (307.9 [F80.9]). Each disorder differs based on the area of communication that is most impacted.

ASD is diagnosed when a dyad of symptoms is present. Specifically, the individual must demonstrate: A. marked, ongoing social communication and social interaction deficits in addition to B. patterns of behaviour, interests, or activities that are restricted or repetitive in nature. Criterion A manifests as deficits in social-emotional reciprocity, non-verbal communicative behaviours used for social interaction, and difficulties in understanding and maintaining relationships appropriate to developmental level. To satisfy criterion B, an individual must exhibit at least two from the following four criteria: motor movements, use of objects, or speech that is stereotyped or repetitive; an insistence on sameness, inflexibility with routine, or ritualised patterns of verbal or non-verbal behaviour; restricted interests with an abnormal intensity or focus; hyper- or hyposensitivity to sensory input. Severity levels are rated on an ascending scale ranging from level 1 requiring support, level 2 requiring substantial support, and level 3 requiring very substantial support. For diagnosis, symptoms must have a significant impact on daily functioning.

Attention deficit hyperactivity disorder (ADHD) diagnostic criteria are impairment caused by at least two symptoms from one or both of 1. inattention and/or 2. hyperactivity-impulsivity that have persisted for more than 6 months and interfere with functioning. This disorder is classified in three ways: combined presentation (314.01 [F90.2]) if both 1 and 2 are present; predominantly inattentive presentation (314.00 [F90.0]) if criterion 1 is met but not 2; and predominantly hyperactive/impulsive presentation (314.01 [F90.1]) if criterion 2 is met but not 1.

Neurodevelopmental motor disorders include three subclassifications. Developmental coordination disorder (315.4 [F82]) is diagnosed when children acquire motor skills at a slower rate than is expected and when the execution of motor actions is significantly below what is expected from a child of that age. A diagnosis of stereotypic movement disorder (307.3 [F98.4]) is given when repetitive and purposeless motor behaviour occurs which is unable to be controlled by the individual. Tic disorders (307.23 [F95.2], 307.22 [F95.1], 307.21 [F95.0]) include a variety of presentations that appear with sudden, rapid, and recurrent motor movements or vocalisations.

Specific learning disorder is diagnosed when there are difficulties learning and using academic skills that persist despite targeted intervention. Where the disorder is coded to include impairment in reading (315.00 [F81.0]), the alternate term "dyslexia" may be used. For a coding that includes impairment in mathematics (315.1 [F81.2]), it may be termed "dyscalculia." A third coding is used when there is impairment with written expression (315.2 [F81.81]).

It is common for neurodevelopmental disorders to co-occur and diagnosis may depend on an excess of certain behaviours (such as repetitive interests in ASD or excessive talking in ADHD) in addition to deficits and delays. Unlike previous versions of the DSM which were hierarchical in nature, children may be diagnosed with more than one of these disorders.

Australia

The incidence and prevalence rates vary dramatically across the range of neurodevelopmental disorders. Research regarding ASD prevalence for children aged 0 to 16 years in Australia is summarised by Williams and colleagues in their 2008 paper (Williams et al., 2008). They conclude that variations in estimates from previous work prevent reliable rates from being calculated but suggest that the prevalence rate in 2003–2004 for children aged 6–12 years was between 9.6 and 40.8/10 000. In a more recent paper, prevalence rates in Western Australia are estimated at 51.0 per 1000 children (Parner et al., 2011). However, variations between states in Australia and across age groups are expected and are likely impacted by the differences in diagnostic processes and waiting times for a diagnosis (0 to 24 months; Williams et al., 2008).[2]

Using the *DSM-IV* criteria, Ebejer and colleagues estimate ADHD Australian prevalence rates in adulthood to be 1.1% (Ebejer et al., 2012); however, when the age of onset criteria is ignored prevalence rates increased to 2.3%.[3] This is lower than

---

[2] The changes to the diagnostic criteria for ASD made in 2013 produce some challenges regarding estimations of incidence and prevalence. As most of the published information regarding incidence and prevalence contains data collected prior to these changes, it is possible that the rates reported here do not reflect alterations that may have occurred following the changed criterion.

[3] As with autism, the diagnostic criteria for ADHD changed between the fourth and fifth editions which may impact prevalence estimates. Thus, we have included the estimates from the 2012 paper (Ebejer et al., 2012) that ignore the age of onset items from the *DSM-IV* criteria.

estimates of the prevalence of neurodevelopmental communication disorders, though it is difficult to get exact statistics on these. A small number of Australian studies have looked at prevalence rates for speech and/or language impairment (Craig et al., 2002) with one estimate as high as 41% in children in northern Tasmania (Jessup et al., 2008). However, most studies that have considered diagnoses (as opposed to reported impairment) have only done so in relation to speech disorders where a prevalence of 1.3% was found in children aged 0 to 14 years from 1995 Australian Health Survey data (Keating, Turrell, & Ozanne, 2001). Further, a prevalence of 1.51% of primary school students were confirmed to have a speech sound disorder (including stuttering and voice disorders; McKinnon, McLeod, & Reilly, 2007). At present the only large study that has considered prevalence of communication disorders as a whole found 13.04% (in wave 1) and 12.40% (in wave 2) in an Australian primary and secondary schools (McLeod & McKinnon, 2007).

Australian estimates of specific learning disorders have traditionally been hard to compile, largely due to differences in definitions across disciplines (Skues & Cunningham, 2011). Prevalence statistics regarding dyslexia have been as high as 15% (Prior et al., 1995) though cut-off criteria for dyslexia in this study only included being one standard deviation below the year level mean and no indication of intelligence levels. Reliable estimates of occurrence of specific learning disorders according to *DSM-5* are not currently available. Similarly, incidence estimates of neurodevelopmental motor disorders as a group are hard to access and estimates of the Australian prevalence of the subclassifications within this grouping are also uncertain. There is little reason to expect that Australian prevalence rates vary significantly from international samples; however, reliable estimates are not available for many of the subclassifications within this group. Where reliable estimates are available, such as in the case of Tourette's syndrome, international prevalence studies suggest similar prevalence across the range of sampled countries and racial groups except African-American and sub-Sahara black African populations where Tourette's is rarely reported (Robertson, 2008).

Australia has produced a significant amount of research relating to all neurodevelopmental disorders. One example of a particular area of research in Australia relating to a neurodevelopmental disorder involves the use of eye-tracking technology to investigate aspects of ASD. Some of the work done in the area includes investigation of differences in response to expressions of emotions in familiar and unfamiliar faces (Nuske, Vivanti, & Dissanayake, 2014), responsiveness to emotion (Nuske, Vivanti, Hudry & Dissanayke, 2014), modulators of the reduced propensity to imitate (Vivanti & Dissanayake, 2014), reduced monitoring of and responsivity to social cues (Vivanti, Trembath, & Dissanayake, 2014) and the effect of inversion on face recognition (Hedley, Brewer, & Young, 2014).

At present, none of the neurodevelopmental disorders outlined in the American Psychiatric Association's *DSM-5* (2013) has a known cure, though evidence-based treatment guidelines exist for most that aim to target the core symptoms and reduce associated difficulties. In addition to behavioural approaches, genetic, pharmacological, and biological research is also active (e.g., Shaw et al., 2009). For example, the National Health and Medical Research Council (NHMRC, 2012) of Australia provide clinical practice points for the treatment of ADHD. These draw on the evidence that symptoms of ADHD may be reduced, and social skills increased via the use of behavioural modification techniques and parenting support. Additionally, pharmacological treatments have been shown to be beneficial in ADHD (Schachter et al., 2001) and two types of medication are approved for use in Australia (NHMRC, 2012). However, while it is common for children with ADHD to be prescribed medication to assist with symptom management, there is currently no evidence to suggest that ASD or GDD benefit from pharmacological treatment, though there is some evidence to suggest that tic disorders may improve with the use of guanfacine (Scahill et al., 2001).

Australian researchers are also interested in the effective treatment of ASD using behavioural techniques. The Structured Program for Children with Autism (SPECTRA) was created in Adelaide, Australia and uses applied behavioural analysis techniques to target the core deficit areas associated with ASD (Young, Partington, & Goren, 2009). Australian guidelines support the use of targeted behavioural interventions for neurodevelopmental communication disorders (Rosetti, 2001).

At present, there is little research specifically regarding the use of evidence-based treatments for neurodevelopmental disorders in Aboriginal and Torres Strait Islander populations. The NHMRC (2012) notes that while there is some evidence to suggest that culturally tailored programs are acceptable and can have positive effects for both child and family (e.g., Turner, Richards, & Sanders, 2007) generally, there is little work that targets specific issues relevant to this population in the treatment of neurodevelopmental disorders. Prevalence of these disorders in the Indigenous Australian population is also unknown and while concerns have been identified in relation to ASD regarding the barriers to diagnosis and treatment that are likely to impact Aboriginal and Torres Strait Islander community specifically (Wilson & Watson, 2011), particular concerns for this group are not well understood. In 2008, the Australian Government introduced the "Closing the Gap" campaign with a number of initiatives targeted at the preschool population. Although this initiative does not directly target developmental disorders, one of its central aims is to halve the gap in reading, writing, and numeracy achievements for Indigenous children by 2018.

The initial step in assessing a childhood disorder should involve a test of adaptive functioning (e.g., Vineland Adaptive Behavior Scales: Sparrow, Cicchetti, & Balla, 2005; Adaptive Behavior Assessment Schedule-II: Harrison & Oakland, 2013) followed by childhood wellness (e.g., Childhood Behavior Checklist: Achenbach, 1991; Achenbach & Edelbrock, 1983). These provide norm-referenced assessment for delays or atypical presentation. Genetic screening can identify underlying causalities for some presentations but the impact the genetic anomaly may have on the behaviour requires more systematic behavioural assessments.

Specific tools are available for some disorders such as ADHD and ASD. Currently, the gold standard for diagnosing ASD remains the Autism Diagnostic Observation Schedule (ADOS) (Lord et al., 2000) and the Autism Diagnostic Interview-Revised (ADI-R; Le Couteur, Lord, & Rutter, 2003). Although the norms used in these tools are from the US, they are thought to be appropriate within the Australian and New Zealand (NZ) context. A screening tool that has been developed in Australia is called Autism Detection in Early Childhood (Young, 2007) and is widely used for pre-diagnostic screening. It has been shown to have excellent reliability and validity (Nah, Young, & Brewer, 2014; Nah, Young, Brewer, & Berlingeri, 2014), with sensitivity and specificity levels at 1.0 and between 0.74 and 0.90, respectively.

Previously, the Australian Government has funded specialised programs that supported and treated children with a number of neurodevelopmental disorders. For example, specific individual funding packages have been available to support children with ASD access approved interventions (Prior et al., 2011) such as FaHCSIA (Families, Housing, Community Services and Indigenous Affairs), which provided children with up to $12 000 over 2 years. Targeted programs such as the Flinders (University) Early Intervention Research Program were supported by state government funds between 2006 and 2016. However, recent changes mean that these funds are now largely directed towards the National Disability Insurance Scheme which began a trial period in Australia in 2013, with South Australia being the pilot state for children. This scheme aims to deliver financial support to people living with a disability within Australia. Individual packages are tailored to the needs of the person with a disability, their family, and their goals. The full scheme began to take effect in 2016 and those with a neurodevelopmental disorder may benefit.

In many cases, when a diagnosis of a neurodevelopmental disorder is documented, government health funds (Medicare) assist with approved treatment providers (generally psychologists, occupational therapists, speech therapists, audiologists, physiotherapists) in addition to generalised and specialised support provided by medical doctors. At present special education funding is not available in Australia to those with learning disorders (Skues & Cunningham, 2011).

New Zealand

Very little data is available regarding the prevalence of each of the neurodevelopmental disorders in NZ. Using overseas data, it has been estimated that 40 000 New Zealanders have ASD (Ministry of Health and Education, 2008). Regarding ADHD diagnosis, the guidelines published by the Ministry of Health in NZ note that there are a number of methodological issues in assessing prevalence rates for the disorder and suggest interpreting prevalence rates with caution (New Zealand Ministry of Health, 2001). A study of a large range of other *DSM-IV* diagnoses in adults showed comparable rates between NZ and the US and Europe (Wells et al., 2006) for most disorders, suggesting there is no reason to purport that the prevalence rates would be significantly different to those in Australia.

A comprehensive report (Bevan-Brown, 2004) using parents of children with ASD from the Māori population of NZ indicated that these parents had similar experiences to non-Māori parents of children with ASD in relation to accessing, understanding and accepting diagnosis, and obtaining support and treatment. The vast majority of the Māori parents in the study wanted cultural input into their child's service provision (though the extent they required varied) and many noted that deficits associated with ASD restricted inclusion in some cultural activities; therefore, the children and their families were less exposed to culturally valued behaviours (specifically group activities and whakawhanaungatanga, relating to others). Overall, parents wished for more Māori-specific services and were concerned about the expertise of the Māori educationalists in areas related specifically to ASD.

A recent paper relating to visual impairment in children in NZ found a high percentage of those enrolled in special schools for vision-impaired children also had a developmental delay (Chong & Dai, 2013). Additionally, NZ research investigating the use of karyotype analysis after referral for developmental delay found clinically significant increases in chromosomal aberrations (Doherty et al., 2013). This work considered the NZ perspective specifically and proposed a more efficient sequential testing algorithm for this group.

The New Zealand Ministry of Health (2001) has documented guidelines relating to the treatment of ADHD and suggests that medication should be considered (though not necessarily prescribed) in all cases where functioning is significantly impaired as a result of ADHD. They also outline several behavioural approaches that are likely to assist in reducing the impact of symptoms, including parent education and behavioural therapy. Formal recommendations are also documented for the treatment of ASD (Ministry of Health and Education, 2008) and these also include parent education and behavioural intervention. Supplementary information regarding gastrointestinal issues in this population are also available in the NZ context (Broadstock, 2013). As in Australia, there is less formal documentation regarding the treatment of other neurodevelopmental disorders, though it is expected that best practice guidelines would follow evidence-based interventions globally.

There are no published standardised assessments of any neurodevelopmental disorder that include NZ norms. The NZ Ministry of Health recommends the use of standardised assessment tools that have been validated for use with a particular disorder (e.g., New Zealand Ministry of Health, 2001). As in Australia, the gold standard assessment tools for ASD that have US norms are a thought to be appropriate for use in NZ.

Many individuals with diagnosed neurodevelopmental disorders in NZ are eligible for disability support services from their local Needs Assessment and Services Coordination (NASC) organisation. For children who are not achieving their milestones, referral to specialised Child Development Services is appropriate.

Australian case study

This case is a composite example created for illustrative purposes.

Jacob is a 10-year-old boy, born to a mother who was a refugee from Kenya and an Australian father. Jacob was abandoned by his mother when he was 3 years old and went to live with his father, who was unaware he had a son until that time. Using the Autism Diagnostic Interview-Revised, his father reports that initially Jacob had presented as a grizzly toddler who was not interested in interacting. He was a poor sleeper and refused most solid food, preferring pureed food that was plain and white. His language was delayed, he was not interested in his peers and did not like to be cuddled.

Jacob was initially diagnosed with a reactive attachment disorder (RAD) and engaged in play therapy to address this. His father also attended parenting classes in how to parent a child with RAD. However, there was no improvement in Jacob's behaviour. He has become more isolated socially, and although his speech has developed, it is odd in prosody. He rarely engages in reciprocal conversation and continues to engage in self-stimulatory behaviours such as flapping and pacing. He has an intense interest in geography and continues to have feeding issues. He has been unable to develop friendships.

A diagnosis of ASD is given following unsuccessful intervention for attachment disorder. Jacob is engaged in a social skills training group for young children with ASD and has been referred to the local ASD association for support. His father has been counselled in effective management strategies by a psychologist, and speech therapy is recommended for his feeding issues.

Australia – further information

For further information about neurodevelopmental disorders, contact:
- Telethon Kids Institute, Subiaco, Western Australia (see http://telethonkids.org.au/our-research/brain-behaviour/)
- the Olga Tennison Autism Research Centre, La Trobe University, Melbourne, Victoria (see www.latrobe.edu.au/otarc).

New Zealand – further information

For more information about ASD, contact:
- Autism New Zealand (see www.autismnz.org.nz).

References

Achenbach, T. M. (1991). *Manual for the child behavior checklist/4–18 and 1991 profile.* Burlington: University of Vermont, Department of Psychiatry.

Achenbach, T. M., & Edelbrock, C. (1983). *Manual for the child behavior checklist and Revised Child Behaviour profile.* Burlington: University of Vermont Department of Psychiatry.

American Psychiatric Association. (1994). *Diagnostic and statistical manual of mental disorders* (4th ed.). Washington, DC: Author.

American Psychiatric Association. (2013). *Diagnostic and statistical manual of mental disorders.* (5th ed.). Arlington, VA: Author.

Bevan-Brown, J. (2004). *Māori perspectives of autistic spectrum disorder.* Wellington, NZ: Ministry of Education.

Broadstock, M. (2013). *New Zealand autism spectrum disorder guideline: Supplementary evidence on gastrointestinal problems in young people.* Christchurch: INSIGHT Research.

Chong, C. F., & Dai, S. (2013). Cross-sectional study on prevalence, causes and avoidable causes of visual impairment in Māori children. *New Zealand Medical Journal, 126,* 31–38.

Craig, A., Hancock, K., Tran, Y., Craig, M., & Peters, K. (2002). Epidemiology of stuttering in the community across the entire life span. *Journal of Speech, Language, and Hearing Research, 45*(6), 1097–1105.

Doherty, E., O'Connor, R., Zhang, A., Lim, C., Love, J. M., Ashton, F., et al. (2013). Developmental delay referrals and the roles of Fragile X testing and molecular karyotyping: A New Zealand perspective. *Molecular Medicine Reports, 7,* 1710–1714.

Ebejer, J. L., Medland, S. E., van der Werf, J., Gondro, C., Henders, A. K., Lynskey, M., et al. (2012). Attention deficit hyperactivity disorder in Australian adults: Prevalence, persistence, conduct problems and disadvantage. *PLOS ONE, 7*(10), e47404.

Harrison, P., & Oakland, T. (2003). *Adaptive behavior assessment system (ABAS-II).* San Antonio, TX: The Psychological Corporation.

Hedley, D., Brewer, N., & Young, R. (2014). The effect of inversion on face recognition in adults with autism spectrum disorder. *Journal of Autism and Developmental Disorders, 45*(5), 1–12. http://dx.doi.org/10.1007/s10803-014-2297-1

Jessup, B., Ward, E., Cahill, L., & Keating, D. (2008). Prevalence of speech and/or language impairment in preparatory students in northern Tasmania. *International Journal of Speech-Language Pathology, 10*(5), 364–377.

Keating, D., Turrell, G., & Ozanne, A. (2001). Childhood speech disorders: Reported prevalence, comorbidity and socioeconomic profile. *Journal of Paediatrics and Child Health, 37*(5), 431–436. http://dx.doi.org/10.1046/j.1440-1754.2001.00697.x

Le Couteur, A., Lord, C., & Rutter, M. (2003). *The autism diagnostic interview – revised (ADI-R).* Canada: Western Psychological Services.

Lord, C., Risi, S., Lambrecht, L., Cook Jr, E. H., Leventhal, B. L., DiLavore, P. C., et al. (2000). The Autism Diagnostic Observation Schedule – Generic: A standard measure of social and communication deficits associated with the spectrum of autism. *Journal of Autism and Developmental Disorders, 30*(3), 205–223.

McKinnon, D. H., McLeod, S., & Reilly, S. (2007). The prevalence of stuttering, voice and speech-sound disorders in primary school students in Australia. *Language, Speech, and Hearing Services in Schools, 38,* 5–15.

McLeod, S., & McKinnon, D. H. (2007). Prevalence of communication disorders compared with other learning needs in 14,500 primary and secondary school students. *International Journal of Language and Communication Disorders, 42*(S1), 37–59.

Ministry of Health and Education. (2008). *New Zealand Autism Spectrum Disorder Guideline Summary.* Wellington, NZ: Ministry of Health.

Nah, Y.-H., Young, R. L., & Brewer, N. (2014). Using the Autism Detection in Early Childhood (ADEC) and Childhood Autism Rating Scales (CARS) to predict long-term outcomes in children with autism spectrum disorders. *Journal of Autism and Developmental Disorders, 44*(9), 2301–2310.

Nah, Y.-H., Young, R. L., Brewer, N., & Berlingeri, G. (2014). Autism detection in early childhood (ADEC): Reliability and validity data for a level 2 screening tool for autistic disorder. *Psychological Assessment, 26*(1), 215.

National Health & Medical Research Council. (2012). *Clinical practice points on the diagnosis, assessment and management of attention deficit hyperactivity disorder in children and adolescents.* Canberra: Author.

New Zealand Ministry of Health. (2001). New Zealand guidelines for the assessment and treatment of attention-deficit/hyperactivity disorder. Wellington, NZ. Available: www.health.govt.nz/publication/new-zealand-guidelines-assessment-and-treatment-attention-deficit-hyperactivity-disorder

Nuske, H. J., Vivanti, G., & Dissanayake, C. (2014). Reactivity to fearful expressions of familiar and unfamiliar people in children with autism: An eye-tracking pupillometry study. *Journal of Neurodevelopmental Disorders, 6*(1), 14.

Nuske, H. J., Vivanti, G., Hudry, K., & Dissanayake, C. (2014). Pupillometry reveals reduced unconscious emotional reactivity in autism. *Biological Psychology, 101,* 24–35.

Parner, E., Thorsen, P., Dixon, G., de Klerk, N., Leonard, H., Nassar, N., et al. (2011). A comparison of autism prevalence trends in Denmark and Western Australia. *Journal of Autism and Developmental Disorders, 41*(12), 1601–1608. http://dx.doi.org/10.1007/s10803-011-1186-0

Prior, M., Roberts, J. M. A., Rodger, S., Williams, K., & Sutherland, R. (2011). *A review of the research to identify the most effective models of practice in early intervention of children with autism spectrum disorders: Australian Government Department of Families, Housing,* Australia: Community Services and Indigenous Affairs.

Prior, M., Sanson, A., Smart, D., & Oberklaid, F. (1995). Reading disability in an Australian community sample. *Australian Journal of Psychology, 47*(1), 32.

Robertson, M. M. (2008). The prevalence and epidemiology of Gilles de la Tourette syndrome: Part 1: The epidemiological and prevalence studies. *Journal of Psychosomatic Research, 65*(5), 461–472.

Rosetti, L. M. (2001). *Communication intervention: Birth to three.* Melbourne: CengageLearning.

Scahill, L., Chappell, P. B., Kim, Y. S., Schultz, R. T., Katsovich, L., Shepherd, E., et al. (2001). A placebo-controlled study of guanfacine in the treatment of children with tic disorders and attention deficit hyperactivity disorder. *American Journal of Psychiatry, 158*(7), 1067–1074.

Schachter, H. M., King, J., Langford, S., & Moher, D. (2001). How efficacious and safe is short-acting methylphenidate for the treatment of attention-deficit disorder in children and adolescents? A meta-analysis. *Canadian Medical Association Journal, 165*(11), 1475–1488.

Shaw, P., Sharp, W. S., Morrison, M., Eckstrand, K., Greenstein, D. K., Clasen, L. S., et al. (2009). Psychostimulant treatment and the developing cortex in attention deficit hyperactivity disorder. *American Journal of Psychiatry, 166*(1), 58–63.

Skues, J. L., & Cunningham, E. G. (2011). A contemporary review of the definition, prevalence, identification and support of learning disabilities in Australian schools. *Australian Journal of Learning Difficulties, 16*(2), 159–180. http://dx.doi.org/10.1080/19404158.2011.605154

Sparrow, S. S., Cicchetti, D. V., & Balla, D. A. (2005). *Vineland Adaptive Behavior Scales* (2nd ed.). Circle Pines, MN: American Guidance Service.

Turner, K. M., Richards, M., & Sanders, M. R. (2007). Randomised clinical trial of a group parent education programme for Australian Indigenous families. *Journal of Paediatrics and Child Health, 43*(6), 429–437.

Vivanti, G., & Dissanayake, C. (2014). Propensity to imitate in autism is not modulated by the model's gaze direction: An eye tracking study. *Autism Research, 7*(3), 392–399.

Vivanti, G., Trembath, D., & Dissanayake, C. (2014). Atypical monitoring and responsiveness to goal-directed gaze in autism spectrum disorder. *Experimental Brain Research, 232*(2), 695–701.

Wells, J. E., Browne, M. A. O., Scott, K. M., McGee, M. A., Baxter, J., Kokaua, J., & for the New Zealand Mental Health Survey Research, T. (2006). Prevalence, interference with life and severity of 12 month DSM-IV disorders in Te Rau Hinengaro: The New Zealand Mental Health Survey. *Australian & New Zealand Journal of Psychiatry, 40*(10), 845–854. http://dx.doi.org/10.1111/j.1440-1614.2006.01903.x

Williams, K., MacDermott, S., Ridley, G., Glasson, E. J., & Wray, J. A. (2008). The prevalence of autism in Australia. Can it be established from existing data? *Journal of Paediatrics and Child Health, 44*(9), 504–510. http://dx.doi.org/10.1111/j.1440-1754.2008.01331.x

Wilson, K., & Watson, L. (2011). Autism spectrum disorder in Australian Indigenous families: Issues of diagnosis, support and funding. *Aboriginal and Islander Health Worker Journal, 35*(5), 17.

World Health Organisation. (2011). *International Statistical Classification of Diseases and Related Health Problems 2010 Edition (ICD-10)*. Geneva: Author. Available: www.who.int/classifications/icd/en/

Young, R. L. (2007). *Autism detection in early childhood (ADEC) manual*. Camberwell, Vic.: ACER Press.

Young, R. L., Partington, C. A., & Goren, T. (2009). *SPECTRA: Structured program for early childhood therapists working with autism*. Camberwell, Vic.: ACER Press.

Recommendations for further reading/resources

Relevant websites:

- Autism CRC: http://autismcrc.com.au/research-programs/education
- Olga Tennison Autism Research Centre: www.latrobe.edu.au/otarc
- Autism and Related Disorders, Telethon Kids Institute: http://autism.telethonkids.org.au/

Author acknowledgements

Thanks to Simon Hobson for his advice regarding the New Zealand schooling system and Māori culture.

9

Schizophrenia and related psychotic disorders

Vaughan Carr, Melissa J Green, and Elliot M Bell

Introduction

Initially termed "dementia praecox," schizophrenia was first described by the German psychiatrist Emil Kraepelin in the late 19th century. Kraepelin distinguished dementia praecox from manic depressive illness, primarily a mood disorder, on the basis of differences in course and outcome: schizophrenia was observed to have a chronic and deteriorating course with a poor outcome, while manic depression was seen to have a cyclic "relapsing-remitting" course, with a more favourable long-term outcome. The name schizophrenia (literally "split mind") was coined in the early 20th century by the Swiss psychiatrist Eugen Bleuler, and much later manic depression was renamed bipolar disorder. However, problems in the distinctions between these two conditions were soon identified and noted by Kraepelin himself in his later writings. Considerable overlap was seen in clinical features, course, and outcome. The more recent diagnostic category of schizoaffective disorder may be seen to encompass composite forms of mood and schizophrenic disorders. Schizophrenia is now more commonly regarded as a clinical syndrome rather than a single disease entity; there is significant heterogeneity in clinical expression, and considerable overlap of both clinical and biological features with other psychiatric conditions. Scientific efforts are yet to delineate the causes and pathophysiology of schizophrenia, although some significant advances in understanding the neurobiology and treatment mechanisms have been made in the past 50 years.

A strong genetic basis for schizophrenia is indicated by family and molecular genetic studies. However, a clear role for environmental influences in the development of schizophrenia is also well established. Current molecular genetic studies of schizophrenia encompassing worldwide consortia have been able to account for an increasing but minor fraction of risk for schizophrenia in common genetic loci. Rare genetic variations, such as copy number deletions and duplications, are also emerging as important risk indicators. High overlap in the heritability of bipolar and schizoaffective disorder within families has also been shown in large-scale epidemiological research.

In terms of impact and incidence, schizophrenia ranks among the top 10 causes of disability in developed countries and incidence is estimated at 15.2/100 000, with current prevalence estimated at 4.6/1000 (McGrath et al., 2008). The mortality rate is 2.5 times that of the general population, such that life expectancy is curtailed by 12–15 years, and premature mortality appears to be increasing (Saha, Chant & McGrath, 2007). Suicide occurs in 5%.

Clinical features

The clinical features of schizophrenia are listed in Table 9.1, alongside an abbreviated and paraphrased summary of the *Diagnostic and Statistical Manual of Mental Disorders*

Table 9.1 Clinical features and *DSM-5* diagnostic criteria (paraphrased) for schizophrenia

Clinical features	*DSM-5* diagnostic criteria (paraphrased)
1. Positive symptoms • delusions • hallucinations (typically auditory but may occur in other modalities) • formal thought disorder (e.g., loose associations, incoherence, neologisms) • disorganised behaviour (e.g., mannerisms, posturing, bizarre dress)	A. Two or more of the following, present for a significant time during a 1-month period; at least one should be 1, 2 or 3: 1. delusions 2. hallucinations 3. disorganised speech 4. grossly abnormal psychomotor behaviour (e.g., catatonia)
2. Negative symptoms • flattened affect (restricted or blunted) • avolition (apathy, amotivation) • asociality (social withdrawal) • alogia (poverty in amount or content of speech) • anhedonia (loss of the capacity to experience or the motivation to seek pleasure)	5. negative symptoms (i.e., restricted affect, avolition, and asociality)
3. Cognitive impairments • general intelligence (IQ) • selective and/or sustained attention • working memory • verbal memory • language (verbal fluency, naming, and comprehension) • processing speed • executive control (flexibility in problem-solving) • social cognition (ability to identify and respond appropriately to social cues)	B. Social/occupational dysfunction; decline from pre-onset levels of at least one of work functioning, interpersonal relations, or self-care C. Duration of 6 months, including at least 1 month of symptoms from Criterion A; this may include periods of prodromal or residual symptoms D. Exclusion of schizoaffective and mood disorder E. Exclusion of the direct effects of a substance (drug of abuse or medication) or a general medical condition F. If there is a history of autism or other pervasive developmental disorder, the diagnosis of schizophrenia is made only if prominent delusions or hallucinations are also present for at least a month

(5th ed.; *DSM-5*; American Psychiatric Association, 2013) diagnostic criteria. Significant impairment in social and/or occupational functioning is essential in making the diagnosis. The *DSM-5* and the *International Statistical Classification of Diseases and Related Health Problems 2010 Edition (ICD-10*; WHO, 2011) codes, respectively, for schizophrenia are 295.90 and F20, and for schizoaffective disorder are 295.70 and F25.

Hallmark symptoms of psychosis include delusions, hallucinations, and/or severely disorganised thoughts, speech, and behaviour. These clinical phenomena have come to be known as the "positive" symptoms of schizophrenia, reflecting an "excess" of (aberrant) function, in contrast to "negative" symptoms that, at least overtly, reflect an "absence" or diminution of function.

Positive symptoms typically include delusions of reference, persecutory and grandiose delusions, and hallucinations, most often auditory verbal – hearing voices – but they can occur in any sensory modality. Particular psychotic symptoms said to be more discriminatory for schizophrenia compared to other psychoses are called first-rank symptoms. These include experiences of thought insertion, thought withdrawal and thought broadcast, delusions of alien control, and particular auditory hallucinations such as thoughts spoken aloud and voices commenting on, or discussing, the individual in the grammatical third person. Disorganised thinking and behaviour are also regarded as positive symptoms. The former refers to such phenomena as loose associations, thought blocking, incoherent speech, and neologisms, whereas the latter includes strange mannerisms, posturing, bizarre attire, and catatonia. Inappropriate affect, in which emotional expression is incongruous with the context, is also regarded as disorganisation symptom in schizophrenia.

While positive symptoms tend to be conspicuous and bring the person to the attention of others, negative symptoms are less obvious, but account for much of the disability associated with schizophrenia. They include restricted or blunted affect, avolition (lack of motivation), anhedonia (inability to experience pleasure), alogia (poverty of speech) and asociality (loss of social competence). Negative symptoms are often associated with cognitive impairments in selective and sustained attention, working memory, verbal memory, processing speed, and executive functions.

Schizophrenia spectrum

As intimated earlier in this chapter, the clinical overlap between schizophrenia and bipolar disorder has long suggested that the traditional diagnostic distinction between the two is not entirely accurate. However, not only has schizoaffective disorder emerged as a category to account for intermediate forms with features of both disorders, the relationship between schizophrenia and other non-affective psychoses remains unclear. For example, schizophreniform disorder is identical to schizophrenia, except that it is of brief (less than 6 months) duration. Delusional disorder consists of a single, circumscribed delusion (e.g., paranoid, grandiose, hypochondriacal, jealous) without hallucinations, negative symptoms, or other features of schizophrenia. Brief psychotic disorder is a transient psychosis of short duration, often occurring in relation to severe stress of some kind. Diagnostically, these are all grouped together as schizophrenia-related psychoses, but the boundaries between them are indistinct, and each may sometimes evolve over time to meet the diagnostic criteria for schizophrenia itself.

Similarly, there is some overlap between features of schizophrenia and non-affective, non-psychotic disorders. Certain personality disorders (schizotypal, paranoid, and schizoid) bear a close resemblance to schizophrenia, given their subclinical expressions of thought disorder, intense suspiciousness, and social aversion. These personality disorders often run in families with schizophrenia, and show similarities in neurophysiological profiles. The concept of schizophrenia spectrum has thus been evoked to encompass these phenomena, but it is unclear whether this concept is valid.

Biological and environmental causes

Recent molecular genetics research has identified over 100 common genetic variants associated with schizophrenia, each of small effect. These genetic loci are distributed across the genome, and together account for about a quarter to one-third of the heritability of schizophrenia. The fact that they are common genetic variants means that they are widely distributed in the general population, such that different combinations of these variants, or their inheritance in the context of non-genetic risk factors, may be necessary to manifest as a clinical disorder. Most identified loci are involved in neuronal development and synaptic functioning, and in immune processes. In addition, some rare genetic variants, of larger effect, have been identified; however, owing to their rarity they can only account for a very small percentage of cases.

In addition to genetic risk factors, a number of environmental risks have also been identified. These include maternal stress and infections during pregnancy, obstetric or perinatal complications (especially those resulting in foetal hypoxia), childhood infections, child maltreatment, urban upbringing, immigration, and cannabis use. However, none of these risk factors is unique to schizophrenia, just as many of the genetic risk factors for schizophrenia are shared with other disorders. Attention is now being paid to the effects of interactions between genetic and environmental risk factors.

Treatment

Standard practice generally involves a combination of pharmacological and psychological treatments. Considerable evidence indicates that the longer the duration of untreated psychosis the worse the clinical outcome, thus early detection and treatment is encouraged. Various psychological and psychosocial approaches can be useful at different stages of illness, and indeed, a combination of medication and psychosocial treatments is highly effective in reducing symptoms and relapse rates. Using combinations of two or more different antipsychotic medications is not uncommon, but has no scientifically demonstrated advantage and increases the likelihood of adverse effects.

Pharmacological treatment

All antipsychotic medications used in the treatment of schizophrenia and related disorders, including both first-generation (typical) and second-generation (atypical) drugs, are of approximately equal effectiveness for positive symptoms, but none impact significantly on negative symptoms or cognitive deficits. Second-generation drugs are generally better tolerated, but failures in treatment adherence occur with all antipsychotics, leading to treatment discontinuation in around three-quarters of cases within 18 months. The drug clozapine, which has superior efficacy for positive symptoms, is reserved for treatment-resistant cases (i.e., severe and persistent positive and/or negative symptoms following adequate trials of two or more antipsychotic drugs). Its use is subject to strict monitoring owing to its potential for causing serious depletion of white blood cells and heart disease.

Choice of drug primarily centres on individual differences in tolerability. Common adverse effects include movement disorders (extrapyramidal effects and akathisia), which are more likely with (but not exclusive to) first-generation antipsychotics, whereas weight gain and metabolic complications are more likely with (but not exclusive to) second-generation agents (especially clozapine and olanzapine). Other common adverse effects include sedation, hyperprolactinaemia (causing gynaecomastia and galactorrhoea) and sexual dysfunction. Usually treatment is started with a low dose that is titrated upwards over 1 to 4 weeks. Treatment is best initiated with oral preparations with short-acting injectable forms reserved for psychosis-related behavioural emergencies. Long-acting injectable (LAI) preparations are available and useful in long-term maintenance treatment if medication adherence is poor.

Psychosocial treatments

There are several psychosocial interventions with a sound evidence base supporting their efficacy.

Supportive family psychoeducation and problem-solving

Individual or group-based interventions for families that are effective in reducing relapse rates, the likelihood of hospital readmission and improving levels of functioning are those that focus on providing psychosocial support and psychoeducation about the nature of schizophrenia, its treatment, and outcome, together with pragmatic assistance in problem-solving and coping strategy development in managing the ill family member. It appears to have these effects by reducing high levels of angry and critical remarks ("expressed emotion") in families and improving treatment adherence.

Cognitive behaviour therapy

There is strong and consistent evidence that this form of therapy is useful in reducing symptoms, especially delusions, and may be more effective than other forms of psychological treatment long term. There is good quality evidence that it may improve overall functioning, mood, feelings of hopelessness, insight, and relapse rates. Moderate quality evidence indicates that this therapy can also improve coexisting social anxiety and depression, and help to retain clients with comorbid substance abuse in treatment.

Cognitive and social cognitive remediation

Cognitive remediation is a behavioural learning-based intervention that aims to improve deficits in memory, attention, and problem-solving capacities, as well as social cognitive skills (e.g., emotion recognition and the capacity to correctly infer others' intentions and beliefs). Deficits in these domains of cognition are known to significantly impair psychosocial functioning, and remediation programs emerging worldwide have demonstrated efficacy in improving cognitive and social cognitive skills, with moderate effects on daily functioning. More traditional treatment programs that involve training in social interactions, social perception, self-management skills, community participation, and workplace skills can improve social competence and produce benefits in communal functioning and reduced symptom levels (including negative symptoms) and relapse rates.

Vocational rehabilitation

Supported employment programs that use an "individual placement and support" model are more effective than other forms of vocational rehabilitation in increasing rates of competitive employment, hours worked per week, total earnings, and duration of employment.

Detecting the first episode of psychosis

Very often a first psychotic episode will not fit a typical diagnostic pattern: features of schizophrenia may not be obvious; manic, depressive, or other symptoms (e.g., anxiety, obsessive-compulsive phenomena) may appear prominent; and often the initial presentation occurs in the context of psychoactive substance abuse, misleading the clinician to assume the psychosis has been caused entirely by drugs. Any young person suspected of experiencing psychological distress of any kind should be asked, among other things, whether they have experienced delusions or hallucinations. Questions such as those listed in Table 9.2 may be used to assist in detecting psychotic symptoms. A positive response to any one of these questions is enough to suggest that further clinical enquiry should be conducted to establish the duration of the symptom(s), the degree of conviction as to their reality, the extent of emotional distress associated with the symptoms and whether the person feels compelled to act upon them.

With the diagnostic uncertainty usually inherent in a first episode of psychosis, it is important not to foreclose prematurely on a specific diagnosis, but to keep diagnostic options open and treat the condition on the basis of its symptom profile. A thorough history, mental status assessment, and physical examination must be undertaken. Certain medical investigations should be performed to identify potential physical health problems. Assessment of cognitive functioning ought to occur and be taken into

Table 9.2 Psychosis screening questions

Symptoms	Questions
Delusional mood	Have there ever been times when you felt that something strange and unexplainable was going on; things that other people would find it very hard to believe?
Grandiose delusions	Have you ever felt that you had special powers or talents that other people lack, and are not shared by any group of people?
Delusions of persecution	Have you ever felt that people were too interested in you, singling you out, or deliberately trying to harm you?
Delusions of reference	Have you ever felt that things were arranged, or happened, or said in a way so as to have a special meaning or message just for you?
Delusions of control; thought interference; passivity	Have you ever felt that your thoughts were being directly interfered with or controlled by another person in a way that people would find hard to believe, for instance, through telepathy?
Hallucinosis	Have there ever been times when you heard voices or noises when there was no one around and no ordinary explanation seemed possible?
	Or have you ever seen visions or things that other people could not see?

Source: Bebbington & Nayani, 1995

consideration in planning and conducting psychosocial treatments and rehabilitation, including the resumption of work or education.

An assessment of the client's risk of suicide, self-harm, and danger to others is critical, and the need for hospitalisation evaluated in light of the available resources and services, as well as the extent of family and other social supports. Although community-based treatment is preferred as a less-restrictive location for treatment, if a client is too severely ill to be managed in the community, represents a significant risk of harm to themselves or others, and/or does not have the degree of family or other social support necessary to help ensure their wellbeing, then hospital admission is indicated to initiate treatment. This may require involuntary hospital admission under the relevant Mental Health Act for that jurisdiction.

Barriers to treatment adherence

A crucial factor that is often overlooked in the treatment of psychotic disorders, and without which treatment invariably fails, is *engagement of the client* (McCabe et al., 2002). This requires particular attention in schizophrenia. Engagement means the establishment of a working therapeutic relationship between client and clinician, marked by mutual respect and commitment to working on the task of getting and staying well in the long term. Similarly, engagement of the client's family is critical for long-term treatment, as families frequently provide essential social and emotional support that may be unavailable elsewhere.

Other barriers to engagement in young people with psychotic disorders include the impairment of insight that often accompanies psychosis, and the low motivation that is an integral component of the negative symptoms of schizophrenia. Cognitive deficits can contribute to poor comprehension and retention of the information needed to manage the illness effectively (e.g., remembering to take medication), as well as to poor problem-solving skills. Immaturity in young people may contribute to impulsivity, poor judgement, and rebelliousness that all interfere with engagement. Psychotic content in conversation with the clinician can hamper engagement as it can impede reality-based communications and interfere with the development of empathy. In particular, it often generates discomfort in the listener and a tendency to try to avoid such topics or bring the consultation to a close, in spite of the client's need to give expression to their psychotic experiences.

Overcoming these barriers can be difficult. It requires listening attentively to the patient's worries and concerns, including psychotic material, while controlling one's own discomfort. Responding empathically to emotional cues is very important in fostering the client's sense of being understood, showing an interest in all aspects of the person, not just their symptoms.

Information for the general public

There are several sources of information about schizophrenia that are available online for consumers, carers, and others. The following provide useful information about schizophrenia and other mental disorders, including advice on seeking treatment:

- SANE Australia (www.sane.org)
- Mind Australia (www.mindaustralia.org.au)
- The Schizophrenia Fellowship of Australia (www.schizophrenia.org.au)
- headspace, National Youth Mental Health Foundation (http://headspace.org.au/)
- Supporting Families in Mental Illness (www.supportingfamilies.org.nz).

Australia

In Australia, the 1-month treated prevalence of schizophrenia/schizoaffective disorder is 2.12 per 1000 population aged 18–64 years (males 2.89, females 1.35 per 1000), as revealed in a national epidemiological survey of psychotic individuals living in the community that was conducted in 2010 (Morgan et al., 2014). In the study, the average age of onset was 24 years, and other non-affective psychoses were much less common (0.14 per 1000). This study also showed that, among persons with schizophrenia, 90% rely on a government pension for their income, only 30% have completed high school education, 69% are unemployed and 12% homeless in a given year, and 71% are single or have never been in a married/de facto relationship, especially males. Two-thirds continue to suffer psychotic symptoms, almost half have severe negative symptoms and

43% have made a suicide attempt at least once. In terms of physical health, 75% are obese or overweight, 67% smoke cigarettes and 58% suffer from the metabolic syndrome (combinations of abdominal obesity, raised blood lipids and glucose, high blood pressure). There are high rates of substance abuse with 51% having lifetime alcohol abuse or dependence; the figures for cannabis and other substances are 54% and 32%, respectively. Moderate or severe disability is reported by 55% (Morgan et al., 2014).

Australian research has led the worldwide clinical emphasis on attempting to reduce the duration of untreated psychosis by means of early psychosis detection (i.e., prior to onset of psychotic symptoms) and intervention services, with long-term follow-up studies of these original "ultra-high risk" (UHR) cohorts now emerging (Henry et al., 2010; Lin et al., 2013; Nelson et al., 2013). While the clinical utility of the UHR criteria in predicting transition to psychosis remains debatable (Yung et al., 2010), the study of these original UHR cohorts has shown the predictive utility of cognitive disturbances (Lin et al., 2013) and significant brain volume loss (Sun et al., 2009), which are evident in the earliest stages of psychosis. Other national epidemiological studies have contributed to the discovery of novel genetic risk variants (Hallmayer et al., 2005; Morar et al., 2010; Ripke et al., 2014), childhood antecedents (Welham et al., 2010), and environmental risk factors for schizophrenia (Jablensky et al., 2005; McGrath, 2010).

Standard practice/treatment recommendations within the Australian context

In Australia, clinical practice guidelines for schizophrenia have been prepared by the Royal Australian and New Zealand College of Psychiatrists (RANZCP; Galletly et al., 2016). These give mostly an overview of current expert opinion on treatment, but their lack of methodological rigour and transparency puts their reliability in some doubt. Very good treatment guidelines that have been rigorously developed are available from the British National Institute for Health and Care Excellence (NICE: www.nice.org.uk/guidance/cg178).

Standard clinical assessments developed in Australia include the Diagnostic Interview for Psychosis (DIP; Castle et al., 2006) and the Comprehensive Assessment of At-Risk Mental States (CAARMS; Yung et al., 2005). The DIP is a semi-structured clinical interview from which diagnoses of schizophrenia or other psychotic or affective mood disorders can be distinguished according to current diagnostic nomenclature. The CAARMS is used in Australian youth mental health services for the early detection of high risk for the development of psychotic disorders.

Government funding of specialised early psychosis prevention and intervention centres sits alongside the depression-focused Australian beyondblue and other crisis contacts such as Lifeline. Although most psychotic disorders are treated in the Australian state-based public mental health services, the Australian Government is currently in the process of rolling out early psychosis detection and intervention services under the national headspace initiative, a community-based youth mental health service.

New Zealand

There is limited data available regarding the patterns and effects of schizophrenia and related disorders in the New Zealand (NZ) population. An early epidemiological study using structured interviews administered by trained laypeople reported a lifetime prevalence for schizophrenia and schizophreniform disorders of 0.6%, with highest rates reported for those aged 25–44 (Wells et al., 1989). This study did not survey people who were homeless or living in institutions, where people with schizophrenia are commonly considered to be over-represented. This was borne out in a subsequent national study examining the prevalence of psychiatric disorders in NZ prisons, which found lifetime schizophrenia prevalence estimates of 8.5% for female and 6.6% for male sentenced inmates (Brinded et al., 2001). There was no difference in prevalence rates observed across ethnic groups (i.e., European/other, Māori, and Pacific Island people) within the national prison sample (Simpson et al., 1999). Of note, only 37% of prison inmates meeting diagnostic criteria for schizophrenia were receiving treatment when interviewed (Brinded et al., 2001).

A more recent NZ survey using the same methodology as a community survey by Wells et al. (1989) did not report findings for psychotic disorders. This was due to findings within the literature indicating that layperson-administered structured interviews lack sufficient reliability and validity for diagnosing these conditions (Oakley-Brown, Wells, & Scott, 2006). However, Kake, Arnold, and Ellis (2008) have reported prevalence estimates of schizophrenia for both Māori and non-Māori New Zealanders using capture-recapture statistical analysis. They estimated 12-month prevalence rates of 0.97% for Māori, and 0.32% for non-Māori.

Research undertaken in NZ has made important contributions to additional aspects of the understanding of schizophrenia. Two large-scale ongoing longitudinal studies have been particularly significant. The Christchurch Health and Development Study (CHDS) has tracked 1265 children born in that city in 1977, while the Dunedin Multidisciplinary Health and Development Study (DMHDS) has followed a 1972–1973 birth cohort of 1037 individuals. The DMHDS in particular has helped clarify three areas of interest in schizophrenia research. First, it has examined the complex relationship between cannabis use and psychosis. Findings have contributed to the contemporary view that cannabis use in adolescence increases risk of developing schizophrenia (Arseneault et al., 2002; Arseneault et al., 2004), and have demonstrated interaction between genetic vulnerability to the negative effects of cannabis and risk of psychosis (Caspi et al., 2005). Second, the DMHDS has also explored the nature of links between schizophrenia and violence (e.g., Arseneault, Moffitt et al., 2002); for example, higher rates of adult violence in DMHDS participants with a history of psychotic symptoms have been reported, but appear to be mediated by conduct disorders in childhood (Arseneault et al., 2000; Arseneault et al., 2003). This is consistent with current findings in the literature which note that the vast majority of people with schizophrenia are not violent; in this context, violent behaviour tends to be associated with psychiatric comorbidities and demographic factors unrelated to the illness (Silverstein et al., 2015).

Third, the DMHDS has revealed signs and symptoms of mental illness in childhood that might be predictive of schizophrenia in adulthood. In general, childhood diagnoses of mental disorder were strong predictors of adult psychiatric illness (Kim-Cohen et al., 2003; Koenen et al., 2009), and early DMHDS studies found evidence of specific links between psychotic symptoms in childhood and adult schizophrenia (Cannon et al., 2002; Poulten et al., 2000). However, outcomes from a more recent report on the cohort at age 38 were consistent with findings from other researchers (see Murray & Jones, 2012) in which childhood psychotic symptoms were associated with broader mental health problems in adulthood, and not schizophrenia specifically (Fisher et al., 2013).

Standard practice/treatment recommendations within the New Zealand context

With RANZCP being a trans-Tasman professional association, the clinical practice guidelines mentioned in this chapter have been developed for both countries. While no best practice guidelines have been produced by the professional bodies or registration authority for psychologists, the RANZCP document has multidisciplinary relevance (Galletly et al., 2016).

A variety of assessment measures are used in clinical practice in NZ with people who have schizophrenia, though published local norms are rarely available. Examples of measures used include the Positive and Negative Syndrome Scale (PANSS; Kay, Opler, & Fizbein, 2006) which evaluates the broad range of symptoms of schizophrenia. The CAARMS is also used in NZ, as are the Psychotic Symptom Rating Scales (PSYRATS; Haddock et al., 1999), for more specific assessment of delusions and hallucinations. Additionally, all users of public (district health board) mental health services in NZ complete the Health of the Nation Outcome Scale (HoNOS), a clinician-administered measure of social and health functioning (Wing, Curtis, & Beevor, 1996).

General guidelines pertaining to the use of psychometric tests have been produced by the New Zealand Psychologists Board, and these apply to using psychological tests with people who have schizophrenia (www.psychologistsboard.org.nz/best-practice-documents-and-guidelines2). The guidelines emphasise the importance of: being competently trained in the use of the tests being administered; triangulating test data with collateral information; avoiding over-testing clients; and interpreting results with caution where culturally relevant norms are not available.

In NZ, many people with schizophrenia receive their mental health treatment in primary care settings through a general practitioner. Some may also consult with psychiatrists, clinical psychologists, or other therapists in private practice. When the most intensive support is needed, people with schizophrenia are usually cared for in public mental health services within local district health boards (DHBs). Many DHBs include specialty "early psychosis" or "early intervention" services which target early psychotic presentations in young people (typically mid-teens to mid-twenties).

New Zealand case study

This case has been created as an example for illustrative purposes.

Tamahou is a 29-year-old Māori man who has spent the last 3 months at an inpatient psychiatric rehabilitation facility. He was initially admitted to the local acute ward under the Mental Health Act, then transferred to the rehabilitation unit due to a concern that he needed longer-term inpatient care. Tamahou had multiple brief admissions previously in the context of psychotic episodes associated with a diagnosis of schizophrenia. His current admission followed a period of medication non-adherence and substance use resulting in a deterioration in his mental state. When admitted, he presented with auditory hallucinations involving his hearing male voices criticising him, telling him not to trust people and to be ready to defend himself against them. Tamahou also showed signs of disorganised thinking, with his speech being difficult to follow. Finally, he described both paranoid and grandiose delusions. These revolved around beliefs that he was a Christian prophet and was being persecuted because of this.

Tamahou identified that he began feeling distressed 6 months ago when his mother died, after which he withdrew from community mental health services and increased his cannabis and alcohol use.

Most of Tamahou's symptoms remitted very quickly while in the acute admitting ward, a low stimulus environment, where he had no access to substances and was able to restart his pharmacotherapy. The latter included antipsychotic and mood stabilising medications. He has also had access to benzodiazepines as needed. The only ongoing psychotic symptom that was apparent was infrequent and low-level auditory hallucinations. Tamahou was able to identify these as such and did not feel any compulsion to respond to them.

With the settling of his psychotic symptoms, Tamahou has become clearer in his thinking and more communicative with nursing staff, sharing that he feels depressed about the loss of his mother and confused with regard to his spirituality and cultural identity. He has positive childhood memories of his time at a Catholic Māori boys boarding school, but has lost contact with the friends he made there, and also with family (whanau) on his mother's side. Following review with a psychiatry registrar, Tamahou has been diagnosed with comorbid mild depression, prescribed a selective serotonin reuptake inhibitor (SSRI) and referred to the ward clinical psychologist for cognitive behaviour therapy both for the depression and to help manage the residual auditory hallucinations. His rehabilitation program also includes individual and group work with the Kaimaanaki (Māori mental health worker) around exploring and strengthening his Māori identity, sessions with the hospital chaplain to help him distinguish between healthy and illness-related spiritual beliefs, and social work input to assist in rebuilding whanau connections.

The Australian Schizophrenia Research Bank

A large national consortium of scientists has established the Australian Schizophrenia Research Bank (ASRB) (Loughland et al., 2010). The ASRB is a repository of diagnostic, demographic, and clinical data on psychosis cases and controls that includes measures of cognitive functioning, genetic data derived from blood samples and structural brain images for a majority of the sample. The ASRB resource is open for access by scientists around the world. It has contributed to the discovery of novel genetic risk variants in large international collaborations (e.g., Schizophrenia Psychiatric Genome-Wide Association Study [GWAS] Consortium, 2011; Ripke et al., 2014). Studies by Australian scientists have used the ASRB to delineate genetic alterations and brain imaging features of cognitive subtypes of schizophrenia (Green et al., 2013, Gould et al., 2014, Wu et al., 2016), as well as showing genetic interactions with other factors such as childhood maltreatment impacting symptoms (e.g., auditory hallucinations and negative symptoms) and/or cognitive features of the illness (Green et al., 2014; Green et al., 2015; McCarthy-Jones et al., 2014). The high-level phenotyping of the ASRB sample provides a unique opportunity to understand the complexity of schizophrenia through the study of subgroups of patients identified by biological features and/or shared environmental exposures.

New Zealand – social cognition and interaction training

For those with schizophrenia, social cognitive impairments are increasingly recognised as impacting functional and vocational outcomes as well as quality of life. Often these difficulties continue after the overt clinical symptoms have been treated successfully by pharmacotherapy. This has resulted in the emergence of cognitive remediation programs targeting social cognitive skills. As such, their use is increasingly entering clinical practice in Australia and NZ.

One such intervention is the Social Cognition and Interaction Training (SCIT) tool (Roberts, Penn & Combs, in press; Roberts et al., 2014). This program is currently being run at one of the inpatient mental health rehabilitation services of the Capital and Coast District Health Board in Wellington, by clinical psychologists Jared Watson and Phoebe Naismith-Thomass, and occupational therapist Eve Grant.

The SCIT is a manualised 20-session group program in which participants learn specific social cognitive strategies to analyse social cognitive stimuli (e.g., video vignettes) and practice applying these in their lives. Aspects of social cognition targeted include emotion perception, attribution style and "theory of mind" (i.e., the capacity to correctly infer others' mental states and intentions). The SCIT groups are run weekly, with sessions taking

60 to 90 minutes each. The sessions proceed through three "modules": 1. "introducing emotions"; 2. "figuring out situations"; and 3. "checking it out". Participant progress in the program can be assessed by rating social functioning, specific domains of social cognition, or symptom levels.

Jared Watson chose to use the SCIT on the basis of its strong theoretical rationale and the fit it provides for the needs of clients completing inpatient rehabilitation. The team has also received positive feedback from clients taking part in the program, consistent with research findings noting the importance that people with schizophrenia place on their social functioning.

Bibliography

Kraepelin, E. (1916a). *Dementia praecox and paraphrenia. 1916*. Translated by R. M. Barclay and edited by G. M. Robertson, 1919. Chicago: Chicago Medical Book Company.

Kraepelin, E. (1916b). *Manic-depressive insanity and paranoia. 1916*. Translated by R. M. Barclay and edited by G. M. Robertson, 1920. Chicago: Chicago Medical Book Company.

Laurens, K. R., Luo, L., Matheson, S. L., Carr, V. J., Raudino, A., Harris, F., & Green, M. J. (2015). Common or distinct pathways to psychosis? A systematic review of evidence from prospective studies for developmental risk factors and antecedents of the schizophrenia spectrum disorders and affective psychoses. *BMC Psychiatry, 15*, 205.

Matheson, S. L., Shepherd, A., & Carr, V. (2014). How much do we know about schizophrenia and how well do we know it? Evidence from the Schizophrenia Library. *Psychological Medicine, 44*, 3387–3405.

Schizophrenia Working Group of the Psychiatric Genetics Consortium. (2014). Biological insights from 108 schizophrenia-associated genetic loci. *Nature, 511*, 421–427.

Sullivan, P. F., Kendler, K. S., & Neale, M. C. (2003). Schizophrenia as a complex trait. Evidence from a meta-analysis of twin studies. *Archives of General Psychiatry, 60*, 1187–1192.

References

American Psychiatric Association. (2013). *Diagnostic and statistical manual of mental disorders* (5th ed.). Arlington, VA: Author.

Arseneault, L., Cannon, M., Murray, R. M., Poulton, R., Caspi, A., & Moffitt, T. E. (2003). Childhood origins of violent behaviour in adults with schizophreniform disorder. *British Journal of Psychiatry, 183*, 520–525.

Arseneault, L., Cannon, M., Poulton, R., Murray, R. M., Caspi, A., & Moffitt, T. E. (2002). Cannabis use in adolescence and risk for adult psychosis: Longitudinal prospective study. *British Medical Journal, 325*, 1212–1213.

Arseneault, L., Cannon, M., Witton, J., & Murray, R. M. (2004). Causal association between cannabis and psychosis: examination of the evidence. *British Journal of Psychiatry, 184*, 110–117.

Arseneault, L., Caspi, A., Moffitt, T. E., Taylor, P. J., & Silva, P. A. (2000). Mental disorders and violence in a total birth cohort: Results from the Dunedin Study. *Archives of General Psychiatry, 57*, 979–986.

Arseneault, L., Moffitt, T. E., Caspi, A., & Taylor, A. (2002). The targets of violence committed by young offenders with alcohol dependence, marijuana dependence and schizophrenia-spectrum disorders: findings from a birth cohort. *Criminal Behavior and Mental Health, 12*, 155–168.

Bebbington, P., & Nayani, T. (1995). The psychosis screening questionnaire. *International Journal of Methods in Psychiatric Research, 5*, 11–19.

Brinded, P. M. J., Simpson, A. I. F., Laidlaw, T. M., Fairley, N., & Malcolm, F. (2001). Prevalence of psychiatric disorders in New Zealand Prisons: A national study. *Australian & New Zealand Journal of Psychiatry, 35*, 166–173.

Cannon, M., Caspi, A., Moffitt, T. E., Harrington, H. L., Taylor, A., Murray, R. M., & Poulton, R. (2002). Evidence for early-childhood, pan-developmental impairment specific to schizophreniform disorder: Results from a longitudinal birth cohort. *Archives of General Psychiatry, 59*, 449–456.

Caspi, A., Moffitt, T. E., Cannon, M., McClay, J., Murray, R. M., Harrington, H. L., Taylor, A., Arseneault, L., Williams, B. S., Braithwaite, A., Poulton, R., & Craig, I. (2005). Moderation of the effect of adolescent-onset cannabis use on adult psychosis by a functional polymorphism in the COMT gene: Longitudinal evidence of a gene x environment interaction. *Biological Psychiatry, 57*, 1117–1127.

Castle, D. J., Jablensky, A., McGrath, J., Carr, V., Morgan, V., Watterreus, A., Valuri, G., Stain, H., McGuffin, P., & Farmer, A. (2006). The diagnostic interview for psychosis (DIP): Development, reliability and applications. *Psychological Medicine, 36*, 69–80.

Fisher, H. L., Caspi, A., Poulton, R., Meier, M. H., Houts, R., Harrington, H. L., Arseneault, L., & Moffitt, T. E. (2013). Specificity of childhood psychotic symptoms for predicting schizophrenia by 38 years of age: A birth cohort study. *Psychological Medicine, 43*, 2077–2086.

Galletly, C., Castle, D., Dark, F., Humberstone, V., Jablensky, A., Killackey, E., Kulkarni, J., McGorry, P., Nielssen, O., Tran, N. (2016). Royal Australian and New Zealand College of Psychiatrists clinical practice guidelines for the management of schizophrenia and related disorders. *Australian & New Zealand Journal of Psychiatry, 50*, 410–472.

Gould, I, Shepherd, A., Laurens, K. R., Cairns, M. J., Carr, V. J., & Green, M. J. (2014). Multivariate neuroanatomical classification of cognitive subtypes in schizophrenia: A support vector machine learning approach. *Neuroimage Clinical, 6*, 229–236.

Green, M. J., Cairns, M. J., Wu, J., Dragovic, M., Jablensky, A., Tooney, P. A., Scott, R., & Carr, V. J. (2013). Genome-wide supported variant MIR137 and severe negative symptoms predict membership of an impaired cognitive subtype of schizophrenia. *Molecular Psychiatry, 18*(7), 774–780.

Green, M. J., Chia, T-. Y., Cairns, M. J., Wu, J. Q., Tooney, P., Scott, R. J., & Carr, V. J. (2014). Catechol-O-Methyl Transferase (COMT) genotype modulates the effects of childhood adversity on cognition and symptoms in schizophrenia. *Journal of Psychiatric Research, 49*, 43–50.

Green, M. J., Raudino, A., Cairns, M. J., Wu, J., Tooney, P. A., Scott, R. J., & Carr, V. J. (2015). Do FK506 binding protein 5 (FKBP5) genotypes moderate the effects of childhood maltreatment on cognition in schizophrenia and healthy controls? *Journal of Psychiatric Research, 70*, 9–17.

Haddock, G., McCarron, N., Tarrier, N., & Faragher, E. B. (1999). Scales to measure the dimensions of hallucinations and delusions: The Psychotic Symptom Rating Scales. *Psychological Medicine, 29*, 879–889.

Hallmayer, J. F., Kalaydjieva, L., Badcock, J., Dragovic, M., Howell, S., Michie, P. T., Rock, D., Vile, D., Williams, R., Corder, E. H., Hollingsworth, K., Jablensky, A. (2005). Genetic evidence for a distinct subtype of schizophrenia characterized by pervasive cognitive deficit. *American Journal of Human Genetics, 77*(3), 468–476.

Henry, L. P., Amminger, G. P., Harris, M. G., Yuen, H. P., Harrigan, S. M., Prosser, A. L., Schwatrz, O. S., Farrelly, S. E., Herrman, H., Jackson, H. J., & McGorry, P. D. (2010). The EPPIC follow-up study of first-episode psychosis: Longer-term clinical and functional outcome 7 years after index admission. *Journal of Clinical Psychiatry, 71*(6), 716–728.

Jablensky, A. V., Morgan, V., Zubrick, S. R., Bower, C., & Yellachich, L. A. (2005). Pregnancy, delivery, and neonatal complications in a population cohort of women with Schizophrenia and major affective disorders. *American Journal of Psychiatry, 162*(1), 79–91.

Kake, T. R., Arnold, R., & Ellis, P. (2008). Estimating the prevalence of schizophrenia amongst New Zealand Māori: a capture-recapture approach. *Australian & New Zealand Journal of Psychiatry, 42*, 941–949.

Kay, S. R., Opler, L. A., & Fizbein, A. (2006). *Positive and Negative Syndrome Scale*. Toronto: Multi-Health Research Systems.

Kim-Cohen, J., Caspi, A., Moffitt, T. E., Harrington, H. L., Milne, B. J., & Poulton, R. (2003). Prior juvenile diagnoses in adults with mental disorder: Developmental follow-back of a prospective-longitudinal cohort. *Archives of General Psychiatry, 60*, 709–719.

Koenen, K., Moffitt, T. E., Roberts, A., Martin, L., Kubzansky, L., Harrington, H. L., Poulton, R., & Caspi, A. (2009). Childhood IQ and adult mental disorders: A test of the cognitive reserve hypothesis. *American Journal of Psychiatry, 166*, 50–57.

Lin, A., Yung, A. R., Nelson, B., Brewer, W. J., Riley, R., Simmons, M., Pantelis, C., & Wood, S. J. (2013). Neurocognitive predictors of transition to psychosis: Medium- to long-term findings from a sample at ultra-high risk for psychosis. *Psychological Medicine, 43*(11), 2349–2360.

Loughland, C., Draganic, D., McCabe, K., Richards, J., Nasir, A., Allen, J., Catts, S., Jablensky, A., Henskens, F., Michie, P., Mowry, B., Pantelis, C., Schall, U., Scott, R.,

Tooney, P., & Carr, V. (2010). Australian Schizophrenia Research Bank: A database of comprehensive clinical, endophenotypic and genetic data for aetiological studies of Schizophrenia. *Australian and New Zealand Journal of Psychiatry, 44*(11), 1029–1035.

McCabe, R., Heath, C., Burns, T., & Priebe, S. (2002). Engagement of patients with psychosis in the consultation: Conversation analytic study. *British Medical Journal 325*, 1148–1151.

McCarthy-Jones, S., Green, M. J., Scott, R. J., Tooney, P., Cairns, M. J., Wu, J. Q., & Carr, V. J. (2014). Preliminary evidence of an interaction between the FOXP2 gene and childhood emotional abuse predicting likelihood of auditory verbal hallucinations in schizophrenia. *Journal of Psychiatric Research, 50*, 66–72.

McGrath, J. (2010). Is it time to trial vitamin D supplements for the prevention of Schizophrenia? *Acta Psychiatrica Scandinavica, 121*(5), 321–324.

McGrath, J., Saha, S., Chant, D., & Welham, J. (2008). Schizophrenia: A concise overview of incidence, prevalence and mortality. *Epidemiologic Reviews, 30*, 67–76.

Morar, B., Dragovic, M., Waters, F. A. V., Chandler, D., Kalaydjieva, L., & Jablensky, A. (2010). Neuregulin 3 (NRG3) as a susceptibility gene in a Schizophrenia subtype with florid delusions and relatively spared cognition. *Molecular Psychiatry, 16*(8), 860–866.

Morgan, V. A, McGrath, J. J., Jablensky, A., Badcock, J. C., Waterreus, A., Bush, R., Carr, V., Castel, D., Cohen, M., Galletly, C., Harvey, C., Hocking, B., McGorry, P., Neil, A. L., Saw, S., Shah, S., Stain, H. J., & MacKinnon, A. (2014). Psychosis prevalence and physical, metabolic and cognitive co-morbidity: Data from the second Australian national survey of psychosis. *Psychological Medicine, 44*, 2163–2176.

Murray, G. K., & Jones, P. B. (2012). Psychotic symptoms in young people without psychotic illness: Mechanisms and meaning. *British Journal of Psychiatry, 201*, 4–6.

Nelson, B., Yuen, H. P., Wood, S. J., Lin, A., Spiliotacopoulos, D., Bruxner, A., Broussard, C., Simmons, M., Foley, D. L., Brewer, W. J., Francey, S. M., Amminger, G. P., Thompson, A., McGorry P. D., & Yung, A. R. (2013). Long-term follow-up of a group at ultra high risk ("prodromal") for psychosis: the PACE 400 study. *JAMA Psychiatry, 70*(8), 793–802.

Oakley-Brown, M. A., Wells, W. E., & Scott, K. M. (eds.) (2006). *Te Rau Hinengaro: The New Zealand mental health survey.* Wellington: Ministry of Health.

Poulton, R., Caspi, A., Moffitt, T. E., Cannon, M., Murray, R. M., & Harrington, H. L. (2000). Children's self-reported psychotic symptoms and adult schizophreniform disorder: A 15-year longitudinal study. *Archives of General Psychiatry, 57*, 1053–1058.

Ripke, S., et al. on behalf of the Schizophrenia Working Group of the Psychiatric Genetics Consortium. (2014). Biological insights from 108 Schizophrenia-associated genetic loci. *Nature, 511*, 421–427.

Roberts, D. L., Combs, D. R., Willoughby, M., Mintz, J., Gibson, C., Betty Rupp, B., & Penn, D. L. (2014). A randomized, controlled trial of Social Cognition and Interaction Training (SCIT) for outpatients with schizophrenia spectrum disorders. *British Journal of Clinical Psychology, 53*, 281–298.

Roberts, D. L., Penn, D. L., & Combs, D. R. (in press). *Social cognition and interaction training (SCIT): Treatment manual.* New York: Oxford University Press.

Saha, S., Chant, D., & McGrath, J. (2007). A systematic review of mortality in schizophrenia: Is the differential mortality gap worsening over time? *Archives of General Psychiatry, 64*, 1123–1131.

Schizophrenia Psychiatric Genome-Wide Association Study. (GWAS) Consortium. (2011). Genome-wide association study of schizophrenia identifies five novel loci. *Nature Genetics*, *43*, 969–976.

Silverstein, S. M., Del Pozzo, J., Roche, M., Boyle, D., & Miskimen, T. (2015). Schizophrenia and violence: realities and recommendations. *Crime Psychology Review*, *1*, 21–42.

Simpson, A., Brinded, P., Fairley, N., Laidlaw, T., & Malcolm, F. (1999). Does ethnicity affect need for mental health service among New Zealand Prisoners? *Australian & New Zealand Journal of Psychiatry*, *37*, 728–734.

Sun, D., Phillips, L., Velakoulis, D., Yung, A., McGorry, P. D., Wood, S. J., van Erp, T. G. M., Toga, A. W., Cannon, T. D., & Pantelis, C. (2009). Progressive brain structural changes mapped as psychosis develops in "at risk" individuals. *Schizophrenia Research*, *108*(1–3), 85–92.

Welham, J., Scott, J., Williams, G. M., Najman, J. M., Bor, W., O'Callaghan, M., & McGrath, J. (2010). The antecedents of non-affective psychosis in a birth-cohort, with a focus on measures related to cognitive ability, attentional dysfunction and speech problems. *Acta Psychiatrica Scandinavica*, *121*(4), 273–279.

Wells, J. E., Bushnell, J. A., Hornblow, A. R., Joyce, P. R., & Oakley-Brown, M. A. (1989). Christchurch psychiatric epidemiology study, Part I: Methodology and lifetime prevalence for specific disorders. *Australian & New Zealand Journal of Psychiatry*, *23*, 315–326.

Wing, J. K., Curtis, R. H., & Beevor, A. S. (1996). HoNOS: *Health of the nation outcome scales: Report on research and development July 1993-December 1995*. London: Royal College of Psychiatrists.

World Health Organisation. (2011). *International statistical classification of diseases and related health problems 2010 edition (ICD-10)*. Geneva: Author. Available: www.who.int/classifications/icd/en/

Wu, J. Q., Green, M. J., Gardiner, E. J., Tooney, P. A., Scott, R. J., Carr, V., & Cairns, M. J. (2016). Transcriptome analysis in schizophrenia patients with cognitive impairment reveals down-regulated neural signaling pathways in peripheral blood mononuclear cells. *Schizophrenia Research*.

Yung, A. R, Huen, H. P., McGorry, P. D., Phillips, L. J., Kelly, D., Dell'Olio, M., Francey, S. M., Cosgrave, E. M., Killackey, E., Stanford, C., Godfrey, K., & Buckby, J. (2005). Mapping the onset of psychosis: The comprehensive assessment of at-risk mental states. *Australian & New Zealand Journal of Psychiatry*, *39*, 964–971.

Yung, A. R., Nelson, B., Thompson, A. D., & Wood, S. J. (2010). Should a "Risk Syndrome for Psychosis" be included in the DSM-V? *Schizophrenia Research*, *120*(1–3), 7–15.

Recommendations for further reading/resources

Schizophrenia Library (www.schizophreniaresearch.org.au/library)

10

Depressive disorders

Gavin Beccaria

Introduction

Depression is a common yet potentially serious mental health condition that affects many Australians and New Zealanders. Although most people feel sad or down from time to time, a depressive illness or clinical depression is characterised by a sustained period of low mood and anhedonia (i.e., loss of pleasure), as well as other cognitive, emotional, and biological markers. The *Diagnostic and Statistical Manual of Mental Disorders* (5th ed.; *DSM-5*; American Psychiatric Association, 2013), has now listed only unipolar depressive disorders within its own chapter. This deviates from previous editions (*DSM-III* through to *DSM-IV-TR*) where depressive disorders appeared in a mood disorders chapter and were listed in the same chapter as bipolar disorders.

In the *DSM-5*, two new depressive disorders have been added: disruptive mood dysregulation disorder and pre-menstrual dysphoric disorder. Major depressive disorder (MDD), dysthymia, substance-induced depressive disorder, and depressive disorder due to a medical condition have been retained with some minor variations in some of the diagnostic criteria. Most people diagnosed with a depressive disorder would have MDD. Generally, when clinicians and public health policymakers discuss depressive disorders, they mean MDD. This chapter will mostly focus on MDD (the term "clinical depression" is used interchangeably with MDD in this chapter).

To be diagnosed with MDD, the individual must have five or more of the following features for a 2-week period: the presence of low mood and/or anhedonia (one of these is mandatory); significant weight loss or weight gain; disturbed sleep; psychomotor agitation or slowing; listlessness; feelings of self-deprecation or guilt; poor concentration; and reoccurring thoughts of death and/or suicide (this may include a plan for suicide).

Australian and New Zealand (NZ) governments have recognised the personal, social, and economic ramifications of depression over the last decade. MDD has been directly linked to suicide, as well as family and relationship issues including parenting difficulties, poorer physical health (including diabetes and heart disease), poorer work productivity, greater workers' compensation claims, and greater sick leave. Organisations in both Australia and NZ have adopted numerous initiatives to increase the public understanding of depression, reduce the stigma associated with depression, and ultimately prevent and treat depression.

Australia

The Australian Bureau of Statistics (ABS, 2009) indicates mood disorders affect 6.2% of people aged between 16 and 85. More recently, beyondblue (2015) reported that one in six Australians will experience a depressive episode within their lifetime. This includes one in five women and one in eight men. At any one time, one million Australians may experience depression. Depression often first emerges in adolescence and one in five young Australian will experience a depressive episode before they turn 18 (beyondblue, 2015; headspace, 2014; Kessler et al., 2005; Rutter, 1995). Depression also has a significant impact on the workplace, costing six million working days (beyondblue, 2015) and nearly $11 billion a year in Australia (Harvey et al., 2014). Depression increases the risk of cardiovascular disease (Black Dog Institute, 2013) so treating the condition can improve length of life (Musselman, Evans, & Nemeroff, 1998). While there is no clear data on the epidemiology of depression for Aboriginal and Torres Strait Islander people, 31% of Indigenous Australians report a high level of distress (ABS, 2010). These rates are particularly high among those who have: experienced violence; a disability or chronic health condition; experienced discrimination; or been removed from their natural family. Suicide accounts for 4.2% of all registered deaths of Aboriginal and Torres Strait Islander peoples, compared to 1.6% of all Australians (ABS, 2012). Most Indigenous suicides are by men aged 20–40. Considerable work still remains to bridge the mental health gap between Indigenous and non-Indigenous Australians. Finally, immigrants to Australia, particularly refugees that may have had repeated exposure to traumatic events, will have increased likelihood of developing depression (Liddell et al., 2013; Silove et al., 1998). As Australia becomes more culturally diverse, clinicians and researchers will need to have culturally appropriate prevention and treatment programs for depression.

The beyondblue, Black Dog Institute, and headspace websites provide a wealth of further information about depression. beyondblue takes a public health approach to assist with depression and anxiety, the Black Dog Institute is also involved in public health research, while headspace targets mental health in 12–25 year olds and has treatment centres across Australia. These and other groups are non-government organisations that provide community awareness about mental illness, conduct important research and, in some cases, provide treatment for the public.

Assessment of depression

Mental health clinicians normally assess depression through a clinical interview. They use information from the client, direct observation, and collateral information. Clinicians sometimes use a Structured Clinical Interview (e.g., SCID; American Psychiatric Association, 2007), but most often use the information from the interview to assess the client alongside diagnostic criteria (Morrison, 2008). To assess the severity, clinicians may use self-report measures such as the Kessler-10 (Kessler, 2002), the Beck Depression Inventory (Beck & Steer, 1992), or the Depression Anxiety and Stress Scales (DASS; Lovibond & Lovibond, 1995). The DASS has become a popular measure for three possible reasons: it is relatively cheap to administer; it has good psychometric properties; and it has been normed and standardised in Australia (Crawford et al., 2011; Crawford & Henry, 2003; Henry & Crawford, 2005).

Aetiology of depression

Given that the diagnostic criteria for MDD is specific, there are some commonalities for all people diagnosed with clinical depression; for example, most people will occasionally have symptoms of dysphoria and/or anhedonia, sleep disturbance, low motivation, and poor concentration. Nevertheless, there may be some individual differences; for example, not every person diagnosed with clinical depression will have irritability, have feelings of guilt, or attempt suicide (American Psychiatric Association, 2013; Sadock, 2007). Similarly, many factors may contribute to depression, including biological/hereditary factors, chronic illness, temperament/personality, and environmental factors such as childhood experiences, relationship breakdown, and work dysfunction/pressures (American Psychiatric Association, 2013). Although there is a plethora of literature available on the aetiology of depression, the role of work as a both a contributor (Harvey et al., 2014) and a preventer (Hoare & Machin, 2010) has received increased attention in recent years. Harvey et al. also noted the importance of a functional and productive workforce in modern Australia and that the workplace had a responsibility in preventing role overload which may lead to depression.

The aetiology of depression is multifactorial and complex, caused by an interplay of biological, psychological, and social factors. As a result, there are a broad range of treatments available, with the number increasing in recent years. Listing all treatments is well beyond the scope of this chapter. Several studies have looked at which therapy is most efficacious for different types and severity levels of depression. Some found that combining antidepressant medication with psychotherapy is most effective (Keller et al., 2000) particularly for acute and severe depression (Craighead & Dunlop, 2014). The next subsection will summarise the best practice guidelines for the treatment of depression recommended by the Australian Psychological Society (2010). There will be a focus on psychological as opposed to biological therapies (e.g., medication and electroconvulsive therapy) which are considered the domain of the medical profession.

Best psychological practice in treatment of depression in Australia

The Australian Psychological Society (2010) developed the *Evidence-based Psychological Interventions in the Treatment of Mental Disorders: A Literature Review.* This document is available to all Australian Psychological Society members and student subscribers. It is a well-designed systematic review of psychological therapies for both adults and minors (children and adolescents) for a wide range of disorders including depression. This review draws on a variety of sources including common databases (i.e., PsycINFO, Cochrane, and Medline) and peak bodies (i.e., Royal Australian and New Zealand College of Psychiatrists, National Institute for Clinical Excellence, American Psychiatric Association, and British Psychological Society). Therapies are classified according to levels of evidence as recommended by the National Health and Medical Research Council (see NHMRC, 1999) ranging from Level I (Systematic review of all relevant randomised controlled trials) through to Level IV (Case series, either post-test, or pre-test and post-test). Therapies that are listed as Level I Evidence for the treatment of depression in adults are cognitive behaviour therapy (CBT), interpersonal psychotherapy, psychodynamic therapy, and self-help. Therapies that are listed as Level I Evidence for the treatment of depression in children and adolescents include CBT, interpersonal psychotherapy (for adolescents), and family therapy.

CBT is arguably the most researched psychological treatment, with the largest evidence base for treating depression. Most universities in Australia would have academics who have conducted research using CBT. A growing area of CBT in Australia is online therapy (Andrews et al., 2010). CBT is well suited to online therapies because of its structured nature. It also suits people in rural areas with limited access to face-to-face psychological services (March, Spence, & Donovan, 2009). The Clinical Research Unit for Anxiety and Depression (CRUfAD), based in Sydney and affiliated with the University of New South Wales and St Vincent's Hospital, is one of the leaders in developing and trialling online treatment programs for depression (see www.crufad. org). In one study conducted out of CRUfAD, Williams et al. (2013) a combined 1-week internet cognitive bias modification (CBM-I) program follow by a 10-week internet-based CBT (iCBT) program for participants diagnosed with MDD. Findings indicated that compared to waitlist control participants, participants who completed the program had significant improvements over the waitlist group both at the end of CBM-I and iCBT. The effect sizes for differences between groups were medium at the end of CBM-I and large at the end of iCBT.

Narrative therapy has not been recognised as a Level I therapy for the general population; however, it is recognised as a therapy of choice for Aboriginal and Torres Strait Islander peoples (Vicary & Westerman, 2004). Narrative therapy involves telling the story and then re-constructing stories in terms of people's strength and mastery (Corey, 2009). Vicary and Westerman argued that the "yarning" that is used in narrative approaches is more in keeping with Indigenous communication styles. They also strongly recommend that non-Indigenous counsellors have cultural competency training before providing counselling to Indigenous Australians.

Services for the treatment of depression in Australia

From 2007, Australians could receive psychological services funded under the Medicare scheme. The federal government recognised the costs of mental illness to the community and the benefit of ready access to psychological therapies. There continues to be research into the cost benefits of psychological therapies (Mathews, 2014), and research is needed to evaluate more efficient and effective treatments of depression. The Better Access for Mental Health Scheme (or Medicare) recognises Level I therapies for treating depression. There is a growing recognition that narrative therapy may be beneficial to Indigenous Australians (Australian Psychological Society, 2015b). Another federally funded scheme is the Access to Allied Psychological Services (ATAPS) scheme (Australian Psychological Society, 2015a). This program is managed through local general practitioner (GP) networks but may be brokered to private practitioners. For both Medicare and ATAPS, the client's GP assumes primary care for the client.

For severe depression and acute suicide risk, public hospitals and integrated mental health services provide multidisciplinary support to mental health consumers (Commonwealth Department of Health and Ageing, 2002). State or territory governments operate these services, which are free to Australian citizens or permanent residents. Demand is high and generally reserved for the people with the most severe presentations of mental illness. Alternatively, people with private health cover who require hospitalisation may elect to go to a private hospital to be treated by a private psychiatrist and allied health professionals.

Non-government organisations such as Lifeline, Centacare and headspace may provide counselling and support for depression either directly (e.g., refugee support services) or indirectly through family support schemes. These schemes are often government funded. There are also specific programs such as WorkCover and Department of Veterans Affairs that may fund treatment for depression. Finally, many employers provide employee assistance schemes that can help staff with a range of personal and interpersonal issues such as depression.

New Zealand

Depression is also a significant concern to New Zealanders. According to the Health Promotion Agency (2015), one in six New Zealanders will experience clinical depression in their lifetime, one in seven before the age of 24. Depression rates are higher for women (one in five) than men (one in eight), and rural men have higher rates of depression than urban men. According to the NZ Ministry of Health (2015) depression is often underdiagnosed and undertreated. Depression is the leading causal factor for suicide and chronic disease, and costs approximately 0.6% of gross domestic product (GDP). Currently, there are 500 New Zealanders who die due to suicide each year. While Māori people are not overrepresented as a proportion of total suicides, like Aboriginal and Torres Strait Islander Australians (ABS, 2012), they are overrepresented as consumers of mental health services (Ministry of Health, 2013). The prevalence of major depression in NZ is as high as, or perhaps slightly higher than, in other developed nations (Bromet et al., 2011).

The NZ Government developed the National Depression Initiative (NDI) in 2004–2005, as a public health response to identifying, treating, and managing depression. The NDI has a number of specific public health initiatives including: the Lowdown website (https://thelowdown.co.nz/) to assist in understanding and managing depression; and a rural initiative to assist farmers and rural workers in identifying and managing depression (Ministry of Health, 2015).

Standard practice/treatment recommendations within the New Zealand context

As part of the NDI, the Ministry of Health has developed best practice guidelines for managing depression. The *Identification of Common Mental Disorders and Management of Depression in Primary Care* document (New Zealand Guidelines Group, 2008) has treatment algorithms for identifying and managing moderate and severe depression for children, adults, and older people. It also has guidelines for managing postpartum depression, and outlines cultural competence for service delivery to Māori and Pacific Islanders.

In recent years, there have been some interesting developments in psychological treatments in NZ. Jordon et al. (2014) found that both CBT and metacognitive therapy were equally effective in treating depression among outpatient adults with affective disorder. The authors concluded that a larger study was needed in the future. There has also been a CBT program adapted for Māori people (Bennett, Flett, & Babbage, 2014); however, this study only had 16 participants and would require replication. Perhaps one of the more widely cited pieces of research out of NZ is the behavioural genetics study by Capsi et al. (2003). This longitudinal study has added a genetic component to the diathesis stress hypothesis, by investigating whether the presence of a short allele in the serotonin transporter (5-HT T) gene as opposed to a long allele is more likely to result in depression after stressful events. In a representative cohort of 1037 Caucasian, non-Māori children, participants were divided into having two copies of the short allele, one copy of the short allele, or two copies of the long allele. While there were no differences between groups in the experiences of stressful life events in the ages between 21 and 26, those with a presence of a short allele were more likely to exhibit depressive symptoms, suicidal ideation, and suicidal behaviours. As with any genetic research, the implications of this study is subject to wide debate; however, the authors note that replication is essential to support or refute these findings.

Australian case study

The following is the fictional case of Jack who presented to his GP for low mood and, more recently, confusion. He was brought to the clinic by his eldest daughter.

Jack is a 64-year-old Aboriginal man who lives alone in a Queensland rural town. His wife Mary, who was also an Aboriginal woman died with complications relating to diabetes six months ago. Jack has two daughters, both live about two hours away.

Since the death of Mary, both of Jack's daughters have noted a decline in his self-care. They have also noted that he has taken less interest in domestic duties and his social life. Initially, Jack's daughters thought that he was grieving for Mary and would improve, but in recent weeks they have noted that Jack is becoming confused and has recently had a fall. Jack explained to his GP that he has dysphoria, anhedonia, poor concentration, crying spells, and thoughts of wanting to just go away. He has also lost 5 kg in the last 2 months. Jack been diagnosed with diabetes and his daughters are concerned that he is not managing his blood sugar levels.

Jack is on the aged pension. He worked for most of his life as a farm hand or stockman with a number of rural properties in the district. He previously enjoyed a good relationship with some of the families he had worked for and would attend the local RSL about once a month to meet one of his old bosses, Frank Kelly. Last week Frank contacted Jack's eldest daughter because he was concerned that Jack has not attended for some months and when he visited Jack at home in the afternoon, the lawn was unkempt, and Jack was still in his pyjamas.

Jack had a difficult childhood. His mother was part of the stolen generation and he never knew his father. Jack was removed from his mother's care when he was 6 and was placed in foster care. Jack went to several group homes and foster families, some he described as "okay" but at others he was beaten. At 14 he ran away and was then involved in property offences. When he was 15, he was placed in Westbrook Training Centre where he found that he had a natural aptitude for farm work. He also had developed a good relationship with one of the training officers who knew the Kelly family and after 6 months went and worked on Frank's family property. There were a number of Indigenous men who worked on this property. Jack often told his daughters that the Kelly family paid all the workers the same regardless of race – this did not occur at all properties. Jack met Mary when he was 20 and they were married at 21. Jack and Mary enjoyed a good marriage, although Jack's work meant that he would be away at "camp" for weeks at a time. Jack did experience racism in his adult life from time to time, but would gravitate towards those who were "fair."

Before the GP can come to a diagnosis of depression, physical ailments must be ruled out and treated first. Confusion may be associated with depression but it is not one of the diagnostic criteria. Jack's confusion may be a result of the diabetes or another physical cause (e.g., dehydration or a urinary tract infection). The physical cause may have been an indirect result of the depression (i.e., the neglect) but unless it is treated first it is difficult to know for sure. Finally, in the *DSM-IV-TR* bereavement was part of the exclusion criteria for depression; however, this has been removed from the *DSM-5*. It is most likely that Jack has depression but his physical ailments complicate matters.

Jack's medical condition will require treatment first. The GP should then consider medication and/or counselling. If counselling is to be used, CBT or interpersonal psychotherapy may be used. Narrative therapy could also be considered. Any form of counselling should consider Jack's strengths and natural support system.

Australia – Indigenous Network Suicide Intervention Skills Training (INSIST) project

The Indigenous Network Suicide Intervention Skills Training (INSIST) project was funded by the National Health and Medical Research Council in 2014. The project leader is Dr Maree Toombs from the University of Queensland. This project uses mobile apps to assist trained gatekeepers who can respond to young people with suicidal ideation or behaviours and when necessary put the person in contact with a primary care or mental health service. See www.uq.edu.au/news/article/2014/09/smartphone-app-tackles-indigenous-youth-suicide for more information.

New Zealand – The Lowdown

The Lowdown is part of the National Depression Initiative that is aimed at reducing depression and suicide among young New Zealanders. This website provides education about depression as well has information and online support to assist people to receive the help they need. It even includes a tab for people who require immediate assistance. See https://thelowdown.co.nz/ for more information.

References

American Psychiatric Association. (2007). *Structured clinical interview for DSM disorders*. Arlington, VA: American Psychiatric Pub Inc. Retrieved 31 January 2012 from: http://www.scid4.org/faq/clinician_version.html

American Psychiatric Association. (2013). *Diagnostic and statistical manual of mental disorders* (5th ed.). Arlington, VA: Author.

Andrews, G., Cuijpers, P., Craske, M. G., McEvoy, P., & Titov, N. (2010). Computer therapy for the anxiety and depressive disorders is effective, acceptable and practical health care: a meta-analysis. *PloS one, 5*(10), e13196.

Australian Bureau of Statistics. (2009). Mental health. *4102.0 – Australian Social Trends, March 2009.* Canberra: Author. Retrieved 4 March 2015 from: www.abs.gov.au/ AUSSTATS/abs@.nsf/Lookup/4102.0Main+Features30March%202009

Australian Bureau of Statistics. (2010). The health and welfare of Australia's Aboriginal and Torres Strait Islander Peoples. *Press Release.* Canberra: Author. Available: www.abs.gov. au/ausstats/abs@.nsf/mediareleasesbytitle/3C18155D35250456CA2574390029C0E5? OpenDocument

Australian Bureau of Statistics. (2012). *Aboriginal and Torres Strait Islander suicide deaths.* Canberra: Author. Retrieved 4 March 2015 from: www.abs.gov.au/ausstats/abs@.nsf/ Products/3309.0~2010~Chapter~Aboriginal+and+Torres+Strait+Islander+suicide+deat hs?OpenDocument

Australian Psychological Society. (2010). *Evidence-based psychological interventions in the treatment of mental disorders: A literature review* (3rd ed.). Melbourne, Australia: Author.

Australian Psychological Society. (2015a). *Better outcomes in mental health care.* Melbourne: Author.

Australian Psychological Society. (2015b). *The mental health medicare items for psychologists.* Melbourne: Author.

Beck, A. T., & Steer, R. A. (1992). *The Beck Depression Inventory -II.* San Antonio, TX: The Psychological Corporation.

Bennett, S. T., Flett, R. A., & Babbage, D. R. (2014). Culturally adapted cognitive behaviour therapy for Māori with major depression. *The Cognitive Behaviour Therapist, 7,* e20. http://dx.doi.org/10.1017/S1754470X14000233

beyondblue. (2015). *Depression.* Retrieved 4 March 2015 from: www.beyondblue.org.au

Black Dog Institute. (2013). *Depression in the medically ill.* Retrieved 4 March 2015 from: www.blackdoginstitute.org.au/public/depression/inthemedicallyill. cfm#riskillnesses

Bromet, E., Andrade, L., Hwang, I., Sampson, N., Alonso, J., de Girolamo, G., et al. (2011). Cross-national epidemiology of DSM-IV major depressive episode. *BMC Medicine, 9*(1), 90.

Capsi, A., Stugden, K., Moffitt, T, E., Taylor, A., Craig, I. W, Harrington, H., et al. (2003). Influence of the life stress on depression: moderation by polymorphism in the 5-HTT gene. *Science, 301*(5631), 386–389. http://dx.doi.org/10.1126/science.1083968

Commonwealth Department of Health and Ageing. (2002). *National practice standards for the mental health workforce.* Canberra: Commonwealth of Australia.

Corey, G. (2009). *Theory and practice of counseling and psychotherapy* (8th ed.). Belmont, London: Wadsworth; CengageLearning.

Craighead, W. E., & Dunlop, B. W. (2014). Combination psychotherapy and antidepressant medication treatment for depression: For whom, when, and how. *Annual Review of Psychology, 65*(1), 267–300. http://dx.doi.org/10.1146/annurev. psych.121208.131653

Crawford, J. R., Cayley, C., Lovibond, P. F., Wilson, P. H., & Hartley, C. (2011). Percentile norms and accompanying interval estimates from an Australian general adult population sample for self-report mood scales (BAI, BDI, CRSD, CES-D, DASS, DASS-21, STAI-X, STAI-Y, SRDS and SRAS). *Australian Psychologist, 46*(1), 3–14. http://dx.doi.org/10.1111/j.1742-9544.2010.00003.x

Crawford, J. R., & Henry, J. D. (2003). The Depression Anxiety Stress Scales (DASS): Normative data and latent structure in a large non-clinical sample. *British Journal of Clinical Psychology, 42*(2), 111.

Harvey, S. B., Joyce, S., Tan, L., Johnson, A., Nguyen, H., Modini, M., & Groth, M. (2014). *Developing a mentally healthy workplace: A review of the literature*. Sydney: Black Dog Institute.

headspace. (2014). *What works? Research & information*. Retrieved 4 March 2014 from: www.headspace.org.au/about-headspace/contact-us/contact-details

Health Promotion Agency. (2015*). Is this depression?* Retrieved 10 March 2015 from: www.depression.org.nz/depression

Henry, J. D., & Crawford, J. R. (2005). The short-form version of the Depression Anxiety Stress Scales (DASS-21): Construct validity and normative data in a large non-clinical sample. *British Journal of Clinical Psychology, 44*, 227–239.

Hoare, P. N., & Machin, M. A. (2010). The impact of reemployment on access to the latent and manifest benefits of employment and mental health. *Journal of Occupational and Organizational Psychology, 83*(3), 759–770. http://dx.doi.org/10.1348/096317909X472094

Jordan, J., Carter, J. D., McIntosh, V. V., Fernando, K., Frampton, C. M., Porter, R. J., et al. (2014). Metacognitive therapy versus cognitive behavioural therapy for depression: A randomized pilot study. *Australian & New Zealand Journal of Psychiatry, 48*, 932–943. http://dx.doi.org/10.1177/0004867414533015

Keller, M. B., McCullough, J. P., Klein, D. N., Arnow, B., Dunner, D. L., Gelenberg, A. J., et al. (2000). A comparison of nefazodone, the cognitive behavioral-analysis system of psychotherapy, and their combination for the treatment of chronic depression. *New England Journal of Medicine, 342*(20), 1462–1470. http://dx.doi.org/10.1056/NEJM200005183422001

Kessler, R. C. (2002). Epidemiology of Depression. In: I. H. Gotlib, & C. L. Hammen (Eds.), *Handbook of depression* (3rd vol., pp. 23–42). New York: Guilford.

Kessler, R. C., Berglund, P., Demler, O., Jin, R., Merikangas, K. R., & Walters, E. E. (2005). Lifetime prevalence and age-of-onset distributions of DSM-IV disorders in the national comorbidity survey replication. *Archives of General Psychiatry, 62*(6), 593–602.

Liddell, B. J., Chey, T., Silove, D., Phan, T. T. B., Giao, N. M., & Steel, Z. (2013). Patterns of risk for anxiety-depression amongst Vietnamese-immigrants: A comparison with source and host populations. *BMC Psychiatry, 13*(1), 1–22. http://dx.doi.org/10.1186/1471-244X-13-329

Lovibond, S. H., & Lovibond, P. F. (1995). *Manual for the Depression Anxiety Stress Scales*. Sydney: University of New South Wales.

March, S., Spence, S. H., & Donovan, C. L. (2009). The efficacy of an internet-based cognitive-behavioral therapy intervention for child anxiety disorders. *Journal of Pediatric Psychology, 34*(5), 474–487.

Mathews, R. (2014). Cost-effectiveness of psychological interventions: International perspectives. *InPysch*, October.

Ministry of Health. (2013). *PRIMHD standards*. Retrieved 26 July 2013 from: www.health.govt.nz/nz-health-statistics/national-collections-and-surveys/collections/primhd-mental-health-data/primhd-standards

Ministry of Health. (2015). *National depression initiative*. Retrieved 10 March, 2015, from www.health.govt.nz/our-work/mental-health-and-addictions/national-depression-initiative

Morrison, J. R. (2008). *The first interview* (3rd ed.). New York: Guilford Press.

Musselman, D. L., Evans, D. L., & Nemeroff, C. B. (1998). The relationship of depression to cardiovascular disease: Epidemiology, biology, and treatment. *Archives of General Psychiatry, 55*(7), 580–592. http://dx.doi.org/10.1001/archpsyc.55.7.580

National Health and Medical Research Council. (1999). *A guide to the development, implementation and evaluation of clinical practice guidelines*. Canberra: Author.

New Zealand Guidelines Group. (2008). *Identification of common mental disorders and management of depression in primary care. An evidence-based best practice guideline*. Wellington: New Zealand Guidelines Group.

Rutter, M. (1995). Relationships between mental disorders in childhood and adulthood. *Acta Psychiatrica Scandinavica, 91*, 73–85. http://dx.doi.org/10.1111/j.1600–0447.1995.tb09745.x

Sadock, B. J. (2007). *Kaplan & Sadock's synopsis of psychiatry: Behavioral sciences clinical psychiatry* (10th ed.). Philadelphia, PA: WolterKluwer/Lippincott Williams & Wilkins.

Silove, D., Steel, Z., McGorry, P., & Mohan, P. (1998). Trauma exposure, postmigration stressors, and symptoms of anxiety, depression and post-traumatic stress in Tamil asylum-seekers: Comparison with refugees and immigrants. *Acta Psychiatrica Scandinavica, 97*(3), 175–181. http://dx.doi.org/10.1111/j.1600-0447.1998.tb09984.x

Vicary, D., & Westerman, T. (2004). "That's just the way he is": Some implications of Aboriginal mental health beliefs. *Australian e-Journal for the Advancement of Mental Health, 3*, 103–12. http://dx.doi.org/10.5172/jamh.3.3.103

Williams, A. D., Blackwell, S. E., Mackenzie, A., Holmes, E, A., & Andrews, G. (2013). Combining imagination and reason in the treatment of depression: A randomized controlled trial of internet-based cognitive-bias modification and internet-CBT for depression. *Journal of Consulting and Clinical Psychology, 81*, 793–799. http://dx.doi.org/10.1037/a0033247

Recommendations for further reading/resources

General

Eckermann, A-. K., Dowd, T., & Chong, E. (2010). *Binan Goonj: Bridging cultures in Aboriginal health*. Chatswood, Australia: Elsevier Health Sciences APAC.

National Institute for Health and Care Excellence, www.nice.org.uk/guidance/cg90

Australia

Australian Psychological Society. (2010). *Evidence-based Psychological Interventions in the Treatment of Mental Disorders: A Literature Review* (3rd ed.). Melbourne, Australia: Author.

Relevant websites:

- beyondblue: www.beyondblue.org.au
- Black Dog Institute: www.blackdoginstitute.org.au
- headspace: www.headspace.org.au

New Zealand

New Zealand Guidelines Group. (2008). *Identification of common mental disorders and management of depression in primary care. An evidence-based best practice.* Auckland, New Zealand: Author.

Relevant websites:

- National Depression Initiative: www.depression.org.nz
- Depression, Ministry of Health: www.health.govt.nz/your-health/conditions-and-treatments/mental-health/depression
- The Lowdown: https://thelowdown.co.nz

Acknowledgements

I would like to thank Associate Professor Peter McIlveen for reading and providing critical feedback to this chapter and Mrs Gill Scrymgeor for providing input into the second case study.

11

Bipolar disorders

Tanya Hanstock and Samson Tse

Introduction

Bipolar disorder is a mood disorder characterised by alternating periods of euthymia, hypomania, mania, mild depression, and/or major depression. Individuals unaffected by a mood disorder tend to have a more consistent euthymic mood state. People with bipolar disorder can experience a high and low mood simultaneously, which is called a mixed episode. Bipolar disorder can be associated with psychotic features such as hallucinations, which are often mood congruent. While bipolar disorder is predominantly viewed as a mood disorder, its symptoms are more far-reaching, including changes in sleep, speech, cognitions, and physical functioning. Bipolar disorder occurs in around 1% to 3% of the population. It has a high genetic loading, with a 10% chance of inheriting it if one parent has the condition and 40% chance if both parents have it. Bipolar disorder is considered one of the most severe mental illnesses as it is lifelong, tends to be chronically relapsing for some, and is associated with a large amount of morbidity combined with a large number of episodes of self-harm, suicide attempts, and suicide completions. The most common comorbidities for bipolar disorder are anxiety and substance use. The World Health Organisation's (WHO) "burden of disease" report in 1996 (Murray & Lopez) ranked bipolar disorder as sixth in terms of overall disability among those aged 15–44 years. People with bipolar disorder die much earlier than the general population, often due to preventable health-related disorders such as smoking-related health issues, cardiovascular disease, and diabetes. Bipolar disorder is associated with a 20% to 50% risk of a suicide attempt (Jamieson, 2000).

Diagnostic criteria

The *Diagnostic and Statistical Manual of Mental Disorders* (5th ed.; *DSM-5*; American Psychiatric Association, 2013) recognises that bipolar disorder occurs on a spectrum of disorders including cyclothymic disorder, bipolar II disorder, bipolar I disorder, and other specified bipolar disorder. The *DSM-5* criteria for depression and mild depression are discussed in Chapter 10. The elevated moods in bipolar disorder are hypothymia and mania as distinguished by severity, with mania the more severe elevated mood. Hypomania is an elevated state lasting up until four days whereas mania lasts more than 1 week and is associated with impaired functioning, hospitalisation, and psychotic features. Cyclothymia is diagnosed when individuals experience at least 2 years (1 year for children) of both hypomanic and depressive episodes, but never experience a full episode of mania or major depression. Bipolar II disorder is diagnosed when an individual experiences at least one episode of major depression and at least one hypomanic episode. Bipolar II disorder is no longer regarded as the less severe disorder compared to bipolar I disorder as individuals can have long periods of depression which, combined with mood instability, can be associated with impaired functioning (Parker, 2012). Bipolar I disorder is considered the classic Kraepelin disorder. Individuals with bipolar I disorder experience at least one episode of mania and one episode of major depression (American Psychiatric Association, 2013). It is more commonly associated with psychotic symptoms and hospitalisation. Other specified bipolar is when symptoms match almost all the criteria of a bipolar disorder subtype, but is missing one criterion such as length of duration of an elevated mood state. The specifiers for bipolar disorder include: with anxious distress (mild to severe); with mixed, melancholic, atypical, and/or psychotic (mood congruent or incongruent) features; with catatonia; with postpartum onset; and/or with seasonal pattern as well as in partial or full remission. Bipolar disorder also requires a severity level rating of mild, moderate, or severe.

Australia

The 2007 National Survey of Mental Health and Wellbeing indicated that 0.9% of Australians have major symptoms of bipolar disorder in any 12-month period and 1.3% over their lifetime (Mitchell et al., 2009). The prevalence rate for specific mental health disorders in Aboriginal and Torres Strait Islander populations is unknown. However, the limited research available suggests that mental illness is very high in Indigenous Australian populations (AIHW, 2009). When looking at hospitalisations for mental health-related conditions in the period July 2005 to June 2007 in most Australian states, mood disorders accounted for 15% of these in Indigenous Australian populations (AIHW, 2009). The average delay from the symptom onset (age 17.5 years) of bipolar disorder to diagnosis is 12.5 years (Berk et al., 2007). Most adult patients with bipolar disorder present in a depressed state and spend more time in this state than the elevated states (Mitchell et al., 2009), similar to international findings (American Psychiatric Association, 2013). Australian research has also focused on detecting and managing women with bipolar disorder in the perinatal period, which is a vulnerable time for onset and relapse (Austin, Highet, & the Guidelines Expert Advisory Committee, 2011).

Australian researchers have also been interested in the early warning signs and onset of bipolar disorder in young people (Hanstock et al., 2012). Orygen Youth Services in Victoria, Australia has been working with young people diagnosed as having "first-episode mania" (the individual's first instance of a manic episode; Macneil et al., 2010) in an attempt to highlight the need for early intervention. Hirneth et al. (2015) have been studying the *DSM-IV* subtypes of bipolar disorder in young people. In comparison to international samples of paediatric bipolar disorder, their sample consisted mainly of adolescent females, with a higher rate of internalising disorders and more consistently higher levels of clinical severity. Perich et al. (2015) looked at young people with a genetic risk of developing bipolar disorder and found that behavioural and affective disorders may be indicators for future episodes of bipolar disorder. Health-related conditions in bipolar disorder are beginning to gain more research attention in Australia. This is due to the earlier mortality of people with bipolar disorder due to preventable health-related issues (Goodrich & Kilbourne, 2010). Health-related issues can also lead to worsening of bipolar disorder symptoms.

Individuals with bipolar disorder in Australia are often managed by a general practitioner (GP) and/or psychiatrist. They can access private or federally funded treatment with psychologists via a mental healthcare plan provided by Medicare. Often clients can only access a limited number of these psychology sessions per year. Adult clients (18 years or over) can be treated by their local community mental health team and young people (under 18) by the Child and Adolescent Mental Health Service (CAMHS), generally when in an acute episode. headspace is a federal government initiative that provides a number of youth-friendly centres across Australia for young people aged 12–25 with mild to moderate severity of mental health issues (including bipolar disorder) and alcohol and substance use. Individuals with private health insurance are more likely to see psychologists and psychiatrists in the private sector. When acutely unwell, with either depression or hypomania/mania, individuals can be admitted to a psychiatric hospital (either a private or public facility). If acutely unwell and suicidal, individuals can be placed in a public psychiatric inpatient unit either as a voluntary patient or as an involuntary patient under their state/territory's Mental Health Act. If they are less severe and have private health insurance, they may be able to be managed in a private adult psychiatric unit. If individuals with bipolar disorder cannot work due to their illness, they can apply for a Disability Support Pension (DSP) via Centrelink.

In terms of medication, Australian psychiatrist John Cade made one of the most significant discoveries in psychiatry generally, and bipolar disorder specifically, in the late 1940s. He originally thought that urea was a causal factor in mental illness and began using lithium urate to change its toxicity. However, he discovered that lithium was acting as a protective agent against urea toxicity. He conducted trials on guinea pigs and himself, and found no side effects. Cade then administered lithium to patients with mania, schizophrenia, and depression. He found that it was most effective for those with mania. Other Australian researchers extended Cade's research, leading to important clinical studies in bipolar disorder in the 1950s (Mitchell et al., 2014). Further studies on the therapeutic vs. toxic blood levels of lithium helped make it one of the most effective medications for bipolar disorder. Malhi et al. (2009) produced "Clinical practice guidelines for bipolar disorder," which outlines a number of easy-to-remember acronyms to help clinicians assess and treat people with bipolar disorder. Mood stabilisers such as lithium and sodium valproate are still commonly used in Australia along with newer antipsychotic medications such as quetiapine (Malhi et al., 2009). Electroconvulsive therapy (ECT) is considered a treatment option where there is high severity and risk for a patient (Malhi et al., 2009).

Psychological treatment for bipolar disorder in Australia often involves a cognitive behaviour therapy (CBT) approach. Several programs enhance CBT with a family focus in young people (Macneil et al., 2010) or a mindfulness focus in adults (Perich et al., 2014). The main benefit of mindfulness-based CBT in bipolar disorder may be for the comorbid anxiety symptoms (Perich et al., 2013). The Black Dog Institute's psychology educational program promotes the importance of psychoeducation and wellbeing plans for individuals with bipolar disorder, to help prevent relapse (www. blackdoginstitute.org.au/). Also becoming popular are internet-based treatments such as the beyondblue funded self-help program for people with bipolar disorder available at www.moodswings.net.au (Lauder et al., 2007).

Australian clinicians and researchers often use the Young Mania Rating Scale (YMRS; Young et al., 1978) to measure hypomanic and manic symptoms, and the Bipolar Depression Rating Scale (BDRS; Berk et al., 2007) to measure depressive symptoms (Malhi et al., 2009). For young people the Child Behaviour Checklist is also used as it is in America (Hirneth et al., 2015). A large amount of community education and research on bipolar disorder exists in Australia. For example, beyondblue (www. beyondblue.org.au) is an Australian service that provides education about mood disorders and anxiety disorders. Pharmaceutical companies, the National Health and Medical Research Council (NHMRC) and smaller funding bodies such as Rotary Health mainly provide the funding for research into bipolar disorder. The main conference on bipolar disorder in Australia is held biannually. It is called the Australasian Society for Bipolar and Depressive Disorders (ASBDD; http://bipolardisorders.com.au/), a subgroup of the International Society for Bipolar Disorders (ISBD; www.isbd.org) which also meets biennially. Both conferences have many different health and research professionals presenting as well as individuals and their family members (also known as consumers) with bipolar disorder.

New Zealand

The New Zealand Mental Health Survey (NZMHS) published in 2006 (field data were collected between 2004 and 2005) found that the overall 12-month prevalence of bipolar disorder (using a broad definition) among people aged 16 and above was 2.2%

(Oakley-Browne, Wells, & Scott, 2006). The 12-month prevalence rates for BPD-I and BPD-II were 0.6% and 0.4%, respectively. These figures were comparable to an international review of 12-month prevalence rates for bipolar I disorder (0.4%) and bipolar II disorder (0.3) in a combined sample of 61 382 adults (18 years old and above) from 11 countries (Merikangas et al., 2011). In the New Zealand (NZ) study, prevalence declined with age. The median age of onset was 23 years; 25% of people had onset of bipolar disorder by age 17, 50% by age 23, and 75% by age 37. There was no significant difference between men and women (2.1% compared with 2.3%; $p = 0.5$). Most people with bipolar disorder have comorbid mental disorder, particularly anxiety disorder and substance use disorder. With regard to ethnic comparisons for bipolar disorder in NZ, Māori people suffered the highest prevalence (3.4%), followed by Pacific people (2.7%), with both higher than the "Other" composite ethnic group (1.9%). These ethnic differences could not be accounted for by age, gender, educational qualifications, and equalised household income (Oakley-Browne et al., 2006).

After the NZMHS published its results on ethnic differences, Mellsop and colleagues examined the data from another large NZ mental health project titled Case-mix Outcome Study (CAOS) (Mellsop, Dutu, & El-Badri, 2007). They compared the clinical profiles of Māori and European ("Pākehā") patients diagnosed with bipolar disorder and presenting for hospitalised treatment. The Māori patients had higher levels of hyperactivity or disruptive aggressive behaviours, and alcohol and drug use, than the Europeans but were rated as significantly less depressed. The researchers concluded that the:

> ethnic differences in prevalence rates raise the possibility of cultural differences in the experience and reporting of key symptomatology ... It may be seriously postulated that in the presence of prominent overactivity behaviour the threshold for the diagnosis of bipolar disorder, particularly mania, is more readily reached. (Mellsop et al., 2007, p. 394)

It is crucial that clinicians are more culturally sensitive when working with patients from ethnically diverse backgrounds and take into account their cultural background and beliefs (Anonymous, 2010).

People with bipolar disorder who experienced only depression in the past 12 months reported the severity of interference with their lives similarly to people with major depressive disorder (5.4 out of 10-point self-reported scale where 0 = *none*, 1–3 = *mild*, 4–6 = *moderate*, 7–9 = *severe*, and 10 = *very severe*):

> Those with mania or hypomania only were on the border between mild and moderate interference. Those who had both highs and lows experienced significantly more interference with life than was reported *for* any other disorder with a mean of 7.4, in the severe range 7–9. (Oakley-Browne et al., 2006, p. 45)

Along this line of investigation, it was found that the 12-month prevalence rates were 0.3% for people with frequent mood episodes of highs and lows (FMEs, four episodes or above) and 0.7% with no FME (1 to 3 episodes; Wells et al., 2010). The FME group experienced the highest number of days out of role and severe role impairments in the worst month of the past 12 months. Although bipolar disorder has such serious dysfunction, people commonly do not seek early treatment. The NZMHS found that only about 12% of people with bipolar disorder would seek treatment in the first year of onset. The median duration of delay in seeking treatment was 13 years compared to 1 year for depression or 5 years for dysthymia.

The Australian and NZ clinical practice guidelines for treating bipolar disorder (Royal Australian New Zealand College of Psychiatrists Clinical Practice Guidelines Team for Bipolar Disorder, 2004) provides evidence-based recommendations to care for individuals affected by bipolar disorder by phase of illness namely acute mania, mixed episodes, bipolar depression and prophylaxis of such episodes covering assessment, pharmacological treatment (including adverse effects), and psychological treatments (such as psychoeducation and cognitive therapy). The guidelines also deal with the topic of suicide prevention and working with women in pregnancy and breastfeeding. A helpful summary of guidelines for monitoring medicines used in bipolar disorder is included in another paper (Anonymous, 2014) specifically written for GPs. They are often the first clinician to suspect a person has bipolar illness and are involved in providing repeat of prescriptions and monitoring the person's adherence to treatment and recovery. Finally, cost-effectiveness analyses modelled on 14 global subregions (including Western Pacific [A]; e.g., Australia, NZ and Japan) of WHO epidemiological data have confirmed that community-based interventions for bipolar disorder are more efficient than hospital-based care (Chisholm et al., 2005).

Australian case study

This case is a composite example created for illustrative purposes.

Eva was a 26-year-old female who was 3 months pregnant when she presented to a rural headspace centre for psychological monitoring of her bipolar not other specified disorder (*DSM-IV-TR* diagnosis). Eva had recently moved to the large rural town. She was no longer in a relationship with the baby's father and had limited social support. She had been receiving ongoing psychiatric monitoring and two previous inpatient admissions in a larger city. Eva had very good insight into her bipolar disorder. She had ceased taking her medication when she found out she was pregnant as she was worried that it was affecting her baby's development. Eva saw a clinical psychologist weekly and saw a psychiatrist monthly at the local adult community mental health team. Eva described a period of 3 years of having bipolar disorder. She could not identify any periods of depression, which was confirmed by her past treating psychiatrist. Eva had two university degrees and was a teacher. She was not working at time of presentation and was living in a rental unit. Seven months into her pregnancy, Eva quickly became manic and had to be admitted to the local psychiatric inpatient unit. She was placed in the high dependency unit. She was refusing oral medication and therefore received sedation via antipsychotic injections. Eva eventually worked with her community treating clinical psychologist and psychiatrist to agree to take oral medication rather than receive ECT, which was suggested. A large case conference occurred with all treating team members including the perinatal staff at the local hospital and Family and Community Services (FACS) to plan for Eva's maternity care at the hospital and post-birth.

Within 2 weeks of recommencing oral antipsychotic medication, Eva's mental state greatly improved and she was changed to a day patient at the psychiatric unit. She delivered a healthy baby full-term with no complications in the maternity ward of the local hospital. She continued her community follow-up with a clinical psychologist at headspace and her psychiatrist at the adult mental health team following discharge. FACS was satisfied with her ability to care for her child and was no longer involved with her case. In a follow-up appointment, Eva told her treating team she did not regret being off her psychiatric medication for the first 7 months of her pregnancy as she had been worried about possible side effects to her developing baby. She had been surprised that she had managed to go 7 months without having a manic episode. Weekly follow-up with her treating team and Eva's good insight when well helped her stay well for the first 7 months of her pregnancy.

Australia – the Black Dog Institute

The Black Dog Institute (www.blackdoginstitute.org.au) is a not-for-profit organisation that specialises in the diagnosis, treatment, and prevention of mood disorders such as depression and bipolar disorder. The Black Dog Institute has many resources on the detection, assessment, and management of mood disorders for both consumers and health professionals. It also raises the awareness of mood disorders in the community and media. An example of this is through its writing, poetry, and photo competitions. It also provides clinics for depression and bipolar disorder for diagnostic clarification and illness management. The Institute offers a number of education workshops and presentations by experienced clinicians in the area of mood disorders. It has a large emphasis on e-therapy and mHealth (mobile-based health) to help improve access to psychoeducation and intervention of mood disorders in young people and adults.

New Zealand – Balance NZ

Balance NZ (www.balance.org.nz) is a charitable trust that makes a difference in the lives of those affected by mental health issues. The organisation provides information online on bipolar illness, depression, Wellness Recovery Action Plan (WRAP, in English and Māori language – Te Reo WRAP), the art of facilitating self-determination, and also online support groups. The target users are individuals with personal experience of bipolar disorder, young people, parents, and spouses.

Bibliography

Baker, A., Kay-Lambkin, F., Richmond, R., Filla, S., Castle, D., Williams, J., et al. (2011). Study protocol: A randomised controlled trial investigating the effect of a healthy lifestyle intervention for people with severe mental disorders. *BMC Public Health*, *11*, 10.

Jorm, A. F. (2006). National surveys of mental disorders: Are they researching scientific facts or constructing useful myths? *Australian & New Zealand Journal of Psychiatry*, *40*(10), 830–834.

Mental Health & Drug & Alcohol Office. (2010). *Mental health act guide book (4th ed.)*. State Health Publication No: (CMH) 031151. Parramatta: NSW Institute of Psychiatry.

References

American Psychiatric Association. (2013). *Diagnostic and statistical manual of mental disorder* (5th ed.). Arlington, VA: Author.

Anonymous. (2010). Recognising and managing mental health problems in Māori. *Best Practice Journal*, *28*, 9–17.

Anonymous. (2014). Bipolar disorder: Identifying and supporting patients in primary care. *Best Practice Journal*, *62*, 6–17.

Austin, M.-P., Highet, N., & the Guidelines Expert Advisory Committee. (2011). *Clinical practice guidelines for depression and related disorders – Anxiety, bipolar disorder and puerperal psychosis – In the perinatal period. A guide of primary care health professionals*. Melbourne: beyondblue: the National Depressive Initiative.

Australian Institute of Health and Welfare. (2009). *Measuring the social and emotional wellbeing of Aboriginal and Torres Strait Islander peoples*. Cat. no. AIHW 24. Canberra: Author.

Berk, M., Malhi, G. S., Cahill, C., Carman, A. C., Hadzi-Pavlovic, D., Hawkins, M. T., et al. (2007). The Bipolar Depression Rating Scale (BDRS): Its development, validation and utility. *Bipolar Disorders*, *9*, 571–579.

Chisholm, D., Van Ommeren, M., Ayuso-Mateos, J.-L., & Saxena, S. (2005). Cost-effectiveness of clinical interventions for reducing the global burden of bipolar disorder. *British Journal of Psychiatry*, *187*(6), 559–567.

Goodrich, D. E., & Kilbourne, A. M. (2010). A long time coming: The creation of an evidence base for physical activity prescription to improve health outcomes in bipolar disorder. *Mental Health and Physical Activity*, *3*, 103.

Hanstock, T., Hirneth, S., Cahill, C., & Macneil, C. (2012). Bipolar disorder in young people. *InPsych*, *34*, 16–17.

Hirneth, S. J., Hazell, P. L., Hanstock, T. L., & Lewin, T. J. (2015). Bipolar subtypes in children and adolescents: Demographic and clinical characteristics from an Australian sample. *Journal of Affective Disorders*, *175*, 98–107.

Jamieson, K. R. (2000). Suicide and bipolar. *Journal of Clinical Psychiatry, 61*, 47–51.

Lauder, S., Berk, M., Castle, D., Dodd, S., & Chester, A. (2007). Online psychosocial interventions for bipolar disorder: www.moodswings.net.au. *Australian & New Zealand Journal of Psychiatry, 41*(Suppl 2), A389.

Macneil, C., Hasty, M., Conus, P., Berk, M., & Scott, J. (2010). *Bipolar disorder in young people: A psychological intervention manual.* Cambridge: Cambridge University Press.

Malhi, G. S., Adams, D., Lampe, L., Paton, M., O'Connor, N., Newton, L. A., et al. (2009). Clinical practice recommendations for bipolar disorder. *Acta Psychiatrica Scandinavica, 119*(Suppl 439), 27–46.

Mellsop, G., Dutu, G., & El-Badri, S. (2007). CAOS contribution to understanding cultural/ethnic differences in the prevalence of bipolar affective disorder in New Zealand. *Australian & New Zealand Journal of Psychiatry, 41*(5), 392–396.

Merikangas, K. R., Jin, R., He, J.-P., Kessler, R. C., Lee, S., Sampson, N. A., et al. (2011). Prevalence and correlates of bipolar spectrum disorder in the world mental health survey initiative. *Archives of General Psychiatry, 68*(3), 241–251.

Mitchell, P. B., Ball, J., Manicavasagar, V., & O'Kearney, R. (2014). Mood disorders. In E. Reiger (Ed.), *Abnormal psychology: Leading research perspectives (3rd ed.)* (pp. 89–132). Sydney: McGraw-Hill.

Mitchell, P., Johnston, A., Slade, T., Hadzi-Pavlovic, D., Frankland, A., Roberts, G., & Corry, J. (2009). Bipolar disorder in Australia: The 2007 National Survey of Mental Health and Wellbeing. *Bipolar Disorders, 11*, 779.

Murray, C. J. L., & Lopez, A. D. (1996). *The global burden of disease: A comprehensive assessment of mortality and disability from diseases, injuries, and risk factors in 1990 and projected to 2020.* Cambridge, MA: Harvard University Press on behalf of the World Health Organisation and the World Bank.

Oakley-Browne, M., Wells, J. E., & Scott, K. M. (2006). *Te Rau Hinengaro: The New Zealand mental health survey.* Wellington, NZ: Ministry of Health.

Parker, G. (Ed.). (2012). *Bipolar II disorder. Modelling, measuring and managing* (2nd ed.). Cambridge, UK: Cambridge University Press.

Perich, T., Lau, P., Hadzi-Pavlovic, D., Roberts, G., Frankland, A., Wright, A., Green, M., Breakspear, M., Corry, J., Radlinska, B., McCormack, C., Joselyn, C., Levy, F., Lenroot, R., Nurnberger, Jnr J. I., & Mitchell, P. R. (2015). What clinical features precede the onset of bipolar disorder? *Journal of Psychiatric Research, 62*, 71–77.

Perich, T., Manicavasagar, V., Mitchell, P. B., & Ball, J. (2014). Mindfulness-based approaches in the treatment of bipolar disorder: Potential mechanisms and effects. *Mindfulness, 5*, 186–191.

Royal Australian New Zealand College of Psychiatrists Clinical Practice Guidelines Team for Bipolar Disorder. (2004). Australian and New Zealand clinical practice guidelines for the treatment of bipolar disorder. *Australian & New Zealand Journal of Psychiatry, 38*(5), 280–305.

Wells, J. E., McGee, M. A., Scott, K. M., & Browne, M. A. O. (2010). Bipolar disorder with frequent mood episodes in the New Zealand mental health survey. *Journal of Affective Disorders, 126*(1), 65–74.

Young, R. C., Biggs, J. T., Ziegler, V. E., & Meyer, D. A. (1978). A rating scale for mania: Reliability and sensitivity. *British Journal of Psychiatry, 133*, 429–435.

Recommendations for further reading/resources

Berk, L., Berk, M., Castle, D., & Lauder, S. (2008). *Living with bipolar: A guide to understanding and managing the disorder.* Sydney: Allen & Unwin.

Eyers, K., & Parker, G. (2008). *Mastering bipolar disorder: An insider's guide to managing mood swings and finding balance.* Sydney: Allen & Unwin.

Galvez, J. F., Thommi, S., & Ghaemi, S. N. (2011). Positive aspects of mental illness: A review in bipolar disorder. *Journal of Affective Disorders, 128*(3), 185–190.

Grande, I., Berk, M., Birmaher, B., & Vieta, E. (2016). Bipolar disorder. *Lancet, 387*(10027), 1561–72.

Harrison, P. J., Cipriani, A., Harmer, C. J., Nobre, A. C., Saunders, K., Goodwin, G. M., & Geddes, J. R. (2016). Innovative approaches to bipolar disorder and its treatment. *Annals of the New York Academy of Sciences, 1366*(1), 76–89.

Tse, S., Murray, G., Chung, K. F., Davidson, L., Ng, K. L., & Yu, C. H. (2014). Exploring the recovery concept in bipolar disorder: A decision tree analysis of psychosocial correlates of recovery stages. *Bipolar Disorders, 16*(4), 366–377.

Wang, G. Y., & Henning, M. (2013). Family involvement in Chinese immigrants with bipolar disorder in New Zealand. *New Zealand Medical Journal, 126*(1368), 45–52.

Yatham, L. N., Kennedy, S. H., Parikh, S. V., Schaffer, A., Beaulieu, S., Alda, M., et al. (2013). Canadian Network for Mood and Anxiety Treatments (CANMAT) and International Society for Bipolar Disorders (ISBD) collaborative update of CANMAT guidelines for the management of patients with bipolar disorder: Update 2013. *Bipolar Disorders, 15*(1), 1–44.

Relevant websites:
- Collaborative Research Team for the study of Bipolar Disorder (CREST.BD): www.crestbd.ca
- List of resources available to people with Bipolar Disorder or their whanau (extended family group), caregivers: www.bipolarcaregivers.org/wp-content/uploads/2012/12/Ways-to-support-the-person-with-bipolar-disorder-.pdf (hosted by the University of Melbourne) and www.helpguide.org/articles/bipolar-disorder/helping-a-loved-one-with-bipolar-disorder.htm (hosted by HelpGuide, in collaboration with Harvard Medical School)
- The Spectrum Centre for Mental Health Research: www.lancaster.ac.uk/shm/research/spectrum

12

Anxiety disorders

Amanda Hutchinson

Introduction

Anxiety disorders are characterised by excessive fear, anxiety, or worry, and are associated with significant distress or impaired functioning. The anxiety disorders are presented here in an order consistent with the *Diagnostic and Statistical Manual of Mental Disorders* (5th ed.; *DSM-5;* American Psychiatric Association, 2013). A brief description of each follows, along with the shared *DSM-5/ICD-10* code. However, refer to the *DSM-5* for a full description of the diagnostic criteria.

- Separation anxiety disorder (F93.0) is characterised by excessive fear or anxiety about separation from particular individuals or from home. Symptoms include excessive distress, worry, or physical symptoms when anticipating or experiencing separation, reluctance to sleep away from home or away from attachment figures, nightmares about separation, reluctance or refusal to go out, or worry about untoward events that would cause separation from attachment figures.
- Selective mutism (F94.0) describes a failure to speak in specific situations where it is expected, despite being able to speak in other social situations. This failure is not due to lack of familiarity or knowledge of the language or a communication disorder.
- Specific phobia (F40.2) is associated with intense fear or anxiety in the presence of a specific object or situation (code varies according to the specific phobia). Examples include fear of animals (e.g., spiders), blood, or injections, and flying on an aeroplane. Individuals with specific phobia avoid feared stimuli or situations or endure intense anxiety when exposed to them.
- Social anxiety disorder (F40.10) involves excessive fear or anxiety of social situations in which an individual may be evaluated. This includes social interactions, performance anxiety, and other situations where others observe an individual and there is the potential for embarrassment or negative assessment. The fear is out of

proportion to the threats these situations pose, causes distress, and often leads to avoidance of social situations.

- Panic disorder (F41.0) describes recurrent panic attacks, which are intense periods of fear or discomfort that include a range of physical and cognitive symptoms. These symptoms include palpitations, sweating, sensations of shortness of breath or choking, chest pain, nausea, dizziness, and a fear of losing control. They are exacerbated by misinterpretations of these symptoms (e.g., "I'm having a heart attack," "I'm going to die," or "I'm going crazy"). These panic attacks are accompanied by worry about their recurrence, their meaning (e.g., "going crazy"), and behaviour changes to prevent or minimise future panic attacks.
- Agoraphobia (F40.00) is fear or anxiety about at least two of a range of situations including using public transport, being in open spaces, being in enclosed spaces, standing in line, being in a crowd, and leaving home alone. These situations are avoided due to fears about difficulty escaping or accessing help. People will sometimes endure the intense anxiety in these situations or take someone along to help them cope.
- Generalised anxiety disorder (GAD; F41.1) is also characterised by excessive anxiety, but in this case associated with several everyday events or activities. The worry is excessive, causes distress, and results in at least three of the following symptoms: restlessness, being easily fatigued, difficulty concentrating, irritability, muscle tension, and sleep problems.
- Substance/medication-induced anxiety disorder (code varies according to specific substance) describes symptoms of panic or anxiety thought to result from the effects of a drug of abuse, medication, or exposure to a toxic substance. This may be comorbid with a substance use disorder. Substances include alcohol, caffeine, opioids, amphetamines, hallucinogens, cannabis, and cocaine among others.

Australia

Prevalence

A meta-analysis of studies on the prevalence of anxiety disorders reported that 7.3% of the world's population has an anxiety disorder at any one time (Baxter et al., 2013). Furthermore, prevalence was found to vary according to region and culture, with Western cultures (including Australasia) displaying higher risk for anxiety disorders than non-Western cultures.

Australian prevalence estimates based on the 2007 National Survey of Mental Health and Wellbeing (NSMHW) indicated a 12-month prevalence of 11.8% and a lifetime prevalence of anxiety disorders of 20.0% (McEvoy, Grove, & Slade, 2011). The most common anxiety disorder based on 12-month prevalence estimates was social phobia (4.2%), followed by GAD (1.9%), panic disorder (1.8%), and agoraphobia (1.2%). Increased risk for an anxiety disorder was associated with being female, single, unemployed, and having a physical condition, a history of smoking, or a family history of anxiety. These rates of anxiety disorders are concerning, particularly when the increase in anxiety over time is considered. Reavley et al. (2011) calculated a National Anxiety Index for Australia, based on results of the National Health Surveys and the National Surveys of Mental Health and Wellbeing, and found evidence for an increase in risk of anxiety between 1997 and 2007, particularly for women aged 45–64.

Comorbidity

It is not uncommon for people to meet criteria for multiple anxiety disorders. McEvoy et al. (2011) found that among those meeting criteria for an anxiety disorder in the past 12 months, approximately one-third met criteria for at least one other anxiety disorder. Furthermore, they were 13 times more likely to meet criteria for another affective disorder, with comorbid major depression and dysthymia the most common. In addition to affective disorders, anxiety disorders were also associated with increased likelihood of alcohol dependence. Comorbidity is clearly a significant concern for people with an anxiety disorder, so it is important that health practitioners consider a range of issues in their treatment plans depending on the specific comorbidities their patient exhibits.

Age of onset

Anxiety disorders can begin at a wide range of ages. In Australia, the median age of onset has been reported as 19 (McEvoy et al., 2011). In general, prevalence increases with age through young adulthood and adulthood and then declines from the age of 45. GAD has the latest onset with a median onset of 33 years of age.

Gender

Females are more than twice as likely to be diagnosed with an anxiety disorder than males (Baxter et al., 2013). Although rates are highest during middle age, women are also at risk of affective disorders postpartum. A large Australian study of women 6 months after they had given birth found that although the rate of postpartum anxiety was lower than that for depression, 12.7% of women had anxiety above the normal range and a further 8.1% had comorbid depression and anxiety above the "normal" range as defined by the Depression and Anxiety Stress Scales (Yelland, Sutherland, & Brown, 2010). Although not directly comparable with the DSM rates presented earlier, these results indicate high rates of anxiety in this group. Recent stressful life events and being born overseas in a country where English is not the primary language spoken were associated with increased likelihood of anxiety symptoms in these women. To support new mothers and their babies, health professionals must consider postpartum anxiety as well as depression during routine health checks. If they identify anxiety and/ or depression, a referral to a psychologist or other mental health professional may be appropriate.

Rural and regional Australia

High rates of mental health concerns in rural areas in Australia have been recognised. A study of 1524 South Australian and Victorian adults living in rural areas found that approximately 11% of both men and women scored above the "normal" range for anxiety as indicated by the Hospital Anxiety and Depression Scale. Prevalence was highest in those aged 45–54 (Kilkkinen et al., 2007). This is of particular concern due to the low use of mental health services in rural areas. Green, Hunt, and Stain (2012) found among adults living in rural areas in New South Wales who were previously diagnosed with a depressive or anxiety disorder that there was an average delay of 18 years between symptom onset and seeking professional help. This is clearly an unacceptable delay and may contribute to the high suicide rates in rural areas. Importantly, however, the delay in seeking help varies by disorder. Green et al. (2012) found that while half the participants with panic disorder sought help in the first year of symptoms, only 19% and 9.3% of participants with GAD and social phobia respectively sought help during the same time frame. Furthermore, living in a remote or very remote region was associated with delays of more than a year.

In summary, those living in rural or remote regions experience high rates of anxiety and are likely to delay seeking help, possibly with the exception of panic disorder. This is likely due to the common misattribution of symptoms to a physical health condition (e.g., a heart attack or stroke) for which medical treatment is considered necessary and urgent.

Indigenous Australians

Indigenous Australians are at greater risk of mental health disorders than non-Indigenous Australians (Chenhall & Senior, 2009). These mental health problems are likely related to the impact of colonisation, the disintegration of families, loss of culture, loss of identity, unemployment, poverty, racism, substance use, and limited access to healthcare (Bulman & Hayes, 2011; Chenhall & Senior, 2009).

Indigenous populations may attribute mood states to externalised causes rather than feelings. It has also been suggested that low mood is indicative of anxiety in Aboriginal people rather than with depression as is often observed in other populations. Intervention within this population may differ from mainstream approaches such as cognitive behaviour therapy (CBT) and may include narrative approaches with personal stories or "yarning", activities, art, and connection to the land. Trust of broader networks or community leaders may also be important in treatment and can take time to establish (Davies, 2011). The importance of these factors and acceptability of specific approaches will vary from person to person as there is significant diversity among Aboriginal Nations and many Aboriginal people value both traditional and modern influences (Axleby-Blake et al., 2013; Bulman & Hayes, 2011; Davies, 2011).

As with many areas of mental health, further research involving Indigenous community members is needed to develop and evaluate culturally appropriate approaches to intervention (Bulman & Hayes, 2011). Participation action research involves the community in all stages of research and therefore offers a promising avenue for future endeavours. Furthermore, more Indigenous mental health professionals and psychologists are needed to increase trust and understanding and to overcome cultural and language barriers (Axleby-Blake et al., 2013). Existing screening tools need to be validated for use with Indigenous people (Bowen et al., 2014) to allow for valid and reliable assessments of anxiety when evaluating efforts to address anxiety disorders.

Treatment

Treatment for anxiety by a psychologist or clinical psychologist currently attracts a Medicare rebate in Australia if a general practitioner (GP) has referred the client for Focused Psychological Services under a Mental Health Care Plan. Focused Psychological Services include psychoeducation and motivational interviewing, CBT, relaxation strategies, skills training, and interpersonal therapy. Narrative therapy is also included for working with Indigenous Australians.

CBT is arguably the most widely applied form of psychotherapy used to treat anxiety disorders due to its strong evidence base. Anxiety disorders are often characterised by fear and avoidance of situations, bodily sensations, thoughts, or feelings that are perceived as threatening. This avoidance is often maintained by beliefs and assumptions about anxiety, physical sensations, or one's ability to cope. For example, an individual may interpret chest pain as an indication of a heart attack, or anxiety as an indication of losing control or "going crazy." Behavioural responses to anxiety, including avoidance, are enacted in order to keep the person safe. However, these behaviours reinforce beliefs about the client's inability to cope with anxiety without engaging in these behaviours. For example, "I'm safe, because I stayed home." This type of avoidance also significantly narrows the individual's social interactions and contact with their support network. Treatment is likely to involve psychoeducation about the nature of anxiety, including the fight or flight response. Case conceptualisation typically identifies the specific thoughts, beliefs, and behaviours associated with the client's experience of anxiety. These thoughts and beliefs can then be addressed using cognitive restructuring. Exposure to avoided stimuli or situations is commonly employed under the guidance of the therapist and safety behaviours may be challenged. Finally, relaxation techniques and problem-solving are commonly incorporated into CBT approaches to the treatment of anxiety disorders.

Acceptance and commitment therapy (ACT) is also gaining recognition. Although it is not specifically listed under Medicare's Focused Psychological Services, evidence for its efficacy is growing (Landy, Schneider, & Arch, 2015; Smout et al., 2012). ACT is considered a third-wave CBT because although it incorporates aspects of behaviour therapy and CBT, mindfulness is a central component. It is further distinguished from these earlier therapies by considering the context rather than the specific content of thoughts. A systematic review found support for ACT in treating anxiety disorders, with most studies reporting moderate treatment effects. ACT was concluded to be superior to no treatment or control conditions and equivalent to other therapeutic approaches. However, the lack of power, heterogeneity in definitions of anxiety disorders, and specific therapeutic techniques used limits the conclusions that can be drawn based on current evidence (Swain et al., 2013).

Online interventions

CBT interventions delivered online have been shown to be effective for GAD, social phobia, and panic disorder in Australian adults (Johnston et al., 2011; Mewton, Wong, & Andrews, 2012). Low completion rates are a concern with online interventions; however, automated emails or guidance by phone or messaging have been shown to increase participation (Johnston et al., 2011; Titov et al., 2013). Furthermore, positive outcomes have been observed for videoconference-based CBT in a small Australian study with significant improvements in anxiety that equated to improvements obtained through therapy delivered in person (Stubbings et al., 2013). Videoconferencing and online interventions may be particularly useful for those in rural or remote regions who lack access to services and those who find it difficult to leave the house due to their anxiety.

Australian interest groups and associations

Although not directly related to anxiety, the Australian Psychological Society has several interest groups that may be relevant to members working with people with anxiety disorders. These are Acceptance and Commitment Therapy and Psychology, Aboriginal and Torres Strait Islander Peoples and Psychology, and Narrative Theory and Practice in Psychology. The Australian Association for Cognitive and Behaviour Therapy also provides a range of resources and training opportunities for members.

Assessment

Anxiety is commonly measured by self-report using questionnaires. There are many measures of anxiety available but few have specifically Australian norms. Crawford et al. (2011) have provided Australian percentile norms for a range of commonly used self-report scales including the Beck Anxiety Inventory, the Depression Anxiety and Stress Scale (DASS), DASS-21, the Self-Rating Scale for Anxiety and the State-Trait Anxiety Inventory. A program is available to calculate percentile ranks for Australian adults' scores on these measures (Crawford et al., 2011).

The DASS is a 42-item questionnaire that provides separate scores for depression, anxiety, and stress. Scores on each domain are then classified as normal, mild, moderate, or severe (Lovibond & Lovibond, 1995).

Commonly used measures of anxiety may not be appropriate with all populations. The Geriatric Anxiety Inventory was developed in Australia (Pachana et al., 2007) and was designed for use with older adults. This scale has 20 items and has less items related to somatic symptoms. A short form has also been developed, consisting of only five items for use in primary care and acute medical settings. Commonly used measures of anxiety may also be inappropriate for use with Indigenous Australians. The Westerman Aboriginal Symptoms Checklist – Youth is one screening tool for Indigenous youth that includes an anxiety subscale (Westerman, 2000).

Screening measures of anxiety can be used to identify those in need of treatment or referral, or to measure progress during treatment. Measures are typically used by psychologists during the initial session and then repeated after a period of intervention. This information also provides valuable feedback to general practitioners when clients have been referred under a Mental Health Care Plan.

New Zealand

Prevalence

Prevalence estimates based on the New Zealand Mental Health Survey (NZMHS) conducted in 2003 and 2004 indicate similar rates of anxiety disorders to those reported in Australia, with 12-month prevalence of 14.8% and lifetime prevalence of 24.9%. Specifically, 12-month prevalence was 5.1% for social phobia, 2.0% for GAD, 1.7% for panic disorder and 0.6% for agoraphobia. Lifetime prevalence was 9.4% for social phobia, 6.0% for GAD, 2.7% for panic disorder and 1.2% for agoraphobia (McEvoy et al., 2011; Wells et al., 2006b; Wells et al., 2006a). Anxiety disorders were more prevalent in females than males (Wells et al., 2006b).

Comorbidity

Comorbidity is a significant issue for people with anxiety disorders in New Zealand (NZ). Among those who reported meeting criteria for an anxiety disorder in the past 12 months in the NZMHS, 37% had a comorbid disorder. Mood disorders and substance use disorders were common comorbidities (Scott et al., 2006).

Age of onset

Anxiety disorders can occur at any age. However, specific phobias start earliest, with the NZMHS finding that half of cases developed before the age of 7 (Oakley Browne, Wells, & Scott, 2006). Consistent with Australian data, GAD had the latest onset with a median age of onset of 32 years (Oakley Browne et al., 2006). Prevalence declined with age for each anxiety disorder with the exception of GAD and agoraphobia in which prevalence was highest in the 25- to 44-year-old age group (Wells et al., 2006b).

Māori

Māori culture is collectivistic, and highly values social relationships, extended family, family background, and cultural identity. Approximately 15% of NZ's population are Māori and the prevalence of anxiety disorders is higher among this group (Tapsell &

Mellsop, 2007). The NZMHS reported a 12-month prevalence of anxiety disorders of 19.4% and lifetime prevalence estimates indicated that almost 1 in 3 Māori will experience an anxiety disorder during their lifetime (31.3%; Baxter et al., 2006).

Interestingly, a study of cultural factors and mental health in Māori employees found that higher collectivism was significantly associated with lower anxiety (Brougham & Haar, 2013). This study indicated that collectivism and cultural identity play an important role in mental health for Māori.

It should be noted that Pacific peoples in NZ also have increased risk of an anxiety disorder and, of further concern, underuse mental health services (Foliaki et al., 2006).

Over time, significant changes have occurred to Māori healthcare such as developing a Māori model of health recognising the importance of spiritual, cognitive, and emotional, physical, and social/family dimensions of health (Durie, 2011). However, cultural and clinical approaches still need further integration. Furthermore, health services which can provide early intervention, perhaps by using the networks of Māori health practitioners, is needed to reduce the delay in accessing mental health services (Durie, 2011). Finally, research is needed to establish the reliability and validity of assessment tools for use with Indigenous people including Māori (Williamson et al., 2014). The extent to which *DSM-5* classifications of mental health relate to Indigenous populations also needs to be carefully considered.

Treatment

Treatment recommendations are consistent with those reported for Australia with evidence-based approaches such as CBT, ACT, and interpersonal therapy common. Family therapy may also be more suited to Māori and other cultural groups where social relationships and extended family play an important role in health (Kumar et al., 2012).

Consistent with Australia and many countries, use of services varies. As discussed, Pacific peoples often do not seek specialist help. Similarly, those in rural areas have less contact with mental health services and there are significant unmet needs in young people (Oakley Browne et al., 2006).

The delay between onset and seeking help also varies according to the specific anxiety disorder. The NZMHS indicated that panic disorder was associated with the highest percentage of sufferers seeking treatment with an average delay of 3 years between onset and treatment. In contrast, social phobia was associated with a delay of 28 years and specific phobia a delay of 38 years before seeking help (Oakley Browne et al., 2006).

Assessment

Few tools have been specifically validated with NZ populations. However, one study indicated that NZ students did not differ from norms on the Profile of Mood States. However, performance on the Symptom Checklist-90-Revised differed from normative data and revealed significant cultural differences (Barker-Collo, 2003).

Australian case study

This case has been created as an example for illustrative purposes.

Hannah is a 19-year-old university student in Melbourne. She has completed the first year of a computer science degree. Hannah lives at home with her parents and her 16-year-old brother, James. Hannah performed well throughout high school and was a straight-A student. She has always been proud of her academic performance and enjoyed school but university has proven more challenging.

Since commencing university, Hannah has become anxious about attending tutorials and being called on to answer questions or contribute to class discussions as she believes her friends will think she is stupid and she will be humiliated. Her fear causes an increased heart rate, dizziness, and rapid breathing during tutorials. Hannah is particularly concerned that her classmates or lecturers will notice her distress and her fast breathing. This would focus even more attention on Hannah, making her more embarrassed. She worries that her classmates and tutor will think she is not smart enough to be at university. She worries that she has nothing intelligent to contribute to the discussion and avoids any eye contact so that she isn't called upon in class. The last time the tutor asked her a question, she felt so self-conscious she was unable to speak. She felt herself blushing and the tutor directed her question to another student. Hannah knows that her fear is excessive but she has started skipping tutorials. She is often unable to sleep the night before her tutorials because she is worried that her class will notice her anxiety. She worries that if she is asked to speak, she will freeze up, everyone will stare at her, and her classmates will exclude her because she is "weird." Her grades are starting to suffer but Hannah feels worse each time she considers returning. Hannah's symptoms are consistent with a diagnosis of social anxiety disorder.

CBT is an evidence-based approach for the treatment of social phobia and would likely include challenging thoughts and beliefs related to Hannah's academic performance and associated self-worth. Alternatively, ACT might involve achieving some distance or diffusion from these thoughts and engaging in mindfulness techniques to manage thoughts and feelings.

Australia – resources

- **Australian Psychological Society:** www.psychology.org.au
  - The Australian Psychological Society (APS) is an organisation for psychologists in Australia that supports the profession and promotes community wellbeing.
- **Australian Association for Cognitive and Behaviour Therapy**
  - The Australian Association for Cognitive and Behaviour Therapy is a multidisciplinary association that supports research and practice of CBT to achieve emotional, cognitive, and behavioural change.

- **beyondblue:** www.beyondblue.org.au
  - beyondblue is a national organisation in Australia that aims to increase awareness and reduce the impact and stigma associated with depression and anxiety. The website includes useful information about symptoms of anxiety and where to seek help.
- **headspace:** www.headspace.org.au
  - headspace is the National Youth Mental Health Foundation, and provides information and support for young people experiencing difficulties including anxiety. It specifically targets 12–25 year olds.
- **Mental Health Online:** www.mentalhealthonline.org.au
  - Mental Health Online provides automated online assessment, information, self-help resources, and therapist-assisted programs for mental health problems including anxiety.

New Zealand – resources

- **The New Zealand Psychological Society:** www.psychology.org.nz
  - The New Zealand Psychological Society (NZPsS) is a professional association for psychologists in Aotearoa/New Zealand that aims to promote wellbeing and advance the field of psychology.
- **The Aotearoa New Zealand Association for Cognitive Behavioural Therapies:** www.cbt.org.nz/
  - The Aotearoa New Zealand Association for Cognitive Behavioural Therapies (ANZACBT) promotes CBT through research and training in Aotearoa New Zealand.
- **Health Navigator:** www.healthnavigator.org.nz
  - Health Navigator provides information and resources for a range of health issues including specific information related to anxiety symptoms, treatment, and resources.
- **Anxiety Support Canterbury:** www.anxietysupport.org.nz
  - This organisation provides information and support for people experiencing anxiety.
- **The Mental Health Foundation of New Zealand:** www.mentalhealth.org.nz
  - The Mental Health Foundation of New Zealand provides a range of resources on their website including a list of helplines offering support to individuals and their family and friends.

References

American Psychiatric Association. (2013). *Diagnostic and statistical manual of mental disorders* (5th ed.). Arlington, VA: Author.

Axleby-Blake, T., Bilney, P., Elliott, P., Evans, C., Fitz, J., Graham, S., & Malin, M. (2013). A pilot investigation into Aboriginal people's understandings of depression and anxiety. *Advances in Mental Health, 11*, 293–301.

Barker-Collo, S. L. (2003). Culture and validity of the Symptom Checklist-90-Revised and Profile of Mood States in a New Zealand student sample. *Cultural Diversity & Ethnic Minority Psychology, 9*, 185–196.

Baxter, A. J., Scott, K. M., Vos, T., & Whiteford, H. A. (2013). Global prevalence of anxiety disorders: A systematic review and meta-regression. *Psychological Medicine, 43*, 897–910. http://dx.doi.org/10.1017/s003329171200147x

Baxter, J., Kingi, T. K., Tapsell, R., Durie, M., McGee, M. A., & New Zealand Mental Health Survey Research, T. (2006). Prevalence of mental disorders among Māori in Te Rau Hinengaro: The New Zealand Mental Health Survey. *Australian & New Zealand Journal of Psychiatry, 40*, 914–923. http://dx.doi.org/10.1111/j.1440-1614.2006.01911.x

Bowen, A., Duncan, V., Peacock, S., Bowen, R., Schwartz, L., Campbell, D., & Muhajarine, N. (2014). Mood and anxiety problems in perinatal Indigenous women in Australia, New Zealand, Canada, and the United States: A critical review of the literature. *Transcultural Psychiatry, 51*, 93–111. http://dx.doi.org/10.1177/1363461513501712

Brougham, D., & Haar, J. M. (2013). Collectivism, cultural identity and employee mental health: a study of New Zealand Māori. *Social Indicators Research, 114*, 1143–1160.

Bulman, J., & Hayes, R. (2011). Mibbinbah and spirit healing: Fostering safe, friendly spaces for Indigenous males in Australia. *International Journal of Men's Health, 10*, 6–25. http://dx.doi.org/10.3149/jmh.1001.6

Chenhall, R., & Senior, K. (2009). "Those young people all crankybella": Indigenous youth mental health and globalization. *International Journal of Mental Health, 38*, 28–43.

Crawford, J., Cayley, C., Lovibond, P. F., Wilson, P. H., & Hartley, C. (2011). Percentile norms and accompanying interval estimates from an Australian general adult population sample for self-report mood scales (BAI, BDI, CRSD, CES-D, DASS, DASS-21, STAI-X, STAI-Y, SRDS, and SRAS). *Australian Psychologist, 46*, 3–14.

Davies, M. (2011). Anxiety in children: Remote area sensitivities and considered changes in structuring a Cool Kids approach. *Australasian Psychiatry: Bulletin of Royal Australian and New Zealand College of Psychiatrists, 19*, Suppl 1, S23–S25. http://dx.doi.org/10.3109/10398562.2011.583055

Durie, M. (2011). Indigenizing mental health services: New Zealand experience. *Transcultural Psychiatry, 48*, 24–36. http://dx.doi.org/10.1177/1363461510383182

Foliaki, S. A., Kokaua, J., Schaaf, D., Tukuitonga, C., & New Zealand Mental Health Survey Research (2006). Twelve-month and lifetime prevalences of mental disorders and treatment contact among Pacific people in Te Rau Hinengaro: The New Zealand Mental Health Survey. *Australian & New Zealand Journal of Psychiatry, 40*, 924–934. http://dx.doi.org/10.1111/j.1440-1614.2006.01912.x

Green, A. C., Hunt, C., & Stain, H. J. (2012). The delay between symptom onset and seeking professional treatment for anxiety and depressive disorders in a rural Australian sample. *Social Psychiatry and Psychiatric Epidemiology, 47*, 1475–1487. http://dx.doi.org/10.1007/s00127-011-0453-x

Johnston, L., Titov, N., Andrews, G., Spence, J., & Dear, B. F. (2011). A RCT of a transdiagnostic internet-delivered treatment for three anxiety disorders: Examination of support roles and disorder-specific outcomes. *PLoS One, 6*, e28079. http://dx.doi.org/10.1371/journal.pone.0028079

Kilkkinen, A., Kao-Philpot, A., O'Neil, A., Philpot, B., Reddy, P., Bunker, S., & Dunbar, J. (2007). Prevalence of psychological distress, anxiety and depression in rural communities in Australia. *The Australian Journal of Rural Health*, *15*, 114–119. http://dx.doi.org/10.1111/j.1440-1584.2007.00863.x

Kumar, S., Dean, P., Smith, B., & Mellsop, G. W. (2012). Which family – what therapy: Māori culture, families and family therapy in New Zealand. *International Review of Psychiatry*, *24*, 99–105. http://dx.doi.org/10.3109/09540261.2012.656303

Landy, L. N., Schneider, R. L., & Arch, J. J. (2015). Acceptance and commitment therapy for the treatment of anxiety disorders: A concise review. *Current Opinion in Psychology*, *2*, 70–74. http://dx.doi.org/10.1016/j.copsyc.2014.11.004

Lovibond, S. H., & Lovibond, P. F. (1995). *Manual for the Depression Anxiety Stress Scales* (2nd ed.). Sydney: Psychology Foundation.

McEvoy, P. M., Grove, R., & Slade, T. (2011). Epidemiology of anxiety disorders in the Australian general population: Findings of the 2007 Australian National Survey of Mental Health and Wellbeing. *Australian & New Zealand Journal of Psychiatry*, *45*, 957–967. http://dx.doi.org/10.3109/00048674.2011.624083

Mewton, L., Wong, N., & Andrews, G. (2012). The effectiveness of internet cognitive behavioural therapy for generalized anxiety disorder in clinical practice. *Depression and Anxiety*, *29*, 843–849. http://dx.doi.org/10.1002/da.21995

Oakley Browne, M. A., Wells, J. E., & Scott, K. M. (2006). *Te Rau Hinengaro: The New Zealand mental health survey.* Wellington, NZ: Ministry of Health.

Pachana, N. A., Byrne, G. J., Siddle, H., Koloski, N., Harley, E., & Arnold, E. (2007). Development and validation of the Geriatric Anxiety Inventory. *International Psychogeriatrics*, *19*, 103–114. http://dx.doi.org/10.1017/S1041610206003504

Reavley, N. J., Jorm, A. F., Cvetkovski, S., & Mackinnon, A. J. (2011). National depression and anxiety indices for Australia. *Australian & New Zealand Journal of Psychiatry*, *45*, 780–787. http://dx.doi.org/10.3109/00048674.2011.607130

Scott, K. M., McGee, M. A., Oakley Browne, M. A., Wells, J. E., & New Zealand Mental Health Survey Research, T. (2006). Mental disorder comorbidity in Te Rau Hinengaro: The New Zealand mental health survey. *Australian & New Zealand Journal of Psychiatry*, *40*, 875–881. http://dx.doi.org/10.1111/j.1440-1614.2006.01906.x

Smout, M. F., Hayes, L., Atkins, P. W. B., Klausen, J., & Duguid, J. E. (2012). The empirically supported status of acceptance and commitment therapy: An update. *Clinical Psychologist*, *16*, 97–109. http://dx.doi.org/10.1111/j.1742-9552.2012.00051.x

Stubbings, D. R., Rees, C. S., Roberts, L. D., & Kane, R. T. (2013). Comparing in-person to videoconference-based cognitive behavioral therapy for mood and anxiety disorders: Randomized controlled trial. *Journal of Medical Internet Research*, *15*, e258. http://dx.doi.org/10.2196/jmir.2564

Swain, J., Hancock, K., Hainsworth, C., & Bowman, J. (2013). Acceptance and commitment therapy in the treatment of anxiety: A systematic review. *Clinical Psychology Review*, *33*, 965–978. http://dx.doi.org/10.1016/j.cpr.2013.07.002

Tapsell, R., & Mellsop, G. (2007). The contributions of culture and ethnicity to New Zealand mental health research findings. *The International Journal of Social Psychiatry*, *53*, 317–324.

Titov, N., Dear, B. F., Johnston, L., Lorian, C., Zou, J., Wootton, B., et al. (2013). Improving adherence and clinical outcomes in self-guided internet treatment for anxiety and depression: Randomised controlled trial. *PLoS One, 8*, e62873. http://dx.doi.org/10.1371/journal.pone.0062873

Wells, J. E., Oakley Browne, M. A., Scott, K. M., McGee, M. A., Baxter, J., Kokaua, J., & New Zealand Mental Health Survey Research, T. (2006a). Te Rau Hinengaro: The New Zealand Mental Health Survey: Overview of methods and findings. *Australian & New Zealand Journal of Psychiatry, 40*, 835–844. http://dx.doi.org/10.1111/j.1440-1614.2006.01902.x

Wells, J. E., Oakley Browne, M. A., Scott, K. M., McGee, M. A., Baxter, J., Kokaua, J., & New Zealand Mental Health Survey Research, T. (2006b). Prevalence, interference with life and severity of 12 month DSM-IV disorders in Te Rau Hinengaro: The New Zealand Mental Health Survey. *Australian & New Zealand Journal of Psychiatry, 40*, 845–854. http://dx.doi.org/10.1111/j.1440-1614.2006.01903.x

Westerman, T. G. (2000). The development of a comprehensive assessment process for Aboriginal youth (aged 13 to 17) at risk of depression, suicidal behaviours and anxiety. *The Westerman Aboriginal Symptoms Checklist for Youth Manual.* Perth: Indigenous Psychological Services.

Williamson, A., Andersen, M., Redman, S., Dadds, M., D'Este, C., Daniels, J., et al. (2014). Measuring mental health in Indigenous young people: A review of the literature from 1998–2008. *Clinical Child Psychology and Psychiatry, 19*, 260–272. http://dx.doi.org/10.1177/1359104513488373

Yelland, J., Sutherland, G., & Brown, S. J. (2010). Postpartum anxiety, depression and social health: Findings from a population-based survey of Australian women. *BMC Public Health, 10*, 771. http://dx.doi.org/10.1186/1471-2458-10-771

Recommendations for further reading/resources

Harris, R. (2007). *The happiness trap: Stop struggling, start living.* Wollombi, NSW: ExislePublishing.

Howell, C., & Murphy, M. (2011). *Release your worries: A guide to letting go of stress and anxiety.* Wollombi, NSW: ExislePublishing.

13

Obsessive-compulsive and related disorders

Rebecca Anderson and David Garratt-Reed

Introduction

The obsessive-compulsive and related disorders span a range of conditions marked by perseverative thinking and the urge to engage in repetitive behaviours. These disorders include obsessive compulsive disorder (OCD), body dysmorphic disorder (BDD), hoarding disorder, trichotillomania (hair pulling), and excoriation (skin picking). While often comorbid, and having similar maintaining factors and treatment approaches, the underlying distinctions between these disorders include different cognitive distortions, foci of the urges, emotional experiences, and types of behaviour. OCD is the most common of these disorders and is more frequently represented in psychological research studies. The *Diagnostic and Statistical Manual of Mental Disorders* (5th ed.; *DSM-5;* American Psychological Association, 2013) defines these disorders as follows.

OCD is characterised by the presence of obsessions and/or compulsions. *Obsessions* are defined as recurrent and persistent thoughts, urges, or images that a person experiences as intrusive, unwanted, and distressing. Once experienced, a person will often avoid known triggers of obsessional thinking. However, if triggered, compulsive attempts will be made to ignore, supress, or neutralise such thoughts and urges, and to restore a sense of safety. *Compulsions* may include overt repetitive behaviours (e.g., cleaning, checking) or covert mental acts (e.g., praying, counting) performed to reduce anxiety or prevent some dreaded outcome, often according to rigid rules. Examples of common obsessions and compulsions are presented in Table 13.1. Many people experience intrusive, unwanted thoughts and engage in the types of behaviours observed in OCD. A diagnosis of OCD requires that the obsessions and/or compulsions are time consuming (e.g., take over 1 hour per day), cause considerable distress, and significantly interfere with an individual's functioning.

Table 13.1 Examples of common obsessions and compulsions

Obsessions	Compulsions
• Thoughts of being contaminated with germs, dirt, or faecal matter • Thoughts of causing or failing to prevent harm to oneself or a loved one • Sexual, blasphemous, or violent images or urges that are inconsistent with one's values • An urge for symmetry with items in one's environment, or with body posture or movements • Superstitious beliefs	• Repeated and prolonged showering, hand-washing, or household cleaning • Repeated checking via touch, visual observation, or mental recall • Counting items or repeating behaviours a particular number of times or until it feels "just right" • Ordering and arranging household items until they appear symmetrical • Mentally "neutralising" unwanted thoughts by counting, praying, or chanting a mantra

BDD, trichotillomania, and excoriation all involve repetitive behaviours about some aspect of the body. BDD involves the preoccupation with a perceived defect or physical flaw that may be unnoticeable or only minimally noticeable to others. Common concerns include imperfect skin, thinning or excessive hair, or that facial features or body parts are too large, too small, or asymmetrical. Individuals with BDD perform repetitive behaviours such as mirror checking, excessive grooming, camouflaging with make-up or clothing, picking at perceived skin defects, and mentally comparing their appearance with others. Trichotillomania and excoriation (respectively) involve compulsive hair pulling and skin picking involving any area of the body. In both disorders there is often initial anxiety or boredom, followed by an increasing sense of tension. The act of hair pulling or skin picking may then bring about a sense of relief, gratification, or pleasure. These behaviours can cause irreversible physical damage.

Once considered a subtype of OCD and a trait associated with obsessive-compulsive personality disorder, the *DSM-5* now recognises hoarding disorder as a standalone diagnosis. The key features include the persistent inability to discard possessions, regardless of their value, which results in the accumulation of items that clutter and compromise living spaces. The clutter may also impact yards, vehicles, and other family members' homes. Any attempt to discard items is associated with significant distress. Family and council intervention may occur when hoarding has led to health, fire, falling, or sanitation risks.

OCD and related disorders in the Australian context

While Australian epidemiological studies have not explored OCD-related disorders, the 2007 National Survey of Mental Health and Wellbeing comprehensively assessed the prevalence and impact of OCD in Australia. Participants included approximately 8800 Australians aged 16–85 years, assessed using the World

Health Organisation's World Mental Health – Composite International Diagnostic Interview (WMH-CIDI). The National Survey found a 12-month prevalence rate for *DSM-IV* diagnosed OCD of 2.7%, and lifetime prevalence of 3.8% (McEvoy, Grove, & Slade, 2011). These figures were higher than reported 12-month and lifetime prevalence rates in other countries, such as for New Zealand (NZ, 0.6% and 1.2%, respectively) and in the United States (US, 1.0% and 1.6%). However, McEvoy et al. (2011) noted that this discrepancy was possibly due to an error in earlier implementations of the WMH-CIDI OCD questions. Prevalence rates from the National Survey were also higher when using *DSM-IV* criteria than when *International Statistical Classification of Diseases and Related Health Problems 2010 Edition (ICD-10)* (WHO, 2011) criteria were applied (1.9% and 2.8%, respectively; Australian Bureau of Statistics [ABS], 2007).

The National Survey (ABS, 2007) found that OCD affected females at a slightly higher rate and noted a median age of onset at 19 years, consistent with prior international reporting (see American Psychiatric Association, 2013). OCD had significant impacts on daily functioning, with 24.7% of those affected reporting severe or very severe interference with an important life domain. On average, individuals with OCD reported an inability to perform their normal daily duties on 6.3 days out of 30 because of the disorder. OCD was also associated with high levels of service utilisation, with 50.2% of those diagnosed having used mental health services in the prior 12 months.

Aetiology of OCD and related disorders

Recent Australian research has contributed to the advancement of biological and cognitive aetiological models. For example, López-Solà et al. (2014) recently examined data from the Australian Twin Registry to obtain estimates of heritability for OCD-related disorders. They found moderate heritability rates for obsessive compulsive, hoarding, and body dysmorphic symptoms, providing support for genetic models of the disorder. Silk et al. (2013) used neuroimaging techniques to observe correlations between white matter microstructure and OCD severity in children, providing support for neurobiological models of the disorder. Furthermore, Labuschagne et al. (2013) examined neurocognitive deficits in OCD and BDD and found similarities in neuropsychological performance on a number of cognitive tasks when compared with controls, providing support for executive functioning deficits in the aetiology of these disorders.

Cognitive models of OCD have long posited that intrusive, unwanted thoughts are a universal phenomenon. However, it is not having these thoughts that drives OCD, but rather misinterpreting them as dangerous/threatening, and maladaptive attempts to control them (Rachman & de Silva, 1978; Salkovskis, 1985). Australian researchers recently contributed to an international conglomerate examining the nature of intrusive thoughts in 13 countries across six continents. These studies supported prior findings that over 90% of the population report intrusive thoughts (Radomsky et al., 2014). Furthermore, they found that the maladaptive appraisals and control strategies observed in individuals with OCD were endorsed across all sites, and were moderate to strongly correlated with perceived importance and persistence of intrusive thoughts, and distress (Moulding et al., 2014). Collectively, these studies provided cross-national and cross-cultural support for key aspects of the cognitive model.

Treatment of OCD and related disorders

Recent reviews by Australian authors (Kyrios, Moulding, & Bhar, 2014; Rees & Anderson, 2013a; Watson, Anderson, & Rees, 2010) identified that exposure and response prevention (ERP) is the most evidence-based approach to treating OCD despite several newer biological and psychological therapies currently undergoing evaluation (e.g., deep brain stimulation, transcranial magnetic stimulation, acceptance and commitment therapy, mindfulness-based therapy). ERP produces significant improvement in approximately 70% of individuals who comply (Kyrios, 2003), but the anxiety-provoking nature of ERP can lead to treatment non-compliance. Australian researchers have developed novel treatment approaches to address these compliance issues.

University of Sydney researchers created danger ideation reduction therapy (DIRT); a cognitive therapy program designed to reduce threat expectancies but without needing aversive ERP exercises. Randomised controlled trials have shown DIRT and ERP had comparable outcomes for obsessive-compulsive checking and cleaning subtypes, with DIRT demonstrating greater improvement on some outcome measures (Krochmalik, Jones, Menzies, & Kirkby, 2004; Vaccoro et al., 2014). Rees and Anderson (2013b) have also identified emerging evidence for a role of metacognitive therapy in treating OCD, which also does not require ERP exercises. Curtin University researchers conducted pilot trials of metacognitive therapy in group format and via videoconferencing, finding large treatment effects (Fitt & Rees, 2012; Rees & van Koesveld, 2008).

Research into barriers to treatment seeking among individuals with OCD in Australia found that cost, a preference for handling problems alone, and lack of knowledge about treatment options were central themes (Gentle, Harris, & Jones, 2014). Fortunately, Australian researchers have done significant work to improve treatment accessibility via evaluations of group and technology-based approaches to ERP delivery. Anderson and Rees (2007) evaluated group vs. individual ERP in a randomised controlled trial and found no difference in rates of recovery at follow-up, supporting the continued use of the cost-effective group format. Australian researchers are also contributing to the evaluation of cost-effective and highly accessible online therapies, potentially increasing specialist services to those living in rural and remote areas. Wootton et al. (2011) found preliminary evidence that internet-based cognitive behaviour therapy (CBT) with ERP components and telephone support significantly improved OCD symptoms. Two further trials are currently being undertaken. Rees and Anderson at Curtin University are trialling *OCD? Not Me!* for adolescents with OCD (see www.ocdnotme.com.au; Rees, Anderson, & Finlay-Jones, 2015) and Kyrios and colleagues at Swinburne University are evaluating *OCD Stop!* for adults with OCD (www.mentalhealthonline.org.au).

Australian assessment and treatment guidelines

Clinical assessment and formulation should be used to establish differential diagnosis between the OCD-related disorders, and across common comorbid conditions and other diagnoses. Clinical severity and treatment outcome may then be measured by the Yale-Brown Obsessive Compulsive Scale (YBOCS-II) (Storch et al., 2010), with variations available to assess children (Scahill et al., 1997), and body dysmorphic symptoms (Phillips et al., 1997). The Padua Inventory (Burns, 1995) can also assess a broad range of obsessive-compulsive symptoms and has normative Australia data (Kyrios, Bhar, & Wade, 1996).

Consistent with other major worldwide bodies, such as the National Institute for Clinical Excellence (United Kingdom) and the American Psychiatric Association, the Australian Psychological Society (APS) recognises CBT with an emphasis on ERP as the first-line treatment approach for OCD (see Australian Psychological Society, 2013). The APS also recognises the role of other professionals, such as psychiatrists or general practitioners, for medication or referral under a Medicare plan.

Crino (2014) summarises the key elements of CBT for OCD as follows.

- Psychoeducation: to normalise the intrusive thoughts and explain the maintenance of symptoms for the individual.
- Cognitive therapy: to target dysfunctional beliefs, particularly relating to appraisal of intrusive thoughts.
- Behavioural therapy (graded ERP or behavioural experiments): to break the negatively reinforced cycle of obsessions and compulsions and to disconfirm core fears. Alternative beliefs are generated as the person engages in previously avoided activities/situations.
- Relapse prevention: to promote independent future application of the treatment techniques so that clients "become their own therapist."

While ERP is used in BDD and hoarding disorder treatment, international experts recommend additional disorder-specific strategies. For BDD, this includes cognitive strategies to address maladaptive appearance-related beliefs and attention training to reduce selective attention to perceived flaws (Wilhelm et al., 2014). For hoarding disorder, this includes organisational and problem-solving skills training to target sorting and discarding difficulties, cognitive restructuring to address problematic possession-related beliefs, and a range of motivational interviewing techniques to address ambivalence and low insight (see Steketee & Frost, 2014). Treatment for trichotillomania and excoriation does not include ERP, but rather emphasises increasing one's awareness of urges, controlling internal and external cues to the unwanted behaviours, and engaging in competing behaviours (e.g., squeezing a stress ball when an urge is experienced; see Franklin & Tolin, 2007).

While there are no current OCD and related disorders treatment guidelines specific to working with Aboriginal and Torres Strait Islander peoples, more general guidelines for working with anxiety in these populations have been developed with funding support from the Australian Department of Health and Ageing (see Purdie, Dudgeon, & Walker, 2010). Historical reports have noted myth-driven ritualistic behaviours in some Aboriginal Australian groups, including sub-incision and blood-letting rites linked to irrational fears (e.g., "magical" rape, castration, or dismemberment), and shaving and bathing rituals linked to fertility beliefs (see Dulaney & Fiske, 1994). Assessment should therefore distinguish culturally normative beliefs and rituals from OCD symptoms.

Australian specialised programs

Specialist ERP programs for OCD are available at the psychology clinics of Curtin University (Perth) and Swinburne University (Melbourne), and specialist inpatient treatment is available at the Melbourne Clinic. For those unable to access such programs, free online treatments are currently available including the following.

- OCD? Not Me! is an online CBT program for young people aged 12–18 years and their families. It has been developed by Curtin University and is funded by the Commonwealth Department of Health and Ageing (www.ocdnotme.com.au).
- OCD Stop! is a 12-week automated self-help or therapist-assisted online CBT program, developed by Swinburne University and funded by a National Health and Medical Research Council grant (www.ocdstop.org.au).
- Building Body Acceptance consists of self-help based online modules for managing body dysmorphic disorder, developed by the Centre for Clinical Interventions, Department of Health Western Australia (www.cci.health.wa.gov.au/resources/consumers.cfm).

OCD and related disorders in the New Zealand context

The prevalence and impact of OCD, but not the OCD-related disorders, was assessed for individuals aged 16 years and over in the New Zealand Mental Health Survey (Oakley-Browne, Wells, & Scott, 2006). The survey found 12-month prevalence rates of 0.6% and lifetime prevalence of 1.2%. Among the Māori population, 12-month and lifetime prevalence were 1% and 2.6% respectively, and among Pacific people were 0.7% and 1.1%. It is unclear if the survey measure (the Composite International Diagnostic Interview: CIDI 3.0) was culturally appropriate for these populations (Oakley-Browne et al., 2006). In addition, the CIDI 3.0 lacked sensitivity to detect milder cases of OCD. This survey therefore likely underreported OCD prevalence in NZ (Oakley-Brown et al., 2006). Earlier studies reported higher 12-month prevalence rates of 1.1% to 4%, comparable to those obtained across the globe (Horwath & Weissman, 2000; Wells et al., 1989). Higher rates of OCD have been noted among NZ prison inmates, with 4.3% of female inmates, 4.8% of sentenced men and 5.0% of remanded men meeting the criteria for OCD in the past month (Brinded et al., 2001). OCD prevalence among the prisoners did not vary based on ethnicity (Simpson et al., 2003).

In the New Zealand Mental Health Survey, age of onset varied; however, 50% of individuals reported onset of OCD symptoms by age 18, 25% by age 14 and 5% by age 8 (Oakley-Browne et al., 2006). These statistics are similar among the Māori population, with Baxter (2008) reporting that 50% experienced symptoms by age 18 and 25% by age 13, with a spike in prevalence from ages 12–13. OCD affected females at slightly higher rates. In research examining the meaning attributed to OCD symptoms by individuals in NZ, Campbell and Longhurst (2013) found that women viewed their experience of OCD as a journey, whereas men perceived it as a battle. The survey also found that OCD was associated with greater interference with work, home, and study domains than any anxiety disorder, and suicidal ideation was present for 27.3% of those who met 12-month OCD criteria (Oakley-Browne et al., 2006). In a study tracking a NZ cohort from birth to 18 years, a high proportion of individuals with OCD had comorbid psychological health problems, including depression, social phobia, and substance dependence (Douglass et al., 1995).

Aetiology of OCD and related disorders

NZ OCD researchers have focused primarily on the cognitive appraisal processes involved in the disorder. Inflated responsibility (IR) and thought-action fusion (TAF) are cognitive appraisals that have been suggested to be involved in the maintenance of OCD symptoms (e.g., Rachman, 1997; Salkovskis, 1985). Researchers from the University of Canterbury, Christchurch, investigated whether IR and TAF beliefs were specific to OCD in a NZ clinical sample (O'Leary, Rucklidge, & Blampied, 2009). Results indicated that individuals diagnosed with OCD had higher levels of responsibility beliefs than other anxious individuals or non-clinical control participants. This indicates that individuals with OCD perceive themselves as responsible for preventing potential harm from occurring (e.g., through performing compulsive behaviours), and that this cognitive bias is specific to OCD, rather than being common across anxiety disorders. However, TAF was elevated in the OCD and anxious control groups, suggesting it might be involved in psychopathology in general, rather than OCD specifically (O'Leary et al., 2009).

It has long been speculated that OCD is closely related to eating disorders, particularly anorexia nervosa (AN) and bulimia nervosa (BN). In an article published in the *New Zealand Journal of Psychology*, Bulik (1995) summarised the evidence suggesting that individuals with AN and BN have high levels of obsessionality and that many individuals with AN or BN have previously received a diagnosis of OCD. Roberts (2006) investigated the link between OCD symptoms and disordered eating symptoms in a female undergraduate sample (76% Pākehā, 12.5% Asian, 5.7% Māori/Pacific Islands) at the Victoria University of Wellington. Among a final sample of 141, the OCD symptom of ordering/arranging was strongly predictive of eating disorder symptomatology, so that people who engaged in high levels of ordering/arranging behaviours were more likely to display eating disorder symptoms.

On the basis of clinical reports and empirical studies suggesting that individuals with schizophrenia often exhibit obsessions and compulsions, Prakash (2002) examined the case histories of individuals with OCD comorbid with a psychotic disorder at a NZ rural mental health clinic. In general, OCD had not been recognised and was therefore untreated for a lengthy period in the context of a psychotic disorder. However, once treated, in most cases OCD symptoms improved significantly. Prakash (2002) suggested that obsessions and psychotic symptoms may relate in several ways. In some cases, OCD and psychosis coexist by chance. However, in other instances obsessions can become delusions or vice-versa (e.g., a reactive delusion can develop in response to an obsession), or obsessions and delusions can trigger one another. Prakash (2002) therefore suggested that treating OCD might improve the outcomes for people with treatment-resistant comorbid psychosis.

New Zealand assessment and treatment guidelines

Similar to Australia, the YBOCS and its variants are commonly used to assess symptoms of OCD and related disorders across different ages. In the absence of NZ norms, researchers use the standard manual norms (e.g., McLachlan & Starkey, 2011). However, the validity of using overseas norms is unclear. Barker-Collo (2003) found that NZ students scored significantly higher than American norms on the obsessive-compulsive scale of the Symptom Checklist-90-Revised (SCL-90-R). This scale may therefore over-identify cases of OCD if used in NZ. In addition, individuals who identified as Māori scored higher than those who identified as Pākehā. Therefore, more research is needed examining the validity of using existing norms for the SCL-90-R and other OCD symptom measures with individuals from different cultural backgrounds in NZ.

The Obsessive-Compulsive Inventory – Revised (OCI-R) has been examined in NZ. Roberts and Wilson (2008) found that the intended factor structure of the 18-item OCI-R (Checking, Ordering, Hoarding, Obsessing, Cleaning, and Neutralising, driven by one overarching factor) was appropriate in a sample of 282 subclinical participants. Roberts and Wilson reported acceptable internal consistency for all OCI-R scales and argued that their results support the use of the OCI-R to screen for OCD in NZ. Roberts (2006) found results consistent with this among a non-clinical NZ sample, and reported no differences between Pākehā, Māori and Asian individuals on the OCI-R.

Consistent with international practice, the New Zealand Ministry of Health (www. health.govt.nz) and Mental Health Foundation of New Zealand (www.mentalhealth. org.nz) advocate graded ERP and medication to manage OCD and BDD symptoms. The importance of using treatment that is consistent with cultural beliefs is widely recognised. Treatment evidence from other western cultures can be applied to Pākehā New Zealanders; however, "… knowledge of how to integrate psychological theory and practice with Māori cultural and spiritual beliefs is rudimentary" (National Health Committee, 1998, p. 6). If cultural factors are contributing to the presentation of OCD, referral to specialist Māori mental health workers or involving community elders is recommended (National Health Committee, 1998). Therapists in NZ must remember that people from Pacific backgrounds may conceptualise psychological illness differently and psychological symptoms often have physical manifestations (such as fainting and seizures) among this population. In addition, these individuals tend to view healthcare workers as authority figures and are therefore reluctant to challenge their views (National Health Committee, 1998). NZ mental healthcare professionals may require specialised training to optimally meet the mental healthcare needs of individuals from diverse backgrounds.

New Zealand specialised programs

The NZ Ministry of Health (www.health.govt.nz) provides links to online information and services suitable for treating OCD. For Māori people, Kaupapa Māori Mental Health (www.pw.maori.nz) provides online information about OCD and other anxiety disorders, including the common symptoms and who to contact for assistance.

New Zealand case study

This case has been created as an example for illustrative purposes.

Anna is a 67-year-old unemployed woman living alone in social housing in Christchurch. She came to the attention of authorities during an inspection of her two-bedroom unit for structural damage following the Christchurch earthquake. Earthquake commission staff were unable to enter Anna's premises due to the large amounts of clutter throughout the dwelling. Old newspapers, magazines, books, and advertising material were found stuffed in plastic shopping bags, piled several bags deep throughout the unit. Several narrow pathways had been left between the piles enabling Anna to reach her bathroom and bedroom. A cockroach infestation and the presence of rat droppings and urine were noted in the unit.

Anna agrees to a meeting to discuss the state of her unit. A health protection officer from Community and Public Health and a representative of the City Council discuss the need for Anna to remove the clutter from her home and set a date to complete the work. Anna is extremely distressed by the idea of having to let go of her possessions. She reports that she began collecting these items after her husband died 10 years earlier. Anna recalls the distress she experienced when unable to locate key paperwork required to finalise her husband's affairs and to obtain financial assistance. She now retains all paper goods she comes in to contact with "just in case" she needs to prove where she has been and what she has done. Anna agrees to a clinical psychologist attending her home to help decrease the clutter.

Anna meets criteria for hoarding disorder. Her inability to discard paper goods has compromised the use of her living spaces and created risks to her health. Any attempt to discard the goods is met with significant distress.

CBT would be offered to Anna. This involves both in-home and office based sessions, usually over 7 to 12 months. Sessions would focus on motivational interviewing, reducing acquiring, teaching skills of organising and decision-making, practice of discarding items via exposure and response prevention, and restructuring of hoarding related beliefs.

Australia – OCD? Not Me!

OCD? Not Me! is an Australian online treatment program for young people with OCD. Developed by researchers at Curtin University, the program guides young people through the steps of tackling OCD and provides families with strategies and support. The program uses a mountain analogy, suggesting that "OCD mountain" is best tackled in stages and with the support of guides, good equipment, and motivating rewards. See www.ocdnotme.com.au to access the program.

New Zealand – Purapura Whetu

Purapura Whetu (www.pw.maori.nz) offers Kaupapa Māori services to address spiritual and cultural needs of Māori individuals, as well as their psychological health requirements. The organisation promotes personal growth and positive mental health through the use of clinical, cultural, and community services that "embrace the Māori view of wellbeing." The organisation employs counsellors, nurses, and community support workers who "work with tamariki (children), taiohi (teenagers), pakeke (adults) and whanau."

References

American Psychiatric Association. (2013). *Diagnostic and statistical manual of mental disorders* (5th ed.). Arlington, VA: Author.

Anderson, R., & Rees, C. (2007). Group versus individual cognitive-behavioural treatment for obsessive-compulsive disorder: A controlled trial. *Behaviour Research and Therapy, 45,* 123–137.

Australian Bureau of Statistics. (2007). *National survey of mental health and wellbeing: Summary of results.* Australia: Author.

Australian Psychological Society. (2013). Obsessive-compulsive disorder. *Evidence-based quality information for psychologists (eqip).* Melbourne: Author. Available: http://eqip.psychology.org.au/information-sheets/OCD/

Barker-Collo, S. L. (2003). Culture and validity of the Symptom Checklist-90-Revised and Profile of Mood States in a New Zealand student sample. *Cultural Diversity and Ethnic Minority Psychology, 9,* 185–196.

Baxter, J. (2008). *Māori mental health needs profile: A review of the evidence*. Palmerston North: TeRau Matatini.

Brinded, P. M. J., Simpson, A. I. F., Laidlaw, T. M., Fairlet, N., & Malcolm, F. (2001). Prevalence of psychiatric disorders in New Zealand prisons: A national study. *Australian & New Zealand Journal of Psychiatry, 35*(2), 166–173.

Bulik, C. M. (1995). Anxiety disorders and eating disorders: A review of their relationship. *New Zealand Journal of Psychology, 24*, 51–62.

Burns, G. L. (1995). *Padua Inventory-Washington State University Revision*. Pullman, WA: Author.

Campbell, R., & Longhurst, R. (2013). Obsessive-compulsive disorder (OCD): Gendered metaphors, blogs, and online forums. *New Zealand Geographer, 69*, 83–93.

Crino, R. (2014). Treatment guidelines for common mental health disorders: Obsessive-compulsive disorder. *InPsych: The Bulletin of the Australian Psychological Society Ltd*, Oct.

Douglass, H. M., Moffitt, T. E., Dar, R., McGee, R., & Silva, P. (1995). Obsessive-compulsive disorder in a birth cohort of 18-year-olds: Prevalence and predictors. *Journal of the American Academy of Child & Adolescent Psychiatry, 34*, 1424–1431.

Dulaney, S., & Fiske, A. P. (1994). Cultural rituals and obsessive-compulsive disorder: Is there a common psychological mechanism? *Ethos, 22*, 243–283.

Fitt, S., & Rees, C. S. (2012). Metacognitive therapy for obsessive compulsive disorder by videoconference: A preliminary study. *Behaviour Change, 29*, 213–229.

Franklin, M. E., & Tolin, D. F. (2007). *Treating trichotillomania: Cognitive-behavioral therapy for hairpulling and related problems*. New York: Springer.

Gentle, M., Harris, L. M., & Jones, M. K. (2014). The barriers to seeking treatment for obsessive-compulsive disorder in an Australian population. *Behaviour Change, 31*, 258–278.

Horwath, E., & Weissman, M. M. (2000). The epidemiology and cross-national presentation of obsessive-compulsive disorder. *Psychiatric Clinics of North America, 23*, 493–507.

Krochmalik, A., Jones, M. K., Menzies, R. G., & Kirby, K. (2004). The superiority of danger ideation reduction therapy (DIRT) over exposure and response prevention (ERP) in treating compulsive washing. *Behaviour Change, 21*, 251–268.

Kyrios, M. (2003). Exposure and response prevention. In R. G. Menzies & P. de Silva (Eds.), *Obsessive-compulsive disorder: Theory, research and treatment*. London: Wiley & Sons.

Kyrios, M., Bhar, S., & Wade, D. (1996). The assessment of obsessive-compulsive phenomena: Psychometric and normative data on the Padua Inventory from an Australian non-clinical sample. *Behaviour Research and Therapy, 34*, 85–95.

Kyrios, M., Moulding, R., & Bhar, S. (2014). A clinician's quick guide of evidence-based approaches to obsessive-compulsive disorder. *Clinical Psychologist, 18*, 96–97.

Labuschagne, I., Rossell, S. L., Dunai, J., Castle, D. J., & Kyrios, M. (2013). A comparison of executive function in body dysmorphic disorder (BDD) and obsessive-compulsive disorder (OCD). *Journal of Obsessive-Compulsive and Related Disorders, 2*, 257–262.

López-Solà, C., Fontenelle, L. F., Alonso, P., Cuadras, D., Foley, D. L., Pantelis, C., Pujol, J., Yücel, M., Cardoner, N., Soriano-Mas, C., Menchón, J. M., & Harrison, B. J. (2014).

Prevalence and heritability of obsessive-compulsive spectrum and anxiety disorder symptoms: A survey of the Australian Twin Registry. *American Journal of Medical Genetics: Part B, 165B*, 314–325.

McEvoy, P. M., Grove, R., & Slade, T. (2011). Epidemiology of anxiety disorders in the Australian general population: findings of the 2007 Australian National Survey of Mental Health and Wellbeing. *Australian & New Zealand Journal of Psychiatry, 45*, 957–967.

McLachlan, A. D., & Starkey, N. J. (2011). The classification of substance and behavioural addictions. A preliminary investigation. *New Zealand Journal of Psychology, 40*, 7–18.

Moulding, R., Coles, M. E., Abramowitz, J., Alcolado, G. M., Alonso, P., Belloch, A., Bouvard, Clark, D. A., Doron, G., Fernandez-Alvarez, H., Garcia-Soriano, G., Ghisi, M., Gomez, B., Inozu, M., Radomsky, A. S., Shams, G., Sica, C., Simos, G., & Wong, W. (2014). Part 2. They scare because we care: The relationship between obsessive intrusive thoughts and appraisals and control strategies across 15 cities. *Journal of Obsessive Compulsive and Related Disorders, 3*, 280–291.

National Health Committee. (1998). *Guidelines for assessing and treating anxiety disorders.* Wellington, NZ: Author.

Oakley-Browne, M. A., Wells, J. E., & Scott, K. M. (Eds.). (2006). *Te Rau Hinengaro: The New Zealand mental health survey.* Wellington, NZ: Ministry of Health.

O'Leary, E. M., Rucklidge, J. J., & Blampied, N. (2009). Thought-action fusion and inflated responsibility beliefs in obsessive-compulsive disorder. *Clinical Psychologist, 13*, 94–101.

Phillips, K. A., Hollander, E., Rasmussen, S. A., Aronowitz, B. R., DeCaria, C., & Goodman, W. K. (1997). A severity rating scale for body dysmorphic disorder: Development, reliability, and validity of a modified version of the Yale-Brown Obsessive Compulsive Scale. *Psychopharmacology Bulletin, 33*, 17–22.

Prakash, G. (2002). The relationship between obsessive-compulsive disorder and psychosis. *Australasian Psychiatry, 10*, 405–410.

Purdie, N., Dudgeon, P., & Walker, R. (2010). *Working together: Aboriginal and Torres Strait Islander mental health and wellbeing principles and practice.* Canberra: Commonwealth of Australia.

Rachman, S. (1997). A cognitive theory of obsessions. *Behaviour Research and Therapy, 35*, 793–802.

Rachman, S., & de Silva, P. (1978). Abnormal and normal obsessions. *Behaviour Research and Therapy, 16*, 233–238.

Radomsky, A. S., Alcolado, G. M., Abramowitz, J., Alonso, P., Belloch, A., Bouvard, M., Clark, D. A., Coles, M., Doron, G., Fernandez-Alvarez, H., Garcia-Soriano, G., Ghisi, M., Gomez, B., Inozu, M., Moulding, R., Shams, G., Sica, C., Simos, G., & Wong, W. (2014). Part 1. You can run but you can't hide: Intrusive thoughts on 6 continents. *Journal of Obsessive Compulsive and Related Disorders, 3*, 269–279.

Rees, C. S., & Anderson, R. A. (2013a). New approaches to the psychological treatment of obsessive-compulsive disorder in adults. In F. Durbano (Ed.), *New insights into anxiety disorders*, (pp. 427–444). United States: InTech.

Rees, C. S., & Anderson, R. A. (2013b). A review of metacognition in psychological models of obsessive-compulsive disorder. *Clinical Psychologist, 17*, 1–8.

Rees, C. S., Anderson, R. A., & Finlay-Jones, A. (2015). OCD? Not Me! Protocol for the development and evaluation of a web-based self-guided treatment for youth with obsessive-compulsive disorder. *BMJ Open*, *5*, e007486. http://dx.doi.org/10.1136/bmjopen-2014-007486

Rees, C. S., & van Koesveld, K. E. (2008). An open trial of group metacognitive therapy for obsessive compulsive disorder. *Journal of Behavior Therapy and Experimental Psychiatry*, *39*, 451–458.

Roberts, M. E. (2006). Disordered eating and obsessive-compulsive symptoms in a sub-clinical student population. *New Zealand Journal of Psychology*, *35*, 45–54.

Roberts, M. E., & Wilson, M. S. (2008). Factor structure and response bias of the Obsessive Compulsive Inventory Revised (OCI-R) in a female undergraduate sample from New Zealand. *New Zealand Journal of Psychology*, *37*, 2–7.

Salkovskis, P. M. (1985). Obsessional-compulsive problems: A cognitive-behavioural analysis. *Behaviour Research and Therapy*, *23*, 571–583.

Scahill, L., Riddle, M. A., McSwiggin-Hardin, M., Ort, S. I., King, R. A., Goodman, W. K., et al. (1997). Children's Yale-Brown obsessive-compulsive scale: Reliability and validity. *Journal of the American Academy of Child and Adolescent Psychiatry*, *36*, 844–852.

Silk, T., Chen, J., Seal, M., & Vance, A. (2013). White matter abnormalities in pediatric obsessive-compulsive disorder. *Psychiatry Research*, *213*, 154–160.

Simpson, A. I. F., Brinded, P. M., Fairley, N., Laidlaw, T. M., & Malcolm, F. (2003). Does ethnicity affect need for mental health service among New Zealand prisoners? *Australian & New Zealand Journal of Psychiatry*, *37*, 728–734.

Steketee, G., & Frost, R. O. (2014). *Treatment for hoarding disorder: Therapist guide*. New York: Oxford University Press.

Storch, E. A., Larson, M. J., Goodman, W. K., Rasmussen, S. A., Price, L. H., & Murphy, T. K. (2010). Development and psychometric evaluation of the Yale-Brown Obsessive-Compulsive Scale – Second edition. *Psychological Assessment*, *22*, 223–232.

Vaccoro, L., Jones, M., Menzies, R., & Wootton, B. (2014). The treatment of obsessive-compulsive checking: A randomised trial comparing danger ideation reduction therapy with exposure and response prevention. *Clinical Psychologist*, *18*, 74–95.

Watson, H. J., Anderson, R. A., & Rees, C. S. (2010). Evidence-based clinical management of obsessive-compulsive disorder. In R. A. Carlstedt (Ed.), *Handbook of integrative clinical psychology, psychiatry and behavioral medicine: Perspectives, practices, and research* (pp. 411–442). New York: Springer.

Wells, J. E., Bushnell, J. A., Hornblow, A. R., Joyce, P. R., & Oakley-Browne, M. A. (1989). Christchurch psychiatric epidemiology study, part 1: Methodology and lifetime prevalence for specific psychiatric disorders. *Australian & New Zealand Journal of Psychiatry*, *23*, 315–326.

Wilhelm, S., Phillips, K. A., Didie, E., Buhlmann, U., Greenberg, J. L., Fama, J. M., Keshaviah, A., & Steketee, G. (2014). Modular cognitive-behavioral therapy for body dysmorphic disorder: a randomised controlled trial. *Behaviour Therapy*, *45*, 314–327.

Wootton, B. M., Titov, N., Dear, B. F., Spence, J., Andrews, G., Johnston, L., & Solley, K. (2011). An internet administered treatment program for obsessive-compulsive disorder: A feasibility study. *Journal of Anxiety Disorders*, *25*, 1102–7.

World Health Organisation. (2011). *International statistical classification of diseases and related health problems 2010 Edition (ICD-10)*. Geneva: Author.

Recommendations for further reading/resources

General

The following are useful guides to understanding and treating the OCD-related disorders:

- Phillips, K. (2009). *Understanding body dysmorphic disorder*. New York: Oxford.
- Steketee, G., & Frost, R. O. (2014). *Treatment for hoarding disorder: Therapist guide*. New York: Oxford.

Australia

Associate Professor Clare Rees is a leading Australian OCD clinician and researcher from Curtin University. The following book contains expert advice, treatment guidelines, and client worksheets for working with OCD:

- Rees, C. S. (2009). *Obsessive-compulsive disorder: A practical guide to treatment*. East Hawthorn, Australia: IP Communications.

New Zealand

The following New Zealand websites contain information about OCD, and links to treatment and supportive services:

- The Mental Health Foundation of New Zealand (www.mentalhealth.org.nz/get-help/a-z/resource/17/obsessive-compulsive-disorder)
- Health Navigator New Zealand (www.healthnavigator.org.nz/health-a-z/o/obsessive-compulsive-disorder).

14

Trauma- and stressor-related disorders

William Hough

Introduction

Trauma- and stressor-related disorders (TSRD) is a new category in the *Diagnostic and Statistical Manual of Mental Disorders* (5th ed.; *DSM-5;* American Psychiatric Association, 2013). The specific criterion for inclusion in this diagnostic category is the explicit exposure to a traumatic or stressful event.

Several disorders have been incorporated into the TSRD category as individuals exhibit a wide range of reactions following trauma. The disorders in this new category are reactive attachment disorder, disinhibited social engagement disorder, posttraumatic stress disorder (PTSD), acute stress disorders (ASD), and adjustment disorders. Of these, adjustment disorder, ASD, and PTSD are the most prevalent. In order to qualify for a diagnosis of PTSD, explicit exposure to the most severe stress (PTSD Criterion A) is required, while criteria for diagnosis of an adjustment disorder requires exposure to the least level of stress.

Immediately following exposure to a distressing event, a diagnosis of an adjustment disorder or ASD (providing diagnostic criteria are fulfilled) can be established. However, the criterion for ASD is that a short-term reaction that persists from 3 days to 1 month exists. Should symptoms last longer than a month, a diagnosis of PTSD may apply if specific. For the sake of brevity, this chapter will consider only PTSD and ASD.

The development of PTSD may occur following exposure to a traumatic event where severe threat or injury occurred. However, a straightforward trajectory does not always exist. For instance, while most people with ASD also develop PTSD, many with PTSD do not initially display ASD (Bryant et al., 2008). Many develop PTSD more than 6 months post-trauma, a phenomenon known as delayed onset PTSD. McFarlane (2010) argues that a key reason for this is the escalating process of increasing sensitisation, which progresses an over-reactivity to subtle environmental cues associated with the trauma. PTSD can present at any age; however, there are separate diagnostic criteria for children under the age of 6 (Scheeringa, Zeanah, & Cohen, 2011).

Events that may precipitate PTSD include violent assault, natural disasters, wars, or accidents; for example, direct exposure to natural disasters such as bush fires in Australia (McFarlane, 1990; Parslow, Jorm, & Christensen, 2006) and earthquakes in New Zealand (NZ; Fergusson et al., 2014). Intimate interpersonal violence has the highest reported risk factor for developing PTSD (Forbes et al., 2014). Cumulative stress can also precipitate PTSD.

For a diagnosis of PTSD following exposure to trauma, symptoms from each of four clusters must be present. The symptom clusters are:
- intrusion (i.e., memories or dreams)
- avoidance (i.e., memories or reminders)
- negative alterations in cognitions and mood (i.e., persistent negative beliefs or emotional state), and
- alterations in arousal and reactivity (i.e., irritability or hypervigilance).

Two specifications are also included: delayed expression and dissociation.

Despite the considerable revisions to the *DSM-5*, it is estimated that rates of PTSD will be comparable to rates required for the *DSM-IV* criteria (O'Donnell et al., 2014). Rates of PTSD vary depending on biopsychosocial factors. For instance, most of the epidemiological studies now demonstrate that women are twice as likely to have a diagnosis of PTSD (Slade et al., 2007) and for considerably longer.

Diagnostic criteria for PTSD

The *DSM-5* criteria for PTSD 309.81 (ICD-10 F43.10) include symptoms from each of the four clusters previously mentioned following exposure to an actual or threatened death, serious injury, or sexual violence. Additionally, the persistence of symptoms (in Criteria B, C, D and E) exist for more than 1 month, and there is significant symptom-related distress or functional impairment (e.g., social, occupational), and disturbance is not due to medication, substance use, or other illness.

Australia

PTSD has emerged as a worldwide major public health concern, especially in areas experiencing high levels of armed conflict (Davidson, 2000). Published global estimates of the prevalence of PTSD vary because of cultural differences and differing statistical methods of measurement. In Australia, approximately 60% of men and 50% of women will experience an explicit threat or trauma to themselves or another during their lifetime, often repeatedly (Creamer, Burgess, & McFarlane, 2001). Although resilience is the norm, a small percentage will develop PTSD. The respective Australian lifetime and prevalence rates of PTSD are estimated at 7.2% and 4.4% (McEvoy, Grove, & Slade, 2011) or approximately 1 million Australians at any time. Comparative NZ rates for lifetime and 12-month prevalence rates are 6.0% and 3.0% (Oakley Browne, Wells, & Scott, 2006); for the United States the rates are 6.8% and 3.5% (Kessler et al., 2005).

An Australian study which examined the psychological sequelae of those admitted to a major metropolitan hospital suffering traumatic injury found that 10% were likely to have a primary diagnosis of PTSD at both 3 and 12 months and a further 10% with depression. A frequent comorbidity of PTSD is major depression (O'Donnell et al., 2004). A recent longitudinal Australian cohort study across four hospital trauma departments examined the psychiatric sequelae of traumatic injury following admission. The results indicated that at 12 months post-injury, 31% were diagnosed with a psychiatric disorder and of these 6% were diagnosed with PTSD. Those with mild traumatic brain injury (MTBI) were found to have approximately twice the rate of PTSD (Bryant et al., 2010). This finding has significant ramifications for veterans returning from conflicts in the Middle East who have been exposed to improvised explosive devises. Interestingly, the 2010 ADF Mental Health Prevalence and Wellbeing Study Report (McFarlane et al., 2011) noted that the estimated 12-month prevalence rate of PTSD among Australian Defence Force (ADF) personnel was 8.3%, which is significantly higher than in the general Australian community.

Although Australia's Indigenous populations make up approximately 3% of Australia's overall population (Australian Institute of Health and Welfare [AIHW], 2013), almost nothing is known of their rates of psychiatric disorders, especially PTSD. A recent systematic review by Black et al. (2015) of empirical quantitative studies which reported prevalence rates found only four studies of PTSD in this population, and three of these specifically used incarcerated populations. Rates varied between 14.2% of males (current prevalence) to 49.2% for females (1-year prevalence) in the prison samples. The only community sample was of remote Aboriginal communities in Western Australia where PTSD was found to be at lifetime prevalence rates of 55.2% (Nadew, 2012).

Treatment of PTSD

Phoenix Australia – Centre for Posttraumatic Mental Health has recently developed clinical practice guidelines for treating both ASD and PTSD, particularly in Australia. The National Health and Medical Research Council (NHMRC) has ratified these guidelines, and the Royal Australian and New Zealand College of Psychiatrists, Royal Australian College of General Practitioners and the Australian Psychological Society have recognised them as the best evidence-based intervention. The guidelines recommend implementing efficacious trauma-focused psychological therapy. This includes:

- trauma-focused cognitive behaviour therapy (CBT), and
- eye movement desensitisation and reprocessing (EMDR).

The essential feature of trauma-focused therapy is re-engaging trauma memories in a safe, managed, and systematic way until the memory no longer evokes significant distress. This process is particularly emotionally confronting so the patient will need to feel safe, understand the treatment rationale, and learn to manage and reduce their arousal. They must understand the role of both avoidant responses and behaviours in maintaining core PTSD symptoms, and learn to challenge them and the associated memories in a controlled way. Evidence-based therapies are time limited and usually require up to 12 sessions. Complex PTSD may require more sessions. Longer sessions such as 90 minutes are recommended for exposure therapy and EMDR, to reduce distress. While trauma-focused therapies are an effective PTSD treatment, dropout rates are relatively high. Many who complete therapy still retain their PTSD diagnosis (Schnyder, 2005).

Psychological first aid (PFA) is recommended immediately following trauma, not therapy. PFA promotes resilience by providing basic assistance as well as physical and emotional support. It also enhances a sense of safety, calmness, self-efficacy and connectedness, and instils hope. Watchful waiting is advised using a stepped-care approach for the first few weeks following trauma exposure before assessing for ASD (Wade et al., 2013).

Complicating matters is the fact that psychiatric comorbidity frequently presents with PTSD. These conditions include depression, substance abuse, pain, and anxiety disorders. Many of these disorders (such as pain) have a comorbid bidirectional relationship with PTSD which escalates the disorder. For instance, chronic pain may activate memories of the trauma. When these additional conditions are appropriately diagnosed and treated, a successful outcome is more likely (Creamer et al., 2001; Liedl, et al., 2010). Thus, treating PTSD often requires a multi-modal approach.

Speciality treatment guidelines and/or interest groups relevant to PTSD can be found via websites of the following organisations:

- Phoenix Australia, Centre for Posttraumatic Mental Health (http://phoenixaustralia. org/)
- Australia Guidelines (http://phoenixaustralia.org/resources/ptsd-guidelines/) for the treatment of:
  - acute stress disorder
  - posttraumatic stress disorder.
- Australian Psychological Society (Trauma and Psychology Interest Group; https:// groups.psychology.org.au/tapig/).

Structured interviews (CAPS-5 for *DSM-5*)

The clinician-administered PTSD scale (CAPS) is the gold standard diagnostic interview. The CAPS-5 is a 30-item structured interview questionnaire. It is used to determine either a past month or lifetime diagnosis of PTSD, or to assess PTSD symptoms in the previous week. Also available is a version for children and adolescents ages 7 and above (CAPS-CA-5).

The CAPS-5 is similar to previous versions which determined symptom severity ratings from both symptom frequency and intensity but in the current version these scores are combined to produce a single overall severity score. Severity ratings can range from nil, mild, moderate, severe to extreme. Nil notes a respondent's information either did not fulfil the *DSM-5* criteria or reported nil affect, while extreme indicates a respondent describes symptoms that are well above threshold and are distressing, intractable, and ubiquitous.

No Australian norms are currently available for the CAPS-5. The questionnaire and Information on the PSS-I (PTSD Symptom Scale Interview) are available via the National Center for PTSD at www.ptsd.va.gov. Similarly, no Australian norms are currently available for the PSS-I.

To determine PTSD status, each symptom is dichotomised as either present or absent. Symptoms are marked as present if the corresponding severity score is rated 2 or more. According to (Weathers et al., 2013), the *DSM-5* PTSD criteria require the following (along with the time, disturbance and exposure to stressor/trauma criteria previously noted):

- at least one intrusive symptom
- at least one avoidance symptom
- at least two negative alterations in mood/cognitions
- at least two alterations in arousal and reactivity.

Self-report questionnaires

Various self-report measures of PTSD are available, including the following.

- PTSD Checklist for *DSM-5* (PCL-5). This is a 20-item self-report measure that assesses the 20 *DSM-5* symptoms of PTSD. Its uses include monitoring, screening, and provisional diagnosis of PTSD.
- Posttraumatic Diagnostic Scale (PDS). The PDS is a 49-item self-report measure used to measure severity of PTSD symptoms. It assesses the *DSM-IV* criteria.

Other self-report measures include the Davidson Trauma Scale (DTS) and Impact of Event Scale – Revised (IES-R) and are available from the National Center for PTSD at www.ptsd.va.gov. There are no Australian norms currently available for the previously mentioned tests.

Specialist agencies providing treatment for PTSD include the following.

- Phoenix Australia – Centre for Posttraumatic Mental Health.
- Private psychologists funded by Medicare specialising in PTSD. A referral is required from a general practitioner (GP) under the auspices of a GP Mental Health Care Plan.
- The Department of Veterans' Affairs (DVA) and Vietnam Veterans Counselling Service (VVCS) provide counselling for veterans and their families.
- Victims of Crime (VOC) in the relevant states provide counselling for victims and their families.
- WorkCover will fund counselling for injury that has occurred in the workplace. Referral from a GP is required.
- Compulsory Third Party (CTP) insurance scheme may also cover for counselling of road accident trauma. Referral from a GP is required.

New Zealand

Approximately 40% of New Zealanders will incur either a mental illness or substance abuse disorder during their lifetime (Oakley Browne, Wells, Scott, & McGee, 2006). Of these, there is a lifetime prevalence of 6% and 12-month prevalence of 3.0% for PTSD (Oakley Browne, Wells, & Scott, 2006). As reflected in worldwide statistics, females have a significantly higher prevalence of PTSD than males. The 12-month prevalence of PTSD among women is 4.2% compared with 1.6% for men (Oakley Browne, Wells, & Scott, 2006). Among the Māori, lifetime prevalence rates of PTSD are 9.7% and 12-month prevalence rates are 4.5% (Baxter, 2008).

As previously noted, PTSD often presents comorbidly with many other psychiatric disorders. These disorders may predate or evolve with the development of PTSD. Data from the longitudinal Dunedin Multidisciplinary Health and Development Study found that 100% of those diagnosed with past-year PTSD and 93.5% of those with lifetime PTSD at age 26 experienced a different mental disorder between the ages of 11 and 21 (Koenen et al., 2008). This study also found that adverse early childhood factors such as low IQ, antisocial behaviour, and poverty before age 11 predict PTSD in those exposed to trauma in adulthood. It is likely that these factors increase both risk to trauma exposure and PTSD (Koenen et al., 2007). Severe childhood maltreatment alone also significantly increases the risk of PTSD in later life (Breslau et al., 2014). It is likely that the process of sensitisation is a dynamic influence in this outcome.

NZ has a culturally diverse population and a unique geography. Recently, it has experienced a number of serious earthquakes, most notably in Christchurch in 2011 when 185 people died and thousands were injured. The Christchurch Health and Development Study, a longitudinal study of over 35 years' duration, found that the rate of mental disorders in people with high levels of exposure to the earthquakes was appropriately 1.4 times higher than for those not exposed. The study reported increased rates of PTSD, anxiety disorders, major depression, and nicotine dependence (Fergusson et al., 2014). Another study assessed the psychological reactions of adolescent students from six high schools in Christchurch. It took place 6 months after the earthquake and found clinically significant PTSD symptoms for 24% of the sample, with females experiencing significantly greater levels of PTSD (Heetkamp & de Terte, 2015).

Prison inmates in NZ also have high rates of PTSD, up to 45% (Brinded et al., 2001). Also, refugees who have experienced trauma have elevated rates of PTSD; for example, a prevalence rate of 12% among Cambodian refugees in Dunedin (Cheung, 1994).

Treatment of PTSD

As mentioned previously, Phoenix Australia – Centre for Posttraumatic Mental Health presents clinical practice guidelines for treating both ASD and PTSD. The Royal

Australian and New Zealand College of Psychiatrists endorsed these guidelines as relevant for use in both Australia and NZ and published a review of the guidelines in 2013. No NZ norms are available and clinicians should refer to the assessment protocols listed for Australia.

Speciality treatment guidelines and/or interest groups relevant to PTSD can be found via websites of the following organisations:

- New Zealand Psychological Society, Institute of Clinical Psychology (www. psychology.org.nz/membership/member-groups/institute-of-clinical-psychology/#. V7rt5Pl961s)
- Australian and New Zealand Association for the Treatment of Sexual Abuse (ANZATSA; www.anzatsa.org).

NZ has many resources for those requiring specialist psychological treatment. GPs can refer to the local community mental health centre and to ProCare PHO (Primary Health Organisation). Their clients may be eligible for funded GP mental healthcare and access to four to six sessions of psychological intervention and a psychiatric review. Those requiring long-term assistance can access a key worker or a publicly funded psychologist or psychiatrist.

Also the Accident Compensation Corporation (ACC) provides comprehensive, no-fault personal injury cover for all NZ residents and visitors. Those who have experienced sexual abuse or assault may be eligible for ACC support to pay for therapy with a clinical psychologist or psychotherapist. GPs are able to make this referral for a Sensitive Claim.

Finally, for those requiring counselling related to their disability or health condition and in hardship, there is provision via Work and Income (NZ Ministry of Social Development). Work and Income may assist in access and payment for counselling. Those in paid employment may be able to access free counselling through their company's Employee Assistance Programme.

Australian case study

This case has been created as an example for illustrative purposes.

Bob Sample is a 45-year-old man who lived approximately 50 km north-east of Melbourne. The area was heavily wooded with dense undergrowth. He had lived there all of his life and built the home that he lived in. Prior to that Saturday, there had been a long drought and an unprecedented hot spell. Several of the days had recorded temperatures of 45 °C. On that Saturday even the dawn was hot and once the sun rose, the heat quickly became unbearable. Several hours later, it had been reported that there was a bushfire which was threatening homes. The threat soon expanded to the whole district and everyone was ordered to evacuate. Bob thought he could save his home as he had built it and knew that he was very well prepared. He also had a bunker where he could retreat. He was still conflicted as to what he should do and in the meantime sent his family away. Once he saw the billowing clouds in the distance, he knew that the decision had been made for him.

Bob had the generator and water pumps going, and had lowered all of the shutters around the home and cleared all possible debris. He was hosing down the home when he noticed the roar was becoming louder and it was becoming more difficult to breathe. The heat was now at the point of suffocation. He decided that now was the time to make his way to the bunker and it was not a moment too soon. As he got into the bunker and looked out across the field, spot fires were breaking out spontaneously in front of him. He could see fire leaping into the sky, then heard what sounded like an explosion as it hit faster than he could have imagined. At that moment, it was all very intense. The noise was overwhelming and it was dark. Although the bunker was supposed to be airtight, smoke was just billowing into the space while oxygen was being sucked out.

Initially, Bob thought he would be okay but he began to panic and was overwhelmed with fear as his situation became more perilous. He was breathing through a wet towel and lying on the ground gasping for air but realised that if this continued much longer he would perish. He thought about his family and the seemingly needless danger that he was now in. He decided that should he survive he would conduct his life differently. Bob noticed blisters on his exposed skin and wondered who would be the first person to find him. He hoped it would not be his family. Bob wept as he thought about this scenario. Bob remained in the bunker for what seemed like hours but eventually the noise subsided and he ventured out. What confronted him looked like a blackened moonscape.

Within a few weeks, Bob was back trying to negotiate with banks and insurance companies but would often find himself getting into a rage very quickly, especially when negotiating with them. He was becoming increasingly isolated from his family and friends, began experiencing nightmares, and found it difficult to get back to sleep at night. Bob would not talk about his experience in the bunker. It was almost a mystery to his family, as he would evade conversations about it. The family also noticed that Bob was a lot more reactive and would spend more time drinking. One night, Bob almost got into a fight with a local resident, which was completely out of character for him. Bob's family told his GP about their concerns, and as he had other medical issues they got him to agree to make an appointment. After seeing the GP, with whom he had a good relationship, Bob was referred to a local clinical psychologist.

During assessment, Bob completed the CAPS-5 and met the criteria for PTSD. He had also developed a sleep disorder and was displaying symptoms of depression. When Bob heard this he was relieved, as he thought he was losing control of his mind. The treatment rationale was thoroughly explained to him and he understood the procedure. He was taught about sleep hygiene, the importance of exercise, and curtailing his drinking to safe levels. Treatment for PTSD included repeating the trauma memory in a prolonged graded way until it no longer evoked the same level of distress (imaginal exposure); and confronting the situations which he had been avoiding in a prolonged and graded way (in vivo exposure). Finally, Bob was able to unpack in a controlled way the memories and some of the irrational interpretations about his experience that had been restricting his recovery (cognitive therapy).

Following therapy over 6 months, Bob has become significantly less symptomatic and although he still had some signs, he no longer met criteria for PTSD.

Australia – websites

- Further information is available at Phoenix Australia – Centre for Posttraumatic Mental Health, which is the leader in Australia (see http://phoenixaustralia.org).
- Australasian Society for Traumatic Stress Studies provides helpful online resources (see www.astss.org.au).

New Zealand – websites

- The Royal Australian and New Zealand College of Psychiatrists provides some useful links and information (https://www.ranzcp.org/Publications/Guidelines-for-clinical-practice/PTSD-practice-guidelines.aspx).
- Skylight is a national organisation with resources for the community and professionals (http://skylight.org.nz/).

References

American Psychiatric Association. (2013). *Diagnostic and statistical manual of mental disorders* (5th ed.). Arlington, VA: Author.

Australian Institute of Health and Welfare. (2013). *Australia's welfare 2013*. Australia's welfare no. 11. Cat. no. AUS 174 (pp. 3–42). Canberra: Author.

Baxter, J. (2008). *Māori mental health needs profile. A review of the evidence*. Palmerston North: TeRau Matatini.

Black, E., Ranmuthugala, G., Kondalsamy-Chennakesavan, S., Toombs, M., Nicholson, G., & Kisely, S. (2015). A systematic review: Identifying the prevalence rates of psychiatric disorder in Australia's Indigenous populations. *Australian & New Zealand Journal of Psychiatry, 49*(5), 412–429.

Breslau, N., Koenen, K., Swanson, S., Agnew-Blais, M., Houts, R., Poulton, R., & Moffitt, T. (2014). Childhood maltreatment, juvenile disorders and adult post-traumatic stress disorder: A prospective investigation. *Psychological Medicine, 44*(9), 1937–1945.

Brinded. P., Simpson, A., Laidlaw, T., Fairley, N., & Malcolm, F. (2001). Prevalence of psychiatric disorders in New Zealand prisons: A national study. *Australian & New Zealand Journal of Psychiatry, 35*, 166–183.

Bryant, R., Creamer, M., O'Donnell, M., Silove, D., & McFarlane, A. (2008). A multisite study of the capacity of acute stress disorder diagnosis to predict posttraumatic stress disorder. *Journal of Clinical Psychiatry, 69*, 923–929.

Bryant, R., O'Donnell, M., Creamer, M., McFarlane, A., Clark, R., & Silove, D. (2010). The psychiatric sequelae of traumatic injury. *American Journal of Psychiatry, 167*(3), 312–320.

Cheung, P. (1994). Post-traumatic stress disorder among Cambodians in New Zealand. *International Journal of Social Psychiatry, 40*, 17–26.

Creamer, M., Burgess, P., & McFarlane, A. (2001). Post-traumatic stress disorder: Findings from the Australian national survey of mental health and wellbeing. *Psychological Medicine, 31*, 1237–1247.

Davidson, J. (2000). New strategies for the treatment of posttraumatic stress. *Journal of Clinical Psychiatry, 61*, 3–51.

Fergusson, D., Horwood, L., Boden, J., & Mulder, R. (2014). Impact of a major disaster on the mental health of a well-studied cohort. *JAMA Psychiatry, 71*(9), 1025–1031.

Forbes, D., Lockwood, E., Phelps, A., Wade, D., Creamer, M., Bryant, R., McFarlane, A., Silove, D., Rees, S., Chapman, C., Slade, T., Mills, K., Teesson, M., & O'Donnell, M. (2014). Trauma at the hands of another: Distinguishing PTSD patterns following intimate and nonintimate interpersonal and noninterpersonal trauma in a nationally representative sample. *Journal of Clinical Psychiatry, 75*(2), 147–153.

Heetkamp, T., & de Terte, I. (2015). PTSD and resilience in adolescents after New Zealand earthquakes. *New Zealand Journal of Psychology, 44*, 1.

Kessler, R., Berglund, P., Delmer, O., Jin, R., Merikangas, K., & Walters, E. (2005). Lifetime prevalence and age-of-onset distributions of DSM-IV disorders in the national comorbidity survey replication. *Archives of General Psychiatry, 62*(6), 593–602.

Koenen, K., Moffitt, T., Caspi, A., Gregory, A., Harrington, H., & Poulton, R. (2008). The developmental mental-disorder histories of adults with posttraumatic stress disorder: A prospective longitudinal birth cohort study. *Journal of Abnormal Psychology, 117*, 460–466.

Koenen, K., Moffitt, T., Poulton, R., Martin, J., & Caspi, A. (2007). Early childhood factors associated with the development of post-traumatic stress disorder: Results from a longitudinal birth cohort. *Psychological Medicine, 37*, 181–192.

Liedl, A., O'Donnell, M., Creamer, M., Silove, D., McFarlane, A., Knaevelsrud, C., & Bryant, R. (2010). Support for the mutual maintenance of pain and post-traumatic stress disorder symptoms. *Psychological Medicine, 40*(7), 1215–1223.

McEvoy, P., Grove, R., & Slade, T. (2011). Epidemiology of anxiety disorders in the Australian general population: Findings of the 2007 Australian National Survey of Mental Health and Wellbeing. *Australian & New Zealand Journal of Psychiatry, 45*, 957–967.

McFarlane, A. (1990). An Australian disaster: The 1983 bushfires. *International Journal of Mental Health, 19*, 36–47.

McFarlane, A. (2010). The long-term costs of traumatic stress: Intertwined physical and psychological consequences. *World Psychiatry, 9*, 3–10.

McFarlane, A., Hodson, S., Van Hooff, M., & Davies, C. (2011). *Mental health in the Australian Defence Force: 2010 ADF mental health and wellbeing study: Full report*, Canberra: Department of Defence.

Nadew, G. (2012). Exposure to traumatic events, prevalence of posttraumatic stress disorder and alcohol abuse in Aboriginal communities. *Rural and Remote Health, 12*, 1667.

Oakley Browne, M., Wells, J., & Scott, K. (Eds.). (2006). *Te Rau Hinengaro: The New Zealand mental health survey*. Wellington, NZ: Ministry of Health.

Oakley Browne, M., Wells, J., Scott, K., & McGee, M. (2006). Lifetime prevalence and projected lifetime risk of DSM-IV disorders in Te Rau Hinengaro: The New Zealand mental health survey. *The Australian & New Zealand Journal of Psychiatry, 40*(10), 865–874.

O'Donnell, M., Alkemade, N., Nickerson, A., Creamer, M., McFarlane, A., Silove, D., Bryant, R., & Forbes, D. (2014). The impact of the diagnostic changes to posttraumatic stress disorder for DSM-5 and the proposed changes to ICD-11. *British Journal of Psychiatry, 205*, 230–235.

O'Donnell, M., Creamer, M., Pattison, P., & Atkin, C. (2004). Psychiatric morbidity following injury. *American Journal of Psychiatry, 161*, 507–514.

Parslow, R., Jorm, A., & Christensen, H. (2006). Associations of pre-trauma attributes and trauma exposure with screening positive for PTSD: Analysis of a community-based study of 2085 young adults. *Psychological Medicine, 36*, 387–595.

Scheeringa, M., Zeanah, C., & Cohen, J. (2011). PTSD in children and adolescents: Toward an empirically based algorithm. *Depression and Anxiety, 28*, 770–782.

Schnyder, U. (2005). Why new psychotherapies for posttraumatic stress disorder? *Psychotherapy and Psychosomatics, 74*, 199–201.

Slade, T., Johnston, A., Oakley Browne, M., Andrews, G., & Whiteford, H. (2007). National survey of mental health and wellbeing: Methods and key findings Australian and New Zealand. *Journal of Psychiatry, 43*, 594–605.

Wade, D., Howard, A., Fletcher, S., Cooper, J., & Forbes, D. (2013). Early response to psychological trauma: What GPs can do. *Australian Family Physician, 42*, 610–614.

Weathers, F., Blake, D., Schnurr, P., Kaloupek, D., Marx, B., & Keane, T. (2013). The clinician-administered PTSD scale for DSM-5 (CAPS-5). National Center for PTSD. Available: www.ptsd.va.gov

15

Dissociative disorders and somatic symptoms and related disorders

Martin Dorahy and Indra Mohan

Dissociative disorders

Integrating what we see, hear, smell, taste, touch, feel, think, and do into a relatively unified experience is essential for our functioning. Integrating these different psychological, physiological, and behavioural aspects into a web of interacting memories, feelings, and actions fosters a more continuous sense of self (i.e., integration of the personality) and assists smooth and flexible interactions with the self, the environment, and other people. Dissociative disorders are characterised by a failure of this capacity. They are founded in dissociation, a disruption in the ability to bring together aspects of an experience or personality.

The *Diagnostic and Statistical Manual of Mental Disorders* (5th ed.; *DSM-5*; American Psychiatric Association, 2013) contains three discrete dissociative disorders: dissociative amnesia (DA); depersonalisation/derealisation disorder (DRD); and dissociative identity disorder (DID). There are also two broader categories with less discrete and specific criteria: other specific dissociative disorder (OSDD) and unspecified dissociative disorder (USDD). They are used when someone experiences debilitating symptoms that do not meet the previous discrete diagnoses. The core feature of DA (*DSM-5* and ICD shared code F44.0) is the inability to recall information laid down in memory (i.e., encoded) about events one has experienced (e.g., autobiographical). This so-called reversible autobiographical memory loss is more serious and distressing than ordinary forgetfulness and is not caused by neurological injury or substance intoxication. The non-retrieved material is typically stressful in nature, such as the central details of being involved in a car accident where a loved one is killed. The person with DA typically has no problems learning new material or engaging in new or previously learned tasks. Amnesia may be localised, relating to a specific time period in the person's life in which they have little or selective memory (selective amnesia), or more rarely generalised, in which the person has a complete loss of memory for their life history. This total loss is experienced as one-half of the symptom profile for what is called dissociative fugue. Dissociative fugue is a subtype of DA. In addition to generalised amnesia for one's own identity (e.g., losing awareness of one's name, age, and history) it involves purposeful travel away from one's home or work, or wandering in a bewildered daze. DA can be diagnosed with (F44.1) or without (F44.0) dissociative fugue. In the clinical setting, clinicians speak of overt amnesia where the patient presents with dramatic and profound loss of memory (as in fugue) or covert amnesia, where the patient conceals their gaps or losses of memory and the amnesia is less dense. The likelihood of DA seems to increase if the traumatic experience:

- is perpetrated by a loved one, or someone who the person trusts
- involves threats from the perpetrator not to disclose
- is repeated and prolonged, and
- starts younger.

DRD (F48.1) is characterised by depersonalisation and/or derealisation. Depersonalisation is denoted by alterations in an individual's perception of their self. This can mean feeling detached from one's own body, and in extreme cases experiencing your own body as an outside observer. Other depersonalisation experiences include feeling like an automaton, a robot, or in a dream, and having one's movements, thoughts, and feelings initiated outside wilful control. Derealisation revolves around distorted perceptions of one's surroundings, where people and objects appear fuzzy, visually distorted, two-dimensional, or dream-like. DRD can be diagnosed when one or both symptom sets are present, and causes significant distress or impairment in daily functioning. Crucially, while those with DRD experience major alterations in the perception of self and their surroundings, they are aware of this and do not create delusional beliefs to account for their experiences. Thus, their reality testing remains intact. Depersonalisation and derealisation experiences are common in the general population and are particularly heightened during times of intensified, transitory stress (e.g., unexpected death of family member) and in late adolescence when identity is still somewhat unstable. Depersonalisation and derealisation symptoms are common in anxiety and other disorders. Those with DRD often experience comorbid psychiatric conditions, like anxiety and depressive disorders.

DID (F44.81) is reflected in the existence of two or more discrete identities with their own sense of self – their own memories, feelings, abilities to initiate actions, and their ways of engaging with the world. These identities, and how they influence the way the person experiences their self and engages with the world, depletes their ability to cope with variation in their environments. Instead of having one relatively coherent personality and view of the self, they have multiple (often not well formed) views of the self and a relatively incoherent personality representation. Dissociative identities may manifest in quite overt ways, with marked differences in demeanour, speech, gait, maturity level (e.g., age), and interaction style. This is explained as "possession" in some settings. Typically, dissociative identities, and movements between them, are more subtle and less noticeable. Movement between dissociative identities ("switching") can be triggered by increased stress, internal conflicts, threat, and changes in the environment. By nature, dissociative identities and the psychobiophysiological characteristics which make them up, are not well integrated. People with DID can report having no awareness of some, most, or all of their identities. Thus, they report amnesia, typically when identities that the person has less conscious access to are guiding their behaviour. Consequently, memory gaps can encompass everyday events, previous significant non-distressing events, and traumatic experiences. Dissociative identities are more discretely elaborated psychobiological constructions than the different states, action systems, and motivational drives that make up normal personality development. In addition, moving between dissociative identities lacks the continuous sense of self, time, and agency that is evident when non-dissociative individuals move between different feelings (e.g., excitement to terror) or different motivational systems (e.g., caregiving to protection).

OSDD (F44.89) captures dissociative symptom presentations that cause distress but do not meet full diagnostic criteria for DA, DRD, or DID. Examples of symptom presentations under this more nebulous category are:

- having dissociative identities without experiencing DA
- experiencing major confusion about one's identity, associated with prolonged coercive treatment (e.g., torture)
- short-duration dissociative responses to stressful events, and
- trance states where the individual loses awareness of their surroundings.

The OSDD category allows clinicians to specify more clearly why the symptoms do not meet criteria for one of the discrete dissociative disorders. The USDD (F44.9) category is used when the clinician does not wish to state the reasons the symptom presentation fails the criteria for DA, DRD, or DID.

Australia

Internationally, dissociative disorders are highly contentious diagnoses. Disputes centre around whether DID and DA exist as legitimate and discrete diagnostic entities, and how closely they are associated with exposure to overwhelming traumatic events (e.g., Lynn et al., 2012). Questions such as: "Can trauma be forgotten and later remembered?", "Can the human psyche divide itself into multiple (dissociative) identities?" and "Is the presence of dissociative identities associated with an effort to psychologically survive childhood trauma by an attachment figure?" have driven conflicting positions. The weight of scientific data is easing this tension and an empirically derived understanding is taking shape (e.g., Dorahy et al., 2014). However, the controversy over the existence of DID and DA in recent decades has led practitioners to take quite polarised positions.

On the one hand, people denied the existence of DID and DA as diagnostic entities, arguing that overzealous therapists influenced suggestible patients to enact these conditions. Thus, the link to trauma exposure was part of the therapist's explanation for the patient's problems. Through therapy, the patient came to share this understanding; for example, believing they were abused in their childhood (Piper & Merskey, 2004). This position largely ignored the presence of abuse exposure in the patient's life or downplayed its psychological effect. From the alternate perspective, DID and DA were seen as disorders intimately associated with exposure to trauma and abuse. Here, childhood trauma caused the psyche to divide and develop multiple dissociative identities with different memories, feelings, behaviours, views of themselves, and memories (Ross, 1997). For DA, child, and adult traumas, especially those involving an attachment figure (e.g., parent or lover), *may* be separated from consciousness awareness and seemingly not available for voluntary recall (Freyd & Birrell, 2013). Historically, the perspective that trauma leads to dissociation (e.g., DID, DA) has downplayed the role of factors like suggestibility and the influence of the therapist (Dalenberg et al., 2014). The debate about DID and DA has been most evident in the United States (US), but also occurs in Europe. Yet, shifts from these polarised positions have taken place (Dalenberg et al., 2012, 2014; Lynn et al., 2014).

There is some scepticism within mental health ranks in Australia and New Zealand about the legitimacy of dissociative disorders (e.g., Leonard, Brann, & Tiller, 2005). However, both countries have largely avoided the ferocity of sentiment evident elsewhere. Literature on DID and DA has taken a more measured position, exemplified by Warwick Middleton, Australia's foremost expert on dissociative disorders. Middleton (2004, pp. 245–246) identifies six guiding principles when navigating work with patients and professionals around dissociative disorders that hold the middle ground and avoid polarisation.

1. Never extrapolate or make assumptions that go beyond verified clinical data.
2. Don't personalise issues when colleagues hold differing views.
3. With respect to the acceptance of dissociative disorders, as with most issues in life, it is counterproductive to spend time trying to convince people of things they don't want to know.
4. It is unwise to view dissociative patients, or the scientific and clinical issues concerning them, as "special."
5. In having an interest in dissociation, it is unhelpful both clinically and professionally to abandon virtually all other roles, such that one stays perpetually immersed in trauma-related countertransference (i.e., being emotionally impacted on by the horrible experiences of patients).
6. The most effective way of advancing clinical and scientific knowledge about patients in the dissociative spectrum is to do the best clinical work possible, to work with colleagues and staff in developing programs that tangibly improve outcomes and management options, to support and contribute to relevant research, to remain friendly and accessible to all colleagues, and to assist in convening seminars and conferences open to anyone interested.

Treatment and treatment services

Internationally, dissociative disorders have not attracted the broad clinical and research interest that posttraumatic stress disorder has, despite sharing a close association with exposure to trauma and some overlapping symptoms (e.g., flashbacks, DA, and depersonalisation/derealisation; Carlson, Dalenberg, & McDade-Montez, 2012). PTSD is more prevalent, which may account for the greater interest. More subtle dynamics may also be at play – the association between DDs and severe prolonged child abuse confronts both society and health professionals with painful truths that are very hard to face (e.g., Herman, 1992). DDs challenge the notion of humans as mentally unified and coherent beings that underpins western social and philosophical beliefs about people having self-awareness, personal responsibility and agency, and free will (Dorahy et al., 2014). Individuals understand the nature of the human condition through different paradigms, some that adequately account for conditions like DID and others that dismiss or ignore them (Manning & Manning, 2009).

The mainstay treatment for DDs, as outlined in the International Society for the Study of Trauma and Dissociation guidelines (ISSTD, 2011) and deemed most valuable by Australian patients (Leonard et al., 2005), is individual psychotherapy that takes a phase-oriented approach. This approach suggests organising treatment for DDs around three sequential phases that may be repeated, or moved backwards and forwards (Cloitre et al., 2012; ISSTD, 2011; Van der Hart, Nijenhuis, & Steele, 2006). The first phase (establishing safety, stabilisation, and symptom reduction) seeks to stabilise the patient by: helping them with anxiety and depression symptoms; managing any self-harm, addictive, or impulsive behaviours; building skills to tolerate feelings; and learning how to regulate dissociation symptoms and times of overwhelming distress. This phase attempts to build the individual's resources to move towards phase two of treatment (confronting, working through, and integrating traumatic memories), which is focused on dealing with the person's trauma memories from the past (and all the associated fears, feelings, behaviours, and strategies of avoidances) that led them to develop the disorder. The third phase (identity integration and rehabilitation) works to integrate remaining dissociative parts, and help the person engage more fully with daily life, including intimate relationships.

Other forms of therapy may supplement individual psychological therapy, including group therapy, medication use (pharmacotherapy), family or parent–child work, and brief inpatient hospitalisations (Amos, Furber, & Segal, 2011; ISSTD, 2011). In Australia, clinicians and therapists provide most DID treatment on an individual basis. Australia also has a dedicated program for treating DDs, especially DID and OSDD, at Belmont Private Hospital in Brisbane. This Trauma and Dissociation Unit (TDU) has been operating since January 1997, offering a range of treatments (Middleton & Higson, 2004). The unit operates with an ethos of open communication, strong personal and interpersonal boundaries, and an empathic understanding of the complexity of patients' problems, while promoting personal responsibility and general understanding that their problems are no more special and unique than others (Middleton & Higson,

2004). Admission comes via psychiatrists with admitting rights, but patients from all over Australia come for short inpatient stays and are then referred back to their treating therapist.

In the 12 months from October 2013, 76% of inpatients were from the greater Brisbane area, 6% from other parts of Queensland and 18% from interstate (M. Williams, Area Manager, personal communication, 18 December 2014). Inpatient stays allow patients to do focused pieces of psychotherapy, often related to their trauma history or dissociative symptom, with support from highly skilled staff. The inpatient program has 12 beds and focuses on skills building and psychoeducation (L. Seager, Unit Manager, personal communication, 15 December 2014). The average length of stay is 3 weeks, which allows for focused treatment. The numbers of inpatient admissions since October 2008 has ranged from 150 to 160 each year (M. Williams, Area Manager, personal communication, 18 December 2014). The outpatient program runs twice weekly for patients who have completed the inpatient program and involves group and individual work over approximately 6 hours each day. Focus is around support for daily living and ongoing individual therapy, and the program also has a strong psychoeducation component (L. Seager, Unit Manager, personal communication, 15 December 2014). Topics covered include boundaries, shame and guilt, fear and anxiety, balanced lifestyle, internal communication (e.g., communication between dissociative identities), and having fun (Middleton & Higson, 2004). Ninety-five per cent of patients attending the TDU are female. Research from this unit has shown that nursing staff dealing with the chronic trauma histories, complex relationship styles, and complicated symptom presentations of those with DID, are most effective when they demonstrate the capacity to tolerate and regulate strong and frightening feelings and behaviours. Patients also report benefit from staff who foster a safe and containing environment even during times of hostility, and maintain a working and compassionate therapeutic relationship (McAllister et al., 2001).

Research

Australia is notable for producing one of the first case studies on dissociative fugue (Maddison, 1953), during a time when such research had fallen from mainstream interest (see Van der Hart & Dorahy, 2009). Australian therapists published an early treatment report on behaviour therapy for DID (Price & Hess, 1979). Over the last 40 years, efforts to empirically understand dissociative disorders have amplified significantly (Dalenberg et al., 2007) with studies published in the US, Turkey, the United Kingdom, many countries in Europe, China, India, Japan, South Africa, and countries in Central and South America. Australian research has contributed strongly but has also been hamstrung by a lack of funding, a phenomenon shared by other countries. Nonetheless, Australian researchers have been particularly interested in the psychological features that characterise DID. Hopper et al. (2002) ran what they described as the first study of electroencephalogram (EEG) coherence in DID (see also Cocker, Edwards, Anderson, & Meares, 1994 for EEG research in DID). EEG coherence assesses the correlation between electrical activities in different parts of the brain. Having higher levels of coherence suggests higher connectivity between brain regions and is a sign of brain maturation. They examined DID participants in their host identity (the identity primarily in executive control) and in other ("alter") identities. They also assessed age and gender-matched actors mimicking host and alter-personalities. No differences were evident between the actors' host and alter-identities on EEG coherence and they did not differ between DID host identities. But the DID host identities had greater levels of coherence than DID alter-identities in some frontal, parietal, temporal, and central areas of the brain. The findings suggest neurophysiological difference in brain connectivity between DID host and alter-identities that could not be simulated by actors.

Middleton and Butler (1998) carried out the first Australian systematic assessment on 62 DID patients they had assessed (and in many cases treated) over 5 years from 1992 in hospital and private practice settings. All participants reported a history of complex childhood trauma in relationships with adults, typically their caregivers; the vast majority acknowledging sexual (81%) and physical (85%) abuse. Other complicated forms of early trauma include being locked in confined spaces (e.g., cupboards), exposed to extreme neglect (e.g., being locked out of the house), or experiencing emotional abuse (e.g., repeatedly undermined or bullied). Although not sought, in around a third of cases corroborating evidence of the reported abuse was obtained. A small but substantial number had abuse continuing well into adulthood (Middleton, 2013).

Middleton and Butler's Australian sample replicated the complex clinical picture so often seen in phenomenological studies of DID. As well as the expected high levels of dissociative symptoms (e.g., identity alterations, depersonalisation, derealisation, amnesia, trance states), nearly all met diagnostic criteria for past or current depression (94%) and posttraumatic stress disorder (PTSD). Borderline personality disorder criteria were reached in 76% of cases. Somatic symptoms (e.g., psychogenic pain and gastrointestinal problems) were evident in most cases, while disordered eating (35%), alcohol abuse (39%), and drug abuse (24%) were a problem in a significant minority of cases. DID is often misdiagnosed as schizophrenia or some other psychotic disorder. Yet Middleton and Butler (1998) found no evidence of thought disorder or bizarre delusions in any participants. They did find that 98% of their DID participants reported auditory hallucinations, while most also reported visual (74%), somatic (82%), olfactory (64%), and gustatory (52%) hallucinations. Despite the complex symptom profile, which other Australian researchers have replicated (Leonard et al., 2005), Middleton and Butler also noted a common finding that patients typically are not forthcoming about their dissociative symptoms. Perhaps due to shame, fear of being labelled psychotic, or not wanting to get too emotionally invested with another person, those with DID often try to cover up their symptoms. Thus, it becomes imperative to be sensitive when enquiring about dissociative symptoms.

Expanding the line of research on hallucinations in DID, Dorahy et al. (2009) drew DID and schizophrenia samples from Australia and Northern Ireland to compare experiences.

Schizophrenia has long been associated with auditory hallucinations. In the previous edition of the DSM (*DSM-IV*; American Psychiatric Association, 1994) schizophrenia could be diagnosed if voices were present and commenting on the person's behaviour. In line with Middleton and Butler (1998), research has also shown a high level of auditory hallucinations in DID. Because of the link between exposure to trauma and auditory hallucinations (e.g., Anketell et al., 2010), Dorahy et al. (2009) examined hallucinations in three samples: DID ($n = 29$); schizophrenia with a history of child abuse and neglect ($n = 16$); and schizophrenia with no child abuse and neglect history ($n = 18$). About half the participants in each sample reported their voices exclusively being heard internally. The DID group was more likely to report hearing both internal and external voices. Experiencing other forms of hallucinations (e.g., olfactory, visual) around the time of voice hearing incrementally increased in frequency from schizophrenia without abuse, to schizophrenia with abuse, to DID – suggesting a link between early trauma experiences and multiple, concurrent hallucinatory episodes. The DID sample differed from the two schizophrenia groups by having a greater likelihood of voices starting before 18 years of age, hearing more than two voices, and reporting both child and adult voices.

In further phenomenological research using Australian DID participants, Dorahy et al. (2015) explored dissociative, borderline personality, and Schneiderian symptoms. These latter symptoms reflect the first-rank positive symptoms of schizophrenia. Additionally, shame, exposure to child abuse, and complex posttraumatic stress symptoms were also examined. The DID sample ($n = 39$) were compared with a chronic posttraumatic stress disorder group (Chr-PTSD; $n = 13$) and a mixed psychiatric sample with anxiety and mood disorders (MP; $n = 21$). The DID sample had higher dissociative, borderline personality, and Schneiderian symptoms than the Chr-PTSD and MP groups, suggesting that these severe and chronic manifestations of psychopathology differentiate DID from chronic trauma, anxiety, and mood disorders. The DID sample also evidenced higher levels of shame, complex PTSD, and child abuse but only compared to the MP group. The findings offer further support to the complicated and severe symptom profile associated with DID in other studies (e.g., Middleton & Butler, 1998).

Experimental work on the functioning of memory and attention processes has become crucial in the understanding of DID, because of the lapses in autobiographical memory characterising DA (Dorahy, 2001; Huntjens et al., 2003). Bryant's (1995) case report of memory retrieval deficits across different dissociative identities in a 31-year-old Australian woman was one of the early attempts to study amnesia and the characteristics of memory retrieval in DID. Considerable international research has followed from this to understand the nature of reported memory problems in DID. Australian research on the dynamics of cognitive inhibition in DID has contributed to this knowledge base. Cognitive inhibition is associated with the ability to selectively attend to stimuli in the environment by withholding or inhibiting distracting information. Individuals with DID may exhibit a weakening in inhibitory processes (i.e., have less ability to withdraw distracting stimuli) especially when in a state of heightened anxiety (Dorahy, 2007; Dorahy,

Irwin, & Middleton, 2002). Weakened inhibition during increased anxiety may promote greater vigilance by allowing potential threat stimuli in the periphery of vision to be oriented to more quickly. In this way, weakened inhibition during times of threat might be adaptive in DID. However, weakened inhibition might also heighten the likelihood that dissociated mental content could intrude on conscious awareness, heightening flashbacks, and intrusive thoughts. In this case, weakened inhibition during heightened anxiety might underpin dissociative experiences (Dorahy, 2006). Research from the TDU supports the notion of weakened inhibition in DID during times of increased anxiety, with DID samples showing normal cognitive inhibitory operations when assessed in neutral, non-anxiety-provoking contexts, but reduced inhibitory capacity when assessed in contexts with heightened anxiety (i.e., when they were informed threat stimuli would be presented). Other psychiatric and control groups do not show this pattern of performance (Dorahy, Irwin, & Middleton, 2004; Dorahy, Middleton, & Irwin, 2005).

While not focusing specifically on dissociative disorders, much research in Australia has examined the construct of dissociation in both (non-dissociative disorder) clinical and non-clinical populations (Ashworth, Ciorciari, & Stough, 2008; Bryant & Panasetis, 2005; Collins & Ffrench, 1998; Devilly et al., 2007; Gow, Hutchinson, & Chant, 2009; Irwin, 1994b; Pullin, Webster, & Hanstock, 2014; Swannell et al., 2012; see also Collins, 2005). This work has included exploring the association between dissociation and psychotic symptoms, eating disorders, various emotions (e.g., shame, anger, guilt, unresolved grief) and traumatic experiences (e.g., childhood sexual abuse), as well as the link between dissociation and posttraumatic stress disorder (e.g., Bowen et al., 2010; Brown et al., 1999; Bryant et al., 2011; Goren et al., 2012; Hodgson & Webster, 2011; Irwin, 1994a, 1994b, 1996, 1998, 2001; O'Toole et al., 1999; Schumaker et al., 1994). In addition, distinguished Australian psychiatrist Russell Meares has used dissociation as a core component in his influential theory of borderline personality disorder (Meares, 2012).

New Zealand

There have been no systematic studies of dissociative disorders, including DID, in NZ, and no dedicated programs for treating dissociative disorders. Yet Aotearoa provides fertile ground for studying dissociative disorders, as several studies have fruitfully explored the construct of dissociation and both published and anecdotal evidence suggests clinicians and therapists treat dissociative disorders (e.g., Duncan et al., 2013; Gibney et al., 2013; Hooper, Dorahy, Blampied, & Jordan, 2014; Hudson, 2000). For example, in a Christchurch study, Mulder et al. (1998) found that dissociative symptoms were common and higher dissociation was associated directly with child physical abuse and having more concurrent psychiatric illnesses.

In an unpublished honours dissertation, Milne (2013) surveyed 119 NZ psychologists, psychotherapists, and counsellors and found that 19 were currently treating people for a dissociative disorder. Fifteen had treated someone for a dissociative disorder in the past 2 years. The Accident Compensation Corporation (ACC), a government entity administering the country's accidental injury scheme, and which provides funding for mental health problems directly related to childhood sexual abuse, reports currently supporting treatment for cases of dissociative disorder, primarily DID, around NZ, but exact figures do not exist (ACC, personal communication, 9 December, 2014).

Dissociation at a social and cultural level that may lead to inequalities in services like healthcare, has been explored in NZ, with Farrelly, Rudegeair, and Rickard (2005) noting it may have shaped differences in mental health rates and outcomes between Māori and New Zealanders of European descent (i.e., Pākehā). Māori have higher suicide, substance use, and mental illness rates. Farrelly et al. contend that the cultural trauma of colonisation, its intergenerational transmission, and the dissociation it evokes play a role in explaining this inequality.

Somatic symptom and related disorders

Somatoform disorders are ubiquitous in medical and clinical settings. They include a heterogeneous group of disorders with predominant focus on physical symptoms. The term "somatoform" originates from the Greek word *soma*, which means body, and reflects the mind–body dichotomy. Somatisation is a key component of these disorders, as is the manifestation of distress as bodily complaints, associated with physiological changes. These problems are often associated with illness, worry, and seeking help from various professionals and people. Somatoform disorders often have a chronic course and are highly disabling. In the *DSM-5*, somatoform disorders have gone through various changes and have recently metamorphosed into the new category of somatic symptom and related disorders. Mind–body dualism (perceiving the mind and body as two different things) unnecessarily creates the problem of excluding a medical condition from somatoform disorders, leading to significant changes in the *DSM-5* about this category. While somatic symptoms still relate to bodily symptoms without a recognisable physical origin, the focus is now more heavily on distress caused by bodily symptoms rather than on assessing if the bodily symptoms have a strict psychological origin (i.e., cannot be explained by any medical illness). In addition, *DSM-IV* conditions like somatisation disorder, hypochondriasis, somatoform pain disorder, and somatoform autonomic dysfunction (American Psychiatric Association, 1994) have been replaced by somatic symptom disorder. This may allow more inclusive and comprehensive clinical management of this condition.

The disorders included under the *DSM-5* category of somatic symptom and related disorders are:

1. somatic symptom disorder
2. illness anxiety disorder
3. conversion disorder (functional neurological symptom disorder)
4. psychological factors affecting other medical conditions
5. factitious disorder (imposed on self and imposed on other)
6. other specified somatic symptom and related disorder
7. unspecified somatic symptom and related disorder.

This chapter focuses on somatic symptom disorder as the most common diagnosis in this group.

Diagnostic criteria for somatic symptom disorder

The following are the diagnostic criteria for somatic symptom disorder (American Psychiatric Association, 2013):

A. One or more somatic symptoms that are distressing or significantly disrupt daily life.
B. Excessive thoughts, feelings, or behaviours related to the somatic symptoms or associated health concerns as manifested by at least one of the following:
    1. disproportionate and persistent thoughts about the seriousness of the symptoms
    2. persistently high anxiety about health or the symptoms
    3. excessive time and energy spent on the symptoms or health concern.
C. Although any one somatic symptom may not be continuously present, the state of being symptomatic is persistent (typically more than 6 months).

This diagnostic category can specify if existing with predominant pain, persistent, and current severity from mild to moderate to severe.

The onset and continuation of various symptoms generally relates to adverse life events or results from underlying psychological conflict. These patients often present with various complaints and can be frustrating for clinicians, with investigations often producing little benefit. The symptoms can significantly disable some patients to the point they may become dependent on others (Sharpe et al., 1994).

Various clinical and epidemiological studies have shown that patients with bodily symptoms that cannot be explained by a medical condition are present in various outpatient and inpatient settings (Bain & Spaulding 1967; Parker et al., 1984; Wallen et al., 1987). Somatisation disorder (i.e., somatic symptom disorder) is seen more commonly in hospital and primary care settings than in psychological services. The prevalence rate can be as high as 1%, which is similar to schizophrenia (Bhui & Hotopf, 1997).

In traditional cultures, somatic symptoms may be an expression of psychological difficulties including anxiety and depression. Individuals from modern cultures may also focus on somatic complaints when psychologically distressed, or may transform this distress into the body. Each culture has its own values and ways of conduct, so may have its own language to manifest distress. Practitioners need to keep cultural values in mind to understand somatic distress.

Research

Few studies in Australia and NZ have explored the extent of somatic symptom disorder.

Australia

Trauma and attachment difficulties can be an aetiological factor in somatisation disorder (now known as somatic symptom disorder; Haliburn, 2011). Early and repeated trauma can adversely affect the individual and lead to later health problems.

Health anxiety (i.e., illness anxiety disorder) affects a significant proportion of the population. An epidemiological study exploring health anxiety in Australia noted that health anxiety affects about 5.7% of the population across the lifespan and 3.4% met criteria for health (now illness) anxiety disorder at the time of assessment. It was associated with increased impairment and disability and greater health service use (Sunderland et al., 2013).

A study of Australian general practitioners (GP) exploring the strategies they use to manage patients with medically unexplained symptoms noted challenges at both a professional and personal level. They held the uncertainty of no diagnosis and hence no known cure and no clear outcome (Stone, 2013).

An exploratory outpatient study at a pain clinic in Perth, Western Australia, where people with chronic pain were referred to the consultation-liaison psychiatry clinic, examined somatic disorders. Somatoform (somatic symptom) disorder was a common comorbid condition found in patients with chronic pain. Persistent somatoform pain disorder was the commonest somatoform disorder found (Mohan et al., 2014).

The first study in Australia that explored somatoform dissociation (dissociative symptoms that manifest in the body) in adolescents noted a high percentage of somatoform dissociation and that participants with more than one mental health condition had higher levels of somatoform dissociation (Pullin et al., 2014). The few studies conducted in Australia show that somatic disorders reflect significant psychological problems and lead to distress for patients, as well as diagnostic and treatment concerns for practitioners.

New Zealand

There is little epidemiological literature on somatoform disorders in NZ. A somewhat related epidemiological study explored the effects of various adverse life events like childhood and adult physical abuse in the possible causation of medical conditions in a large community sample. Various medical conditions emerged as significantly increased including migraine, heart disease, and diabetes (Romans et al., 2002).

A case example noted a shipping accident resulting from the ship's pilot experiencing a conversion disorder in the form of sudden vision loss. It is difficult to anticipate such an occurrence, even from regular medical screening (Griffiths & Ellis, 2007).

Management

The key feature in managing somatic symptom and related disorders is arriving at a diagnosis by taking a thorough history, including any stressors or conflicts. A thorough review of various tests, investigations, and liaison with the treating physicians is imperative to have a thorough view of the ongoing difficulties. Assessing the psychosocial world of the individual encourages exploring possible perpetuating and precipitating factors, which could be useful in future management. A comorbid psychiatric condition should be also considered and treated assertively.

An open stance towards the condition should be present with a non-judgemental view on the illness and the possible causative factors. Honest and sensitive discussions should ensue with the patient. Negotiate the plan to move forwards and arrange a contract for engagement. Psychoeducation is important and families should be involved wherever possible. Fix appointments and avoid granting unnecessary requests for investigations and tests. Consistent care and coordination is needed and should include families and other health professionals. Maintain communication with allied and other health professionals.

Target a realistic goal, like reducing the impact of ongoing pain or avoiding seeking attention for trivial physical concerns. A biopsychosocial approach involving various members of the multidisciplinary team can improve outcomes. A similar approach noted improvement in physical and psychosocial functioning of adolescents with chronic fatigue syndrome or somatoform disorders over time in a prospective study conducted at Westmead Hospital, Sydney (Klineberg et al., 2014). The long-term gains seen in many people with severe and chronic somatic disorders are in the context of involving multidisciplinary treatment and care (Houtveen et al., 2015). Medications may not be very effective. A recent Cochrane review found very low-quality evidence for new-generation antidepressants and natural products being effective in treating adults with somatic symptoms. It also suggested that the adverse effects of medication may further compound the negative perception of symptoms (Kleinstauber et al., 2014)

Focusing on managing psychosocial stressors is more relevant and important. Cognitive behaviour therapy (CBT) remains the most studied psychological therapy and has been associated with reduced somatic symptoms. It is useful to address excessive preoccupation and fears around the symptoms and altering the behaviours and responses to the symptoms is helpful. A Cochrane review of non-pharmacological interventions noted that all psychological therapies included in the review were superior to usual care in reducing the symptoms, but the psychological therapies were not more effective when compared with the enhanced care (Van Dessel et al., 2014).

The role of a clinical psychologist or a psychotherapist cannot be stressed enough. They can be a containing figure in the lives of patients, and help them achieve stability in daily life. The focus should be to assist in rebuilding their lives.

New Zealand case study

This case has been created as an example for illustrative purposes.

Ms J is a 24-year-old woman of Māori descent who has been admitted to the emergency department after her mother witnessed her having a seizure in her home. In the emergency department, she is poorly responsive to verbal commands but her vital parameters are normal. She was breathing normally and multiple tests reveal no significant pathology. Her brain scan is normal. Her mother does not report any significant medical history and she appears to be a healthy woman. The seizure consisted of random movements with no loss of consciousness and with no preceding aura (i.e., sense that attack was imminent). There is no significant history of alcohol or other substances. The doctor seeks a psychiatric consultation. On review, it is noted that a distant family friend sexually assaulted Ms J a month ago and there has been a lot of shame following the incident in the family. Ms J and her mother have been feeling isolated within the community and two days before the seizure, Ms J had been quiet, was not speaking to her mother, and stayed in her room most of the time. It is concluded that the significant trauma and sense of shame and isolation contributed to an episode of seizure with the diagnosis of conversion disorder. The altered motor function could not be accounted for with a recognised medical or neurological disorder.

Australia – resources

Dissociative disorders:
- Adjunct Professor Warwick Middleton, MD, Trauma and Dissociation Unit, Belmont Private Hospital, Carina, Brisbane.

Somatic symptom and related disorders:
- Professor Alexandar Janca, FRANZCP, MD, School of Psychiatry and Clinical Neurosciences University of Western Australia, Perth.
- Associate Professor Vladan Starcevic, FRANZCP, MD, Nepean Clinical School, University of Sydney.

New Zealand – resources

- For more information about dissociative identity disorders, contact the New Zealand Mental Health Foundation (see www.mentalhealth.org.nz/get-help/a-z/resource/54/dissociative-identity-disorder-did).

Bibliography

Crowe, M., Whitehead, L., Gagan, M. J., Baxter, G. D., Pankhurst, A., & Valledor, V. (2010). Listening to the body and talking to myself – the impact of chronic lower back pain: A qualitative study. *International Journal of Nursing Studies, 47*, 586–592.

Irwin, H. J. (1994b). Paranormal belief and proneness to dissociation. *Psychological Reports, 75*, 1344–1346.

Loewenstein, R. J. (2014). Dissociative amnesia: epidemiology, pathogenesis, clinical manifestations, course, and diagnosis. In D. Spiegel (Ed.), *Dissociative disorders. Uptodate: Topic 14697 Version 2.0*. Wolters Kluwer Health (Electronic Publication). Available: www.uptodate.com/contents/dissociative-amnesia-epidemiology-pathogenesis-clinical-manifestations-course-and-diagnosis?source = search_result&search = dissociative+amnesia&selectedTitle = 1~5

Simeon, D. (2014). Depersonalization derealization disorder: Epidemiology, pathogenesis, clinical manifestations, course, and diagnosis. In D. Spiegel (Ed.), *Dissociative disorders. Uptodate: Wolters Kluwer Health* (Electronic Publication). Available: www.uptodate.com/contents/depersonalization-derealization-disorder-epidemiology-pathogenesis-clinical-manifestations-course-and-diagnosis

Spiegel, D., Loewenstein, R. J., Lewis-Fernández, R., Sar, V., Simeon, D., Vermetten, E., et al. (2011). Dissociative disorders in DSM-5. *Depression and Anxiety, 28*, 824–852.

Staniloiu, A., & Markowitsch, H. J. (2014). Dissociative amnesia. *Lancet Psychiatry*, July 2. http://dx.doi.org/10.1016/S2215-0366(14)70279-2

References

American Psychiatric Association. (1994). *Diagnostic and statistical manual of mental disorders* (4th ed.). Washington, DC: Author.

American Psychiatric Association. (2013) *Diagnostic and statistical manual of mental disorders* (5th ed.). Arlington, VA: Author.

Amos, J., Furber, G., & Segal, L. (2011). Understanding maltreating mothers: A synthesis of relational trauma, attachment disorganization, structural dissociation of the personality, and experiential avoidance. *Journal of Trauma & Dissociation, 12*, 495–509.

Anketell, C., Dorahy, M. J., Shannon, M., Elder, R., Hamilton, G., Corry, M., MacSherry, A., Curran, D., & O'Rawe, B. (2010). An exploratory analysis of voice hearing in chronic PTSD: Potential associated mechanisms. *Journal of Trauma and Dissociation, 11*, 93–107.

Ashworth, J., Ciorciari, J., & Stough, C. (2008). Psychophysiological correlates of dissociation, handedness, and hemispheric lateralization. *Journal of Nervous and Mental Disease, 196*, 411–416.

Bain, S. T., & Spaulding, W. B. (1967). The importance of coding presenting symptoms. *Canadian Medical Association Journal, 97*, 953–959.

Bhui, K., & Hotopf, M. (1997). Somatization disorder. *British Journal of Hospital Medicine*, *58*, 145–149.

Bowen, A., Shelley, M., Helmes, E., & Landman, M. (2010). Disclosure of traumatic experiences, dissociation, and anxiety in group therapy for posttraumatic stress. *Anxiety, Stress & Coping: An International Journal, 23*, 449–461.

Brown, L., Russell, J., Thornton, C., & Dunn, S. (1999). Dissociation, abuse and the eating disorders: Evidence from an Australian population. *Australian and New Zealand Psychiatry, 33*, 521–528.

Bryant, R. A. (1995). Autobiographical memory across personalities in dissociative identity disorder: A case report. *Journal of Abnormal Psychology, 104*, 625–631.

Bryant, R. A., Brooks, R., Silove, D., Creamer, M., O'Donnell, M., & McFarlane, A. C. (2011). Peritraumatic dissociation mediates the relationship between acute panic and chronic posttraumatic stress disorder. *Behaviour Research and Therapy, 49*, 346–351.

Bryant, R. A., & Panasetis, P. (2005). The role of panic in acute dissociative reactions following trauma. *British Journal of Clinical Psychology, 44*, 489–494.

Carlson, E. B., Dalenberg, C., & McDade-Montez, E. (2012). Dissociation in posttraumatic stress disorder, part 1: Definitions and review of research. *Psychological Trauma: Theory, Research, Practice and Policy, 4*, 479–489.

Cloitre, M., Courtois, C. A., Ford, J. D., Green, B. L., Alexander, P., Briere, J., Herman, J. L., Lanius, R., Stolbach, B. C., Spinazzola, J., Van der Kolk, B. A., & Van der Hart, O. (2012). *The ISTSS Expert Consensus Treatment Guidelines for Complex PTSD in Adults*. Available: www.istss.org/ISTSS_Main/media/Documents/ISTSS-Expert-Concesnsus-Guidelines-for-Complex-PTSD-Updated-060315.pdf

Cocker, K. I., Edwards, G. A., Anderson, J. W., & Meares, R. A. (1994). Electrophysiological changes under hypnosis in multiple personality disorder: A two-case exploratory study. *Australian Journal of Clinical & Experimental Hypnosis, 22*, 165–176.

Collins, F. (2005). Dissociation in Australia. In G. Rhoades, & V. Sar (Eds.), *Trauma and dissociation in a cross-cultural perspective: Not just a North American phenomena* (pp. 55–79). Binghamton, NY: Haworth Press.

Collins, F. E., & Ffrench, C. H. (1998). Dissociation, coping strategies and locus of control in a non clinical population: Clinical implications. *Australian Journal of Clinical & Experimental Hypnosis, 26*, 113–126

Dalenberg, C. J., Brand, B. L., Gleaves, D. H., Dorahy, M. J., Loewenstein, R. J., Cardeña, E., et al. (2012). Evaluation of the evidence for the trauma and fantasy models of dissociation. *Psychological Bulletin, 138*, 550–588.

Dalenberg, C. J., Brand, B. L., Loewenstein, R. J., Gleaves, D. H., Dorahy, M. J., Cardeña, E. et al. (2014). Reality vs. fantasy: Reply to Lynn et al. (2014). *Psychological Bulletin, 140*, 911–920.

Dalenberg, C., Loewenstein, R., Spiegel, D., Brewin, C., Lanius, R., Frankel, S., et al. (2007). Scientific study of the dissociative disorders. *Psychotherapy &; Psychosomatics, 76*, 400–401.

Devilly, G. J., Ciorciari, J., Piesse, A., Sherwell, S., Zammit, S., Cook, F., & Turton, C. (2007). Dissociative tendencies and memory performance on directed forgetting tasks. *Psychological Science, 18*, 212–217.

Dorahy, M. J. (2001). Dissociative identity disorder and memory dysfunction: The current state of experimental research, and its future directions. *Clinical Psychology Review, 21,* 771–795.

Dorahy, M. J. (2006). The dissociative processing style: A cognitive organisation activated by perceived or actual threat in clinical dissociators. *Journal of Trauma and Dissociation, 7,* 29–53.

Dorahy, M. J. (2007). A critical evaluation of cognitive inhibition in dissociative identity disorder as inferred by negative priming in the flanker task: Limitations and the episodic retrieval alternative. *Applied and Preventive Psychology, 12,* 115–127.

Dorahy, M., Brand, B., Sar, V., Krüger, C., Stavropoulos, P., Martínez-Taboas, A., et al. (2014). Dissociative identity disorder: An empirical overview. *Australian & New Zealand Journal of Psychiatry, 48*(5), 402–417.

Dorahy, M. J., Irwin, H. J., & Middleton, W. (2002). Cognitive inhibition in dissociative identity disorder (DID): Developing an understanding of working memory function in DID. *Journal of Trauma and Dissociation, 3,* 111–132.

Dorahy, M. J., Irwin, H. J., & Middleton, W. (2004). Assessing markers of working memory function in dissociative identity disorder using neutral stimuli: A comparison with clinical and general population samples. *Australian & New Zealand Journal of Psychiatry, 38,* 47–55.

Dorahy, M. J., Middleton, W., & Irwin, H. J. (2005). The effect of emotional context on cognitive inhibition and attentional processing in dissociative identity disorder. *Behaviour Research and Therapy, 43,* 555–568.

Dorahy, M. J., Middleton, W., Seager, L., McGurrin, P., Williams, M., & Chambers, R. (2015). Dissociation, shame, complex PTSD, child maltreatment and intimate relationship self-concept in dissociative disorder, chronic PTSD and mixed psychiatric groups. *Journal of Affective Disorders, 172,* 195–203.

Dorahy, M. J., Shannon, C., Seagar, L., Corr, M., Stewart, K., Hanna, D., Mulholland, C., & Middleton, W. (2009). Auditory hallucinations in dissociative identity disorder and schizophrenia with and without a childhood trauma history: Similarities and differences. *Journal of Nervous and Mental Disease, 197,* 892–898.

Duncan, E., Dorahy, M. J., Hanna, D., Bagshaw, S., & Blampied, N. (2013). Psychological responses after a major, fatal earthquake: The effect of peritraumatic dissociation and posttraumatic stress symptoms on anxiety and depression. *Journal of Trauma and Dissociation, 14,* 501–518.

Farrelly, S., Rudegeair, T., & Rickard, S. (2005). Trauma and dissociation in Aotearoa: The psyche of a society. In G. Rhoades & V. Sar (Eds.), *Trauma and dissociation in a cross-cultural perspective: Not just a North American phenomenon.* Binghamton, NY: Haworth Press

Freyd, J. J., & Birrell, P. J. (2013). *Blind to betrayal: Why we fool ourselves we aren't being fooled.* Hoboken, NJ: Wiley and Sons.

Gibney, S., Martens, A., Kosloff, S., & Dorahy, M. J. (2013). Examining the impact of obedient killing on peritraumatic dissociation using a bug-kill paradigm. *Journal of Social and Clinical Psychology, 32,* 261–275.

Goren, J., Phillips, L., Chapman, M., & Salo, B. (2012). Dissociative and psychotic experiences of adolescents admitted to a psychiatric inpatient unit. *Journal of Trauma & Dissociation, 13*, 554–567.

Gow, K. M., Hutchinson, L., & Chant, D. (2009). Correlations between fantasy proneness, dissociation, personality factors and paranormal beliefs in experiencers of paranormal and anomalous phenomena. *Australian Journal of Clinical & Experimental Hypnosis, 37*, 169–191.

Griffiths, R. F., & Ellis, P. M. (2007). Visual conversion disorder in a harbor pilot leading to sudden loss of control of a large vessel. *Aviation Space Environ Medicine, 78(1)*, 59–62.

Haliburn, J. (2011). From traumatic attachment to somatization disorder. *Australasian Psychiatry, 19*, 401–405.

Herman, J. L. (1992). *Trauma and recovery*. New York: Basic Books.

Hodgson, R. C., & Webster, R. A. (2011). Mediating role of peritraumatic dissociation and depression on post-MVA distress: Path analysis. *Depression and Anxiety, 28*, 218–226.

Hooper, A. L., Dorahy, M. J., Jordan, J., & Blampied, N. M. (2014). Dissociation, perceptual, and conceptual processing in survivors of the 2011 Christchurch earthquake. *Psychological Trauma: Theory, Research, Practice and Policy, 6*, 668–674.

Hopper, A., Ciorciari, J., Johnson, G., Spensley, J., Sergejew, A., & Stough, C. (2002). EEG coherence and dissociative identity disorder. *Journal of Trauma and Dissociation, 3*, 75–88.

Houtveen, J. H., Van Broeckhuysen-Kloth, S., Lintmeijer, L. L., Buhring, M. E., & Geenen, R. (2015). Intensive multidisciplinary treatment of severe somatoform disorder: A prospective evaluation. *Journal of Nervous and Mental Disease, 203(2)*, 141–148.

Hudson, S. (2000). Working with dissociative identity disorder using transactional analysis. *Transactional Analysis Journal, 30*, 91–93.

Huntjens, R. J. C., Postma, A., Peters, M. L., Woertman, L., & Van der Hart, O. (2003). Interidentity amnesia for neutral, episodic information in dissociative identity disorder. *Journal of Abnormal Psychology, 112*, 290–297.

International Society for the Study of Trauma and Dissociation (ISSTD). (2011). Guidelines for treating dissociative identity disorder in adults, third revision. *Journal of Trauma & Dissociation, 12*, 115–187.

Irwin, H. J. (1994a). Affective predictors of dissociation: I. *The Case of Unresolved Grief. Dissociation, 7*, 86–91.

Irwin, H. J. (1994b). Proneness to dissociation and traumatic childhood events. *Journal of Nervous and Mental Disease, 182*, 456–460.

Irwin, H. J. (1996). Traumatic childhood events, perceived availability of emotional support, and the development of dissociative tendencies. *Child Abuse & Neglect, 20*, 701–707.

Irwin, H. J. (1998). Affective predictors of dissociation II: Shame and guilt. *Journal of Clinical Psychology, 54*, 237–245.

Irwin, H. J. (2001). The relationship between dissociative tendencies and schizotypy: An artifact of childhood trauma? *Journal of Clinical Psychology, 57*, 331–342.

Kleinstauber, M., Witthoft, M., Steffanowski, A., Van Marwijk, H., Hiller, W., & Lambert, M. J. (2014). Pharmacological interventions for somatoform disorders in adults. *The Cochrane Database of Systematic Reviews*, 7 Nov, 11.

Klineberg, E., Rushworth, A., Bibby, H., Bennett, D., Steinbeck, K., & Towns, S. (2014). Adolescent chronic fatigue syndrome and somatoform disorders: A prospective clinical study. *Journal of Paediatrics and Child Health*, *50*(10), 775–781.

Leonard, D., Brann, S., & Tiller, J. (2005). Dissociative disorders: Pathways to diagnosis, clinician attitudes and their impact. *Australian & New Zealand Journal of Psychiatry*, *39*, 940–946.

Lynn, S. J., Lilienfeld, S. O., Merckelbach, H., Giesbrecht, T., McNally, R., Loftus, E., et al. (2014). The trauma model of dissociation: Inconvenient truths and stubborn fictions. Comment on Dalenberg et al. (2012). *Psychological Bulletin*, *140*(3), 896–910.

Lynn, S. J., Lilienfeld, S. O., Merckelbach, H., Giesbrecht, T., & Van der Kloet, D. (2012). Dissociation and dissociative disorders: Challenging conventional wisdom. *Current Directions in Psychological Science*, *21*, 48–53. http://dx.doi.org/10.1177/0963721411429457

Maddison, D. C. (1953). A case of double personality. *The Medical Journal of Australia*, *6*, 814–816.

Manning, M. L., & Manning, R. L. (2009). Convergent paradigms for visual neuroscience and dissociative identity disorder. *Journal of Trauma and Dissociation*, *10*, 405–419.

McAllister, M., Higson, D., McIntosh, W., O'Leary, S., Hargreaves, L., Murrell, L., et al. (2001). Dissociative identity disorder and the nurse-patient relationship in the acute care setting: An action research study. *Australian and New Zealand Journal of Mental Health Nursing*, *10*, 20–32.

Meares, R. (2012). *A dissociation model of borderline personality disorder*. New York: Norton.

Middleton, W. (2004). Dissociative disorders: A personal "work in progress." *Australasian Psychiatry*, *12*, 245–252.

Middleton, W. (2013). Ongoing incestuous abuse during adulthood. *Journal of Trauma and Dissociation*, *14*, 251–272.

Middleton, W., & Butler, J. (1998). Dissociative identity disorder: An Australia series. *Australian & New Zealand Journal of Psychiatry*, *32*, 794–804.

Middleton, W., & Higson, D. (2004). Establishing and running a trauma and dissociation unit: A contemporary experience. *Australasian Psychiatry*, *12*, 338–346.

Milne, B. (2013). *A snap-shot of current mental health practice in New Zealand: The prevalence and distribution of dissociative identity disorder among mental health professionals*. Unpublished Honours Dissertation. Christchurch, NZ: University of Canterbury.

Mohan, I., Lawson-Smith, C., Coall, D. A., Van der Watt, G., & Janca, A. (2014). Somatoform disorders in patients with chronic pain. *Australasian Psychiatry*, *22*, 66–70.

Mulder, R. T., Beautrais, A. L., Joyce, P. R., & Fergusson, D. M. (1998). Relationship between dissociation, childhood sexual abuse, childhood physical abuse, and mental illness in a general population sample. *American Journal of Psychiatry*, *155*, 806–811.

O'Toole, B. I., Marshall, R. P., Schureck, R J., & Dobson, M (1999). Combat, dissociation, and posttraumatic stress disorder in Australian Vietnam Veterans. *Journal of Traumatic Stress*, *12*, 625–640.

Parker, G., Abeshouse, B., Morey, B., et al. (1984). Depression in general practice. *Medical Journal of Australia*, *141*, 154–158.

Piper, A., & Merskey, H. (2004). The persistence of folly: A critical examination of dissociative identity disorder. Part 1. The excess of an improbable concept. *Canadian Journal of Psychiatry*, *49*, 592–600.

Price, J., & Hess, N. C. (1979). Behaviour therapy as precipitant and treatment in a case of dual personality. *Australian & New Zealand Journal of Psychiatry*, *13*, 63–66.

Pullin, M. A., Webster, R. A., & Hanstock, T. L. (2014). Psychoform and somatoform dissociation in a clinical sample of Australian adolescents. *Journal of Trauma & Dissociation*, *15*, 66–78.

Romans, S., Belaise, C., Martin, J., Morris E., & Raffi, A. (2002). Childhood abuse and later medical disorders in women: An epidemiological study. *Psychotherapy and Psychosomatics*, *71(3)*, 141–150.

Ross, C. A. (1997). *Dissociative identity disorder: Diagnosis, clinical features, and treatment of multiple personality* (2nd ed.). New York: Wiley.

Schumaker, J. F., Warren, W. G., Schreiber, G. S., & Jackson, C. C. (1994). Dissociation in anorexia nervosa and bulimia nervosa. *Social Behavior and Personality*, *22*, 385–392.

Sharpe, M., Mayou, R., Seagroatt, V., et al. (1994). Why do doctors find some patients difficult to help? *Quarterly Journal of Medicine*, *87*, 187–193.

Stone, L. (2013). Reframing chaos: A qualitative study of GPs managing patients with medically unexplained symptoms. *Australian Family Physician*, *42*, 501–502.

Sunderland, M., Newby, J. M., & Andrews, G. (2013). Health anxiety in Australia: Prevalence, comorbidity, disability and service use. *British Journal of Psychiatry*, *202*, 56–61.

Swannell, S., Martin, G., Page, A., Hasking, P., Hazell, P., Taylor, A., & Protani, M. (2012). Child maltreatment, subsequent non-suicidal self-injury and the mediating roles of dissociation, alexithymia and self-blame. *Child Abuse & Neglect*, *36*, 572–584.

Van der Hart, O., & Dorahy, M. J. (2009). Dissociation: The history of a construct. In P. Dell. & J. O'Neil (Eds.), *Dissociation and dissociative disorders: DSM V and beyond* (pp. 3–26). New York: Routledge.

Van der Hart, O., Nijenhuis, E. R. S., & Steele, K. (2006). *The haunted self: Structural dissociation and the treatment of chronic traumatization*. New York: Norton & Co.

Van Dessel, N., Den Boeft, M., Van der Wouden, J. C., Kleinstauber, M., Leone, S. S., Terluin, B., et al. (2014). Non-pharmacological interventions for somatoform disorders and medically unexplained physical symptoms (MUPS) in adults. *The Cochrane Database of Systematic Reviews*, 1 Nov, *11*.

Wallen, J., Pincus, H. A., Goldman, H. H., et al. (1987). Psychiatric consultations in short-term general hospitals. *Archives of General Psychiatry*, *44*, 163–168.

Recommendations for further reading resources

Dell, P. F., & O'Neil, J. A. (2009). (Eds.). *Dissociation and the dissociative disorders: DSM-V and beyond*. New York: Routledge.

Ross, C. A. (1997). *Dissociative identity disorder: Diagnosis, clinical features, and treatment of multiple personality*. New York: Wiley.

16

Feeding and eating disorders

Leah Brennan, Sarah Mitchell, and Jake Linardon

Introduction

Feeding and eating disorders involve disturbed eating and eating-related behaviour, altered food consumption and absorption, and impaired physical and psychosocial health and wellbeing. Feeding and eating disorders include pica, rumination disorder, avoidant/restrictive food intake disorder (ARFID), anorexia nervosa (AN); bulimia nervosa (BN), binge eating disorder (BED), other specified feeding or eating disorder (OSFED), and unspecified feeding or eating disorders (USFED).

Specific changes to eating disorder diagnoses from the *DSM-IV* to the *DSM-5* include revised diagnostic criteria for AN and BN, recognition of BED, and inclusion of descriptors of OSFEDs and USFEDs. The other major change is the inclusion of ARFID (previously feeding disorder of infancy or early childhood), pica, and rumination disorder; diagnoses that were previously listed under "disorders usually first diagnosed in infancy, childhood, or adolescence" not retained in the *Diagnostic and Statistical Manual of Mental Disorders* (5th ed.; *DSM-5*; American Psychiatric Association, 2013).

- AN is characterised by persistent energy restriction, fear of weight gain or persistent behaviours that interfere with weight gain, and disturbed self-perceived weight and shape. Specifiers include restricting type (weight loss achieved via dieting, fasting, and excessive exercise, without recurrent binging or purging) or binge eating/purging type (recurrent episodes of binge eating or purging), in partial or full remission, and severity based on body mass index (BMI) criteria. The *DSM-5* changes to diagnostic criteria include removing the term "refusal" in relation to maintaining normal body weight (Criteria A) and requiring amenorrhea (Criteria D).
- BN is characterised by recurrent binge eating episodes, inappropriate compensatory behaviours, and overvaluation of weight and shape. Specifiers include in partial or full remission and severity is based on frequency of compensatory behaviours.

- BED is characterised by recurrent binge eating episodes which involve eating a large amount of food and experiencing lack of control. Specifiers include in partial or full remission and severity is based on frequency of binge eating.
- ARFID is characterised by avoidance or restriction of food intake resulting in failure to meet nutritional and/or energy requirements. There has been refinement of diagnostic criteria from the previous name of feeding disorder of infancy or early childhood. Rumination is characterised by the repeated regurgitation of food after eating, the re-chewed food may be spat out or re-swallowed. Only one of the above diagnoses can be made during a single episode.
- Pica is characterised by the persistent consumption of non-nutritive, non-food substances (e.g., paper, soap, chalk, gum, hair). It can coexist with other eating disorders.
- The OSFEDs include atypical AN (meet all criteria for AN except weight is within normal range), BN of low frequency and/or duration (meet all criteria for BN except frequency and/or duration of binging and compensatory behaviours), BED of low frequency and limited duration (meet all criteria for BN except frequency and/or duration of binge eating), purging disorder (recurrent purging to influence weight/shape without binge eating), and night eating syndrome (waking during the night to eat or excessive eating after the evening meal).
- USFEDs have symptoms consistent with feeding and eating disorders, including the severity of symptoms and distress and impairment, but do not meet the full criteria for any of the feeding and eating disorders diagnoses.

Australia

More than 1 million Australians are expected to have an eating disorder by 2022 (Deloitte Access Economics, 2012). In 2012, it was estimated that over 913 000 Australian people (4% of the total population) had a clinical eating disorder (Deloitte Access Economics, 2012). Of these, 3% had AN, 12% had BN, 47% had BED, and 37% had other eating disorders (*DSM-IV* criteria). Broadening the criteria for BN and including BED, in the *DSM-5* led to a twofold increase in reported prevalence rates of these disorders, while the prevalence for unspecified eating disorders significantly reduced (Hay, Girosi, & Mond, 2015). AN and BN are female-dominated disorders (90%) whereas a much equal gender distribution exists for BED (American Psychiatric Association, 2013). Data for Aboriginal and Torres Strait Islander peoples is scarce; however, one community-based study found that eating disorder behaviours are high in Indigenous Australians (Hay & Carriage, 2012).

No research exists on the epidemiology of feeding disorders in Australia. Global prevalence for pica, rumination disorder, and ARFID in the community is limited and inconclusive (Kelly et al., 2014). International evidence suggests that pica, rumination disorder, and ARFID are more common in younger children and infants as well as individuals with severe intellectual disabilities (Delaney et al., 2014; Kelly et al., 2014).

AN typically emerges during early to mid-adolescence while BN and BED typically emerge during late adolescence and young adulthood (Deloitte Access Economics, 2012; Wade et al., 2006). Eating disorders can also occur during older adulthood (Deloitte Access Economics, 2012). International data suggests that 46% of individuals with AN will recover, 34% will partially recover and 20% will remain chronically ill following treatment (Steinhausen, 2002). Approximately 50% of those with BN recover following treatment (Steinhausen, Weber, & Phil, 2009) and recovery rates for BED are thought to be even higher (Hay et al., 2014). Limited data exists for the developmental trajectories of feeding disorders in Australia. International data indicates that pica typically emerges in childhood, although it can occur during adolescence and adulthood. When onset emerges in adulthood, it is often accompanied by additional psychological disorders or intellectual disability. Pica also increases during pregnancy. Rumination disorder occurs most often during infancy (3–12 months), generally remits without intervention and, if prolonged, can result in medical conditions (e.g., malnutrition). Rumination disorder can also occur during childhood, adolescence, or adulthood. AFRID often emerges in infancy or childhood and can continue on to adulthood (American Psychiatric Association, 2013).

Australian prospective studies have explored risk factors and consequences for eating disorders. Risk factors for early and late-onset eating disorders include: being perceived as overweight by parents (Allen, Byrne, & Crosby, 2014); expressing extreme concerns about weight, shape, and eating (Allen, Byrne, & Crosby, 2014; Allen, Byrne, Oddy, Schmidt, & Crosby, 2014); and experiencing weight-related teasing from peers (Wertheim, Koerner, & Paxton, 2001). Depression, anxiety, and substance-abuse disorders commonly co-occur with eating disorders (Allen et al., 2013; Swinbourne et al., 2012). Individuals with eating disorders report poorer mental, physical and social health and quality of life (Mond et al., 2012). Engaging in binge eating and purging prospectively predicts poorer physical and psychosocial functioning (Mond & Hay, 2007). No Australian data exists for risk factors and consequences for feeding disorders. International data suggests that weight loss, malnutrition, and electrolyte imbalance are consequences of rumination disorder (Pinhas et al., 2011; Rajindrajith, Devanarayana, & Perera, 2012) while consequences of pica include intestinal obstruction and chronic abdominal pain (Altepeter, Annes, & Meller, 2011; O'Callaghan & Gold, 2012). ARFID has been shown to correlate with anxiety disorders, attention deficit disorders, and autism spectrum disorders (Fisher et al., 2014; Timimi, Douglas, & Tsiftsopoulou, 1997).

The Royal Australian and New Zealand College of Psychiatrists (RANZCP) clinical practice guidelines for treating eating disorders (Hay et al., 2014) provide recommendations for assessing and treating AN, BN, BED, OSFED, and ARFID. Due to a lack of evidence, no treatment recommendations were made for ARFID, and pica and rumination disorder were not included. Recommendations are informed by Cochrane reviews of AN and BN treatment authored by Australian researchers Hay and colleagues (Claudino et al., 2007; Hay et al., 2003; Hay et al., 2009; Hay, Claudino, & Kaio, 2001).

The RANZCP guidelines (Hay et al., 2014) note the following principles of care: person-centred informed decision making, involving family and significant others; recovery-oriented practice; least restrictive treatment context; multidisciplinary approach; stepped and seamless care; and dimensional and culturally informed approach to diagnosis and treatment. A harm minimisation approach is recommended for those with chronic eating disorders, particularly AN.

Comprehensive AN assessment includes: presence and history of symptoms; medical risks and complications; psychiatric comorbidities; cognitive impacts of starvation; and possible predisposing, precipitating, and perpetuating factors. Multidisciplinary assessment involving families and carers in young people is recommended. Treatment recommendations for AN included interdisciplinary treatment (i.e., nutrition, medical, psychological), long-term specialised therapist-led manualised psychological treatment, and family-based therapy for young people. Hospitalisation is recommended only when required to manage medical or psychological risk (Hay et al., 2014). Specific Australian guidelines exist regarding inpatient management of eating disorders (Centre for Eating and Dieting Disorders, 2014).

The RANZCP guidelines (Hay et al., 2014) recommend that BN and BED assessment include eating-related behaviours, weight and shape-related cognitions, history of eating disorders (particularly AN), psychiatric comorbidity, and medical assessment. They recommend therapist-led cognitive behaviour treatment for BN and BED, and recognise the role of internet-based and non-specialised guided self-help CBT. Pharmacotherapy (e.g., antidepressant and topiramate) is recommended as an adjunct or alternative treatment (Hay et al., 2014).

These RANZCP guidelines are consistent with the Australian Psychological Society (APS) College of Clinical Psychology review of evidence-based approaches for eating disorders (Wade, Byrne, & Touyz, 2013), the APS's review of evidence-based psychological interventions (2010), and the National Eating Disorders Collaboration (NEDC) evidence review of eating disorder prevention, treatment, and management (National Eating Disorder Collaboration, 2010a). Of note, the NEDC has also published a review of eating disorder information and support resources for Australians (National Eating Disorder Collaboration, 2010b).

There are no studies on the assessment and treatment of eating disorders in Aboriginal and Torres Strait Islander peoples. Treatment should be guided by the broader RANZCP (2012) Australian Indigenous Mental Health document which outlines principles of mental healthcare (Hay et al., 2014).

Structured clinical interview is the gold standard approach to eating disorder identification assessment and diagnosis (Hay et al., 2014). The NEDC recommends the Eating Disorder Examination (Fairburn, 2008) and the Child Eating Disorder Examination (Bryant-Waugh et al., 1996) for this purpose. The Eating Disorders Examination Questionnaire, a self-report questionnaire based on the Eating Disorder Examination interview, is commonly used for screening and assessment, and Australian norms are available (Engel et al., 2006; Mond et al., 2014; Wade, Byrne, & Bryant-Waugh, 2008).

No Australian guidelines or empirical studies exist for screening, assessing, or treating feeding disorders (McAdam et al., 2004). International research is also scarce; no government or professional bodies endorse evidence-based guidelines for assessing or treating these disorders. A number of public health publications provide guidelines on healthy eating behaviours and dietary intake; for example, the Australian Dietary Guidelines (www.nhmrc.gov.au/guidelines-publications/n55), the Australian Guide to Healthy Eating and associated resources, and the National Health and Medical Research Council Infant Feeding Guidelines (NHMRC, 2012, 2013).

In addition to these treatment categories, other support includes:

- support lines such as the Butterfly Foundation (http://thebutterflyfoundation.org.au) and Eating Disorders Victoria (www.eatingdisorders.org.au)
- support groups such as Eating Disorders Association Inc. Queensland (http://eda.org.au) and the Butterfly Foundation
- self-help interventions such as Fursland et al. (2007) and the Body Esteem Program (www.womenshealthworks.org.au/programs/eating-disorders-body-esteem).

Support groups such as the Eating Disorders Association of South Australia (www.edasa.org.au) and Tasmania Recovery from Eating Disorders (www.tred.org.au) and online self-help programs such as Understanding ED Recovery – A Carers Online Program (http://thebutterflyfoundation.org.au/our-services/recovery-programs/emerging-2/) are also available for carers of individuals with eating disorders. Various community-based and professional support organisations exist in Australia that focus on better treatment and management of eating disorders; for example, the National Eating Disorders Collaboration, the Australia & New Zealand Academy for Eating Disorders (www.anzaed.org.au) and the Butterfly Foundation. A recent Australian report identified the limited research examining treatment needs of Aboriginal and Torres Strait Islander peoples who are suffering from an eating disorder and has highlighted this as an important area for future research (Deloitte Access Economics, 2012). Australia does not have specialist services for feeding disorders; however, these disorders are often treated by maternal and child health nurses and associated multidisciplinary teams (e.g., paediatrician, psychologist, dietician, occupational therapists, and speech pathologists) who provide support for the overall health and development of children.

New Zealand

There is limited research on the epidemiology of eating disorders in New Zealand (NZ). Twelve-month prevalence for older pre-*DSM-5* eating disorders has been reported to be 0.5% of the population (0.4% for BN, < 0.01% for AN; Wells et al., 2006). Lifetime prevalence was estimated to be slightly higher (1.7% total, 1.3% for BN, and 0.6% for AN). Those aged 25–44 years had the highest prevalence rates, with females (0.6%) significantly outnumbering males (0.3%; Oakley Browne et al., 2006; Wells et al.,

2006). One study estimated lifetime and 12-month point prevalence for individuals who identify as Māori. Total prevalence rates were 3.1% (0.7% for AN, 2.4% for BN) and 1% (1% for BN), respectively (Baxter et al., 2006). There is no research examining whether prevalence rates of eating disorders have increased over time in NZ. There is no epidemiological research that has explored feeding disorders in NZ populations.

Limited NZ data exists for age of onset for eating and feeding disorders. According to one large national survey, the average age of onset for AN is 17 years and BN is 18 years (Wells et al., 2006). There is no NZ data on the average age of onset for feeding disorders.

Correlates of eating disorders have been rarely investigated in NZ samples. However, there is evidence to suggest that those who experienced childhood sexual abuse are at a greater risk of developing an eating disorder (Romans et al., 2001) while healthy and social family environments serve as protective factors (Wood et al., 2012). Comorbid depression and anxiety, previous suicide attempts, low-self-esteem, and impaired quality of life are higher in NZ women who have an eating disorder or who exhibit eating disorder behaviours (Romans et al., 2001; Rosewall, 2009). No research exists on correlates of eating or feeding disorders in individuals who identify as Māori.

There are no studies on the assessment and treatment of eating disorders in Māori and Pacific peoples. The Te Tiriti o Waitangi (the Treaty of Waitangi) principles apply as per the Medical Council of New Zealand (2006) and the New Zealand Psychologists Board. No NZ guidelines or empirical studies exist for screening, assessing, or treating feeding disorders (McAdam et al., 2004). A number of public health publications provide guidelines on healthy eating behaviours and dietary intake. For example, Food and nutrition guidelines for healthy infants and toddlers (aged 0–2; Ministry of Health, 2008), children and young people (aged 2–18 years; Ministry of Health, 2012a), adults (Ministry of Health, 2003), and older people (Ministry of Health, 2013).

There are three speciality eating disorder services in NZ known as "hubs" (in Auckland, Wellington and Christchurch; Eating Disorders Association of New Zealand, n.d.), which support local districts or "spokes". These "hubs" provide various inpatient, day-patient, and outpatient treatment options, and support services for families, friends, and carers. They provide training, supervision, consultation, and onsite visits to the spokes. Eating disorders liaison clinicians play an important role in each spoke providing treatment in their local area and information about referral pathways. They provide an important point of contact to the hub service. Several community-based and professional support organisations have been established in NZ to focus on supporting clinicians and improving treatment for eating disorders; for example, Eating Disorders Association of New Zealand (www.ed.org.nz), Australia & New Zealand Academy for Eating Disorders (www.anzaed.org.au). Māori and Pacific peoples are underrepresented in eating disorder services. Thus, it is important to identify reasons for low referrals and higher drop-out rates to ensure their needs are met (Recognising and managing mental health disorders in Māori, 2010). Feeding disorders are treated as part of targeted interventions through NZ's Maternity and

Child Health Services (Ministry of Health, 2012b), which comprise practitioners of various disciplines such as general practitioners, well-child nurses, and dieticians. These disorders are also treated through various public and private services by a range of practitioners (e.g., paediatrician, psychologist, dietician, occupational therapists, and speech pathologists).

New Zealand case study

This case is a composite example created for illustrative purposes.

John is a 20-year-old male who presented to a specialist eating disorder treatment service in Auckland. John lives with his mother and father in a socio-economically disadvantaged outer suburb community in NZ. Both of his parents have Māori heritage. John does not work and is studying social work at university.

A comprehensive assessment was undertaken with John during his first visit. Over the past 2 years he has been exercising excessively and has become increasingly preoccupied with developing lean muscle mass and losing fat. He goes long periods without eating (on average 8 hours) and is binge eating and purging an average of five times a week. John has lost 10 kg over the past 2 years. John's BMI at the time of the assessment was 22.4 kg/m^2 and he described feeling that he is overweight. He reports that his body shape is the most important aspect of his self-worth. John expresses experiencing low mood most days and not enjoying several activities he previously enjoyed such as reading and going to the movies. He reports experiencing strong feelings of shame, commenting that he feels he has a "women's illness."

John reported that his mother suffers from depression and his father has always been a heavy drinker. John's father works long hours as a labourer. John was overweight as a child and adolescent and his parents would often comment that he needed to lose weight. He had few friends at primary school and high school and was often bullied for being overweight. John reported experiencing low mood and anxiety during Year 11, which he attributed to increased self-imposed pressure to perform well during the final years at high school. To help manage the stress from school John started running, initially for 15 minutes twice a week. Over the next 3 months, he increased the frequency and duration to 1 hour five times a week. During this time, John lost 7 kg and received compliments from his peers, which he reported made him feel good. He wanted to lose additional weight and so began throwing out his lunch at school. One afternoon during Year 12, John arrived home from school and found that his mother had left a large block of chocolate in the fridge. John ate one piece, then another and then could not stop until he had eaten the whole block of chocolate. He became distressed that he was going to put on weight and made himself vomit to relieve the distress. Subsequently, John began binge eating and purging on average five times a week, usually after going long periods without eating. While John was initially able to hide the disordered eating behaviours from his parents, they soon began noticing food going missing and on occasions heard John vomiting after eating. They called Eating Disorders Association of New Zealand to find out recommendations for treatment.

It is recommended that John undertake CBT for eating disorders (CBT-E) which is a treatment approach that has been shown to be effective for people with various eating disorder psychopathology, particularly BN (Fairburn, 2008). CBT-E consists of 20 sessions divided into four phases of treatment. Phase 1 encourages regular eating and weekly weighing to target the clinical features of restraint, weight checking, and avoidance. Phase 2 is a review of the treatment to date, including any barriers to treatment, and also focuses on planning for phase 3. Phase 3 focuses on key behaviours and cognitions thought to maintain the client's eating disorder, and phase 4 includes maintaining progress and preventing relapse. John's parents have been linked into a Carers Support Group to discuss and share their experience, and to develop strategies to help support John during his recovery journey.

John's diagnosis is bulimia nervosa, current severity moderate. John meets the first two diagnostic criteria for body dysmorphic disorder (preoccupation with an imagined deficit in appearance, clinically significant distress or impairment); however, given the binge eating and compensatory behaviours and that his self-evaluation is unduly influenced by body shape and weight, the symptoms are better accounted for by BN. Further, although he experiences low mood for most days that has been present for the past 6 months, he only meets one other Criterion A symptom for major depressive disorder (loss of interest or pleasure in activities) and therefore his only diagnosis is bulimia nervosa.

Australia – disordered eating

Subdiagnostic disordered eating, including the cognitive and behavioural features of eating disorders, is associated with significant impairments in biopsychosocial functioning and is the strongest risk factor for developing a clinical eating disorder (National Eating Disorder Collaboration, 2010a). The prevalence of disordered eating significantly outnumbers the prevalence of eating disorder cases in Australia. A twofold increase in disordered eating behaviours has been observed since 1995, such that 5% of Australian men and women engage in binge eating, 3.3% diet in an extreme fashion, and 1% purge in attempt to control weight and shape (Mitchison et al., 2012). While these behaviours predict significant impairments in quality of life, there is a lack of research evaluating whether current evidence-based treatments are effective for individuals experiencing disordered eating symptoms. The National Eating Disorders Collaboration website does, however, offer various services and support lines for those who experience symptoms of disordered eating.

New Zealand – anorexia nervosa

Although AN was first described more than 100 years ago, AN treatment has been relatively unsuccessful thus far (Fairburn, 2005; le Grange & Lock, 2005). This has to do with the difficulties in engaging those with AN in treatment, and a lack of published rigorous studies evaluating treatment for AN (le Grange & Lock, 2005). A recent, well-designed New Zealand randomised controlled trial (RCT) compared CBT and interpersonal psychotherapy (IPT) with a non-specific supportive clinical management (SCM) in 50 females with AN (McIntosh et al., 2005). This NZ study was the first to evaluate the longer term effects of treatment for AN (Carter et al., 2011). Findings from this RCT indicate that at post-treatment, SCM produced better outcomes than both CBT and IPT, although around half of the total sample had a poor outcome (defined as not achieving weight gain and presenting with dysfunctional attitudes towards weight, shape, and eating). At long-term follow-up, however, those in either CBT or IPT showed slight improvements in symptoms while symptoms worsened for those in SCM such that there were no differences in treatment outcome across all three groups. This NZ study highlights the urgent need to develop more effective treatments for AN and to consider the longer term effects of treatment. This is particularly important given that AN runs a chronic course and is associated with significant morbidity and mortality.

Bibliography

American Psychiatric Association. (1994). *Diagnostic and statistical manual of mental disorders* (4th ed.). Washington, DC: Author.

References

Allen, K., Byrne, S., & Crosby, R. (2014). Distinguishing between risk factors for bulimia nervosa, binge eating disorder, and purging disorder. *Journal of Youth and Adolescence*, 1–12. http://dx.doi.org/10.1007/s10964-014-0186-8

Allen, K., Byrne, S., Oddy, W., & Crosby, R. (2013). DSM-IV–TR and DSM-5 eating disorders in adolescents: Prevalence, stability, and psychosocial correlates in a population-based sample of male and female adolescents. *Journal of Abnormal Psychology, 122*, 720–732. http://dx.doi.org/10.1037/a0034004

Allen, K., Byrne, S., Oddy, W., Schmidt, U., & Crosby, R. (2014). Risk factors for binge eating and purging eating disorders: Differences based on age of onset. *International Journal of Eating Disorders, 47*, 802–812. http://dx.doi.org/10.1002/eat.22299

Altepeter, T., Annes, J., & Meller, J. (2011). Foam bezoar: Resection of perforated terminal ileum in a 17-year-old with sickle β+ thalassemia and pica. *Journal of Pediatric Surgery, 46*, e31–2. http://dx.doi.org/10.1016/j.jpedsurg.2011.04.017

American Psychiatric Association. (2013). *Diagnostic and statistical manual of mental disorders* (5th ed.). Arlington, VA: Author.

Australian Psychological Society. (2010). *Evidence-based psychological interventions in the treatment of mental disorders: A literature review* (3rd ed.). Victoria: Author. Available: www.psychology.org.au/Assets/Files/Evidence-Based-Psychological-Interventions.pdf

Baxter, J., Kani Kingi, T., Tapsell, R., Durie, M., & McGee, M. A. (2006). Prevalence of mental disorders among Māori in Te Rau Hinengaro: The New Zealand mental health survey. *Australian & New Zealand Journal of Psychiatry, 40*(10), 914–923. http://dx.doi.org/10.1080/j.1440-1614.2006.01911.x

Bryant-Waugh, R. J., Cooper, P. J., Taylor, C. L., & Lask, B. D. (1996). The use of the eating disorder examination with children: A pilot study. *International Journal of Eating Disorders, 19*, 391–397. http://dx.doi.org/10.1002/(SICI)1098-108X(199605)19:4<391::AID-EAT6>3.0.CO;2-G

Carter, F. A., Jordan, J., McIntosh, V. V., Luty, S. E., McKenzie, J. M., Frampton, C., et al. (2011). The long-term efficacy of three psychotherapies for anorexia nervosa: A randomized, controlled trial. *International Journal of Eating Disorders, 44*, 647–654.

Centre for Eating and Dieting Disorders. (2014). Guidelines for the inpatient management of adult eating disorders in general medical and psychiatric settings in NSW. NSW Ministry of Health. Available: http://cedd.org.au/wordpress/wp-content/uploads/2013/09/Final-Print-Version-Adult-Inpatient-Guidelines-2014.pdf

Claudino, A., Hay, P., Silva de Lima, M., Schmidt, U., Bacaltchuk, J., & Treasure, J. (2007). Antipsychotic drugs for anorexia nervosa. *Cochrane Database of Systematic Reviews.* http://dx.doi.org/10.1002/14651858.CD006816

Delaney, C. B., Eddy, K. T., Hartmann, A. S., Becker, A. E., Murray, H. B., & Thomas, J. J. (2014). Pica and rumination behavior among individuals seeking treatment for eating disorders or obesity. *International Journal of Eating Disorders, 48*, 238–248. http://dx.doi.org/10.1002/eat.22279

Deloitte Access Economics. (2012). *Paying the price: The economic and social impact of eating disorders in Australia.* New South Wales: The Butterfly Foundation. Available: http://thebutterflyfoundation.org.au/wp-content/up

Eating Disorders Association of New Zealand. (n.d.). Eating disorders services available in NZ. Retrieved 26 August 2015 from: www.ed.org.nz/getting-help/eating-disorder-services/

Engel, S. G., Wittrock, D. A., Crosby, R. D., Monderlich, S. A., Mitchell, J. E., & Kolotkin, R. L. (2006). Development and psychometric evaluation of an eating disorder-specific health-related quality of life instrument. *International Journal of Eating Disorders, 39*, 62–71.

Fairburn, C. (2005). Evidence-based treatment of anorexia nervosa. *International Journal of Eating Disorders, 37*, S26–S30.

Fairburn, C. (2008). *Cognitive behavior therapy and eating disorders.* New York: Guilford Press.

Fisher, M. M., Rosen, D. S., Ornstein, R. M., Mammel, K. A., Katzman, D. K., Rome, E. S., et al. (2014). Characteristics of avoidant/restrictive food intake disorder in children and adolescents: A "new disorder" in DSM-5. *Journal of Adolescent Health, 55*(1), 49–52. http://dx.doi.org/10.1016/j.jadohealth.2013.11.013

Fursland, A., Byrne, S., & Nathan, P. (2007). *Overcoming disordered eating.* Perth, Western Australia: Centre for Clinical Interventions. Available: www.cci.health.wa.gov.au/about/objectives.cfm

Hay, P., Bacaltchuk, J., Byrnes, R., Claudino, A., Ekmejian, A., & Yong, P. (2003). Individual psychotherapy in the outpatient treatment of adults with anorexia nervosa. *Cochrane Database of Systematic Reviews, 4.* Art. no.: CD003909. http://dx.doi.org/10.1002/14651858.CD003909

Hay, P., Bacaltchuk, J., Stefano, S., & Kashyap, P. (2009). Psychological treatments for bulimia nervosa and binging. *Cochrane Database of Systematic Reviews, 4.* Art. No.: CD000562. http://dx.doi.org/10.1002/14651858.CD000562.pub3

Hay, P., & Carriage, C. (2012). Eating disorder features in Indigenous Aboriginal and Torres Strait Islander Australian Peoples. *BMC Public Health, 12*(1), 233. http://dx.doi.org/10.1186/1471-2458-12-233

Hay, P., Chinn, D., Forbes, D., Madden, S., Newton, R., Sugenor, L., et al. (2014). Royal Australian and New Zealand College of Psychiatrists clinical practice guidelines for the treatment of eating disorders. *Australian & New Zealand Journal of Psychiatry, 48,* 977–1008. http://dx.doi.org/10.1177/0004867414555814

Hay, P., Claudino, A., & Kaio, M. H. (2001). Antidepressants versus psychological treatments and their combination for bulimia nervosa. *Cochrane Database of Systematic Reviews.* http://dx.doi.org/10.1002/14651858.CD003385

Hay, P., Girosi, F., & Mond, J. (2015). Prevalence and sociodemographic correlates of DSM-5 eating disorders in the Australian population. *Journal of Eating Disorders, 3*(1), 1–7. http://dx.doi.org/10.1186/s40337-015-0056-0

Kelly, N. R., Shank, L. M., Bakalar, J. L., & Tanofsky-Kraff, M. (2014). Pediatric feeding and eating disorders: Current state of diagnosis and treatment. *Current Psychiatry Reports, 16,* 1–12. http://dx.doi.org/10.1007/s11920-014-0446-z

le Grange, D., & Lock, J. (2005). The dearth of psychological treatment studies for anorexia nervosa. *International Journal of Eating Disorders, 37,* 79–91.

McAdam, D. B., Sherman, J. A., Sheldon, J. B., & Napolitano, D. A. (2004). Behavioral interventions to reduce the pica of persons with developmental disabilities. *Behavior Modification, 28*(1), 45–72. http://dx.doi.org/10.1177/0145445503259219

McIntosh, V. V., Jordan, J., Carter, F. A., Luty, S. E., McKenzie, J. M., Bulik, C. M., et al. (2005). Three psychotherapies for anorexia nervosa: A randomized, controlled trial. *American Journal of Psychiatry, 162,* 741–747. http://dx.doi.org/10.1176/appi.ajp.162.4.741

Medical Council of New Zealand. (2006). *Statement on best practices when providing care to Māori patients and their Whanau.* Wellington, NZ: Author. Available: www.mcnz.org.nz/assets/News-and-Publications/Statements/Statement-on-best-practices-when-providing-care-to-Maori-patients-and-their-whanau.pdf

Ministry of Health. (2003). *Food and nutrition guidelines for healthy adults: A background paper.* Wellington, NZ: Author. Available: www.health.govt.nz/publication/food-and-nutrition-guidelines-healthy-adults-background-paper

Ministry of Health. (2008). *Food and nutrition guidelines for healthy infants and toddlers (Aged 0–2): A background paper – Partially revised December 2012*. Wellington, NZ: Author. Available: www.health.govt.nz/publication/food-and-nutrition-guidelines-healthy-infants-and-toddlers-aged-0-2-background-paper-partially

Ministry of Health. (2012a). *Food and nutrition guidelines for healthy children and young people (Aged 2–18 years): A background paper – Revised February 2015*. Wellington, NZ: Author. Available: www.health.govt.nz/publication/food-and-nutrition-guidelines-healthy-children-and-young-people-aged-2-18-years-background-paper

Ministry of Health. (2012b). *New Zealand's maternity and child health services: Preconception to 6 years*. Wellington, NZ: Author. Available: www.health.govt.nz/system/files/documents/pages/moh-poster-d5b.pdf

Ministry of Health. (2013). *Food and nutrition guidelines for healthy older people: A background paper*. Wellington, NZ: Author. Available: www.health.govt.nz/publication/food-and-nutrition-guidelines-healthy-older-people-background-paper

Mitchison, D., Hay, P., Slewa-Younan, S., & Mond, J. (2012). Time trends in population prevalence of eating disorder behaviors and their relationship to quality of life. *PloS One, 7*, 1–7. http://dx.doi.org/10.1371/journal.pone.0048450

Mond, J., Hall, A., Bentley, C., Harrison, C., Gratwick-Sarll, K., & Lewis, V. (2014). Eating-disordered behavior in adolescent boys: Eating disorder examination questionnaire norms. *International Journal of Eating Disorders, 47*, 335–341. http://dx.doi.org/10.1002/eat.22237

Mond, J., & Hay, P. (2007). Functional impairment associated with bulimic behaviors in a community sample of men and women. *International Journal of Eating Disorders, 40*, 391–398. http://dx.doi.org/10.1002/eat.20380

Mond, J., Hay, P., Rodgers, B., & Owen, C. (2012). Quality of life impairment in a community sample of women with eating disorders. *Australian & New Zealand Journal of Psychiatry, 46*, 561–568. http://dx.doi.org/10.1177/0004867411433967

National Eating Disorder Collaboration. (2010a). *Eating disorder prevention, treatment and management: An evidence review*. The Commonwealth Department of Health and Ageing. Available: www.nedc.com.au/files/pdfs/NEDC_Evidence%20Review_Final.pdf

National Eating Disorder Collaboration. (2010b). *Eating disorders information & support for Australians*. Crows Nest. Available: http://www.nedc.com.au/files/pdfs/NEDC_Resources%20Review_Final.pdf.

National Health and Medical Research Council. (2012). *Infant feeding guidelines: Information for health workers*. Canberra: Author. Available: www.nhmrc.gov.au/_files_nhmrc/publications/attachments/n56_infant_feeding_guidelines.pdf

NHMRC. (2013). *Australian dietary guidelines: Providing the scientific evidence for healthier australian diets*. Canberra: National Health and Medical Research Council. Available: www.nhmrc.gov.au/_files_nhmrc/publications/attachments/n55_australian_dietary_guidelines_130530.pdf

Oakley Browne, M. A., Wells, J. E., Scott, K. M., & McGee, M. A. (2006). Lifetime prevalence and projected lifetime risk of DSM-IV disorders in Te Rau Hinengaro: The New Zealand mental health survey. *Australian & New Zealand Journal of Psychiatry, 40*(10), 865–874. http://dx.doi.org/10.1080/j.1440-1614.2006.01905.x

O'Callaghan, E. T., & Gold, J. I. (2012). Pica in children with sickle cell disease: Two case reports. *Journal of Pediatric Nursing, 27*, e65–70. http://dx.doi.org/10.1016/j.pedn.2012.07.012

Pinhas, L., Morris, A., Crosby, R. D., & Katzman, D. K. (2011). Incidence and age-specific presentation of restrictive eating disorders in children: A Canadian paediatric surveillance program study. *Archives of Pediatrics & Adolescent Medicine, 165*, 895–899. http://dx.doi.org/10.1001/archpediatrics.2011.145

Rajindrajith, S., Devanarayana, N. M., & Perera, B. J. C. (2012). Rumination syndrome in children and adolescents: A school survey assessing prevalence and symptomatology. *BMC Gastroenterology, 12*(1), 163.

Royal Australian and New Zealand College of Psychiatrists. (2012). *Aboriginal and Torres Strait Islander mental health workers.* Available: www.wpanet.org/uploads/News-Zonal-Representatives/wpa-policy-papers-from-zone-18/ZONE%20 18-RANZCP.50_PS-2012-Aboriginal-and-Torres-Strait-Islander-Mental-Health-Workers-GC-2012-3-R36.pdf

Recognising and managing mental health disorders in Māori. (2010). *Best Practice Journal, 28*, 8–17. Available: www.bpac.org.nz/BPJ/2010/June/docs/BPJ_28_mentalhealth_pages8-17.pdf

Romans, S. E., Gendall, K. A., Martin, J. L., & Mullen, P. E. (2001). Child sexual abuse and later disordered eating: A New Zealand epidemiological study. *International Journal of Eating Disorders, 29*, 380–392.

Rosewall, J. M. (2009). *Prevalence, correlates and moderators of eating pathology in New Zealand women, adolescent and preadolescent girls.* Doctor of Philosophy in Psychology. Christchurch, NZ: University of Canterbury.

Steinhausen, H.-C. (2002). The outcome of anorexia nervosa in the 20th century. *American Journal of Psychiatry, 159*, 1284–1293.

Steinhausen, H.-C., Weber, S., & Phil, C. (2009). The outcome of bulimia nervosa: Findings from one-quarter century of research. *American Journal of Psychiatry, 166*, 1331–1341.

Swinbourne, J., Hunt, C., Abbott, M., Russell, J., St Clare, T., & Touyz, S. (2012). The comorbidity between eating disorders and anxiety disorders: Prevalence in an eating disorder sample and anxiety disorder sample. *Australian & New Zealand Journal of Psychiatry, 46*, 118–131. http://dx.doi.org/10.1177/0004867411432071

Timimi, S., Douglas, J., & Tsiftsopoulou, K. (1997). Selective eaters: A retrospective case note study. *Child Care, Health and Development, 23*, 265–278. http://dx.doi.org/10.1111/j.1365-2214.1997.tb00968.x

Wade, T., Bergin, J. L., Tiggemann, M., Bulik, C. M., & Fairburn, C. (2006). Prevalence and long-term course of lifetime eating disorders in an adult Australian twin cohort. *Australian & New Zealand Journal of Psychiatry, 40*(2), 121–128. http://dx.doi.org/10.1080/j.1440-1614.2006.01758.x

Wade, T., Byrne, S., & Bryant-Waugh, R. (2008). The eating disorder examination: Norms and construct validity with young and middle adolescent girls. *International Journal of Eating Disorders, 41*, 551–558. http://dx.doi.org/10.1002/eat.20526

Wade, T., Byrne, S., & Touyz, S. (2013). A clinician's quick guide of evidence-based approaches. Number 1: Eating disorders. *Clinical Psychologist, 17*(1), 31–32. http://dx.doi.org/10.1111/cp.12004

Wells, J. E., Oakley Browne, M. A., Scott, K. M., McGee, M. A., Baxter, J., & Kokaua, J. (2006). Prevalence, interference with life and severity of 12 month DSM-IV disorders in Te Rau Hinengaro: The New Zealand mental health survey. *Australian & New Zealand Journal of Psychiatry, 40*, 845–854.

Wertheim, E. H., Koerner, J., & Paxton, S. J. (2001). Longitudinal predictors of restrictive eating and bulimic tendencies in three different age groups of adolescent girls. *Journal of Youth and Adolescence, 30*(1), 69–81. http://dx.doi.org/10.1023/A:1005224921891

Wood, A., Utter, J., Robinson, E., Ameratunga, S., Fleming, T., & Denny, S. (2012). Body weight satisfaction among New Zealand adolescents: Findings from a national survey. *International Journal of Adolescent Medicine and Health, 24*, 161–167. http://dx.doi.org/10.1515/ijamh.2012.024

Recommendations for further reading/resources

General

Fairburn, C. G., Cooper, Z., & Shafran, R. (2003). Cognitive behaviour therapy for eating disorders: A "transdiagnostic" theory and treatment. *Behaviour Research and Therapy, 41*, 509–528.

Fairburn, C. G., & Harrison, P. J. (2003). Eating disorders. *The Lancet, 361*, 407–16.

Hoek, H. W., & Van Hoeken, D. (2003). Review of the prevalence and incidence of eating disorders. *International Journal of eating disorders, 34*(4), 383–396.

Australia

Hay, P. J., Mond, J., Buttner, P., & Darby, A. (2008). Eating disorder behaviors are increasing: Findings from two sequential community surveys in South Australia. *PloS one, 3*, e1541.

Mond, J., Hay, P., Rodgers, B., & Owen, C. (2012). Quality of life impairment in a community sample of women with eating disorders. *Australian & New Zealand Journal of Psychiatry, 46*, 561–568.

Mond, J. M., Myers, T. C., Crosby, R. D., Hay, P. J., Rodgers, B., Morgan, J. F., et al. (2008). Screening for eating disorders in primary care: EDE-Q versus SCOFF. *Behaviour Research and Therapy, 46*, 612–622.

New Zealand

Baxter, J., Kani Kingi, T., Tapsell, R., Durie, M., & McGee, M. A. (2006). Prevalence of mental disorders among Māori in Te Rau Hinengaro: The New Zealand mental health survey. *Australian & New Zealand Journal of Psychiatry, 40*(10), 914–923. http://dx.doi.org/10.1080/j.1440-1614.2006.01911.x

Wells, J. E., Oakley Browne, M. A., Scott, K. M., McGee, M. A., Baxter, J., & Kokaua, J. (2006). Prevalence, interference with life and severity of 12 month DSM-IV disorders in Te Rau Hinengaro: The New Zealand mental health survey. *Australian & New Zealand Journal of Psychiatry, 40*, 845–854.

17

Elimination disorders

Christine Grove and Chris Hardwick

Introduction

Children normally develop bladder and bowel control by the age of 5. Controlled toileting is a developmental milestone that happens step by step. Babies are born incontinent. They slowly develop control of their bowels at night and during the day, then gradually acquire daytime and night-time bladder continence. Most children can control their bladder and bowel by age 4–5, but some take longer to do so. Five years old is considered the cut-off age for diagnosing encopresis (faecal soiling) and enuresis (wetting).

Encopresis and enuresis are the primary toileting difficulties in childhood. These issues can affect the social and educational development of children, who can be isolated at school, excluded from peers, and face conflict with parents and teachers. They can lead the child to experience low self-esteem, poor academic achievement, and secondary social, emotional, or behavioural issues.

According to the *Diagnostic and Statistical Manual of Mental Disorders* (5th ed.; *DSM-5*; American Psychiatric Association, 2013) children who do not achieve toilet training by age 5 and have repeated bed or clothes wetting twice per week for 3 consecutive months, meet the criteria for enuresis (307.6); specified if: 1. nocturnal only; 2. diurnal only; and 3. nocturnal and diurnal. If the child involuntarily and repeatedly passes faeces in inappropriate places (usually undergarments) the criteria for encopresis (307.7) is met; specified if: 1. with constipation and overflow incontinence; 2. without constipation and overflow incontinence.

According to the *International Statistical Classification of Diseases and Related Health Problems 2010 Edition (ICD-10*; WHO, 2011), children can experience involuntary rejecting of urine, day and night, which is usually not expected considering the child's mental age, and is not a result of a lack of bladder control due to neurological disorder, epilepsy, or unusual abnormality of the urinary tract. This type of toileting issue is known as nonorganic enuresis (F98.0). The child's enuresis may be present from birth or it may have developed after bladder control. The enuresis could be associated with emotional or behavioural difficulties.

The child may experience repeated, voluntary, or involuntary passing of faeces, usually of normal consistency, in places that are not deemed appropriate in the child's sociocultural setting. In the ICD-10 this is known as nonorganic encopresis (F98.1). Nonorganic encopresis may represent an abnormal persistence of everyday infantile incontinence, it may involve a loss of continence following the development or improvement of bowel control, or it may include considered placement of faeces in inappropriate places in spite of normal bowel control. Nonorganic encopresis may occur as a monosymptomatic disorder or it may form part of other developmental disorders, such as emotional disorder or a conduct disorder.

Australian perspective of elimination disorders

In Australia, the prevalence of paediatric bladder incontinence is 16.9% for daytime wetting (Sureshkumar et al., 2009) and 18.8% for nocturnal wetting (Bower, 1996). Australian prevalence of soiling has not been reported but is understood to be similar to that noted internationally as around 30% to 50% (von Gontard et al., 2011). The impact of daytime incontinence varies within the considerably large and diverse ethnic communities in Australia (Deshpande et al., 2012), which underscores the need for a culturally sensitive approach when working with the families. Studies have yet to be conducted specifically within the Australian Aboriginal community. However, the need for sensitivity is reflected by the adaption of parent information resources on incontinence with use of culturally specific language and illustrations (Continence Foundation of Australia, 2015, see www.continence.org.au).

Standard practice and treatment recommendations

Best practice treatment of elimination disorders should adhere to the guidelines established by the International Children's Continence Society (ICCS). There are no guidelines published specifically for Australia; however, some Australian specialists have published internationally reflecting ICCS protocols (Caldwell et al., 2005: Deshpande et al., 2011) while others have documented effective local programmes (Gordon, 2014; Hurst & Walker, 2005).

Paediatric management

Treatment commences with a medical assessment of bowel function and diurnal and nocturnal bladder including medical history, physical examination, bladder capacity and voiding measurements, bladder voiding and fluid intake diary, presence of any urinary tract infection, and related medical conditions. A program to address specific areas of incontinence is developed with an emphasis on parental education.

Daytime wetting

Urotherapy is a structured bladder-retraining program led by a paediatrician, continence nurse, or general practitioner (GP) and sometimes involving a physiotherapist. It includes fluid management, scheduled voiding (maybe using a watch timer), and pelvic floor exercises (Chase et al., 2010) and may be supported by bladder medication. Timed voiding gradually yields to reliance on self-voiding as the child's neurological awareness of a full bladder increases (Christophersen & Friman, 2010). Some multidisciplinary approaches include a significant psychological component. Studies have demonstrated the effectiveness of urotherapy internationally (Schulman et al., 1999; Wiener et al., 2000) and in Australia (Deshpander et al., 2011).

Night-time bed wetting

Nocturnal enuresis is treated with alarm training sometimes with medication support (Caldwell, Deshpande, & von Gontard, 2013; Neveus et al., 2010). An alarm worn on the body (or pad and bell alarm) wakes the child as they start to urinate and with this regular prompt rousing them to void, the child learns to wake when the bladder is full (Caldwell, 2005). Studies have demonstrated the effectiveness of alarm training internationally (Neveus et al., 2010) and in Australia (Caldwell et al., 2009; Gim, Lillystone, & Caldwell, 2009).

Soiling

Treatment of soiling and constipation with a bowel program may involve dietary changes, fluid management, laxatives, and scheduled bowel voiding shortly after a major meal. This approach has been shown to be clinically effective (Burgers et al., 2013).

Psychological management

A psychologist is indicated when the urotherapy, alarm training, or bowel program is ineffective due to problems with compliance and motivation (Butler, 2008). In such cases, the psychologist's role is to help the child and family adhere to the medical treatment program. Non-compliance may be due to a range of psychological reasons and may be global or specific to just one or more aspects of the regime. The psychologist should check that a clear treatment program has been established and seek a collaborative relationship with the referring clinician. The psychologist supports, but does not lead, the treatment plan (Carr, 2006). This acknowledges that incontinence is primarily a chronic physiological condition with secondary psychological consequences, or may have arisen with comorbid behavioural vulnerabilities (von Gontard, 2005), rather than the historical view of an elimination disorder as a psychological problem.

Initial assessment

A brief global psychosocial assessment should screen for any significant mental health, developmental, health, family functioning, or social issues that may contribute to medical non-compliance and treatment resistance (American Academy of Child and Adolescent Psychiatry, 2004; von Gontard, 2005). If significant issues are detected, consider whether to treat the incontinence in isolation, or whether to treat the other issues first or concurrently with the incontinence (Equit et al., 2015). Complete this clinical planning in collaboration with the referring clinician and the family.

The initial assessment should determine that the incontinence has arisen typically due to unsuccessful toilet training, rather than the less common secondary incontinence associated with abuse, trauma, or development of anxious avoidance. In both cases, the medical treatment would be the same. However, with the latter, the psychological treatment would be more substantial.

Psychological intervention

Psychological treatment should address any behaviours that reduce compliance with the program regime. These commonly include: void withholding in the day (i.e., not voiding when time to go or when sensing a full bladder); incomplete day emptying of the bladder due to rushing; not voiding having being woken by the alarm at night or being insufficiently woken by the alarm; poor day fluid intake; and less commonly, anxious compulsive voiding.

Supportive education, especially with the parent or carer, is useful. Training the brain to heed a full bladder or bowel is a slow process when there has been chronic incontinence, which can be frustrating for the family. It requires considerable effort and patience and progress may be variable rather than continual. An incontinent child is given a toilet training regime that is developmentally best suited for a toddler undergoing physical self-mastery. Yet they also face a medical program that most adults would find challenging, often with insufficient adult support. Framing the problem as a neurodevelopmental process and discussing the psychological strain on the family and any unrealistic expectations on the child can help positively shift many families.

Psychologists best work with the child and attending parent using motivational counselling, problem solving, parental guidance, and behaviour management suited to the particular family and developmental age of the child. The goal is to increase adherence to the toileting program and remove any emotional and relationship issues caused by the chronic nature of the problem. Periodic appointments and supportive phone or email contact can help support the family during the treatment process, which may take 3 to 6 months to succeed.

For children with night wetting, the supervising adult must be able to check that the child is fully waking to the alarm and voiding, since waking quickly and fully is essential for the brain to learn to detect the full bladder signal.

When soiling and wetting occur together, or when soiling is frequent, psychological support may need to be more intensive and prolonged. Medical investigations may have been more intensive and longer. Medical management using laxatives can often lead to temporary increased soiling before achieving optimal stool consistency. These factors, combined with the increased social aversion to faeces compared to urine, can cause greater stress, frustration, and conflict for the child and family, and less confidence about the medical regime.

Some families are absorbed with seeking medical explanations and investigations the referring doctor does not consider necessary. Others experience overwhelming stress from competing demands, and may not be ready to undertake the continence program. These families can benefit from counselling.

The psychologist will often need to collaborate with the school or educational team and ask for staff support, especially for primary school children, who usually lack the maturity to follow the precise demands of urotherapy on their own. The school can assist by discretely prompting regular drinks and toilet voids and monitoring that the child is following the regime. A bowel program less frequently needs school support, unless the child prefers to empty their bowels in school hours. This may be the best time for stressed families as the child needs a longer period of relaxed voiding, not possible with a rushed morning or evening home regime. The psychologist will need regular contact with the continence clinician to remain aware of changes in the program and the child's progress. The continence clinician will benefit from guidance from the psychologist, so a partnership is mutually beneficial.

The expectations and delivery of the program must change to suit the developmental age of the child and the level of family functioning. The approach should be adjusted to suit any sensory, motor, cognitive, or communication challenges faced by the child.

Less commonly, an anxiety issue may be the underlying cause (e.g., phobic avoidance, anxious over-voiding, or trauma-related secondary enuresis). This typically occurs where there has been some trauma associated with constipation pain or embarrassment during an accident in public. Urotherapy or a bowel program is still appropriate in these cases, but the psychologist would also target anxiety symptoms that may disrupt the regime.

Speciality treatment guidelines/groups

As the established international authority on paediatric incontinence, the ICCS has published guidelines on treatment protocols (Burgers et al., 2013; Chase et al., 2010; Franco, von Gontard, & De Gennaro, 2012; Neveus et al., 2010). The psychologist should be aware that the concurrent medical or nursing intervention should reflect these protocols. The Continence Foundation of Australia (www.continence.org.au) can help access referrals for medical and nursing continence professionals if required, and for families. The Victorian Continence Resource Centre (www.continencevictoria. org.au) can also be helpful for accessing resources for professionals and families in Australia. Overseas, the Education and Resources for Improving Childhood Incontinence provides a useful professional platform for professional and family support (www. eric.org.uk).

Culturally sensitive parent information on bedwetting has been made available for the Aboriginal community by the Continence Foundation of Australia (www.continence.org.au/pages/aboriginal-torres-strait-islander.html) and the Australian Government (www.bladderbowel.gov.au/footer/publications/atsi.htm).

Multidisciplinary treatment manuals have recently become available that are specifically helpful for the psychologist (Equit et al., 2015) or applicable to the special needs population (South Australia Government Disability Services, 2014).

Standard assessment measures

Child-specific treatment-focused assessment tools such as diet, drink, and voiding diaries are essential for urotherapy or bowel programs. Some authors have begun to make manuals about this process (Equit et al., 2015).

Studies have established a significant correlation between incontinence and behavioural disorders. Tools sensitive to behavioural and attention regulation problems are most relevant to this population (von Gontard et al., 2011). They may help discriminate between simple chronic incontinence and complex comorbid conditions. If significant psychopathological comorbidity is suspected, then use standardised screening tools to supplement the clinical assessment, such as questionnaires for anxiety and mood disorders.

The short screening tool for psychological problems developed by Van Hoecke et al. (2007) and recommended by ICCS would be useful for nursing and medical clinicians.

Funding of specialist treatment

In Australia, the only specific funding source for wetting treatment studies is the Australian Bladder Foundation, a grant from the Continence Foundation of Australia (www.continence.org.au). Non-specific project funding has been granted in the past for studies on continence from the National Health and Medical Research Council (NHMRC, www.nhmrc.gov.au) and the Foundation for Children (www.foundationforchildren.com.au).

New Zealand perspective of elimination disorders

Two New Zealand (NZ) studies have shown prevalence data for children with enuresis. One study found that by age 8, around 3.3% of children had not controlled their bladder and around 7.4% had nocturnal enuresis (Fergusson, Horwood, & Shannon, 1986). Fergusson et al. found that the prevalence of children unable to attain bladder control was lower than that of nocturnal enuresis at all ages. By the age of 11, around 6% of children had maintained nocturnal enuresis (Feehan et al., 1990). No studies have been conducted to date regarding prevalence data for children with encopresis in NZ; however, the Kiwi Enuresis Encopresis Association (KEEA) estimates that it affects 1% to 3%.

Standard practice and treatment recommendations

Standard practice and treatment recommendations include four main categories:
1. education; 2. non-pharmacological management; 3. medication management; and
4. therapeutic interventions with psychologist (ICCS). The standardised treatment
plan in NZ follows a similar trajectory plan as within Australia. However, the NZ
context and cultural considerations for Māori and bicultural positions need to be
considered when assessing for elimination disorders and implementing treatment
plans. A few cultural considerations for the Māori people include: acknowledging
role of broader whanau factors; awareness of Māori belief systems, including
views on individual mana, death, and dying; reliance on the family, prayer
(karakia), and traditional healing practices and providers (tohunga); and
practices of tapu/noa (Medical Council of New Zealand, 2008). Learning about
existing support mechanisms, such as kaiatawhai, whanau, and kaumātua,
can support practitioners when providing treatment for elimination disorders.
The principles of working with Māori people and their whanau are considered
generalisable to working with people from all cultures in NZ (Elder, 2015; Glynn
& Macfarlane, 2002).

Speciality treatment guidelines and/or groups

The New Zealand Continence Association helps support families and children with
wetting and/or soiling problems:
- New Zealand Continence Association, helpline 0800 650 659 (www.continence.org.nz).

Standard assessment measures

Standard assessment measures for elimination disorders are usually conducted by
a paediatrician and follow the guidelines of the ICCS. The assessments include a
thorough bodily examination observing body habitus and nutritional state as well
as psychosocial observations of self-confidence, posture, and gait. There are no
NZ norms available for these assessments; usually extensive physical exams are
implemented.

Behavioural assessments for psychosocial, emotional, or behavioural difficulties can
be used to identify other issues occurring simultaneously or as a secondary problem
to the elimination disorder (i.e., Strengths and Difficulties Questionnaire [SDQ],
Depression, Anxiety Stress Scale [DASS], and Behavior Assessment System for Children
[BASC]).

Funding of specialised treatment

The New Zealand Chiropractors' Association (NZCA) has provided free continence
education sessions to 1600 carers, nurses, and other health professionals. Community
incontinence services are typically delivered through district health boards (DHB)

and from privately managed services (e.g., psychologists). To date there are no specific funded treatment plans for elimination disorders in NZ.

New Zealand case study

This case has been created as an example for illustrative purposes.

An 8-year-old male has been referred to a psychologist from his paediatrician for help managing encopresis. The referral also notes social skills difficulties as he struggles to keep a strong friendship group and has trouble concentrating at school on tasks at hand. The boy is Māori, living with parents, and an only child.

His toileting difficulties were noted throughout his life. His parents reported that he had never learnt to use the toilet for bowel movements. He would soil his pants several times a day. His encopresis may be maintained through learned helplessness and low self-efficacy beliefs, also by anxiety and embarrassment associated with interactions around soiling. Important to note are the protective factors in this case which include support from an extended network of family (whanau), good physical health, easy temperament, and an optimistic attributional style.

He has been diagnosed by a paediatrician for meeting the *DSM-5* criteria for encopresis. That is, he had not achieved toilet training by age 5 and has repeated involuntarily passing faeces in his undergarments at home and school. Specifically, he meets encopresis (307.7) (i) with constipation and overflow incontinence.

If elimination is part of a wider set of adjustment difficulties and the problem is in the child's family network, treatment needs to address all the issues. For example, if a child presents with encopresis that is secondary to a trauma, a management program which addresses the trauma and a medical and psychological program for elimination problems would be the most appropriate intervention. However, in this case there appears to be no history of trauma, rather a cultural misunderstanding about appropriate toileting.

In order to support cultural awareness and understanding of the client's Māori background, the first session would entail a parent psychoeducation. This session could include creating an environment where the child can be treated with:
- acknowledging the role of broader whanau factors (reliance on extended family members)
- using prayer (karakia) to support client in treatment
- reflecting traditional healing practices and providers (tohunga), and practices of tapu/noa, to support the client's toileting
- using kaiatawhai, kaumātua with the parents to support practitioners
- viewing encopresis as a problem, which is non-intentional and uncontrollable.

Evidence-based treatment suggests that parents should offer praise for small gains in toileting, and provide a supportive environment: 20 minutes a day engage in supportive play or prayer (karakia) together and help the boy to maintain a regular predictable routine of eating, sleeping, and exercising. Collaboration with a paediatrician is needed to regularly manage laxative use and remove faecal mass as the client's encopresis diagnosis specifies constipation. The paediatrician would also most likely set up a bowel program following ICCS guidelines (sitting schedule, correct relaxed sitting/straining, and diet/fluid management) and liaise closely with the psychologist.

Recommended reading for parents

Clayden, G., & Agnarsson, V. (1992). Constipation in childhood: Information booklet for children and parents. In Appendix A of Buchanan, A. (Ed.). *Children who soil. Assessment and treatment.* Chichester: Wiley.

Recommended reading for client

Galvin, M., & Ferrero, S. (1991). *Clouds and clocks: A story for children who soil.* Washington, DC: Magination Press.

Culture-specific recommendations

For extra support for the parents, a referral for a Māori-sensitive practitioner to support the psychologist in session is made through the Kiwi Enuresis and Encopresis Association – Awhinatia Tamariki (KEEA), particularly for awareness and understanding around routines and systems in place to teach toileting and hygiene.

Australia – resources

Continence Foundation of Australia (CFA, www.continence.org.au) is the major professional body in Australia providing education, raising public awareness, and providing resources and referral information in support of child and adult incontinence. Contact the CFA on 1800 33 00 66 or info@continence.org.au

New Zealand – resources

Kiwi Enuresis and Encopresis Association – Awhinatia Tamariki (KEEA, www.continence.org.nz) is the children's division of New Zealand Chiropractors' Association, supporting parents, children and health professionals who are living with and/or managing the continence issues of childhood. KEEA was registered as a NZ charity in 2001, and has since merged with the New Zealand Continence Association. It is the only program support of its kind in NZ which provides guidance regarding encopresis and enuresis. KEEA provides information and support to families and health professionals on bedwetting (nocturnal enuresis) daytime wetting and soiling. Contact KEEA on 0800 650 659 or email info@continence.org.nz

Bibliography

Philichi, L. (2008). When the going gets tough: Paediatric constipation and encopresis. *Gastroenterology Nurse, 31*(2), 121–130.

von Gontard, A., Heron, J., & Joinson, C. (2011). Family history of nocturnal enuresis and urinary incontinence: Results from a large epidemiological study. *Journal of Urology, 185*(6), 2303–2306.

von Gontard, A., & Neveus T. (2006). *Management of disorders of bladder and bowel control in children.* London: MacKeithPress.

Zink, S., Freitag, C. M., & von Gontard, A. (2008). Behavioral comorbidity differs in subtypes of enuresis and urinary incontinence. *Journal of Urology, 179*(1), 295–298.

References

American Academy of Child and Adolescent Psychiatry. (2004). Practice parameters for the assessment and treatment of children and adolescents with enuresis. *Journal of the American Academy of Child and Adolescent Psychiatry, 43*(12), 1540–1550.

American Psychiatric Association. (2013). *Diagnostic and statistical manual of mental disorders* (5th ed.). Arlington, VA: Author.

Bower, W. F., Moore, K. H., Shepherd, R. B., & Adams, RD. (1996). The epidemiology of childhood enuresis in Australia. *British Journal of Urology, 78*(4), 602–606

Burgers, R. E., Mugie, S. M., Chase, J., Cooper., C. S., von Gontard., A., Riting, C. S., Homsy, Y., Bauer, S. B., & Benninga., M. A. (2013). Management of functional constipation in children with lower urinary tract symptoms: Report from the Standardization Committee of the International Children's Continence Society. *Journal of Urology, 190,* 29–36.

Butler, R. (2008). Wetting and soiling. In: A. Thapar, D. Pine, J. Leckman, S. Scott, M. Snowling, & E. Taylor (Eds.), *Rutters child and adolescent psychiatry* (pp. 916–929). Carlton, Vic.: Blackwell.

Caldwell, P., Deshpande, A., & von Gontard, A. (2013). Management of nocturnal enuresis. *British Medical Journal, 347,* 1–6.

Caldwell, P., Edgar, D., Hodson, E., & Craig, J. (2005). Bedwetting and toileting problems in children. *Medical Journal of Australia, 182*(4), 190–195.

Caldwell, P., Edgar, D., Jones, M., Hodson, E., & Craig, J. (2009). Treatment of enuresis: Effectiveness of alarm monotherapy versus combination treatment in a multidisciplinary clinic. *Australian and New Zealand Continence Journal, 13,* 61–67.

Carr, A. (2006). *The handbook of child and adolescent clinical psychology: A contextual approach.* London: Routledge.

Chase, J., Austin, P., Hoebeke, P., & McKenna, P. (2010). The management of dysfunctional voiding in children: A report from the Standardisation Committee of the International Children's Continence Society. *Journal of Urology, 183,* 1296–1302.

Christophersen, E., & Friman, P. (2010). *Elimination disorder in children and adolescents.* Cambridge, MA: Hogrefe.

Continence Foundation of Australia. (2015). *Promoting bladder and bowel health*. Retrieved 25 August 2015 from: www.continence.org.au

Deshpande, A. V., Craig, J. C., Smith, G. H., & Caldwell, P. H. (2011). Factors influencing quality of life in children with urinary incontinence. *Journal of Urology, 186,* 1048–1052.

Deshpande, A. V., Craig, J. C., Smith, G. H., & Caldwell, P. H. (2012). Management of daytime urinary incontinence and lower urinary tract symptoms in children. *Journal of Pediatrics and Child Health, 48*(2), 44–52.

Elder, H. (2015). *A psychiatric registrar's viewpoint: Hinemoa elder.* Accessed 8 January 2015: www.teiho.org.

Equit, H., Sambach, J., Niemczyk, A., & von Gontard, A. (2015). Urinary and fecal incontinence: A training programme for children and adolescents. *A comprehensive structured treatment manual.* Boston: Hogrefe.

Feehan, M., McGee, R., Stanton, W., & Silva, P. A. (1990). A 6 year follow up of childhood enuresis: Prevalence in adolescence and consequences for mental health. *Journal of Paeditrcs. Child Health, 26,* 75–79.

Fergusson, D. M., Horwood, L. J., & Shannon, F. T. (1986). Factors related to attainment of nocturnal bladder control: An 8 year longitudinal study. *Pediatrics, 78,* 884–890.

Franco, I., von Gontard, A., & De Gennaro, M. (2012). Evaluation and treatment of nonmonosymptomatic nocturnal enuresis: A standardization document from the International Children's Continence Society. *Journal of Pediatric Urology, 9,* 234–243.

Gim, C., Lillystone, D., & Caldwell, P. (2009). Efficacy of the bell and pad alarm therapy for nocturnal enuresis. *Journal of Paediatrics and Child Health, 45*(7–8), 405–408.

Glynn, T., & Macfarlane, A. (2002). Māori and bicultural positions: Professional development programme for resource teachers learning and behaviour. *The Proceedings of the National Māori Graduates of Psychology Symposium,* 95–105.

Gordon, D. (2014). PEBBLES*: A family-centred, community-based continence service improving bladder and bowel health in children with disabilities in Western Australia: A protocol paper. *Journal of Stomal Therapy Australia, 34*(3), 8–14.

Hurst, C., & Walker, P. (2005). Tasmanian children are the winners with Wetaway. *Australian and New Zealand Continence Journal, 11*(2), 33–37.

Medical Council of New Zealand. (2008). *Best health outcomes for Māori: Practice implications.* Available: www.mcnz.org.nz/assets/News-and-Publications/Statements/best-health-maoricomplete.pdf

Neveus, T., Eggert, P., Evans, J., Macedo, A., Rittig, S., Tekgul, S., Vande Wall, J., Yeung, C. K., & Robson, L. (2010). Evaluation of and treatment for monosymptomatic enuresis: A standardization document from the International Children's Continence Society. *Journal of Urology, 183,* 441–447.

Schulman, S., Quinn, C., Plachter, N., & Kodman-Jones, A. (1999). Comprehensive management of dysfunctional voiding. *Pediatrics, 103*(3), 1–5.

South Australia Government Disability Services. (2014). *Toilet time; a resource manual for allied health professionals and educators for special needs population.* Retrieved 17 September 2015 from www.shop.service.sa.gov.au

Sureshkumar, P., Jones, M., Cumming, R., & Craig, J. (2009). A population based study of 2,856 school-age children with urinary incontinence. *Journal of Urology, 181,* 808–816.

Van Hoecke, E., Baeyens, D., Vanden Bossche, H., Hoebeke, P., & Vande Walle, K. (2007). Early detection of psychological problems in a population of children with enuresis: Construction and validation of the short screening instrument for psychological problems in enuresis. *Journal of Urology, 178,* 2611–2616.

von Gontard, A. (2005). Elimination disorders: enuresis and encopresis. In C. Gillberg (Ed.), *A clinician's handbook of child and adolescent psychiatry.* Cambridge: University Press.

von Gontard, A., Baeyens, D., Van Hoecke, E., Warzak, W. J., & Bachmann, C. (2011). Psychological and psychiatric issues in urinary and fecal incontinence. *Journal of Urology, 185,* 1432–1437.

Wiener, J., Scales, M., Hampton, J., King, L. R., Surwit, R., & Edwards, C. L. (2000). Long-term efficacy of simple behavioral therapy for daytime wetting in children. *Journal of Urology, 164,* 786–790.

World Health Organisation. (2011). *International statistical classification of diseases and related health problems 2010 edition (ICD-10).* Geneva: Author.

Recommendations for further reading/resources

General

Bonner, L., & Wells, M. (2008). *Effective management of bladder and bowel problems in children.* UK: Class Publishing.

Boswell, S., & Gray, D. (2012). *Applying structured teaching principles to toilet training.* Available: www.teacch.com

Clayden, G., & Agnarsson, V. (1992). Constipation in childhood: Information booklet for children and parents. In A. Buchanan (Ed.), *Children who soil: Assessment and treatment.* Chichester: Wiley.

Fergusson, D. M., & Horwood, L. J. (1994). Nocturnal enuresis and behavioral problems in adolescence: A 15-year longitudinal study. *Pediatrics, 94*(5), 662–668.

Hall, J. (2009). *How to stop bedwetting.* Victoria, Australia: The Five Mile Press.

Kids Incorporated. (2015). "How Teachers can Help" abridged from Bowel Group. Retrieved 17 September 2015 from www.bgk.org.au

National Institute for Health and Clinical Excellence. (2010). *Constipation in children and young people.* May. London: Author. Available: www.nice.org.uk/guidance/qs62

South Australia Government Disability Services. (2015). *Are you ready?* DVD animation Resource. Retrieved 17 September 2015 from: www.shop.service.sa.gov.au

Victorian Continence Resource Centre. (2010). *One step at a time – A parent's guide to toilet skills for children with special needs.* Available: www.continencevictoria.org.au/one-step-at-a-time

Multimedia applications

- The New Potty and Once Upon a Potty (www.oceanhousemedia.com)
- See Me Go Potty (www.avakid.com)
- Little Star Toilet and Potty Training Story (www.apps.littlestarearlylearning.com)

Australia

Queensland Health. (2012). *Conquering wees and poos. A learning resource for allied health and nursing professionals working in the field of paediatric continence*. South Brisbane: Queensland Health and Royal Children's Hospital Foundation.

Royal Children's Hospital Melbourne. (November 2010). *Clinical practice guideline: Chronic constipation*. Retrieved 8 January 2015 from: www.rch.org.au/clinicalguide/cpg.cfm?doc_id=11659

New Zealand

Feehan, M., McGee, R., Stanton, W., & Silva, P. A. (1990). A 6 year follow up of childhood enuresis: Prevalence in adolescence and consequences for mental health. *Journal of Paediatric Child Health*, *26*, 75–79.

Fergusson, M. D., & Horwood, L., J. (1994). Nocturnal enuresis and behavioral problems in adolescence: A 15-year longitudinal study. *Pediatrics*, *94*(5), 662–668.

Medical council of New Zealand. (2008). *Best health outcomes for Māori: Practice implications*. Available: www.mcnz.org.nz/assets/News-and-Publications/Statements/best-health-maoricomplete.pdf

New Zealand Psychological Society. Bicultural resources: Implications for practice. Available: www.psychology.org.nz/nga-kete/bicultural-resources/#.VK3MOR2Ue90

Acknowledgements

Thanks to Dr Patrina Caldwell, Staff Specialist, Department of Nephrology, Children's Hospital at Westmead, Sydney and Fiona Davis, Psychologist, Specialist Children's Services, Department of Education and Training, Victoria, for assistance with the Australian content.

18

Sleep-wake disorders

Kurt Lushington and Silvia Pignata

Introduction

The *Diagnostic and Statistical Manual of Mental Disorders* (5th ed.; *DSM-5*; American Psychiatric Association, 2013) contains 10 sleep-wake disorders: insomnia; hypersomnolence; narcolepsy; breathing related; circadian rhythm; non-rapid eye movement (NREM) sleep arousal; nightmare; rapid eye movement (REM) sleep behaviour; restless legs syndrome; and substance/medication-induced sleep difficulties. The *DSM-5* nosology incorporates recent advances in our understanding of the physiological and genetic factors underpinning disordered sleep, the impact of lifespan development on sleep and pathology, and findings from treatment studies. Diagnostic formulations incorporate validated polysomnographic and neurobiologic biomarkers, which distinguish the diagnosis of sleep from most other psychiatric disorders. Unfortunately, it is not possible to review all 10 *DSM-5* sleep-wake disorders in one summary chapter. As a result, this chapter will focus on those most often addressed via psychological interventions. Readers interested in a review of the full range of sleeping disorders are referred to the companion academic supplementary materials available for the current textbook.

Common to all the *DSM-5* sleep-wake disorders is dissatisfaction with the quality, timing, and amount of sleep, together with evidence of impact or distress in everyday functioning. Diagnosis also depends on the sleep problem being primary in origin and not secondary to a known medical condition, disease, or health impairment. However, identifying the primary disorder can be complicated by the bidirectional and often mutually exacerbating relationship that exists between disordered sleep (e.g., insomnia, excessive sleepiness, early morning wakefulness) and many psychiatric and medical conditions. Sleep problems typically do not occur in isolation, but there is good evidence that treating sleep disorders can lead to gains, even when secondary to other medical problems.

Two distinguishing features of the sleep disorders field are: 1. the diversity of disorders; and 2. the degree to which psychological treatments play a role in therapy.

Some sleep disorders are more properly addressed via medical and pharmaceutical interventions, such as narcolepsy with stimulant medication and obstructive sleep apnoea hypopnea disorder with continuous positive airway pressure (CPAP) apparatus, although cognitive behaviour therapy (CBT) has been shown to increase CPAP adherence (Agudelo et al., 2014; Richards et al., 2007).

Prevalence and cost of sleep disorders

The prevalence of sleep disorders in Australia and New Zealand (NZ) is high. A 2011 report commissioned by the Sleep Health Foundation estimated they affect 1.5 million adult Australians (about 9% of the population; Deloitte Access Economics, 2011). A recent study of Australian adult sleeping habits estimated that up to 35% report one or more persistent symptoms of disrupted sleep, insufficient sleep, daytime fatigue, excessive sleepiness, or irritability (Mansfield et al., 2013). Patients also rank problematic sleep highly as a reason for seeking treatment. For example, in a 2007 survey of Australian general practice consultations, an estimated 1.7 million cases were for managing disordered sleep, most for insomnia (Britt et al., 2008; Knox et al., 2008).

The prevalence of specific sleep disorders in Australian and NZ children is not well documented, but the general consensus is that while sleep problems are common (e.g., bedtime resistance and/or inadequate sleep), in most cases this does not generalise to a sleep disorder. The frequency of moderate–severe sleep problems in Australian children is estimated to range from 18% in the first few months of life to 7% by age 7 (Quach et al., 2013). Notwithstanding the high frequency in infants, sleep problems are also surprisingly common in older children and especially sleep insufficiency and daytime sleepiness. Up to 37% of NZ teenagers are reported to have a significant sleep problem lasting more than a month (Fernando et al., 2013) and comparable estimates are reported in Australian teenagers (Gradisar, Gardner, & Dohnt, 2011). Sleep problems early in life are known to adversely impact schooling and daytime functioning and are also predictive of reduced mental health later in life. For example, in a sample of 4460 Australian children aged 6–7 years, at transition to school poor sleep was predictive of lower health quality-of-life, behaviour, language, and learning scores. In a sample of 943 NZ children aged 6–9 years, 13% were reported to have a significant sleep problem which was strongly predictive of anxiety at 26 years of age (Gregory et al., 2005; Quach et al., 2009).

Nosology: *DSM-5* sleep-wake disorders

The following section presents a brief outline of the key features of some select sleep-wake disorders across age groups, latest research developments, and prevalence and treatment approaches with a focus on psychological interventions and CBT.

Insomnia disorder

The key feature of insomnia disorder is dissatisfaction with the quantity or quality of sleep together with impaired interpersonal, occupational, academic, or behavioural functioning. The *DSM-5* distinguishes three subtypes of insomnia: sleep-onset (initial) insomnia characterised by difficulty falling asleep at bedtime; sleep maintenance (middle) insomnia indicated by awakening frequently or problems returning to sleep after wakening; and (late) insomnia characterised by early awakening and the inability to return to sleep. Insomnia disorder is diagnosed if the sleep difficulty occurs at least three nights per week, for at least 3 months, despite adequate opportunities for sleep. Insomnia disorder may be diagnosed in children if they report dissatisfaction with the quantity or quality of sleep, cannot settle to sleep, or have difficulty returning to sleep without their caregiver's attention.

Insomnia causes increased daytime irritability, poor concentration, fatigue, decreased motivation and attention, and emotional lability. Individuals may also become preoccupied with sleep and not sleeping, which can provoke anxiety and affect sleep. The counterproductive thoughts surrounding sleeplessness are the focus of the cognitive component of CBT (Harvey, 2002). The long-term consequences of insomnia include: an increased risk of a major depressive disorder; hypertension; myocardial infarction; reduced quality of life; increased risk for accidents, injury, and work absenteeism; and reduced productivity. Insomnia may occur as a primary disorder but is commonly comorbid with other physical or mental disorders; for example, approximately 50% of patients with depression are reported to have comorbid insomnia (Cunnington, Junge, & Fernando, 2013; Roth, 2007).

Insomnia is a significant public health issue affecting up to 25% of adults, with a higher prevalence in females and the aged (Ohayon, 2002; Zhang & Wing, 2006). About 13% to 33% of adult Australians have regular difficulty in getting to sleep or staying asleep (Cunnington et al., 2013; Hillman & Lack, 2013). An estimated 13% of adult New Zealanders report at least one insomnia symptom, 25% report a chronic sleep problem and 45% report having the symptoms of insomnia at least once per week with higher frequency in Māori populations (O'Keeffe et al., 2011; Paine et al., 2005; Wilsmore et al., 2013). Although less well researched, insomnia is also common in adolescents. An estimated 7.8% of Australian adolescents are reported to have insomnia while 37.2% of NZ adolescents report significant sleep symptoms lasting longer than 1 month and 17.2% insomnia (Dohnt, Gradisar, & Short, 2012; Fernando et al., 2013).

In contrast to adults, the prevalence of insomnia in Australian and NZ children is not well documented. Overseas data indicates that childhood behavioural insomnia, which involves bedtime problems and night waking, affect 20% to 30% of infants and toddlers and 5% of school-aged children, with a higher frequency among children with developmental disorders (Blader et al., 1997; Owens et al., 2000). Australian data indicates that 17% of infants and 14% of preschool-aged children have moderate to severe sleep problems (Martin et al., 2007), while in a combined sample of Australian and NZ parents, 30.7% perceived that their child (aged 0–3 years) had a sleep problem (Teng et al., 2012). These frequencies are likely to be underestimates as sleep problems in children are both under-reported by parents and underdiagnosed by practitioners (Blunden et al., 2004).

Treatment paradigms for insomnia include relaxation therapy, stimulus control therapy, sleep restriction therapy, cognitive restructuring, biofeedback, and sleep hygiene education. Recent innovations include internet-assisted self-help therapies, coaching-assisted self-help treatment, and therapist-guided e-therapy for insomnia (Cheng & Dizon, 2012; Cuijpers et al., 2009). CBT for insomnia is well validated in adults (Morgenthaler et al., 2006) and moderately validated in children (Meltzer & Mindell, 2014; Meltzer et al., 2014). In adolescents, treatment often requires attention to particular risk factors such as anxiety and delayed sleep phase syndrome and in adults to stressors such as concerns with relationships, work/career, finances, and shiftwork schedules (Taylor et al., 2014).

Australian researchers have contributed to several innovations in treating insomnia, such as intensive sleep retraining (a single night of sleep deprivation followed by brief nap opportunities; Harris et al., 2007), and bright light therapy in the morning for sleep-onset insomnia (Harris et al., 2007) and in the evening for early morning awakening insomnia (Lack & Wright, 1993).

Hypersomnolence disorder

The *DSM-5* criteria for hypersomnolence disorder is excessive sleepiness despite adequate sleep of at least 7 hours. It is associated with: recurrent periods of sleep or lapses into sleep within the same day; feeling unrefreshed despite sleeping for more than 9 hours per day; or having difficulty being fully awake after awakening abruptly (sleep inertia). The disorder is diagnosed if the excessive sleepiness occurs at least three times per week for at least 3 months. The consequences of hypersomnolence disorder include reduced alertness and concentration, poor daytime memory (often leading to significant distress and dysfunction in social relationships and employment such as arriving at work late), and an increased risk for accidents and mood disorders (de Pinho et al., 2006; Kaplan & Harvey, 2009).

Psychological stress and alcohol use may temporarily increase hypersomnolence, which can also be associated with viral infections such as human immunodeficiency virus (HIV) pneumonia. Hypersomnolence increases the risk for substance-related disorders, particularly self-medication with stimulants. It is estimated to affect up to 25% of adults with 5% to 10% seeking treatment for daytime sleepiness (Adenuga & Attarian, 2014; Masri, Gonzales, & Kushida, 2012). A community survey of sleep habits in Australian adults indicated that one-fifth of people are chronically sleep restricted and 11.7% are chronically sleepy (Bartlett et al., 2008). In Australian adolescents, up to 49.1% reported being sleepy and 20.0% said they missed class in the last month because they overslept (less than once per week = 11.1% and more than once per week = 8.3%; Lushington et al., 2015; Short et al., 2013). In contrast to adolescents, the frequency of hypersomnolence is less well established in Australian and NZ children, but a United States (US) sample estimated that up to 15% of children are excessively sleepy during the day (Calhoun et al., 2011).

Hypersomnolence disorder is persistent, with an increasing severity of symptoms. Individuals reported an average night-time sleep duration of about 9.5 hours. The disorder rarely occurs in children and people are often diagnosed 10–15 years after the first symptoms appear. Often, the disorder fully manifests in late adolescence or early adulthood with a mean age at onset of 17–24 years.

Non-drug treatment options for hypersomnolence are limited to sleep hygiene education, especially establishing a regular sleep-wake pattern, optimising opportunities for sleep, and short 15- to 30-minute naps timed in the mid-afternoon to prevent sleep disruption (Conroy, Novick, & Swanson, 2012). Severe cases may require pharmaceutical support (for more information see www.hypersomnolenceaustralia. com; Mignot, 2012).

Circadian rhythm sleep-wake disorders

The *DSM-5* classification of circadian rhythm sleep-wake disorders comprises the five subtypes of: delayed sleep phase (DSPD); advanced sleep phase (ASPD); irregular sleep-wake; non-24-hour sleep-wake; and shiftwork. To diagnose the disorders, individuals must report a persistent pattern of sleep disruption due to an alteration of the circadian rhythm and the individual's required sleep-wake schedule, which leads to excessive sleepiness and/or insomnia and reduced daytime functioning. The circadian system ensures the body's various physiological processes are synchronised with each other, with the external light/dark cycle, and with the 24-hour cycle. This system ensures that humans sleep at night. The "clock" responsible for timing the circadian system is in the suprachiasmatic nucleus of the hypothalamus which receives input from specialised light-sensitive cells in the eye (Dijk & Lockley, 2002). Light exposure in the evening delays the "clock" and morning light exposure advances the "clock," thus regulating the synchrony between the rhythms of the body and the 24-hour day-night cycle (Czeisler et al., 1986).

One example of a circadian difficulty is shiftwork sleep disorder. This refers to insomnia during the major sleep period and excessive sleepiness (and inadvertent sleep) at work during the major awake period associated with the shiftwork schedule. Indeed, falling asleep at work at least once a week occurs in 32% to 36% of shiftworkers (Rajaratnam, Howard, & Grunstein, 2013). Diagnosis is based on a history of the individual regularly working outside the normal daytime schedule of 8.00 am to 6.00 pm. The disorder affects an estimated 5% to 10% of those who work at night, higher for those over 50 and worsening with age, as the circadian phase shift disrupts sleep for older adults more so than younger adults. In Australia, nearly 1.5 million do shiftwork, which represents 16% of the working population (Rajaratnam et al., 2013). Shiftwork is associated with adverse health outcomes (especially cardiometabolic diseases and mood disturbance), an increased risk of accidents at work and driving home, and psychosocial deficits (especially impaired interpersonal relationships and drug/alcohol misuse; Rajaratnam et al., 2013). Treatment of shiftwork sleep disorder is typically aimed at facilitating circadian adjustment with sleep hygiene education, behavioural scheduling, light therapy and chronobiotics; and promoting night-time alertness with prophylactic napping, stimulants (e.g., caffeine), and bright light therapy (Wright, Bogan, & Wyatt, 2013). Strategies that address work and organisational factors can also help in roster scheduling and managing fatigue (Gander et al., 2011).

Absent in the *DSM-5* nosology is jet lag (i.e., the sleep-wake disruption arising from time-zone travel). Although included in the *DSM-IV*, because it is perceived to be a normal physiological response to travel across time-zones and its transient, short-lived and self-correcting nature it was not thought to warrant inclusion. Management of jet lag includes those strategies that facilitate circadian adjustment (e.g., behavioural scheduling, light therapy and chronobiotics such as melatonin; Waterhouse et al., 2007).

Parasomnias

The parasomnias classification comprises disorders that are characterised by "abnormal behavioural, experiential or physiological events occurring in association with sleep, specific sleep stages, or sleep-wake transitions" (American Psychiatric Association, 2013, p. 399). The classification includes NREM sleep arousal disorder, nightmare disorder, and REM sleep behaviour disorder.

Sleepwalking is an example of a parasomnia and involves repeated episodes of an individual rising from bed during sleep and walking about with a blank staring face, being difficult to awake, and unresponsive to others. Individuals may be initially confused and disoriented after waking, but normal cognitive function and behaviour soon returns. Two subtypes of sleepwalking are distinguished: 1. sleep-related eating behaviour (most common in females); and 2. sleep-related sexual behaviour (more common in males). Many people have isolated or infrequent episodes of sleepwalking, particularly children. Estimates from studies conducted outside of Australia and NZ suggest that 10% to 30% of children have had at least one episode of sleepwalking, 2% to 3% often sleepwalk and 1% to 5% meet a diagnosis of sleepwalking disorder, while 1.6% to 2.4% of individuals over 15 years often sleepwalk (Bixler et al., 1979; Hublin et al., 1997; Ohayon, Guilleminault, & Priest, 1999). However, because of the dependency on external report (i.e., parent or partner) and the absence of objective data, the reliability of sleepwalking estimates is questionable. In general, sleepwalking is reported to be more common in females (Ohayon et al., 1999) and is thought to have a strong heredity component (Hublin et al., 1997). Unlike the pattern typically seen in slow wave sleep, there is activation of the cingulate cortex and no deactivation of the thalamus, explaining the mental confusion and motor activation (Bassetti et al., 2000). Little is known about the two subtypes of sleepwalking other than case study reports. The initial onset of sleepwalking in adults may be associated with obstructive sleep apnoea and hypopnea (OSAH), nocturnal seizures, major depressive episodes, and obsessive-compulsive disorder or medication (Ohayon et al., 1999). Sleep restriction, alcohol, stress, medications, and fever are reported to exacerbate symptoms (Pressman, 2007; Rosen, Mahowald, & Ferber, 1995). Non-drug treatments for sleepwalking include scheduled awakenings (Frank et al., 1997), ensuring adequate sleep, and supportive psychotherapy (Pressman, 2007).

Another parasomnia is sleep terrors or recurring episodes of awakening accompanied by abrupt terror often characterised by a panicky scream, displays of intense fear with signs of autonomic arousal (such as dilated pupils, a fast heart rate, rapid breathing, and sweating) and a lack of response to carers. In addition, little or no dreams are recalled, there is no memory of the episode and it causes significant distress in social, occupational, or daily functioning. Noticeably, an individual's eyes will often be open during an arousal, which are typically brief but can last up to an hour, especially in children. Sleep terror disorder decreases with age and is more common in males. An estimated 37% of children at 18 months of age are reported to have experienced a sleep terror, decreasing to 20% at 30 months of age, and further to 2.2% by adulthood (Ohayon et al., 1999). Sleep terrors have a strong hereditary component (Hublin et al., 1997), are exacerbated by sleep restriction, and are often accompanied by anxiety and depression (Ohayon et al., 1999). Non-drug treatments include scheduled awakenings (Lask, 1988) and hypnosis (Hurwitz et al., 1991).

Nightmares are an REM phenomenon. In contrast to sleep terrors, individuals with nightmare disorder usually awaken easily with vivid recollections of their dreams. Nightmares occur more frequently in the second half of the night when REM density peaks. Nightmare disorder can be diagnosed if an individual reports repeated occurrences of extended, distressed, and well-remembered dreams that occur during the second half of the night-time sleep period, often involving imminent threats to survival, security, or physical integrity. The distressing emotions may contribute to difficulty in returning to sleep and, in turn, significant daytime distress or impaired functioning.

Nightmares are often associated with acute or chronic psychosocial stressors (Spoormaker, Schredl, & van den Bout, 2006). The frequency of nightmares increases through childhood. Overseas data indicate that 1.3% to 3.9% of parents report that their pre-school child often or always has nightmares and 22% for children aged 6–12 years (Simard et al., 2008; Vela-Bueno, 1985). The prevalence of nightmares peaks in young adulthood with a higher frequency in females before steadily decreasing with age. Figures are not available for Australia and NZ, but data from the US indicate that 6% of adults report monthly nightmares and 1% to 2% frequent nightmares (Bixler et al., 1979). CBT for nightmare disorder includes systematic desensitisation, imagery rehearsal, relaxation techniques, fear extinction, and eye movement desensitisation (Sadeh, 2005). Pharmaceutical intervention may also be recommended especially for nightmares associated with posttraumatic stress disorder (Aurora et al., 2010).

Australian case study

This case has been created as an example for illustrative purposes.

Tom is a 17-year-old student with a history of taking a long time to fall asleep and excessive daytime tiredness. On examination, Tom is of normal height and weight for his age, denies any mood or health problems and reports few conflicts with his parents other than around the timing of his sleep. Tom presents as a quiet youth, mature for his age, and reports a reasonably strong peer network. However, most of his socialisation is on the weekend and because of school absences he is less engaged with school peers than previously. He reports that his school performance has deteriorated recently and that this is affecting his mood.

From a history of his sleep patterns over childhood, it is revealed that Tom's parents have been fairly relaxed about setting limits for bedtime and since early adolescence he has been responsible for setting his bedtime. Tom reports that this has generally not been a problem, but in the last year he has been falling asleep progressively later and later and correspondingly finding it more difficult to get up in the morning. This is proving especially problematic on school days and in the last month he reports having missed at least one day of schooling per week because of having overslept. This has led to school notices for poor attendance and resulted in increased family tension. In addition, Tom reports that even when he does attend school, he finds it difficult to concentrate because of sleepiness. Both of Tom's parents leave early to go to work and are therefore not able to supervise him in the morning. Tom reports that despite going to bed earlier, he does not fall asleep. Moreover, despite setting several alarms he often sleeps through. He has not used prescription medications but has tried a herbal remedy containing St John's Wort to improve his sleep, without much effect.

The first step of Tom's treatment plan was to monitor his sleep pattern using a sleep diary to document when he goes to bed, when he falls asleep, when he finally wakes up, and when he gets up out of bed. In addition, Tom was asked prior to going to bed to review the day and rate the level of his daytime tiredness. He was asked to maintain the diary for 2 weeks. A review of his sleep diary revealed that on average he went to bed at 1.15 am but did not fall asleep until 3.25 am. On school days, he reported that on the days he attended school he generally was out of bed by 8.30 am, but was always tired and often late for class. Of note is that on weekend days he would fall asleep around 3.30 am but in contrast to school days he would wake-up around 1.30 pm feeling refreshed and active.

Upon further questioning, it was revealed that on school holidays when Tom was allowed to follow his own inclinations for going and getting up out of bed, he would settle into a routine of falling asleep by 4.00 am and getting up around 2.00 pm. He reported that this was not a struggle and that he felt good during the day. His mother reported that ever since he was a baby, he always liked to go to bed late. She described him as the owl in the family.

Tom was diagnosed with delayed sleep phase syndrome. He was prescribed a chronotherapy treatment regime to reset his "clock" to better align the timing of his sleep-wake pattern with his daily living activities. This consisted of asking Tom to stay in his bedroom from midnight to 2.00 pm without exposure to sunlight for 3 days to establish a baseline. He was then instructed every 3 days to reset his bed and rise times. Specifically, he was asked to go to bed 1 hour earlier and get up out of bed 1 hour earlier. As well, after getting up he was instructed to immediately expose himself to sunlight either by sitting outside or sitting in a sunlit room. Over the treatment period, Tom kept a sleep diary and attended the sleep clinic weekly to monitor his progress. The intervention was scheduled over the school holidays to allow for the later rise times and the whole protocol took 21 days to complete.

Tom has been able to successfully reset the timing of his sleep-wake pattern. After treatment, he reports on school days that he is able to fall asleep between 11.00–12.00 pm and wake up between 7.00–8.00 am. The pattern is similar for weekends and he tends to lie-in but not later than 10.00 am. To prevent relapse, he is further instructed not to oversleep on weekends or holidays beyond 10.00 am and during school time not to go to bed later than 12.00 pm on weekend nights.

Research in Australia and New Zealand

The Australian and NZ sleep health landscape is currently fragmented and under-resourced. There is a need for greater education and to raise awareness in the community, health professionals, and public policy makers of sleep disorders, their causes and treatment, impact on health, and the consequences for productivity and workplace safety. Further research and development is also needed to improve our understanding as to the prevalence of sleep disorders (especially in children), to better evaluate the cost effectiveness of prevention, treatment and management options, and to explore the link between sleep disorders and other illnesses and, similarly, the impact of sleep disorders on workplace productivity and occupational health and safety (especially motor vehicle accidents). Research is also needed on the broad sociocultural changes affecting modern societies and the rise of the 24/7 world and its impact on sleep and health. For more information, see Deloitte Access Economics (2011, www.sleephealthfoundation.org.au/pdfs/news/Reawakening#Australia.pdf).

Despite the advances in sleep medicine, much remains a mystery. We do not understand why humans and animals need to sleep and we are only just beginning to understand the impact of disordered sleep, sleep loss, and displaced sleep (e.g., shiftworkers) on social, physical, and mental wellbeing. More research into the functions of sleep, the pathophysiology of sleep, and the treatment of sleep disorders is needed. Despite clinicians and researchers in Australia and NZ being early and active contributors to the field of sleep, basic research remains to be undertaken. In both countries there is a need for population studies to determine what is "normal sleep," epidemiological studies to explore the prevalence rates of the various sleep disorders, and longitudinal studies to examine treatment efficacy. Given the demand for services, also needed is a great recognition of sleep as a unique health discipline and thereby the requirement for specialist training and treatment centres to manage what is an underserviced area of health need. For more information, see Sleepdex, Scientific research into sleep (www.sleepdex.org/future.htm).

References

Adenuga, O., & Attarian, H. (2014). Treatment of disorders of hypersomnolence. *Current Treatment Options in Neurology, 16*(9), 1–12.

Agudelo, H. A. M., Correa, U. J., Sierra, J. C., Pandi-Perumal, S. R., & Schenck, C. H. (2014). Cognitive behavioral treatment for narcolepsy: Can it complement pharmacotherapy? *Sleep Science, 7*(1), 30–42.

American Psychiatric Association. (2013). *Diagnostic and statistical manual of mental disorders* (5th ed.). Arlington, VA: Author.

Aurora, R. N., Zak, R. S., Auerbach, S. H., Casey, K. R., Chowdhuri, S., Karippot, A., Maganti, R. K., Ramar, K., Kristo, D. A., & Bista, S. R. (2010). Best practice guide for the treatment of nightmare disorder in adults. *Journal of Clinical Sleep Medicine, 6*(4), 389–401.

Bartlett, D., Marshall, N., Williams, A., & Grunstein, R. (2008). Sleep health New South Wales: Chronic sleep restriction and daytime sleepiness. *Journal of Internal Medicine, 38*(1), 24–31.

Bassetti, C., Vella, S., Donati, F., Wielepp, P., & Weder, B. (2000). SPECT during sleepwalking. *The Lancet, 356*(9228), 484–485.

Bixler, E. O., Kales, A., Soldatos, C. R., Kales, J. D., & Healey, S. (1979). Prevalence of sleep disorders in the Los Angeles metropolitan area. *The American Journal of Psychiatry. 136*(10), 1257–1262.

Blader, J. C., Koplewicz, H. S., Abikoff, H., & Foley, C. (1997). Sleep problems of elementary school children: A community survey. *Archives of Pediatrics and Adolescent Medicine, 151*(5), 473–480.

Blunden, S., Lushington, K., Lorenzen, B., Ooi, T., Fung, F., & Kennedy, D. (2004). Are sleep problems under-recognised in general practice? *Archives of Disease in childhood, 89*(8), 708–712.

Britt, H., Harrison, C., Miller, G., & Knox, S. (2008). Prevalence and patterns of multimorbidity in Australia. *Medical Journal of Australia, 189*(2), 72–77.

Calhoun, S. L., Vgontzas, A. N., Fernandez-Mendoza, J., Mayes, S. D., Tsaoussoglou, M., Basta, M., & Bixler, E. O. (2011). Prevalence and risk factors of excessive daytime sleepiness in a community sample of young children: The role of obesity, asthma, anxiety/depression, and sleep. *Sleep, 34*(4), 503–507.

Cheng, S. K., & Dizon, J. (2012). Computerised cognitive behavioural therapy for insomnia: A systematic review and meta-analysis. *Psychotherapy and Psychosomatics, 81*(4), 206–216.

Conroy, D. A., Novick, D. M., & Swanson, L. M. (2012). Behavioral management of hypersomnia. *Sleep Medicine Clinics, 7*(2), 325–331.

Cuijpers, P., Marks, I. M., van Straten, A., Cavanagh, K., Gega, L., & Andersson, G. (2009). Computer aided psychotherapy for anxiety disorders: A meta analytic review. *Cognitive Behaviour Therapy, 38*(2), 66–82.

Cunnington, D., Junge, M. F., & Fernando, A. T. (2013). Insomnia: Prevalence, consequences and effective treatment. *Medical Journal of Australia, 199*(8), S36–S40.

Czeisler, C. A., Allan, J. S., Strogatz, S. H., Ronda, J. M., Sanchez, R., Rios, C. D., Freitag, W. O, Richardson, G. S., & Kronauer, R. E. (1986). Bright light resets the human circadian pacemaker independent of the timing of the sleep-wake cycle. *Science, 233*(4764), 667–671.

de Pinho, R. S., da Silva-Junior, F. P., Bastos, J. P. C., Maia, W. S., de Mello, M. T., de Bruin, V. M., & de Bruin, P. F. C. (2006). Hypersomnolence and accidents in truck drivers: A cross-sectional study. *Chronobiology International, 23*(5), 963–671.

Deloitte Access Economics. (2011). *Re-awakening Australia: The economic cost of sleep disorders in Australia.* Canberra. Available: http://www.sleephealthfoundation.org.au/pdfs/news/Reawakening%20Australia.pdf

Dijk, D. J., & Lockley, S. W. (2002). Invited review: Integration of human sleep-wake regulation and circadian rhythmicity. *Journal of Applied Physiology, 92*(2), 852–862.

Dohnt, H., Gradisar, M., & Short, M. A. (2012). Insomnia and its symptoms in adolescents: Comparing DSM-IV and ICSD-II diagnostic criteria. *Journal of Clinical Sleep Medicine, 8*(3), 295–299.

Fernando, A. T., Samaranayake, C. B., Blank, C. J., Roberts, G., & Arroll, B. (2013). Sleep disorders among high school students in New Zealand. *Journal of Primary Health Care, 5*(4), 276–282.

Frank, N. C., Spirito, A., Stark, L., & Owens-Stively, J. (1997). The use of scheduled awakenings to eliminate childhood sleepwalking. *Journal of Pediatric Psychology, 22*(3), 345–353.

Gander, P., Hartley, L., Powell, D., Cabon, P., Hitchcock, E., Mills, A., & Popkin, S. (2011). Fatigue risk management: Organizational factors at the regulatory and industry/company level. *Accident Analysis and Prevention, 43*(2), 573–590.

Gradisar, M., Gardner, G., & Dohnt, H. (2011). Recent worldwide sleep patterns and problems during adolescence: A review and meta-analysis of age, region, and sleep. *Sleep Medicine, 12*(2), 110–118.

Gregory, A. M., Caspi, A., Eley, T. C., Moffitt, T. E., O'Connor, T. G., & Poulton, R. (2005). Prospective longitudinal associations between persistent sleep problems in childhood and anxiety and depression disorders in adulthood. *Journal of Abnormal Child Psychology, 33*(2), 157–163.

Harris, J., Lack, L., Wright, H., Gradisar, M., & Brooks, A. (2007). Intensive sleep retraining treatment for chronic primary insomnia: A preliminary investigation. *Journal of Sleep Research, 16*(3), 276–284.

Harvey, A. G. (2002). A cognitive model of insomnia. *Behaviour Research and Therapy, 40*(8), 869–893.

Hillman, D. R., & Lack, L. C. (2013). Public health implications of sleep loss: The community burden. *Medical Journal of Australia, 199*(8), S7–S10.

Hublin, C., Kaprio, J., Partinen, M., Heikkila, K., & Koskenvuo, M. (1997). Prevalence and genetics of sleepwalking: A population-based twin study. *Neurology, 48*(1), 177–181.

Hurwitz, T. D., Mahowald, M. W., Schenck, C. H., Schluter, J. L., & Bundlie, S. R. (1991). A retrospective outcome study and review of hypnosis as treatment of adults with sleepwalking and sleep terror. *Journal of Nervous and Mental Disease, 179*(4), 228–233.

Kaplan, K. A., & Harvey, A. G. (2009). Hypersomnia across mood disorders: A review and synthesis. *Sleep Medicine Reviews, 13*(4), 275–285.

Knox, S. A., Harrison, C. M., Britt, H. C., Henderson, J. V., Knox, S., Harrison, C., Britt, H. C., & Henderson, J. (2008). Estimating prevalence of common chronic morbidities in Australia. *Medical Journal of Australia, 189*(2), 66–70.

Lack, L., & Wright, H. (1993). The effect of evening bright light in delaying the circadian rhythms and lengthening the sleep of early morning awakening insomniacs. *Sleep, 16*(5), 436–443.

Lask, B. (1988). Novel and non-toxic treatment for night terrors. *British Medical Journal, 297*(6648), 592.

Lushington, K., Wilson, A., Biggs, S., Dollman, J., Martin, J., & Kennedy, D. (2015). Culture, extracurricular activity, sleep habits and mental health: A comparison of senior high school Asian-Australian and Caucasian-Australian adolescents. *International Journal of Mental Health, 44*(1–2), 139–157.

Mansfield, D. R., Hillman, D. R., Antic, N. A., McEvoy, R. D., & Rajaratnam, S. (2013). Sleep loss and sleep disorders. *Medical Journal of Australia, 199*(8), 5–6.

Martin, J., Hiscock, H., Hardy, P., Davey, B., & Wake, M. (2007). Adverse associations of infant and child sleep problems and parent health: An Australian population study. *Pediatrics, 119*(5), 947–955.

Masri, T. J., Gonzales, C. G., & Kushida, C. A. (2012). Idiopathic hypersomnia. *Sleep Medicine Clinics, 7*(2), 283–289.

Meltzer, L. J., & Mindell, J. A. (2014). Systematic review and meta-analysis of behavioral interventions for pediatric Insomnia. *Journal of Pediatric Psychology, 39*(8), 932–948.

Meltzer, L. J., Plaufcan, M. R., Thomas, J. H., & Mindell, J. A. (2014). Sleep problems and sleep disorders in pediatric primary care: Treatment recommendations, persistence, and health care utilization. *Journal of Clinical Sleep Medicine, 10*(4), 421–426.

Mignot, E. J. (2012). A practical guide to the therapy of narcolepsy and hypersomnia syndromes. *Neurotherapeutics, 9*(4), 739–752.

Morgenthaler, T., Kramer, M., Alessi, C., Friedman, L., Boehlecke, B., Brown, T., Coleman, J., Kapur, V., Lee-Chiong, T., & Owens, J. (2006). Practice parameters for the psychological and behavioral treatment of insomnia: An update. An American Academy of Sleep Medicine report. *Sleep, 29*(11), 1415–1419.

Ohayon, M. M. (2002). Epidemiology of insomnia: What we know and what we still need to learn. *Sleep Medicine Reviews, 6*(2), 97–111.

Ohayon, M. M., Guilleminault, C., & Priest, R. G. (1999). Night terrors, sleepwalking, and confusional arousals in the general population: Their frequency and relationship to other sleep and mental disorders. *Journal of Clinical Psychiatry, 60*(4), 268–276.

O'Keeffe, K. M., Gander, P. H., Scott, W. G., & Scott, H. M. (2011). Insomnia treatment in New Zealand. *New Zealand Medical Journal, 125*(1349), 46–59.

Owens, J. A., Spirito, A., McGuinn, M., & Nobile, C. (2000). Sleep habits and sleep disturbance in elementary school-aged children. *Journal of Developmental and Behavioral Pediatrics, 21*(1), 27–36.

Paine, S. J., Gander, P. H., Harris, R. B., & Reid, P. (2005). Prevalence and consequences of insomnia in New Zealand: Disparities between Māori and non-Māori. *Australian and New Zealand Journal of Public Health, 29*(1), 22–28.

Pressman, M. R. (2007). Factors that predispose, prime and precipitate NREM parasomnias in adults: Clinical and forensic implications. *Sleep Medicine Reviews, 11*(1), 5–30.

Quach, J., Gold, L., Hiscock, H., Mensah, F., Lucas, N., Nicholson, J., & Wake, M. (2013). Primary healthcare costs associated with sleep problems up to age 7 years: Australian population-based study. *BMJ Open, 3*(5), e002419.

Quach, J., Hiscock, H., Canterford, L., & Wake, M. (2009). Outcomes of child sleep problems over the school-transition period: Australian population longitudinal study. *Pediatrics, 123*(5), 1287–1292.

Rajaratnam, S. M. W., Howard, M. E., & Grunstein, R. R. (2013). Sleep loss and circadian disruption in shift work: Health burden and management. *The Medical Journal of Australia, 199*(8), 11–15.

Richards, D., Bartlett, D. J., Wong, K., Malouff, J., & Grunstein, R. R. (2007). Increased adherence to CPAP with a group cognitive behavioral treatment intervention: A randomized trial. *Sleep, 30*(5), 635–640.

Rosen, G., Mahowald, M., & Ferber, R. (1995). Sleepwalking, confusional arousals, and sleep terrors in the child. In R. Ferber & M. Kryger (Eds.), *Principles and practice of sleep medicine in the child* (pp. 99–106). Philadelphia: WB Saunders.

Roth, T. (2007). Insomnia: Definition, prevalence, etiology, and consequences. *Journal of Clinical Sleep Medicine, 3*(5 Suppl), S7–S10.

Sadeh, A. (2005). Cognitive–behavioral treatment for childhood sleep disorders. *Clinical Psychology Review, 25*(5), 612–628.

Short, M. A., Gradisar, M., Lack, L. C., Wright, H. R., & Dohnt, H. (2013). The sleep patterns and well-being of Australian adolescents. *Journal of Adolescence, 36*(1), 103–110.

Simard, V., Nielsen, T. A., Tremblay, R. E., Boivin, M., & Montplaisir, J. Y. (2008). Longitudinal study of bad dreams in preschool-aged children: Prevalence, demographic correlates, risk and protective factors. *Sleep, 31*(1), 62–70.

Spoormaker, V. I., Schredl, M., & van den Bout, J. (2006). Nightmares: From anxiety symptom to sleep disorder. *Sleep Medicine Reviews, 10*(1), 19–31.

Taylor, D., Gehrman, P., Dautovich, N. D., Lichstein, K. L., & McCrae, C. S. (2014). *Handbook of insomnia.* London: Springer.

Teng, A., Bartle, A., Sadeh, A., & Mindell, J. (2012). Infant and toddler sleep in Australia and New Zealand. *Journal of Paediatrics and Child Health, 48*(3), 268–273.

Vela-Bueno, A. (1985). Prevalence of night terrors and nightmares in elementary school children: A pilot study. *Research Communications in Psychology, Psychiatry and Behavior, 10*(3), 177–185.

Waterhouse, J., Reilly, T., Atkinson, G., & Edwards, B. (2007). Jet lag: Trends and coping strategies. *The Lancet, 369*(9567), 1117–1129.

Wilsmore, B. R., Grunstein, R. R., Fransen, M., Woodward, M., Norton, R., & Ameratunga, S. (2013). Sleep habits, Insomnia, and daytime sleepiness in a large and healthy community-based sample of New Zealanders. *Journal of Clinical Sleep Medicine, 9*(6), 559–566.

Wright, K. P., Bogan, R. K., & Wyatt, J. K. (2013). Shift work and the assessment and management of shift work disorder (SWD). *Sleep Medicine Reviews, 17*(1), 41–54.

Zhang, B., & Wing, Y. (2006). Sex differences in insomnia: A meta-analysis. *Sleep, 29*(1), 85–93.

Recommendations for further reading/resources

General

Relevant websites:

- Australasian Sleep Association: www.sleep.org.au
- Australasian Chronobiology Society: www.australasianchronobiology.org
- Asia Pacific Paediatric Sleep Alliance (APPSA): www.appsasleep.org/educational-material
- International Pediatric Sleep Society: www.pedsleep.org
- Teenage Sleep e-book: http://vuir.vu.edu.au/467/
- International Parkinson and Movement Disorder Society, Restless Legs Syndrome: www.movementdisorders.org/MDS/About/Movement-Disorder-Overviews/Restless-Legs-Syndrome.htm
- World Association of Sleep Medicine (WASM): www.wasmonline.org
- World Sleep Federation: http://worldsleepfederation.org

Australia

Relevant websites:

- Hypersomnolence Australia: www.Hypersomnolenceaustralia.com
- Narcolepsy and Overwhelming Daytime Sleep Society of Australia (NODSS): www.nodss.org.au/index.html
- National Health and Medical Research Council: www.nhmrc.gov.au
- Restless Legs Syndrome Australia: www.rls.org.au
- Sleep Disorders Australia: www.sleepoz.org.au
- Sleep Health Foundation: www.sleephealthfoundation.org.au
- Australian Sleep Association, Reawakening the nation: www.sleep.org.au/information/sleep-documents/reawakening-the-nation

New Zealand

Relevant websites:

- Sleep Apnoea Association of New Zealand: www.grownups.co.nz/sleepapnoea-association/
- The Thoracic Society of Australia & New Zealand: www.thoracic.org.au

19

Disruptive, impulse-control, and conduct disorders

Vicki McKenzie and Kelly Allen

Introduction

This chapter deals with problems of conduct, commonly considered as externalising disorders, which involve self-control of emotions and behaviours. "Problem behaviour," "challenging behaviour," "severely challenging behaviour," and "emotional disorders" or "behavioural disorders" are all terms that describe behaviours that create problems at home, at school, and in the community.

Mental health problems presenting in young people have been broadly categorised into externalising and internalising problems and behaviours (Wilmshurst, 2005). Internalising behaviour difficulties are defined as those "problems that negatively impact the child's internal psychological world rather than the external environment" (Fite et al., 2008, p. 64). Externalising problems include impulsive and antisocial behaviours, such as distracting others, disobeying teachers, and aggression towards others, along with behaviours associated with inattention, and hyperactivity (Achenbach & Rescoria, 2001). Externalising behaviour has also been related to other mental health issues (Sawyer et al., 2000).

Teachers are often less accepting of students with social, emotional, and behavioural difficulties, so they are strongly associated with negativity in the student–teacher relationship (Baker, Grant, & Morlock, 2008). Furthermore, the association between disruptive behaviour and low achievement is well established, particularly with males (Hinshaw, 1992; Prior et al., 1999). As externalising behaviours have been associated with subsequent development of antisocial behaviours, difficulty in negotiating social relationships, substance abuse, and early school leaving, they are of considerable concern to educators and health professionals (Baker et al., 2008; Hunter, 2003).

Disruptive behaviour disorders are evident in behaviours that violate the rights of others or bring the individual into conflict with social norms or authorities (*Diagnostic and Statistical Manual of Mental Disorders*, 5th ed.; *DMS-5*; American Psychiatric

Association, 2013). The disorders include oppositional defiant disorder, (ODD), conduct disorder (CD), and intermittent explosive disorder. They can be considered on a spectrum according to the emphasis on emotion or behaviour, as seen in Table 19.1.

Table 19.1 The major behaviour disorders

Contrasting focus on emotional or behavioural regulation		
Conduct disorder	Oppositional defiance disorder	Intermittent explosive disorder
Poorly controlled behaviours	Symptoms relate to emotion and behaviour	Poorly controlled emotional reactivity
Violate rights or norms; may be overt or covert behaviours	Anger and defiance; overt and non-destructive behaviour	Reaction not matched to stimulus

Many of the symptoms that are used to identify behavioural disorders occur in typical development; however, the frequency, persistence, intensity, and impact on functioning are key factors in diagnosing significant variation from the norm. Age and stage of development are important factors to consider.

The disruptive behaviour disorders emerge in childhood or adolescence, with greater frequency in males than females (American Psychiatric Association, 2013). Age of onset for ODD occurs at 4–8 years, and CD more frequently appears in the adolescent years (Wilmshurst, 2005). Most children with ODD do not develop CD (*DSM-5*). The risk factors for developing disruptive disorders are the quality of caregiving, an avoidant attachment, low socio-economic status (SES) and the level of stress and depression in the caregiver in the first 3 years of development (Aguilar et al., 2000). Both ODD and CD have common features – 75% of children with ODD do not progress to CD; however, 90% of young people who are identified with CD have previously been diagnosed with ODD. The disorders are explained in more detail below.

Oppositional defiant disorder

Children presenting with ODD are difficult to manage due to their confrontational personalities, which impacts powerfully at home, school, and in employment.

Features

ODD is one of a group of behavioural disorders that presents as a persistent pattern (for at least 6 months) of negative, hostile, disobedient, and defiant behaviour in a child or adolescent without serious violation of the basic rights of others. ODD typically begins by age 8, can occur in multiple settings and may develop into other disorders. Comorbidity concerning ODD is common, existing alongside other conditions such as attention deficit hyperactivity disorder (ADHD), learning disabilities, mood disorders, and anxiety disorders. Young people diagnosed with ODD are at heightened risk for a number of adjustment problems in adulthood.

Assessment

Assessment of ODD typically relates to the frequency and severity of symptoms relating to a set of criteria (Table 19.2), usually collected across a range of settings (e.g., home and school). Gender may impact the presentation of the disorder; for example, girls may tend to be untruthful and cooperative, while boys tend to lose their temper and argue with adults. Assessment is made by a medical practitioner and/or paediatrician, psychiatrist, or psychologist.

Table 19.2 *DSM-5* diagnostic criteria for oppositional defiant disorder

A. At least 4 symptoms of:

Angry irritable mood
- Often loses temper
- Often easily annoyed by others
- Often angry and resentful

Argumentative/defiant behaviour
- Often argues with adults
- Often actively defies or refuses to comply with adult's requests
- Often deliberately annoys people
- Often blames others for mistakes or misbehaviour

Vindictiveness
- Often spiteful or revengeful (at least twice in the past 6 months)

B. Behaviours impact negatively on the individual or others, and on social, educational, occupational, or other important areas of functioning

C. The behaviours do not occur exclusively during the course of a psychotic, substance abuse, depressive or bipolar disorder, and do not meet the criteria for disruptive mood dysregulation.

Severity:

Symptoms occur in:
- One setting – Mild
- 2+ settings – Moderate
- 3+ settings – Severe

Source: Adapted from American Psychiatric Association, 2013

Prevalence

Little evidence exists for the prevalence of ODD in preschool age groups. Symptoms usually appear in late childhood and early adolescence. ODD occurs in up to 11% of the population with an average of approximately 3.3% (American Psychiatric Association, 2013). The disorder is more common in males than in females in younger years, evening out in older children and adolescents. Over 80% of children with ODD have comorbid ADHD, while 65% of children with ADHD have ODD (Wilsmhurst, 2005).

Treatment

Early intervention is advocated for the treatment of ODD. Treatment is mostly offered in school or clinic-based programs and focuses on social skills training and development, behavioural therapy, and academic tutoring. It is recommended that parents or caregivers are included in treatment, with input on creating improved communication with the child, teaching how to make positive choices, setting goals, giving positive reinforcement, and setting and enforcing appropriate boundaries. The management of behaviour across settings (e.g., school and home) should be consistently applied by the primary adults and caregivers within the young person's life.

Treatment efficacy

It has been reported that 67% of children diagnosed with ODD who received treatment were symptom free after 3 years (American Academy of Child and Adolescent Psychiatry, 2007); however, other research has indicated that 30% of children diagnosed with ODD were later diagnosed with CD (Connor, 2002).

Conduct disorder

Conduct disorder is the most severe of the disruptive behaviour disorders, involving aggressive action directed at the rights of others and/or social rules and customs. Young people with this disorder are likely to be aggressively dealing with others, using bullying and fighting, and possibly manipulating others through lying, deception, and false promises, from an early age. Often teachers and parents are dismayed by the lack of guilt or concern they express for their victims. There are high rates of comorbidity, again with ADHD, learning disabilities, mood disorders, and anxiety disorders, as well as substance use and depression. People with CD frequently misperceive the intentions of others, reading them as hostile and threatening, and hence act with a degree of aggression that they believe is justified.

Assessment is made by establishing the presence of 3 out of 15 symptoms considered against the diagnostic criteria (See Table 19.3).

Australian prevalence rates have been estimated from 2% and 10%, with a median of 4%. It is generally agreed that 3% to 6% of students in Australian schools present with emotional or behaviour disorders (Carter, Clayton, & Stephenson, 2008). CD is one of the most frequent diagnoses of young people who attend mental health clinics. Males are more frequently identified, but gender differences in manifestation have been noted. Males are more likely to have symptoms of vandalism, physical fighting, theft, and poor school behaviour, while females express their CD in running away, substance use, truancy and prostitution (Carter et al., 2008). Australian research suggests that nearly one in six students will experience a clinically significant emotional or behavioural health problem in their school years.

A recent national survey of Australian children aged 4–17 years placed prevalence rates for internalising at 12.8%, externalising at 12.9% and total mental health problems at 14.1%, with some of these aspects being present comorbidly (Sawyer et al., 2000). These figures echo the growing concern in the community about increasing violence and problematic behaviour in young people with assaults,

Table 19.3 *DSM-5* diagnostic criteria for conduct disorder

A. Repetitive and persistent pattern of behaviour, where basic rights of others or major norms are broken in at least 3 of the 15 criteria in the last year, and at least 1 in last 6 months
- Aggression to people and animals
  - Frequently bullies, threatens, or intimidates others
  - Often starts fights
  - Uses a harmful weapon
  - Physical cruelty to people
  - Physical cruelty to animals
  - Stolen while confronting person
  - Forced sexual activity on person
- Destruction of property
  - Deliberately set fires
  - Deliberately destroyed property
- Deceitfulness or theft
  - Breaks into a house or building
  - Lies to obtain favours or to avoid obligations
  - Steals items of non-trivial value
- Serious violations of rules
  - Stays out at night without permission beginning before age 13
  - Has run away from home at least once
  - Is often truant from school

> **Onset can be:**
> *Childhood onset* – at least one symptom prior to age 10 years.
> *Adolescent onset* – no symptoms pre age 10 years.
> *Unspecified onset* – insufficient information to establish onset

> **Can range in severity:**
> Mild – few symptoms causing minor harm
> Moderate
> Severe – many symptoms present

B. Behaviour causes clinically significant impairment – social academic or social

C. If 18 years+ not assessable as antisocial personality disorder

May also show limited prosocial emotions:
- Lack of remorse or guilt
- Callous, lack of empathy
- Lack of concern about performance
- Shallow or deficient affect

Source: Adapted from American Psychiatric Association, 2013

vandalism, and burglaries occurring in schools, even at the primary school level (Tomazin, 2009).

Problems with these externalising behaviours are complicated by the frequency of comorbid conditions which make intervention more difficult (Sawyer et al., 2000). One study estimated that 25.5% of children had two or more mental health diagnoses (Costello, Eggar, & Angold, 2005). However, when stringent definitions were applied, these numbers have been disputed (Carter et al., 2008). Teachers appear to be more concerned about boys. Arbuckle and Little (2004) reported that teachers suggested 18.2% of male students and 7.25% of female students in their classes needed additional management assistance. The ratio of teacher concerns about boys compared with girls is 9:1 (Carter et al., 2008). Problem behaviours are highly associated with academic difficulty and present a substantial challenge in school classrooms.

Treatment

In reviewing 165 studies of school-based treatment, Wilson, Gottfredson, and Najaka, (2001) found that interventions ranged from counselling individuals and behaviour modification, to wider scale whole-school programs. Student problems included substance use, school dropout, and nonattendance. The meta-study demonstrated that interventions reduced alcohol and drug use, and other conduct problems, but with small effect sizes. Consistently positive effects came from school-based cognitive behavioural and behavioural instructional methods, and non-instructional cognitive behavioural and behavioural methods programs. Promoting self-control and social competency was an important part of these programs. Environmentally focused interventions (e.g., norms and expectations across school classes, whole school discipline management) appeared to be particularly effective for reducing delinquency and drug use. Non-cognitive behaviour counselling, social work, and other therapeutic interventions did not show similar effects. Analysis proved difficult as a result of the vague depiction of elements of effective activities, and the wide range of prevention strategies used compared with the narrow set of strategies that are supported by research evidence (Wilson et al., 2001). There are also inconclusive findings about useful combinations of interventions or specific programs.

Methods and structures that enable young people to feel supported in their educational settings do appear important. For example, Australian researchers Cunningham, Werner, and Firth (2004) examined the links between coping and connectedness. The students who demonstrated successful coping had developed these responses through experiencing warmth and acceptance from teachers and peers, through appropriate supervision, and through safe situations where they could demonstrate their competencies, and in particular where they could gain a sense of perceived control. There is increasing evidence that violence can be prevented though a range of strategies, including those that:

- help to develop safe, stable, and nurturing relationships between children and their parents and caregivers
- reduce the availability and harmful use of alcohol
- reduce access to guns, knives, and pesticides, and
- promote gender equality to prevent violence against women (World Health Organisation, 2015).

Interventions for children with CD and related antisocial problems focus on working with parents and families, as well as containing the escalation of existing problems. Parenting training programs for children aged between 3–11 years, as well as child-focused social and cognitive problem-solving programs using a cognitive behavioural model, are recommended by the National Institute for Clinical Excellence (2013). For older children (aged between 11 and 17), multimodal interventions such as multisystemic therapy are recommended.

Anger management is widely used for aggressive and violent clients, with correctional and forensic mental health services across Australia delivering intensive group treatment programs for the more serious offenders. These approaches use cognitive behavioural models based on the understanding of antisocial or aggressive behaviour in terms of socio-cognitive deficits which significantly impair reasoning capacity. Lacking social problem-solving skills necessary to identify and deal with everyday living problems, the client resorts to aggression or violent action. Accordingly, intervention targets change in maladaptive cognitions or cognitive distortions. Prevention programs to reduce domestic violence focus on changing the beliefs and attitudes towards women that lead to aggressive and violent behaviour in the perpetrators. Treatment is typically delivered in small group settings, and using a Socratic method the group members are encouraged to confront and challenge these unhelpful cognitive distortions. In some cases, progress in developing evidence-based intervention programs for reducing domestic violence in groups from Aboriginal and Torres Strait Islander backgrounds has been slow, although frameworks for culturally specific and culturally safe violence prevention programs have been developed (Day et al., 2012).

Anger management can produce reliable clinical change. Beck and Fernandez (1998), in their meta-analysis of 50 outcome studies, concluded that individuals receiving cognitive behavioural anger management were 75% advantaged, in terms of anger reduction, compared to untreated controls. However, there is less evidence of successful anger management programs for those who have extended histories of serious violence (Heseltine, Howells, & Day, 2010).

Four core components of anger management are considered important.

1. Exposure to provocation (either overt or covert) that leads to some level of emotional arousal.
2. Cognitive change, given that anger arousal is commonly mediated by the presence of automatic thoughts and beliefs.
3. Self-management skills to help develop appropriate coping skills.
4. Relaxation to help to reduce physiological arousal and to manage stress. Anger management programs increasingly incorporate acceptance-based approaches that teach clients to more fully feel emotions and bodily sensations.

Anger management programs increasingly incorporate acceptance-based approaches that teach clients to more fully feel emotions and bodily sensations.

Other relevant disorders

Far less research is available for antisocial personality disorder and intermittent explosive disorder, compared with the other disorders in this class. This is especially lacking in the Australian and New Zealand (NZ) contexts.

Intermittent explosive disorder

Features

The central features of intermittent explosive disorder include: failure to control aggressive outbursts and behaviour, impulsivity, rapid onset of outbursts lasting for less

Chapter 19 Disruptive, impulse-control, and conduct disorders

than 30 minutes, and unpredictable aggressive behaviour that often results from minor provocation from a close intimate or associate. Intermittent explosive disorder can be associated with other conditions; for example, mood disorders, anxiety disorders, and substance use disorders. Individuals with a history of other disorders with disruptive behaviours may be at greater risk of comorbid intermittent explosive disorder.

With the introduction of the *DSM-5*, the criteria for intermittent explosive disorder now include verbal and non-destructive/non-injurious physical aggression rather than purely physical (see Table 19.4).

Table 19.4 *DSM-5* diagnostic criteria for intermittent explosive disorder

DSM-5 criteria for intermittent explosive disorder

A. Recurrent outbursts (unable to control aggressive impulses), for example:
   a. verbal aggression
   b. three behavioural outbursts involving damage or destruction of property or assault within a 12-month period.

B. Outburst out of proportion to provocation or stressor.
C. Not premeditated and without preconceived plan.
D. Outbursts cause distress or are associated with personal legal or occupational consequences.
E. Age at least 6 years.
F. Not otherwise explained by another mental disorder.

Source: Adapted from American Psychiatric Association, 2013

Assessment

Age of onset is commonly in late childhood or adolescence, and rarely begins over 40 years. Core features tend to continue over many years. In the very young, it can be difficult to distinguish from normal temper tantrums of young children, hence diagnosis is from 6 years and above. The course of the disorder may be chronic and persistent over many years, often with episodic periods of impulsive aggressive outbursts. There is evidence of genetic influence, and recent neurobiological research points to some serotonergic abnormalities in the brain.

Prevalence

The data is not strong on prevalence of this disorder, it is more frequent in younger individuals, compared with those over 50 years, and is rare in persons with extended education. There is inconclusive information about gender differences in prevalence.

Treatment

There is a strong focus on working with parents and different stakeholders. Treatment modalities are similar to those listed previously, in particular using a cognitive behavioural model with direct treatment of anger. The challenge in treatment can be engaging the client in behaviour change. Further details can be obtained from

UpToDate (www.uptodate.com/contents/intermittent-explosive-disorder-in-adults-treatment-and-prognosis).

Antisocial personality disorder

Features

Antisocial personality disorder is dual coded in the *DSM-5* and appears in the disruptive, impulse-control, and CD grouping due to the close connection with the externalising CD. This disorder is also classified under personality disorders and may be evident in pyromania and kleptomania. In order to meet criteria for diagnosis, an individual must be at least 18 years or older, demonstrate a pattern of pervasive disregard and violation of the rights of others occurring since the age of 15, and have a history of CD before the age of 15. Studies have demonstrated a link between antisocial behaviour in childhood and adulthood as from young as three years (e.g., Stevenson & Goodman, 2001).

Prevalence

Extrapolated data suggests that approximately 3% of males and 1% of females display antisocial personality disorder. However, prevalence and incidence rates vary markedly from country to country. Antisocial personality disorder rates are highest in the specialised populations for individuals with substance abuse issues (e.g., intravenous drug users 71%, Darke et al., 2004) and criminal offenders (47% of males and 21% of females).

New Zealand case study

The following case study is of a young girl diagnosed with oppositional defiant disorder.

Cherry is a 10-year-old child of Māori ethnicity who lives with her parents and maternal grandmother in NZ.

Cherry's mother reports that her behaviour has been disruptive from the age of approximately 2 years. Specifically, her mother describes Cherry as having difficulty following instructions, complying with basic requests, following house rules and boundaries, and controlling her temper. Cherry is angry and resentful towards her parents and blames them for her unhappiness. While her parents describe her as irritable, aggressive, argumentative, and temperamental, Cherry's teachers do not identify this behaviour, stating that she draws little attention for conduct issues at school.

In this case behaviour at school is better than that described at home, which is not uncommon for individuals with oppositional defiant disorder, who tend to present differently in different contexts. Teachers report few concerns and describe Cherry as a solitary child. If asked about her reasons for not socialising, Cherry reports that "it is because they annoy her." She is sometimes invited to sleepovers but claims she does not want to spend more time with her peers than she has to. When her parents invite children to their home, Cherry loses her temper easily, is resentful, and avoids contact.

Cherry was diagnosed with oppositional defiant disorder. Her behaviour is atypical and causes disturbance and distress within her day-to-day family relationships as well as her social functioning at school. The specific behavioural criteria related to her temper, irritability, resentment towards her parents, argumentative and rule-breaking behaviour, and tendency to blame others and rationalise her misbehaviour.

Due to Cherry's age, behaviour management training for her parents and teachers would help them consistently support improving Cherry's behaviour. Strategies may include a structured reward system, self-esteem building, and consistently following up on uncooperative behaviour. At school, this could include social and emotional programs that promote managing and identifying emotions, monitoring self-talk, self-regulation, and general wellbeing. Intervention needs to integrate individual, school, and family settings through multisystemic treatment. Multisystemic treatment is an intensive, integrative approach that emphasises how an individual's conduct problems are reinforced by, and can be changed within, a broader context.

It is also recommended that Cherry's parents would benefit from participating in a parent support group with other parents with children with similar presenting issues. Cherry is also encouraged to receive individual psychological support, counselling, cognitive behaviour therapy, and social skills training. Parents should be encouraged to involve the support of Cherry's teachers who may encourage her to participate in group activities with other children.

Australia – parenting programs

Parenting programs can positively assist the management of children with disruptive, impulsive control, and CDs. Examples include the following.

- Child behavior research clinic parenting program: https://myparenting.com.au/About-The-Program
- Triple P Parenting: www.triplep.net/glo-en/home
- The Incredible Years: http://incredibleyears.com

New Zealand – schools

Schools are an important part of a multisystemic approach. The Ministry of Education offers specialised resources available from their website.

- www.education.govt.nz/ministry-of-education/specific-initiatives/pb4l/
- Like Minds, Like Mine: www.likeminds.org.nz

References

Achenbach, T. M., & Rescoria, L. A. (2001). *Manual for the ASEABA school-age forms and profiles*. Burlington, VT: University of Vermont, Research Center for Children, Youth & Families.

Aguilar, B., Sroufe, L. A., Egeland, B., & Carlson, E. (2000). Distinguishing the early-onset/persistent and adolescence-onset antisocial behavior types: From birth to 16 years. *Development and Psychopathology, 12*, 109–132.

American Academy of Child and Adolescent Psychiatry. (2007). Adolescent psychiatry's practice parameter for the assessment and treatment of children and adolescents with oppositional defiant disorder. *Journal of the American Academy of Child & Adolescent Psychiatry, 46*(1), 126–141.

American Psychiatric Association. (2013). *Diagnostic and statistical manual of mental disorders* (5th ed.). Arlington, VA: Author.

Arbuckle, C., & Little, E. (2004). Teachers' perceptions and management of disruptive classroom behaviour during the middle years (years five to nine). *Australian Journal of Educational & Developmental Psychology, 4*, 59–70.

Baker, J. A., Grant, S., & Morlock, L. (2008). The teacher-student relationship as a developmental context for children with internalising or externalizing behaviour problems. *School Psychology Quarterly, 23*(1), 3–15.

Beck, R., & Fernandez, E. (1998) Cognitive-behavioral therapy in the treatment of anger: A meta-analysis. *Cognitive Therapy and Research, 22*(1), 63–74.

Carter, M., Clayton, M., & Stephenson, J. (2008). Students with severe challenging behaviour in regular classrooms: Support and impacts. *Australian Journal of Guidance and Counselling, 9*(1), 141–159.

Connor, D. F. (2002). *Aggression and antisocial behavior in children and adolescents: Research and treatment*. New York: The Guilford Press.

Costello, E. J., Eggar, H., & Angold, A. (2005). 10-year research update review: The epidemiology of child and adolescent psychiatric disorders: I. Methods and public health burden. *Journal of the American Academy of Child & Adolescent Psychiatry, 44*(10), 972–986. http://dx.doi.org/10.1097/01.chi.0000172552.41596.6f

Cunningham, E., Werner, S. C., & Firth, N. V. (2004). Control beliefs as mediators of school connectedness and coping outcomes in middle adolescence. *Australian Journal of Guidance and Counselling, 14*(2), 139–150.

Darke, S., Williamson, A., Ross, J., Teeson, M., & Lynskey, M. (2004). Borderline personality disorder, antisocial personality disorder and risk-taking among heroin users: Findings from the Australian treatment outcome study. *Journal of Psychiatric Research, 38*, 619–635.

Day, A., Jones, R., Nakata, M., & McDermott, D. (2012). Indigenous family violence: An attempt to understand the problems and inform appropriate and effective responses to criminal justice system intervention. *Psychiatry, Psychology and Law, 19*, 104–117.

Fite, P. J., Stoppelbein, L., Greening, L., & Dhossche, D. (2008). Child internalizing and externalizing behavior as predictors of age at first admission and risk for repeat admission to a child inpatient facility. *American Journal of Orthopsychiatry, 78*, 63–69. http://dx.doi.org/10.1037/0002-9432.78.1.63

Heseltine, K., Howells, K., & Day, A. (2010). Brief anger interventions with offenders may be ineffective: A replication and extension. *Behaviour Research and Therapy, 48*, 246–250.

Hinshaw, S. P. (1992). Externalising behaviour problems and academic achievement in childhood and adolescence: Causal relationships and underlying mechanisms. *Psychological Bulletin, 111*, 127–155.

Hunter, L. (2003). School psychology: a public health framework-III. Managing disruptive behaviour in school: The value of a public health and evidence-based perspective. *Journal of School Psychology, 41*(1), 39–59.

National Institute for Clinical Excellence. (2013). *Antisocial behaviour and conduct disorders in children and young people, recognition, intervention and management, NICE Clinical Guideline, No. 158.* UK: British Psychological Society.

Prior, M., Smart, D., Sanson, A., & Oberklaid, F. (1999). Relationships between learning difficulties and psychological problems in preadolescent children from a longitudinal sample. *Journal of the American Academy of Child and Adolescent Psychiatry, 38*(4), 429–436.

Sawyer, M. G., Arney, F. M., Baghurst, P. A., Clarke, J. J., Graetz, B. W., Kosky, R. L., Nurcombe, B., Patton, G. C., Prior, M. R., Raphel, B., Rey, J., Whaites, L. C., & Zubrick, S. R. (2000). *The mental health of young people in Australia: Child and adolescent component of the national survey of mental health and well-being.* Canberra: Commonwealth of Australia.

Stevenson, J., & Goodman, R. (2001). Association between behaviour at age 3 years and adult criminality. *British Journal of Psychiatry, 179*(3), 197–202.

Tomazin, F. (2009). Sharp rise in student suspension, *The Age*, 15 September.

Wilmshurst, L. (2005). *Essentials of child and adolescent psychopathology* (2nd ed.). Hoboken, NJ: Wiley.

Wilson, D. B., Gottfredson, D. C., & Najaka, S. S. (2001). School-based prevention of problem behaviors: A meta-analysis. *Journal of Quantitative Criminology, 17*(3), 247–272.

World Health Organisation. (2015). *Youth violence*, Fact Sheet No 356. Available: http://www.who.int/mediacentre/factsheets/fs356/en/

Recommendations for further reading/resources

General resources

Relevant websites:

- Better Health Channel, Conduct disorder: www.betterhealth.vic.gov.au/bhcv2/bhcArticles.nsf/pages/Conduct_disorder?open

- Better Health Channel, Oppositional defiant disorder: www.betterhealth.vic.gov.au/health/conditionsandtreatments/oppositional-defiant-disorder-odd
- KidsMatter: www.kidsmatter.edu.au/sites/default/files/public/KMP_C4_CBD_AboutSeriousBehaviourDifficulties.pdf

Australia

Relevant websites:
- Australian Psychological Society, Find a Psychologist service: www.psychology.org.au/findapsychologist
- headspace (National Youth Mental Health Foundation): www.headspace.org.au
- MIND Australia: www.mindaustralia.org.au

New Zealand

Relevant websites:
- Ministry of Education: www.minedu.govt.nz/theMinistry/EducationInitiatives/PositiveBehaviourForLearning.aspx
- Like Minds Like Mine: www.likeminds.org.nz
- Mental Health Foundation: www.mentalhealth.org.nz

Acknowledgements

A special thanks to Juliette Spearman and Lucy Harrison for their time and specialised knowledge of New Zealand resources and referral pathways.

20

Substance-related and addictive disorders

Nicki Dowling, Kate Hall, and Petra K Staiger

Introduction

Substance-related disorders

There are two groups of substance-related disorders in the *Diagnostic and Statistical Manual of Mental Disorders* (5th ed.; *DSM-5*; American Psychiatric Association, 2013): substance-induced disorders and substance use disorders (SUDs). Substance-induced disorders include intoxication, withdrawal, and substance-induced mental disorders. SUDs are problematic symptoms that occur when individuals continue to use substances, despite experiencing impairment or distress. Substance-related disorders are listed separately for each of the 11 substance groups (alcohol, caffeine, cannabis, phencyclidine, other hallucinogens, inhalants, opioids, sedatives, hypnotics and anxiolytics, stimulants, tobacco, and other substances). The *DSM-5* combines the categories of abuse and dependence into the single disorder of SUD with mild, moderate, and severe subclassifications based on the number of criteria met. Anyone meeting any two of the 11 criteria during the same 12-month period receives a SUD diagnosis. The criteria also include a remission specifier (in early remission, in sustained remission, on maintenance therapy, in a controlled environment).

Behavioural addictions

Behavioural addictions, which are characterised by impairment of control rather than physiological dependence, may involve gambling, internet use, video games, shopping, exercise, work, eating, and sex. Behavioural addiction is not included as a diagnostic category in the *DSM-5* due to insufficient evidence to establish diagnostic criteria and course descriptions. However, gambling disorder, which was formerly an impulse control disorder known as pathological gambling, is now included as a substance-related and addictive disorder. Gambling disorder is defined as persistent and recurrent problematic gambling behaviour leading to clinically significant impairment or distress.

The diagnosis requires endorsement of five of nine criteria within the previous 12 months and includes specifiers for course (episodic, persistent), remission (early, sustained) and current severity (mild, moderate, severe). Moreover, internet gaming disorder (IGD) is included as a condition for further study. IGD is defined as repetitive use of internet-based games, often with other players, which leads to significant issues with functioning. The *DSM-5* requires endorsement of five of nine criteria within the previous 12 months and includes current severity specifiers (mild, moderate, and severe).

Australia

Substance-related disorders

A national survey by the Australian Institute of Health and Welfare (AIHW, 2014) indicates tobacco use in Australia has steadily declined since 1993; by 2013, 60% of individuals reported they had never smoked. Nearly 80% (78.3%) reported having consumed alcohol in the previous 12 months, with men (82%) reporting higher rates of alcohol consumption than women (76%). While 15.6% of all drinkers reported drinking at very high risk levels, this was most prevalent among those aged 18–29 years. Illicit drugs were used by 42% of respondents, most commonly by males and those aged 20–29 years. Cannabis was the most frequently used illicit drug (10.2%). In contrast, the use of ecstasy, GHB, and heroin has decreased over time. Although amphetamine rates have remained static, the use of ice has increased. Nearly 5% of Australians had misused a pharmaceutical drug in the past 12 months. Pain killers/analgesics were the most common and although males were more likely to misuse pharmaceuticals, females used them on a more frequent basis. Interestingly, rates of illicit drug use have risen most in individuals over 50 years of age, predominantly due to increased cannabis use by this age group (AIHW, 2014). Individuals who identified as Aboriginal or Torres Strait Islander were more likely to smoke tobacco daily, use cannabis, use illicit drugs, misuse pharmaceuticals, and use alcohol at risky levels than non-Indigenous individuals. It appears, however, that problematic and risky use of alcohol is gradually declining in such populations. Recent figures report increasingly later initiation to alcohol and drugs, with alcohol being first used at 15.6 years, and illicit drugs at 16.3 years (Gao, Ogeil, & Lloyd, 2014).

Australian studies suggest that risk for SUDs has been associated with disrupted and neglectful parental dynamics during childhood, problem behaviours during childhood (Hayatbakhsh et al., 2008), exposure to parental violence (Schiff et al., 2014), and low social cohesion (Loxley et al., 2004). Moreover, twice the number of illicit drug users have a diagnosed mental health disorder than non-drug users (AIHW, 2014). Positive outcomes are associated with good school and social connectedness, positive modelling, and supportive parenting strategies (Ryan, Jorm, & Lubman, 2010), and (later) employment and income. People who inject drugs (PWID) are at additional risk of blood borne viruses (BBV) and injection site complications. Transition to injecting drug use is associated with social disadvantage (Lea et al., 2015). Indigenous persons who inject are at a greater risk of acquiring a BBV than non-Indigenous injectors, due to their increased daily use, sharing of equipment, and poorer knowledge of the transmission and treatment of BBV (Paquette, McEwan, & Bryant, 2013).

The Australian Government's National Drug Strategy 2010–2015 is based on harm minimisation, with strategies to reduce substance demand, supply, and associated harm (Department of Health and Ageing, 2011). The strategy incorporates a number of substrategies, including prioritising Indigenous drug use, pharmaceutical drug misuse, and workforce development and research. Many state governments have developed Ice Action Plans to manage the rising use, and associated harmful sequelae, of methamphetamine use.

The National Health and Medical Research Council (NHMRC, 2009, 2011) has developed screening and assessment guidelines for the risky and harmful use of alcohol and volatile substance use (i.e., inhalants). The National Drug Scheme has resulted in assessment and intervention frameworks regarding the misuse of pharmaceuticals, opioid dependence, and psychoactive substances. In addition, guidelines for managing comorbid substance use and mental health diagnoses have been developed and regularly reviewed (Mills et al., 2010). In Australia, interventions for SUDs are most commonly brief (9% of episodes lasted six months or longer). Most clients of Australian intervention services present for their own use (96%), are predominantly male (68%), and are most often aged 30–39 years (29%). Indigenous clients are slightly younger, predominantly in the 10–29-year age range (49%; AIHW, 2013). Treatment is most commonly counselling (49%); however, education generally targets cannabis use and pharmacotherapy predominantly targets heroin use. Substance use assessment and treatment services in Australia include government, non-government, and not-for-profit organisations. Indigenous-specific organisations have been developed. Key research, health promotion, and advocacy bodies include the Australian Drug Foundation, DrugInfo, the Indigenous Alcohol and Other Drugs Knowledge Centre, the National Indigenous Drug and Alcohol Committee (NIDAC), the National Aboriginal Community Controlled Health Organisation (NACCHO), the Australian Psychological Society (APS) Psychology and Substance Use Interest Group, the Victorian Alcohol and Drug Association (VAADA), and headspace.

Behavioural addictions

Gambling disorder

Approximately 65% of Australian adults gamble at least once per year (Dowling et al., 2015). Lotteries, instant scratch tickets, electronic gaming machines (EGMs, also known as poker machines), and racing are the most popular gambling activities (Dowling et al., 2015). The national participation rate of past year internet gambling is 8.1% (Gainsbury et al., 2014). Australians spend over $20 billion per annum on gambling, or $1167 per capita (Queensland Government Statistician's Office [QGSO], 2014), which represents the largest per capita expenditure in the world (*The Economist*, 2014). Over half of gambling expenditure is lost on EGMs (QGSO, 2014).

State and territory governments, which regulate gambling in Australia, have adopted a public health perspective. This perspective conceptualises gambling problems across a continuum of risk and employs the term "problem gambling" to describe "difficulties in limiting money and/or time spent on gambling which leads to adverse consequences for the gambler, others, or for the community" (Neal, Delfabbro, & O'Neil, 2005). Only 0.6% of adult Australians are classified as problem gamblers, but an additional 2.0% to 3.7% are classified as moderate-risk gamblers (Dowling et al., 2015; Gainsbury et al., 2015). Problem gambling is over-represented in young people (Christensen et al., 2014) and Indigenous populations (Young et al., 2006). The gender gap has narrowed, however, with women comprising 52% of past year gamblers, 27% of low-risk gamblers, 48% of moderate-risk gamblers, and 33% of problem gamblers (Dowling et al., 2015). The incidence of problem gambling in Australia has been estimated to be 0.36% (Victorian Department of Justice, 2011).

Problem gambling in Australia is associated with playing EGMs, gambling for non-social reasons, alcohol and substance use disorders, mood and anxiety disorders, personality disorders, impulsivity, intimate partner violence, parental problem gambling, family conflict, family history of antisocial behaviour, academic failure, low school commitment, rebelliousness, antisocial peers, peer drug use, and antisocial behaviour (Dowling et al., 2016; Dowling et al., 2010; Dowling et al., 2014, 2015; Dowling, Smith, & Thomas, 2005; Dowling, Suomi, et al., 2014; Francis et al., 2015; Lorains et al., 2014; Scholes-Balog et al., 2014). Factors associated with problem gambling in Indigenous populations include older age, early onset, parental problem gambling, alcohol and drug use while gambling, gambling by family and friends, and gambling for non-social reasons (Hing et al., 2014). The pathways model (Blaszczynski & Nower, 2002) is a popular Australian typology which attempts to account for the heterogeneity in problem gambling by integrating disparate research findings from various theoretical frameworks.

Australia has adopted the Problem Gambling Severity Index (PGSI, Ferris, & Wynne, 2001) as the preferred measurement tool (Neal et al., 2005; PGRTC, 2011). The NHMRC guidelines recommend using naltrexone, cognitive behaviour therapy (CBT), motivational interviewing (MI) therapies, and practitioner-delivered interventions (PGRTC, 2011; Thomas et al., 2011). Australian state and territory governments provide funding for free specialised problem gambling treatment, including face-to-face counselling, telephone counselling, online support (Gambling Help Online), financial counselling, peer support, and self-help resources. Most provide services for family members and friends, and some provide specialist programs for specific communities, such as young people and Indigenous people. Self-exclusion from gambling venues is also available. Many Australian governments run awareness campaigns, provide community education, and fund research. The APS has coordinated review and position papers (Australian Psychological Society, 2012; Rickwood et al., 2010) and practitioner resources. The National Association for Gambling Studies, which aims to promote discussion and research, runs an annual national conference.

Internet gaming disorder

Estimates of the prevalence of technology-based addictions in Australian secondary school and university students range from 0% to 6.4% (Dowling & Brown, 2010; King et al., 2013; Thomas & Martin, 2010; Wang, 2001). Moreover, patterns of video gaming problems in adult Australian regular video game players persist across time (King, Delfabbro, & Griffiths, 2013). Technology-based addictions in Australian students have been associated with higher internet use frequency, online group membership, depression, anxiety, panic disorder, separation anxiety, student stressors, loneliness, impulsivity, and lowered psychosocial maturity (Dowling & Brown, 2010; King, Delfabbro et al., 2013; Mottram & Fleming, 2009; Wang, 2011). Systematic reviews by Australian researchers have revealed several limitations of available measures, such as varying cut-off scores, untested or inconsistent dimensionality and inadequate data on predictive validity and inter-rater reliability (King, Haagsma, et al., 2013), and methodological weaknesses in the evidence base for treatments (King & Delfabbro, 2014; King et al., 2011). In a review of treatment outcomes, King and Delfabbro (2014) concluded that there is currently insufficient evidence that IGD interventions display long-term therapeutic benefit.

New Zealand

Substance-related disorders

New Zealanders report high rates of drug (49.0%) and alcohol (85.2%) use (Ministry of Health, 2009, 2010). New Zealand (NZ) substance users are predominantly aged 25–34 years. Cannabis is favoured and substance use is more common in men. Compared to the general population, Māori peoples report similar rates of alcohol use and higher drug use (specifically cannabis, BZP [benzylpiperazine] party pills), while Pacific peoples report lower drug and alcohol use. Māori substance use appears to be increasing over time. SUD risk factors include young age, male gender, low education and income, living in deprived areas, and Māori heritage (Wells, Baxter, & Schaaf, 2007). Problematic drug use in young adults is significantly associated with parental adjustment, childhood exposure to abuse, and childhood/early adolescent adjustment (Fergusson, Boden, & Horwood, 2008). Cannabis use, substance-using peers, and concurrent alcohol use have also been implicated. Comorbidity with other SUDs (30.7% to 45.3%), anxiety disorders (40.0%), mood disorders (29.0%), and suicidality is common (Wells et al., 2007).

NZ's National Drug Policy emphasises a harm minimisation perspective and involves drug seizures, community education, and alcohol and drug treatment services (Ministry of Health, 2013). A number of well-validated substance abuse screening and assessment tools (including the AUDIT, CUDIT-R, ASSIST, and SACS) are commonly used in NZ clinical settings. The Matalafi Matrix is a bio-psychosocial assessment tool developed for use with Māori and Pacific populations (Matua Raki, 2011). NZ governmental treatment guidelines outline best practice for assessing and treating clients with opioid dependence and substance withdrawal. In this country, self-help groups are commonly based on twelve-step programs and non-specialist services provide brief intervention and aftercare. Specialist services include information and supportive phone lines and websites, community-based outpatient assessment and treatment services, day programs, community or inpatient detoxification services, residential treatment, opioid substitution treatment services, and needle exchange services. Some specialist services also target particular groups (e.g., youth, parents, Māori and Pacific peoples, co-existing mental health issues, and criminal justice involved; Matua Raki, 2012). Treatment providers include Community Alcohol and Drug Services and research and advocacy bodies include the New Zealand Drug Foundation and the Health Promotion Agency.

Behavioural addictions

Gambling disorder

Approximately 80% of the NZ adult population gamble at least once per year; lotteries and instant scratch tickets (most commonly Instant Kiwi) are the most popular activities (Abbott et al., 2014a). Internet gambling participation is relatively low, ranging from 0.4% (sports betting) to 5.0% (lotteries; Abbott et al., 2014a). NZ residents spend $2.1 billion per annum on gambling, of which over one-third is lost on EGMs (also known as poker machines) outside casinos (NZDIA, 2014). It currently has the fourth largest expenditure per resident adult in the world (*The Economist*, 2014).

NZ has also adopted a public health perspective and employs the term "problem gambling" to refer to gambling problems that lead to adverse consequences. Although only 0.7% of adults are classified as problem gamblers, an additional 1.8% are classified as moderate risk gamblers (Abbott et al., 2014b). Men are marginally more likely to be problem gamblers, but not moderate-risk gamblers, than women. Although there are few age differences, Pacific Islanders (8.0%), Māori peoples (6.2%), and Asians (1.8%) report the highest rates of problem or moderate-risk gambling. Problem gambling is associated with alcohol and substance use disorders, poor health, low quality of life, life events, deprivation, regular gambling, overseas internet gambling, EGM and casino gambling, multiple gambling activities, high gambling expenditure, and exposure to gambling by family and friends.

NZ has recently employed the PGSI to estimate current problem gambling prevalence (Abbott et al., 2014b). In an NZ publication, Bellringer et al. (2008) recommend a clinical assessment battery comprising the Lie-Bet Questionnaire, the PGSI, questions relating to dollars lost gambling and control over gambling, and brief screens to identify other comorbid behaviours. The Ministry of Health funds free specialised problem gambling treatment services including: face-to-face counselling; support groups; couple and family therapy; telephone counselling; self-help resources; services for family members and friends; specialist services for people from Māori, Pacific Islander, and Asian communities; community education and advocacy; and host responsibility programs. Self-exclusion and third-party exclusion from gaming venues are also available. The Ministry of Health also funds problem gambling monitoring, research, and evaluation and the Gambling and Addictions Research Centre (Auckland University of Technology) runs a biennial international gambling conference and an international think tank.

Internet gaming disorder

There is a paucity of research exploring technological addictions, including IGD, in NZ. Nor are there any NZ screening, assessment, or treatment recommendations.

Australian case study

This case has been created as an example for illustrative purposes.

Tony is a 28-year-old man living in an inner city area of a large Australian city. Tony was raised by his single mother, who had chronic health issues. Tony has very little contact with his father, who is Indigenous, but has close relationships with his mother, sister, as well as cousins and uncles from his father's family.

Tony trained as an electrician and is employed by a large manufacturing company where he oversees maintenance on large machinery. He currently lives with his girlfriend of 8 years, who also has Indigenous heritage. Tony is a bright, ambitious young man who has had a steady relationship with his partner since high school and a supportive and stable group of friends. He is well engaged in his local community through his membership in the local football team, where he was a player/coach on weekends until a serious injury prevented him from playing football for the remainder of the season.

Until 4 weeks ago, Tony was smoking methamphetamine (ice) two to three times per week. What initially started as recreational use on weekends with friends had increased in the past 4 months. Tony's increased use of ice was triggered by ongoing work stressors due to company changes, a significant injury that prevented him from playing football, and relationship difficulties with his partner. He had to use larger quantities and was spending larger amounts of money on ice than he intended. Tony attended work intoxicated on one occasion. He was concerned that he had lost control over his use and ceased ice completely.

Tony's work has a mandatory drug screening process and Tony feared he would lose his job. His ice use had a significant impact on his relationship with his girlfriend, who wants to start a family. Tony had hidden his ice use from his partner, but she had observed him behaving in an agitated way, going for long periods without sleep, and becoming uncharacteristically aggressive. Tony's boss had observed changes in Tony's work ethic including taking multiple sick days without explanation.

Tony is diagnosed with SUD, moderate, stimulant (amphetamine), in early remission. It was recommended that Tony engage in outpatient relapse prevention counselling and/or join a peer recovery network. It is also recommended that Tony recommence his involvement in community activities, such as football, as this is a protective factor. Further, Tony has been encouraged to seek assistance through his company's employee assistance program to help manage work-related stressors in the future.

Australia – the prevention paradox

Over 20% of Australians meet lifetime criteria for alcohol use disorders, yet despite high rates of associated psychological morbidity (such as anxiety or depression) and a poorer quality of life, only one in five seek treatment (Teeson, 2010). Publicly funded treatment services have evolved to meet the needs of the small minority of dependent drinkers who seek help. Many of these treatment seekers also have complex coexisting problems such as medical and psychiatric disorders and/or psychosocial disadvantage such as homelessness and poverty. Therefore, they access many different types of welfare services and require intensive and expensive support alongside their addiction treatment. It is now recognised that it is the population of moderate to heavy problem drinkers, who are unlikely to seek treatment, that cause the greatest cost to society, due to their greater number (Kaner, 2007). This has been termed the "prevention paradox." Consequently, it is critical to consider the entire continuum of alcohol problems when designing public health and specialist interventions for alcohol use disorders. Recent treatment advances are addressing barriers to seeking help for alcohol issues, such as stigma, by providing treatment online or via telephone.

New Zealand – internet gaming disorder research and treatment

There is a paucity of research exploring technological addiction disorders, including internet gaming disorder, particularly in NZ. The prevalence of internet gaming disorder in student or general populations, the course of these disorders across time, or the comorbid conditions and risk factors associated with the development of these disorders is currently unknown. Due to this lack of an evidence base, there are currently no NZ screening, assessment, or treatment recommendations for internet gaming disorder available. There are also no prevention programs or specialist services available to treat individuals with this disorder. There is a clear need to develop a consensus around the most appropriate assessments and interventions for this disorder.

Bibliography

Dowling, N. A. (2014). Commentary on Petry et al. (2014): Issues raised by the DSM-5 internet gaming disorder classification and proposed diagnostic criteria. *Addiction, 109*, 1407–1413.

Grant, J. E., Potenza, M. N., Weinstein, A., & Gorelick, D. A. (2010). Introduction to behavioral addictions. *American Journal of Drug and Alcohol Abuse, 36*, 233–241.

Petry, N. M., Rehbein, F., Gentile, D. A., Lemmens, J. S., Rumpf, H-J., Mößle, T., Bischof, G., Tao, R. Fung, D. S. S., Borges, G., Auriacombe, M., González Ibáñez, A., Tam, P., & O'Brien, C. P. (2014). An international consensus for assessing internet gaming disorder using the new DSM-5 approach. *Addiction, 109*, 1399–1406.

References

Abbott, M., Bellringer, M., Garrett, N., & Mundy-McPherson, S. (2014a). *New Zealand 2012 national gambling study: Overview and gambling participation (report number 1)*. Wellington, NZ: Ministry of Health.

Abbott, M., Bellringer, M., Garrett, N., & Mundy-McPherson, S. (2014b). *New Zealand 2012 national gambling study: Gambling harm and problem gambling (report number 2)*. Wellington, NZ: Ministry of Health.

American Psychiatric Association. (2013). *Diagnostic and statistical manual of mental disorders* (5th ed.). Arlington, VA: Author.

Australian Institute of Health and Welfare. (2013). *Alcohol and other drug treatment services in Australia 2011–2012 (Drug Treatment Series No. 21)*. Canberra: Author.

Australian Institute of Health and Welfare. (2014). *National drug strategy household survey detailed report 2013 (Drug Statistic Series No. 28)*. Canberra: Author.

Australian Psychological Society. (2012). *Gambling-related harm: A position statement prepared for the Australian Psychological Society*. Melbourne: Author.

Bellringer, M., Abbott, M., Volberg, R., Garrett, N., & Coombes, R. (2008). *Problem gambling assessment and screening instruments*. Wellington, NZ: Ministry of Health.

Blaszczynski, A. & Nower, L. (2002). A pathways model of problem and pathological gambling. *Addiction, 97*, 487–499.

Christensen, D. R., Dowling, N. A., Jackson, A. C., & Thomas, S. A. (2014). Gambling participation and problem gambling severity in a stratified random survey: Findings from the second social and economic impact study of gambling in Tasmania. *Journal of Gambling Studies*. [Epub ahead of print.]

Department of Health and Ageing. (2011). *The national drug strategy 2010–2015*. Available: www.nationaldrugstrategy.gov.au/internet/drugstrategy/publishing.nsf/Content/nds2015

Dowling, N. A., & Brown, M. (2010). Commonalities in the psychological factors associated with problem gambling and internet dependence. *Cyberpsychology, Behavior, and Social Networking, 13*(4), 437–441.

Dowling, N. A., Cowlishaw, S., Jackson, A. C., Merkouris, S. S., Francis, K. L., & Christensen, D. R. (2014). The prevalence of comorbid personality disorders in treatment-seeking problem gamblers: A systematic review and meta-analysis. *Journal of Personality Disorders*. Epub ahead of print.

Dowling, N. A., Cowlishaw, S., Jackson, A. C., Merkouris, S. S., Francis, K. L., & Christensen, D. R. (2015). The prevalence of psychiatric comorbidity in treatment-seeking problem gamblers: A systematic review and meta-analysis. *Australian & New Zealand Journal of Psychiatry*, *49*(6), 519–539.

Dowling, N. A., Jackson, A. C., Thomas, S. A., & Frydenberg, E. (2010). *Children at risk of developing problem gambling*. Melbourne: Gambling Research Australia.

Dowling, N. A., Merkouris, S. S., Greenwood, C. J., Oldenhof, E., Toumbourou, J. W., & Youssef, G. J. (2016). Risk and protective factors for youth problem gambling: A systematic review and meta-analysis of longitudinal studies. Prepared for the Ontario Problem Gambling Research Centre.

Dowling, N. A., Smith, D., & Thomas, T. (2005). Electronic gaming machines: Are they the "crack-cocaine" of gambling? *Addiction*, *100*, 33–45.

Dowling, N. A., Suomi, A., Jackson, A. C., Lavis, T., Patford, J., Cockman, S., Thomas, S. A., Bellringer, M. E., Koziol-McLain, J., Battersby, M., Harvey, P., & Abbott, M. (2014). Problem gambling and intimate partner violence: A systematic review and meta-analysis. *Trauma, Violence, and Abuse*. Epub ahead of print.

Dowling, N. A., Youssef, G. J., Jackson, A. C., Pennay, D. W., Francis, K. L., Pennay, A., & Lubman, D. I. (2015). National estimates of Australian gambling prevalence: Findings from a dual-frame omnibus survey. *Addiction*. [Epub ahead of print].

Fergusson, D. M., Boden, J. M., & Horwood, L. J. (2008). Exposure to childhood sexual and physical abuse and adjustment in early adulthood. *Child Abuse and Neglect, 32*, 607–619.

Ferris, J., & Wynne, H. J. (2001). *The Canadian problem gambling index*. Ottawa: Canadian Centre on Substance Abuse.

Francis, K. L., Dowling, N. A., Jackson, A. C., Christensen, D. C., & Wardle, H. (2015). Gambling motives: Validation of the reasons for gambling questionnaire in an Australian population survey. *Journal of Gambling Studies*, *31*(3), 807–823.

Gainsbury, S. M., Russell, A., Hing, N., Wood, R., Lubman, D. I., & Blaszczynski, A. (2014). The prevalence and determinants of problem gambling in Australia: Assessing the impact of interactive gambling and new technologies. *Psychology of Addictive Behaviors, 28*, 769–779.

Gainsbury, S. M., Russell, A., Hing, N., Wood, R., Lubman, D., & Blaszczynski, A. (2015). How the internet is changing gambling: Findings from an Australian prevalence survey. *Journal of Gambling Studies, 31*, 1–15.

Gao, C., Ogeil, R. P., & Lloyd, B. (2014). *Alcohol's burden of disease in Australia*. Canberra: FARE and VicHealth in collaboration with Turning Point.

Hayatbakhsh, M. R., Mamun, A. A., Najman, J. M., O'Callaghan, M. J., Bor, W., & Alati, R. (2008). Early childhood predictors of early substance use and substance use disorders: Prospective study. *Australian & New Zealand Journal of Psychiatry, 42*, 720–731.

Hing, N., Breen, H., Gordon, A., & Russell, A. (2014). Risk factors for problem gambling among Indigenous Australians: An empirical study. *Journal of Gambling Studies, 30,* 387–402.

Kaner, E. F., et al. (2007). Effectiveness of brief alcohol interventions in primary care populations. *Cochrane Database of Systematic Review, 2,* CD004148.

King, D. L., & Delfabbro, P. H. (2014). Internet gaming disorder treatment: A review of definitions of diagnosis and treatment outcome. *Journal of Clinical Psychology, 70,* 942–955.

King, D. L., Delfabbro, P. H., & Griffiths, M. D. (2013). Trajectories of problem video gaming among adult regular gamers: An 18-month longitudinal study. *Cyberpsychology, Behavior, and Social Networking, 16,* 72–76.

King, D. L., Delfabbro, P. H., Griffiths, M. D., & Gradisar, M. (2011). Assessing clinical trials of internet addiction treatment: A systematic review and CONSORT evaluation. *Clinical Psychology Review, 31,* 1110–1116.

King, D. L., Delfabbro, T. Z., Zwaans, T., & Kaptsis, D. (2013). Clinical features and Axis I comorbidity of Australian adolescent pathological internet and video game users. *Australian & New Zealand Journal of Psychiatry, 47,* 1058–1067.

King, D. L., Haagsma, M. C., Delfabbro, P. H., Gradisar, M., & Griffiths, M. D. (2013). Toward a consensus definition of pathological video-gaming: A systematic review of psychometric assessment tools. *Clinical Psychology Review, 33,* 331–342.

Lea, T., Bryant, J., Ellard, J., Howard, J., & Treloar, C. (2015). Young people at risk of transitioning to injecting drug use in Sydney, Australia: Social disadvantage and other correlates of higher levels of exposure to injecting. *Health and Social Care in the Community, 23,* 200–207.

Lorains, F., Stout, J. C., Bradshaw, J. L., Dowling, N. A., & Enticott, P. (2014). Self-reported impulsivity and inhibitory control in problem gamblers. *Journal of Clinical and Experimental Neuropsychology, 36,* 144–157.

Loxley, W., Toumbourou, J. W., Stockwell, T., Haines, B., Scott, K., Godfrey, C., et al. (January 2004). *The prevention of substance use harm in Australia: A review of the evidence.* Canberra, Australia: Australian Government Department of Health and Ageing.

Matua Raki. (2011). *Screening, assessment and evaluation (alcohol and other drug, smoking and gambling).* Wellington, NZ: Author.

Matua Raki. (2012). *A guide to the addiction treatment sector in Aotearoa New Zealand.* Wellington, NZ: Author.

Mills, K. L., Deady, M., Proudfoot, H., Sannibale, C., Teesson, M., Mattick, R., & Burns, L. (2010). *Guidelines on the management of co-occurring alcohol and other drug and mental health conditions in alcohol and other drug treatment settings.* Sydney: National Drug and Alcohol Research Centre (NDARC), University of New South Wales.

Ministry of Health. (2009). *Alcohol use in New Zealand: Key results of the 2007/08 New Zealand alcohol and drug use survey.* Wellington, NZ: Author.

Ministry of Health. (2010). *Drug use in New Zealand: Key results of the 2007/08 New Zealand alcohol and drug use survey.* Wellington, NZ: Author.

Ministry of Health. (November 2013). *Drug policy*. Wellington, NZ: Author. Available: www.health.govt.nz/our-work/mental-health-and-addictions/drug-policy

Mottram, A. J., & Fleming, M. J. (2009). Extraversion, impulsivity, and online group membership as predictors of problematic internet use. *CyberPsychology and Behavior, 12,* 319–321.

National Health and Medical Research Council. (2009). *Australian guidelines to reduce health risks from drinking alcohol.* Canberra: Author.

National Health and Medical Research Council. (2011). *Consensus-based clinical practice guideline for the management of volatile substance use in Australia.* Canberra: Author.

Neal, P., Delfabbro, P., & O'Neil, M. (2005). *Problem gambling and harm: Towards a national definition.* Melbourne: Gambling Research Australia.

New Zealand Department of Internal Affairs. (2014). *Gambling expenditure statistics.* NZ: Author.

Paquette, D., McEwan, M., & Bryant, J. (2013). Risk practices among Aboriginal people who inject drugs in New South Wales, Australia. *AIDS Behaviour, 17,* 2467–2473.

Problem Gambling Research and Treatment Centre. (2011). *Guideline for screening, assessment and treatment in problem and pathological gambling.* Clayton, Monash University: Author.

Queensland Government Statistician's Office. (2014). *Australian gambling statistics* (30th ed.). Qld, Australia: Author.

Rickwood, D., Blaszczynski, A., Delfabbro, P., Dowling, N., & Heading, K. (2010). *The psychology of gambling: APS review paper.* Melbourne: Australian Psychological Society.

Ryan, S. M., Jorm, A. F., & Lubman, D. I. (2010). Parenting factors associated with reduced adolescent alcohol use: A systematic review of longitudinal studies. *Australian & New Zealand Journal of Psychiatry, 44,* 774–783.

Schiff, M., Plotnikova, M., Dingle, K., Williams, G. M., Najman, J., & Clavarino, A. (2014). Does adolescent's exposure to parental intimate partner conflict and violence predict psychological distress and substance use in young adulthood? A longitudinal study. *Child Abuse and Neglect, 38,* 1945–1954.

Scholes-Balog, K. E., Hemphill, S. A., Dowling, N. A., & Toumbourou, J. W. (2014). A prospective study of risk and protective factors for problem gambling among young adults. *Journal of Adolescence, 37,* 215–224.

Teesson, M., et al. (2010). Prevalence and correlates of DSM-IV alcohol abuse and dependence in Australia: Findings of the 2007 National Survey of Mental Health and Wellbeing. *Addiction, 105,* 2085–2094.

The Economist. (2014). Daily chart: The house wins. 3 Feb. Available: www.economist.com/blogs/graphicdetail/2014/02/daily-chart-0

Thomas, N. J., & Martin, F. H. (2010). Video-arcade game, computer game and internet activities of Australian students: Participation habits and prevalence of addiction. *Australian Journal of Psychology, 62,* 59–66.

Thomas, S. A., Merkouris, S. S., Radermacher, H. L., Dowling, N. A., Misso, M. L., Anderson, C. J., & Jackson, A. C. (2011). An Australian guideline for treatment in problem gambling: An abridged outline. *Medical Journal of Australia, 195*(11), 664–665.

Victorian Department of Justice. (2011). *The Victorian gambling study: A longitudinal study of gambling and public health – Wave two findings*. Melbourne: Author.

Wang, W. (2001). Internet dependency and psychosocial maturity among college students. *International Journal of Human-Computer Studies, 55*, 919–938.

Wells, J. E., Baxter, J., & Schaaf, D. (Eds). (2007). *Substance use disorders in Te Rau Hinengaro: The New Zealand mental health survey*. Wellington, NZ: Alcohol Advisory Council of New Zealand.

Young, M., Abu-Duhou, I., Barnes, T., Creed, E., Morris, M., Stevens, M., & Tyler, B. (2006). *Northern Territory gambling prevalence survey 2005*. Darwin: School for Social and Policy Research, Charles Darwin.

Recommendations for further reading/resources

General

Blaszczynski, A., & Nower, L. (2002). A pathways model of problem and pathological gambling. *Addiction, 97*, 487–99.

Dowling, N. A., Cowlishaw, S., Jackson, A. C., Merkouris, S. S., Francis, K. L., & Christensen, D. R. (2015). The prevalence of psychiatric comorbidity in treatment-seeking problem gamblers: A systematic review and meta-analysis. *Australian & New Zealand Journal of Psychiatry, 49*(6), 519–539.

Grant, J. E., Potenza, M. N., Weinstein, A., & Gorelick, D. A. (2010). Introduction to behavioral addictions. *American Journal of Drug and Alcohol Abuse, 36*, 233–241.

King, D. L., Delfabbro, P. H., Griffiths, M. D., & Gradisar, M. (2011). Assessing clinical trials of internet addiction treatment: A systematic review and CONSORT evaluation. *Clinical Psychology Review, 31*, 1110–1116.

Petry, N. M., Rehbein, F., Gentile, D. A., Lemmens, J. S., Rumpf, H-J., Möβle, T., Bischof, G., Tao, R. Fung, D. S. S., Borges, G., Auriacombe, M., González Ibáñez, A., Tam, P., & O'Brien, C. P. (2014). An international consensus for assessing internet gaming disorder using the new DSM-5 approach. *Addiction, 109*, 1399–1406.

Australia

Australian Institute of Health and Welfare. (2014). *National drug strategy household survey detailed report 2013 (Drug Statistic Series No. 28)*. Canberra: Author.

Australian Psychological Society. (2012). *Gambling-related harm: A position statement prepared for the Australian Psychological Society*. Melbourne: Author.

Department of Health and Ageing. (2011). *The national drug strategy 2010–2015*. Available: www.nationaldrugstrategy.gov.au/internet/drugstrategy/publishing.nsf/Content/nds2015

National Health and Medical Research Council. (2009). *Australian guidelines to reduce health risks from drinking alcohol*. Canberra: Author.

Problem Gambling Research and Treatment Centre. (PGRTC). (2011). *Guideline for screening, assessment and treatment in problem and pathological gambling.* Clayton, Australia: Monash University.

New Zealand

Abbott, M., Bellringer, M., Garrett, N., & Mundy-McPherson, S. (2014b). *New Zealand 2012 national gambling study: Gambling harm and problem gambling (Report Number 2).* Wellington, NZ: Author.

Matua Raki. (2011). *Screening, assessment and evaluation (alcohol and other drug, smoking and gambling).* Wellington, NZ: Author.

Matua Raki. (2012). *A guide to the addiction treatment sector in Aotearoa New Zealand.* Wellington, NZ: Author.

Ministry of Health. (2010). *Drug use in New Zealand: Key results of the 2007/08 New Zealand alcohol and drug use survey.* Wellington, NZ: Author.

Acknowledgements

The authors would like to thank Bonnie Albrecht and Emma Lockwood for sourcing some of the relevant data.

21

Neurocognitive disorders

Karen A Sullivan and Alice Theadom

Introduction

The primary feature of the neurocognitive disorders (NCDs) is a decline in cognitive function. Other conditions such as schizophrenia and depression can have associated cognitive impairment, but for the NCDs it is the defining characteristic (e.g., Laughren, 2011). The name – neurocognitive disorders – arguably hides the fascinating diversity within this disorder class. It includes conditions such as Alzheimer's disease with its long, slow, progressive cognitive decline and uncertain aetiology, and Huntington's disease with its relatively rapid course and clear genetic basis. NCDs primarily affect adults, especially older adults. As the population of Australia and New Zealand (NZ) ages, NCDs are likely to become more prevalent. The NCDs are also not without controversy. Some people question whether they should be classified as a mental disorder (Robles et al., 2015). They are unique in that, unlike other diagnoses in the *Diagnostic and Statistical Manual of Mental Disorders* (5th ed.; *DSM-5*; American Psychiatric Association, 2013), the pathology, and in some cases the aetiology of the conditions, is largely known (Ganguli et al., 2011).

The hallmark of a person with a neurocognitive disorder is a decline in one or more formally defined areas of cognition. In the *DSM-5*, these are complex attention, executive function, learning and memory, language, perceptual-motor, or social cognition. The extent of decline separates the two main divisions within this disorder class, of *major or mild* neurocognitive disorder, as per the following example.

- Major NCD refers to disorders previously referred to as dementia or delirium where there is *significant* decline from previous functioning in one or more of the six areas of cognitive functioning. This decline is: 1. noticeable, it is evident to the affected person (they describe it) or a close other (e.g., a knowledgeable informant); 2. demonstrable, when formally assessed; and 3. impactful, it interferes with the person's capacity to do everyday tasks.

- Mild NCD differs in extent only. Mild NCD refers to cognitive difficulties at a level where the person needs to use strategies to function in everyday life.

We all experience cognitive decline as we age, so drawing the line between normal and abnormal decline can be difficult. Some consider the threshold suggested by the *DSM-5* too low. Forensic psychologists anticipate that this low threshold diagnosis will give new legitimacy to brain injury conditions that were previously controversial (Simpson, 2014). However, proponents of this low threshold diagnosis argue it could permit the earlier identification and treatment of conditions such as Alzheimer's disease (Crowe, 2015; Sachs-Ericsson & Blazer, 2014).

The term "neurocognitive disorder" is an overarching one and it masks the reason for the cognitive decline. In the *DSM-5*, specifiers for major NCD can show the presumed reason for the cognitive decline. The neurocognitive disorder may be due to Alzheimer's disease, frontotemporal lobar degeneration, Lewy body disease, vascular dementia, traumatic brain injury, substance/medication abuse, human immunodeficiency virus (HIV) infection, Prion disease, Parkinson's disease, Huntington's disease, another medical condition, multiple aetiologies, or unspecified. This list of specifiers was debated when the *DSM-5* was developed (Laughren, 2011; Sachs-Ericsson & Blazer, 2014) and may grow especially as biomarker knowledge advances (Sachs-Ericsson & Blazer, 2014).

The overarching term "NCD" was deliberately introduced to provide a common term for clinicians and researchers to use, in place of the multiple diagnostic terms (and criteria) that were being used, even for the same pathology (Sachdev et al., 2015; Sachdev, Kalaria et al., 2014). However, this approach has been criticised for prematurely collapsing a range of etiologically distinct disorders into one group which can really only function with the addition of multiple specifiers (Looi & Liberg, 2015). The new *DSM-5* terminology must compete with terms that may be more familiar to, or readily understood by, patients, their families, and in the community, such as dementia. It must also compete with the terminology and diagnostic approach promoted by other agencies and specialist groups (Cuthbert & Insel, 2013; Dubois et al., 2014; Frances, 2014; Sachdev, Blacker et al., 2014).

Given the breadth of presentations encompassed by the neurocognitive disorders, one exemplar from this category is used to guide the rest of the discussion in this chapter. This chapter focuses on major neurocognitive disorder due to *probable* Alzheimer's disease.

Coding NCDs using *DSM-5*

The *DSM-5* code for this disorder is derived as follows. First, the severity of the cognitive decline is determined (e.g., major or minor). For major NCD, a numeric code is applied to designate the presumed aetiology of the NCD. For example, in this case, Alzheimer's disease, 331.0 (*International Statistical Classification of Diseases and Related Health Problems 2010 Edition [ICD-10]* code G30.9). Second, a text code is used to indicate how likely it is that the disorder is due to this pathology (is it *probably* or *possibly* due to it?). Third, a numeric *code indicates* whether or not behavioural disturbance is 294.11, (F01.81), or is not present 294.10 (F02.80). A full list of aetiological codes is available at www.dsm5.org/.

For minor NCD, the code 331.83 (G31.84) is used. There is no need to use an additional code for the aetiological subtype or presence of behavioural disturbance.

Due to cost and practice issues in updating coding systems within hospital services, some services may still use the prior DSM coding system.

Australia

Neurocognitive disorders are on the rise in Australia and NZ. In Australia, the category of dementia and Alzheimer's disease was the third leading cause of death in 2012, claiming the lives of more than 10 000 Australians. This is a significant increase of approximately 140% over the same number a decade ago (Australian Bureau of Statistics [ABS], 2012). Other metrics show a similar rise in rank of this disorder compared to other causes of death or disability. For example, in 1990 Alzheimer's disease was ranked as the 26th cause of premature mortality in Australia, but by 2010 it was the ninth cause of premature death (Institute for Health Metrics and Evaluation, 2013a). There are probably several factors that contribute to this increase, including increasing disorder awareness, as well as the ageing of the population (Kalaria et al., 2008). It is also important to note that the burden of the neurocognitive disorders is probably not evenly borne by subgroups in Australia or NZ (Bramley et al., 2004; Garvey et al., 2011).

In Australia, there has been a significant investment in dementia research. The Australian government has supported dementia research via its Dementia Collaborative Research Centres. These centres have produced research focused on consumers and carers, pathogenesis, and identifying risk factors through population-level research, respectively. The Perth-based Centre of Excellence for Alzheimer's Disease Research and Care has also attracted state government funding, and investment by several Western Australian universities. Perhaps one of the most well-known Australian dementia research enterprises is the landmark multidisciplinary longitudinal Australian Imaging, Biomarker and Lifestyle (AIBL) Flagship Study of Aging. With partners including the Commonwealth Science and Industry Research Organisation, universities, hospitals, and private enterprise, this study has been tracking Australian participants to improve understanding of the cause of, and best method of identifying a precursor of Alzheimer's disease. Originally conceived as a three-year longitudinal study but still going today, the AIBL study is tracking more than 1100 volunteers aged over 65. When it started, it was one of the world's largest pre-clinical biomarker studies to use amyloid imaging from positron emission tomography (PET) to try to identify a pre-clinical biomarker of disease. So far this study has shown that abnormal levels of amyloid-β in the brain are detected 17 years before the onset of dementia symptoms (Burnham, Villemagne, & Macaulay, 2013). The AIBL researchers are also trialling a lower cost blood test equivalent to neuroimaging (Burnham et al., 2014), which would enable more people access to this test. If the best treatment option for Alzheimer's disease is disease-modifying agents as some people argue (Cummings, Doody, & Clark, 2007), despite the challenges of the drug search (Cummings, Morstorf, & Zhong, 2014), then the earlier that amyloid deposition can be identified, the sooner preventive treatments could be tried.

The *DSM-5* prefers but does not insist on standardised neuropsychological assessment to document the decline in cognitive function for the NCDs. In the absence of it, the *DSM-5* accepts another quantified clinical assessment. The manual itself suggests tests for various functions, such as executive function or memory, and the *DSM-5* includes a recommendation about the normative level of performance that would typically accompany the diagnosis. Specific online tools are now also endorsed for use with the *DSM-5* (American Psychiatric Association, 2015).

In terms of cognitive assessment for Alzheimer's disease, many of the generic tools suggested in the *DSM-5* are recommended by others (Foley & Heck, 2014). While this suggests consensus, there is actually little agreement about which tests to use in assessing dementia. A further, and arguably more important and complex challenge than test selection, is the test interpretation. Local normative data may not be available for the measures identified in the *DSM-5* or there may be no prior test result against which to compare a person's performance. Several international and local groups promote their batteries, normative data, or dementia assessment approach. In 2012, the United States' (US) National Institutes of Health (NIH) launched a computerised dementia screen (Weintraub et al., 2013), which it recommends for longitudinal studies. This tool "standardises" and co-norms the measures, it is quick and cheap to administer, and it is suitable for repeat applications with the same person. In Australia, computerised tools such as Cogstate, which is affiliated with the AIBL study, aim for something similar. The NIH toolbox (which also includes cognitive measures) is not currently normed for use in Australia, but if researchers succeed in this line of research, it could be used in international research trials and individual clinical assessments. In Australia the researchers leading the Sydney Memory and Ageing Study recently announced details of their neuro-norms calculator, a new tool that promises real time demographic adjustment for data from commonly used neuropsychological tests of cognitive performance (Kochan et al., 2014).

The federally funded Dementia Collaborative Research Centres have identified the Dementia Outcome Measures (DOMS), which include several tests of cognition and mood. The DOMS' intended audience is primarily non-specialist dementia assessors. There are several other practice guidelines for similar audiences from other Australian government organisations, including state governments. These guidelines have some overlap with each other, and with the tests some psychologists in Australia recommend (Pachana & Helmes, 2010) but there are important differences. For example, two

Victorian Government publications recommend the use of the Mini-Mental State Examination, or the Standardised Mini-Mental State Examination (National Ageing Research Institute, 2011), to assess a key area of functioning, cognition. However, the DOMS and other authors (Dementia Collaborative Research Centres, n.d.; Pachana & Helmes, 2010) recommend the Modified Mini-Mental State Test (the 3MS, Teng & Chui, 1987) or the Addenbroke's Cognitive Examination-Revised (ACE-R, Mioshi et al., 2006). These and other guidelines, such as those of the Royal Australian and New Zealand College of Psychiatrists (New South Wales [NSW] Ministry of Health and Royal Australian and New Zealand College of Psychiatrists, 2013), allow the assessor choice over which tool to use. Students of psychology must be familiar with a range of these commonly encountered tools. This discussion masks a broader question of whether these brief global cognitive screens can realise the objective outlined in the diagnostic standard, especially considering the requirement of decline in at least one *specific* area of cognition from an individual's baseline. In cases with subtle impairment, it is unlikely that general screening tests can provide sensitive measures of specific deficits.

In addition to the assessment of cognition in a person who may have dementia, other aspects of functioning should also be assessed. The guidelines from the Royal Australian and New Zealand College of Psychiatrists, and the DOMS, includes a list non-cognitive measures for this purpose (NSW Ministry of Health and The Royal Australian and New Zealand College of Psychiatrists, 2013). An alternative approach to assessing the behavioural and psychological symptoms of dementia through tools such as the Geriatric Depression Scale (Yesavage et al., 1983) and the Geriatric Anxiety Inventory (Pachana et al., 2007) is to use behavioural assessment. Using these tools can provide a normative comparison, but using behavioural assessment can offer insight to subclinical problems and behaviour modification strategies, and arguably gives a more holistic, context-rich, and individualised perspective on what might be termed *problem* behaviour.

There is currently no known treatment for many of the neurocognitive disorders, including Alzheimer's disease. In Australia, Medicare rebates for psychological services to people in residential care are not available, and neuropsychological services that could assist with diagnosis and early intervention are not rebated. The aim of treatment for the affected person is primarily symptom relief and it is often pharmacological; however, behavioural analysis should be considered to find alternate means of alleviating the distress that a person with dementia, or their caregiver, can experience.

There is growing interest in how to prevent disorders such as Alzheimer's disease, or how to slow its progression. Research groups, including the AIBL team, are vigorously pursuing the early identification of pre-clinical amyloid deposition, which could enable early use of disease-modifying drugs. The everyday advice for people who want to lower or prevent their risk of conditions such as Alzheimer's disease through non-pharmacological means is often phrased as "use it or lose it." This advice is much debated and the evidence for it is contested. There are new trials of individual cognitive stimulation (Yates et al., 2015) that could overcome the limitations of generic "use it or lose it" advice. Australian research also suggests that physical activity could be important in preventing Alzheimer's disease (Lautenschlager et al., 2008).

The Australian Psychological Society has a number of useful tip sheets for working with people with neurocognitive disorders, including dementia. The Australian Psychological Society Ageing and Psychology Interest group, and the Society's College of Clinical Neuropsychology, have members who work with older adults and grapple with the challenges faced by people with a neurocognitive disorder such as Alzheimer's disease including the loss of independent decision-making capacity, and their families.

The Australian Federal Government funds the Dementia Behaviour Management Advisory Service, which provides information and advice to carers of people with dementia who have behavioural and psychological symptoms. Alzheimer's Australia also provides support and resources.

New Zealand

In NZ it is estimated that more 7% of people over the age of 65 (1.1% of the NZ population) are affected by major NCD (Campbell, McCosh, & Reinken, 1983). Most (60%) are female, which may be due to females living on average 5 years longer than their male counterparts (Statistics New Zealand, 2015). The Indigenous populations of NZ, including Māori and Pacific peoples, are believed to experience higher levels of major NCD than NZ Europeans (Dyall, 2014).

Prevalence of NCD is believed to be rising due to both the ageing of the population and a growing number of people with early onset NCD (Lambert et al., 2014). The Māori population is also growing at double the rate of non-Māori (Dyall, 2014). Projections suggest that the prevalence of Alzheimer's disease specifically will increase 2.5 fold by 2031 (Tobias, Yeh, & Johnson, 2008). This is concerning as there is evidence that many cases of major NCD remain undiagnosed (Valcour et al., 2000). It is also of concern that some cultures perceive NCD to be a mental health diagnosis that is shameful, which may prevent people from seeking intervention and treatment.

The significance of this major neurocognitive disorder is growing. In NZ in 1990, Alzheimer's disease was ranked as the 35th cause of premature mortality, but by 2010 it was ranked 9th (Institute for Health Metrics and Evaluation, 2013b). As a result, in 2013 the NZ Ministry of Health outlined key areas of action needed to improve the health, independence, and wellbeing of those with major NCD. This included increasing awareness, reducing the risk, and increasing access to a timely diagnosis. Before 2000, little research in NCD had been completed in NZ but it has been steadily increasing since then, with a focus on using antipsychotic medication, diagnosis and assessment, and managing major NCD in residential facilitates (Prasadarao, 2014).

Recent developments in NZ have included the launch of New Zealand's first in a series of planned NCD research clinics in Auckland in 2014. The program forms part of a Centre of Research Excellence known as Brain Research New Zealand; Rangahau Roro Aotearoa co-hosted by the University of Auckland and University of Otago in partnership with Auckland University of Technology and the University of Canterbury. These clinics aim to test innovative new treatments of the people with mild NCD (with the aim to prevent progression to major NCD). A compilation of NZ research has also been published (Prasadarao, 2014).

NZ researchers have highlighted that there remains considerable stigma and embarrassment to living with NCD. People also report that they are frequently patronised by others in everyday life, highlighting a need for societal attitude change (O'Sullivan, Hocking, & Spence, 2014).

The NZ Framework for Dementia Care was released in 2013 with the aim to move towards a more multi-faceted treatment model, rather than a medical model. As part of this framework, all regional district health boards had to develop their own care pathway. This has been an important shift in healthcare and offers a more responsive approach to meeting the needs of the Indigenous populations. It takes into account the spiritual, family and whanau (essentially "extended family," as "whanau" as a term covers a collective social familial unit with roles and responsibilities for the collective), cultural, economic, social, and occupational needs, as well as the health needs of the person, to maximise their independence and wellbeing. However, this approach has created differences in the treatment model provided depending on where the person lives. Services to support people with mild and major NCD commonly run alongside adult and older adult mental health services. Those experiencing cognitive impairment due to vascular dementia and Alzheimer's tend to be seen within the dementia services. Those experiencing symptoms due to specific conditions such as HIV, brain injury, or Huntington's disease are managed within services for these specific conditions.

Within dementia services, assessments are usually conducted within the person's home, so contextual factors can be considered. Following assessment, routine blood tests, computed tomography (CT) or magnetic resonance imaging (MRI) scans and medical reviews, feedback is given during a face-to-face meeting, to involve the person and their significant others in treatment planning.

There is a neuropsychology special interest group linked to the New Zealand College of Clinical Psychologists. Meetings are held regionally across the country. The groups cover all areas of neuropsychology, and discuss issues about NCD and its treatment. Many services teams also hold regular psychology team forums and peer-supervision meetings, and encourage clinical supervision.

Assessment tools used in NZ can vary depending on the nature of the presenting difficulties and region. Common initial assessments include the Addenbrooke's Cognitive Examination (ACE-III; Hsieh et al., 2013) and the Frontal Assessment Battery (Dubois et al., 2000). If there are challenges in administering these assessments, the Montreal Cognitive Assessment (MoCA; Nasreddine et al., 2005) or the Rowland Universal Dementia Assessment Scale (RUDAS; Storey et al., 2004) are often used. Subtests from the Neuropsychological Assessment Battery (NAB; White & Stern, 2003) can provide a more detailed assessment. In addition to cognitive functioning, other core assessments often include the Neuropsychiatric Inventory (NPI, Cummings et al., 1994), Activities of Daily Living Questionnaire (Johnson et al., 2004) and the Zarit Carer Burden Interview (Zarit, Reever, & Bach-Peterson, 1980) to present a broader picture of how the difficulties impact the person and their families.

Neuropsychological testing can be challenging in people who do not speak English fluently. Interpreters are often available through mainstream services, but this can affect performance on the test. Many people do not want interpreters present while they are being assessed. Often, families feel that as they know the person best, they would prefer to interpret themselves rather than to have a stranger in their home. Alternatively, as people who speak the same language are often well known to each other in NZ, having someone else from the community present can threaten people's sense of privacy.

There are additional challenges in using neuropsychological tests with the Indigenous people of NZ and people from other non-westernised cultures. Cultural factors are known to impact on performance, and individuals who are not from a western culture may be disadvantaged by these tests (Dudley, Wilson, & Barker-Collo, 2014). Little research has been done on the application of these assessments in Māori and Pacific people, although some work is currently underway. Skills in cultural competence and cultural safety are needed to prevent the impact of cultural factors on test performance (Dudley et al., 2014).

It is recognised that, in most cases, there is a dearth of appropriately normed tests for use with New Zealanders. There have been a number of other studies to generate normative standards for older New Zealanders (Harvey & Siegert, 1999; Siegert & Cavana, 1997); however, these studies are now quite dated and many tests still do not have local norms, so those from the US are used. NZ psychologists recognise the need for large local normative data sets to aid the interpretation of neuropsychological tests, including to enable stratification across important variables, such as culture (Feigin & Barker-Collo, 2007).

There are no government subsidies for psychological dementia assessments. There is a local branch of Alzheimer's New Zealand that provides information and links to local resources. Local district health boards provide funding for NCD services.

New Zealand case study

This case is a composite example created for illustrative purposes.

Tainafi Fisu is a 72-year-old man born in Samoa. He moved to NZ with his wife and children when he was 28 to work. He retired from his job as a bus driver aged 64. He is married and has three children. He lives in South Auckland with his wife as well as with his eldest daughter, her husband, and her three children. His other two children and four grandchildren all live nearby. Mr Fisu is able to provide some details of his life, but most information comes from his wife and eldest daughter who are both present at the assessment.

It is difficult to find out about the onset of Mr Fisu's difficulties, which had been gradual over a number of years, although the wife and daughter mentioned a few occasions where Mr Fisu seemed to deteriorate. The family had previously visited their general practitioner (GP) about Mr Fisu's difficulties several times prior to referral. Mr Fisu is now becoming irritable and confused on a daily basis. Mr Fisu has been admitted on several occasions due to complications with his diabetes and high blood pressure. His family are concerned that he is not taking his medication as he should be. Mr Fisu is still driving and is responsible for dropping off and picking up his grandchildren from school.

There are no obvious clues as to the reason for the recent decline in behaviour, which has occurred gradually over time. Referral to the service was made via Mr Fisu's GP.

A neuropsychological assessment has been conducted to determine the nature and extent of difficulties Mr Fisu is experiencing. Mr Fisu was very cooperative with the assessment although became agitated when asked to recall information he had recently been given or to generate information. Difficulties with executive functioning, memory (particularly immediate recall), information processing, and phonemic fluency, were noted on neuropsychological testing. Mr Fisu's CT scan revealed several small infarcts suggesting a diagnosis of major neurocognitive disorder due to vascular disease.

The feedback meeting is attended by his wife and all three children. The geriatrician proposes a course of treatment using donepezil. Medical follow-up will be required. Strategies for supporting Mr Fisu to remember his medication are proposed and the family agree to re-labelling his medication container so that a section can be used for each dose required (as across his current medications he is required to take four doses per day rather than three) so this can be checked by the family and Mr Fisu reminded if necessary. Mr Fisu is advised that he should no longer drive and the family discuss ways this could be managed and identify other activities he can do with the grandchildren. Approaches for helping to prevent and manage Mr Fisu's agitation are discussed and a referral is made to Alzheimer's New Zealand for ongoing support.

Australia – dementia in Indigenous Australians

Research indicates that Aboriginal and Torres Strait Islander peoples are three to five times more likely than the general Australia population to experience dementia (Flicker & Holdworth, 2014). The Kimberly Indigenous Cognitive Assessment (KICA-Cog) was published in 2004 to meet the urgent need for a culturally appropriate tool to aid the assessment of cognition in Indigenous Australians (LoGiudice et al., 2006). The KICA-Cog is described as the only validated dementia assessment tool for Indigenous Australians (Dementia Collaborative Research Centres, 2015), although it is applicable to

continued ›

> **continued ›**
>
> groups other than the Indigenous people from the Kimberley and Northern Territory regions of Australia. The KICA-Cog is described as suitable for adults over the age of 45 years who live in remote communities, when other instruments are not appropriate. The KICA-Cog is an interviewer-administered 18-item questionnaire that is brief (takes approximately 10 minutes to administer) and it has a cut score to signal a positive screen, which should be followed up with further assessment. A modified KICA-Cog was recently described and pilot tested with promising results for use with urban Indigenous Australians (Pulver et al., 2012), and a shorter 10-item form of this test – the KICA-screen – has also begun to be trialled (LoGiudice et al., 2011).

New Zealand – Alzheimer's research

Professor Robert Knight is the neuropsychologist in a team of NZ researchers who are searching for a biomarker for Alzheimer's disease. This research group is also examining the relation between some of the most well-established risk factors for Alzheimer's disease and their cognitive phenotypes. Older persons with the apolipoprotein E (APOE) ε4 genotype typically score lower on neuropsychological tests than those adults who do not have this genotype. Professor Knight's research tested the idea that the relationship between the genotype and phenotype may not be direct. Not all genetic carriers develop Alzheimer's disease, so with his colleagues' help they looked at whether the relationship persisted if those who went on to develop the disease were removed from the study. The study included 241 people over the age of 65 years who did not have dementia, but their genetic profile was known. Group differences between carriers and non-carriers were found on cognitive tests, but when the data from carriers who developed dementia were excluded, these group differences were no longer observed. The authors concluded that if there is no dementia, the presence of the ε4 allele itself is unlikely to lead to an accelerated rate of cognitive decline (Knight et al., 2014).

References

American Psychiatric Association. (2013). *Diagnostic and statistical manual of mental disorders* (5th ed.). Arlington, VA: Author.

American Psychiatric Association. (2015). *Online assessment measures*. Available: www.psychiatry.org/practice/dsm/dsm5/online-assessment-measures

Australian Bureau of Statistics. (2012). *Causes of death, Australia, 2012*. Canberra: Author. Available: www.abs.gov.au/ausstats/abs@.nsf/mf/3303.0/

Bramley, D., Hebert, P., Jackson, R., & Chassin, M. (2004). Indigenous disparities in disease-specific mortality, a crosscountry comparison: New Zealand, Australia, Canada and the United States. *The New Zealand Medical Journal, 117*(1207), 1–16.

Burnham, S. C., Faux, N. B., Wilson, W., Laws, S. M., Ames, D., Bedo, J., ... Australian Imaging, Biomarkers and Lifestyle Study Research Group. (2014). A blood-based predictor for neocortical Aβ burden in Alzheimer's disease: Results from the AIBL study. *Molecular Psychiatry, 19*, 519–526. http://dx.doi.org/10.1038/mp.2013.40

Burnham, S. C., Villemagne, V. L., & Macaulay, S. L. (2013). The AIBL study: Opening the presymptomatic window in Alzheimer disease. *Medical Journal of Australia, 198*(11), 578.

Campbell, A., McCosh, L., & Reinken, J. (1983). Dementia in old age and the need for services. *Age and Aging, 12*, 11–16.

Crowe, S. F. (2015). Assessing the neurocognitive disorders of the diagnostic and statistical manual of mental disorders (5th ed.). *Australian Psychologist, 50*(1), 1–5. http://dx.doi.org/10.1111/ap.12104

Cummings, J. L., Doody, R., & Clark, C. (2007). Disease-modifying therapies for Alzheimer disease: Challenges to early intervention. *Neurology, 69*(16), 1622–1634. http://dx.doi.org/10.1212/01.wnl.0000295996.54210.69

Cummings, J. L., Mega, M., Gray, K., Rosenberg-Thompson, S., Carusi, D. A., & Gornbein, J. (1994). The neuropsychiatric inventory comprehensive assessment of psychopathology in dementia. *Neurology, 44*(12), 2308.

Cummings, J. L., Morstorf, T., & Zhong, K. (2014). Alzheimer's disease drug-development pipeline: Few candidates, frequent failures. *Alzheimer's Research and Therapy, 6*(37). http://dx.doi.org/10.1186/alzrt269

Cuthbert, B. N., & Insel, T. R. (2013). Toward the future of psychiatric diagnosis: The seven pillars of RDoC. *BMC Medicine, 11*(1), 126.

Dementia Collaborative Research Centres. (n.d.). Cognitive assessment measures. Available: www.dementia-assessment.com.au/cognitive/index.html

Dementia Collaborative Research Centres. (2015). Cognition dementia assessment measures. Available: www.dementia-assessment.com.au/cognitive/index.html

Dubois, B., Feldman, H. H., Jacova, C., Hampel, H., Molinuevo, J. L., Blennow, K., et al. (2014). Advancing research diagnostic criteria for Alzheimer's disease: The IWG-2 criteria. *The Lancet Neurology, 13*(6), 614–629.

Dubois, B., Slachevsky, A., Litvan, I., & Pillon, B. (2000). The FAB A frontal assessment battery at bedside. *Neurology, 55*(11), 1621–1626.

Dudley, M., Wilson, D., & Barker-Collo, S. (2014). Cultural invisibility: Māori people with traumatic brain injury and their experiences of neuropsychological assessments. *New Zealand Journal of Psychology, 43*(3), 14–22.

Dyall, L. (2014). Dementia: Continuation of health and ethnic inequalities in NZ. *New Zealand Medical Journal, 127*(1389), 68–80.

Feigin, V. L., & Barker-Collo, S. (2007). Normative neuropsychological data: Do we need them in New Zealand? *New Zealand Family Physician, 34*(6), 441–443.

Flicker, L., & Holdworth, K. (2014). Aboriginal and Torres Strait Islander people and dementia: A review of the research. A report for Alzheimer's Australia (Paper 41 October 2014). Available: https://fightdementia.org.au/files/NATIONAL/documents/Alzheimers-Australia-Numbered-Publication-41.pdf

Foley, J. M., & Heck, A. L. (2014). Neurocognitive disorders in aging: A primer on DSM-5 changes and framework for application to practice. *Clinical Gerontologist, 37*(4), 317–346. http://dx.doi.org/10.1080/07317115.2014.907595

Frances, A. (2014). ICD, DSM and The Tower of Babel. *Australian & New Zealand Journal of Psychiatry, 48*(4), 371–373. http://dx.doi.org/10.1177/0004867414526792

Ganguli, M., Blacker, D., Blazer, D., Grant, I., Jeste, D., Paulsen, J., et al. (2011). Classification of neurocognitive disorders in DSM-5: A work in progress. *The American Journal of Geriatric Psychiatry, 19*(3), 205–210.

Garvey, G., Simmonds, D., Clements, V., O'Rourke, P., Sullivan, K., Gorman, D., et al. (2011). Making sense of dementia: Understanding amongst Indigenous Australians. *International Journal of Geriatric Psychiatry, 26*(6), 649–656. http://dx.doi.org/10.1002/gps.2578

Harvey, J. A., & Siegert, R. J. (1999). Normative data for New Zealand elders on the Controlled Oral Word Association Test, Graded Naming Test, and the Recognition Memory Test. *New Zealand Journal of Psychology, 28*(2), 124–132.

Hsieh, S., Schubert, S., Hoon, C., Mioshi, E., & Hodges, J. R. (2013). Validation of the Addenbrooke's Cognitive Examination III in frontotemporal dementia and Alzheimer's disease. *Dementia and Geriatric Cognitive Disorders, 36*(3–4), 242–250.

Institute for Health Metrics and Evaluation. (2013a). GBD profile: Australia. Available: www.healthdata.org/sites/default/files/files/country_profiles/GBD/ihme_gbd_country_report_australia.pdf

Institute for Health Metrics and Evaluation. (2013b). GBD profile: New Zealand. Available: www.healthdata.org/sites/default/files/files/country_profiles/GBD/ihme_gbd_country_report_new_zealand.pdf

Johnson, N., Barion, A., Rademaker, A., Rehkemper, G., & Weintraub, S. (2004). The activities of Daily Living Questionnaire: A validation study in patients with dementia. *Alzheimer Disease & Associated Disorders, 18*(4), 223–230.

Kalaria, R. N., Maestre, G. E., Arizaga, R., Friedland, R. P., Galasko, D., Hall, K., et al. (2008). Alzheimer's disease and vascular dementia in developing countries: Prevalence, management, and risk factors. *The Lancet Neurology, 7*(9), 812–826. http://dx.doi.org/10.1016/S1474-4422(08)70169-8

Knight, R. G., Tsui, H. S. L., Abraham, W. C., Skeaff, C. M., McMahon, J. A., & Cutfield, N. J. (2014). Lack of effect of the apolipoprotein E ε4 genotype on cognition during healthy aging. *Journal of Clinical and Experimental Neuropsychology, 36*(7), 742–750. http://dx.doi.org/10.1080/13803395.2014.935706

Kochan, N. A., Crawford, J. R., Slavin, M. J., Pont, S., Brodaty, H., Crawford, J., et al. (2014). The neuro-norms calculator for older adults: Demographically adjusted normative data and statistical analysis of neuropsychological test performance. *Alzheimer's & Dementia: The Journal of the Alzheimer's Association, 10*(4), 564–565. http://dx.doi.org/10.1016/j.jalz.2014.05.919

Lambert, M. A., Bickel, H., Prince, M., Fratiglioni, L., Von Strauss, E., Frydecka, D., et al. (2014). Estimating the burden of early onset dementia: Systematic review of disease prevalence. *European Journal of Neurology, 21*(4), 563–569.

Laughren, T. (2011). FDA Perspective on the DSM-5 approach to classification of "cognitive" disorders. *Journal of Neuropsychiatry and Clinical Neurosciences, 23*(2), 126–131.

Lautenschlager, N. T., Cox, K. L., Flicker, L., Foster, J. K., van Bockxmeer, F. M., Xiao, J., et al. (2008). Effect of physical activity on cognitive function in older adults at risk for Alzheimer disease: A randomized trial. *Journal of the American Medical Association*, *300*(9), 1027–1037. http://dx.doi.org/10.1001/jama.300.9.1027

LoGiudice, D., Smith, K., Thomas, J., Lautenschlager, N. T., Almeida, O. P., Atkinson, D., et al. (2006). Kimberley Indigenous Cognitive Assessment tool (KICA): Development of a cognitive assessment tool for older Indigenous Australians. *International Psychogeriatrics*, *18*(2), 269–280. http://dx.doi.org/10.1017/S1041610205002681

LoGiudice, D., Strivens, E., Smith, K., Stevenson, M., Atkinson, D., Dwyer, A., et al. (2011). The KICA Screen: The psychometric properties of a shortened version of the KICA (Kimberley Indigenous Cognitive Assessment). *Australasian Journal of Ageing, 30*, 215–219. http://dx.doi.org/10.1111/j.1741-6612.2010.00486.x

Looi, J. C. L., & Liberg, B. (2015). Between scylla and charybdis: DSM-5/ICD-11 and RDoC in neuropsychiatry? *Australian & New Zealand Journal of Psychiatry*, *49*(1), 82–87.

Mioshi, E., Dawson, K., Mitchell, J., Arnold, R., & Hodges, J. R. (2006). The Addenbrooke's Cognitive Examination-Revised (ACE-R): A brief cognitive test battery for dementia screening. *International Journal of Geriatric Psychiatry*, *21*(11), 1078–1085.

Nasreddine, Z. S., Phillips, N. A., Bédirian, V., Charbonneau, S., Whitehead, V., Collin, I., et al. (2005). The Montreal Cognitive Assessment, MoCA: A brief screening tool for mild cognitive impairment. *Journal of the American Geriatrics Society*, *53*(4), 695–699.

National Ageing Research Institute. (2011). The assessment of older people with dementia and depression of culturally and linguistically diverse backgrounds: A review of current practice and the development of guidelines for Victorian Aged Care Assessment Services. Available: www.health.vic.gov.au/agedcare/downloads/pdf/cald_assessment.pdf

New South Wales Ministry of Health & Royal Australian and New Zealand College of Psychiatrists. (2013). *Assessment and management of people with behavioural and psychological symptoms of dementia (BPSD): A handbook for NSW health clinicians* Available: www.ranzcp.org/Files/Publications/A-Handbook-for-NSW-Health-Clinicians-BPSD_June13_W.aspx

O'Sullivan, G., Hocking, C., & Spence, D. (2014). Dementia: The need for attitudinal change. *Dementia*, *13*(4), 483–497.

Pachana, N. A., Byrne, G. J., Siddle, H., Koloski, N., Harley, E., & Arnold, E. (2007). Development and validation of the Geriatric Anxiety Inventory. *International Psychogeriatrics*, *19*(1), 103–114. http://dx.doi.org/10.1017/S1041610206003504

Pachana, N. A., & Helmes, E. (2010). Role of psychologists in assessing and treating dementia. *InPsych: The Bulletin of the Australian Psychological Society Ltd*, *32*(5), 8–11. Available: http://search.informit.com.au.ezp01.library.qut.edu.au/documentSummary;dn=201011752;res=IELAPA

Prasadarao, P. S. D. V. (2014). Ageing and dementia: A compendium of New Zealand Research Literature. Hamilton, NZ: MHSOP, Waikato District Health Board.

Pulver, L. J., Broe, G. A., Grayson, D., Chalkley, S., Flicker, L., Daylight, G., et al. (2012). Dementia screening for urban Aboriginal Australians: The modified Kimberly Indigenous Cognitive Assessment (mKICA) – Pilot study report.

Robles, R., Fresán, A., Medina-Mora, M. E., Sharan, P., Roberts, M. C., Jesus Mari, J., et al. (2015). Categories that should be removed from mental disorders classifications: Perspectives and rationales of clinicians from eight countries. *Journal of Clinical Psychology, 71*(3), 267–281.

Sachdev, P., Kalaria, R., O'Brien, J., Skoog, I., Alladi, S., Black, S. E., et al. (2014). Diagnostic criteria for vascular cognitive disorders: A VASCOG statement. *Alzheimer Disease & Associated Disorders, 28*(3), 206–218.

Sachdev, P. S. B., Blacker, D., Blazer, D. G., Ganguli, M., Jeste, D. V., Paulsen, J. S., & Petersen, R. C. (2014). Classifying neurocognitive disorders: The DSM-5 approach. *Nature Reviews Neurology, 10*(11), 634–642. http://dx.doi.org/10.1038/nrneurol.2014.181

Sachdev, P. S., Mohan, A., Taylor, L., & Jeste, D. V. (2015). DSM-5 and mental disorders in older individuals: An overview. *Harvard Review of Psychiatry, 23*(5), 320–328.

Sachs-Ericsson, N., & Blazer, D. G. (2014). The new DSM-5 diagnosis of mild neurocognitive disorder and its relation to research in mild cognitive impairment. *Aging & Mental Health, 19*(1), 2–12. http://dx.doi.org/10.1080/13607863.2014.920303

Siegert, R. J., & Cavana, C. M. (1997). Norms for older New Zealanders on the Trail-Making test. *New Zealand Journal of Psychology, 26*(2), 25–31.

Simpson, J. R. (2014). DSM-5 and neurocognitive disorders. *The Journal of the American Academy of Psychiatry and the Law, 42*, 159–164.

Statistics New Zealand. (2015). www2.stats.govt.nz. Wellington, NZ: Author.

Storey, J. E., Rowland, J. T., Conforti, D. A., & Dickson, H. G. (2004). The Rowland universal dementia assessment scale (RUDAS): A multicultural cognitive assessment scale. *International Psychogeriatrics, 16*(1), 13–31.

Teng, E. L., & Chui, H. C. (1987). The modified mini-mental state (MMS) examination. *Journal of Clinical Psychiatry, 48*(8), 314–318.

Tobias, M., Yeh, L. C., & Johnson, E. (2008). Burden of alzheimer's disease: Population-based estimates and projections for New Zealand. *Australian & New Zealand Journal of Psychiatry, 42*(9), 828–836.

Valcour, V. G., Masaki, K. H., Curb, D., & Blanchette, P. L. (2000). The detection of dementia in the primary care setting. *Archives of Internal Medicine, 160*, 2964–2968.

Weintraub, S., Dikmen, S. S., Heaton, R. K., Tulsky, D. S., Zelazo, P. D., Bauer, P. J., et al. (2013). Cognition assessment using the NIH Toolbox. *Neurology, 80*(11 Supp 3), S54–64. http://dx.doi.org/10.1212/WNL.0b013e3182872ded

White, T., & Stern, R. (2003). *Neuropsychological assessment battery*. Lutz, FL: Psychological Assessment Resources.

Yates, L. A., Leung, P., Orgeta, V., Spector, A., & Orrell, M. (2015). The development of individual cognitive stimulation therapy (iCST) for dementia. *Clinical Interventions in Aging, 10*, 95–104. http://dx.doi.org/10.2147/cia.s73844

Yesavage, J. A., Brink, T., Rose, T. L., Lum, O., Huang, V., Adey, M., & Leirer, V. O. (1983). Development and validation of a geriatric depression screening scale: A preliminary report. *Journal of Psychiatric Research, 17*(1), 37–49.

Zarit, S. H., Reever, K. E., & Bach-Peterson, J. (1980). Relatives of the impaired elderly: Correlates of feelings of burden. *The Gerontologist, 20*(6), 649–655.

Recommendations for further reading/resources

General

Kempler, D. (2004). *Neurocognitive disorders in aging*. California: SAGE Publications.

Smith, G. E., & Bondi, M. W. (2013). *Mild cognitive impairment and dementia. Definitions, diagnosis and treatment*. Oxford: American Academy of Clinical Neuropsychology. Oxford Workshop Series.

Australia

Alzheimer's Australia website: https://fightdementia.org.au/

Ragg, M. (2013). *Understanding alzheimer's*. South Melbourne: Macmillan Australia.

New Zealand

Perkins, C. (2014). *The New Zealand dementia guide*. Auckland: Random House New Zealand Ltd.

Acknowledgements

With thanks to Dr Susan Yates, Clinical Psychologist at the Dementia Clinic from Counties Manukau Dementia service, and Ms Lina Karlsson for administrative assistance with this chapter.

22

Personality disorders

Phillip S Kavanagh

Introduction

Personality disorders are a class of mental health problems in which personality traits that are fixed and maladaptive cause significant difficulties in individual psychosocial functioning. This is not the same as stating that an individual's personality is disordered, but rather their behaviours and interactional styles with others cause significant difficulties. The *Diagnostic and Statistical Manual of Mental Disorders* (5th ed.; *DSM-5*; American Psychiatric Association, 2013) defines a personality disorder this way:

> *A Personality Disorder is an enduring pattern of inner experience and behavior that deviates markedly from the expectations of the individual's culture, is pervasive and inflexible, has an onset in adolescence or early adulthood, is stable over time, and leads to distress or impairment* (American Psychiatric Association, 2013, p. 645).

The *DSM-5* lists 10 personality disorders, split into three Clusters (A, B, C).
- Cluster A
  - Paranoid (301.0) – A pattern of distrust and suspiciousness such that others' motives are interpreted as malevolent.
  - Schizoid (301.20) – A pattern of detachment from social relationships and a restricted range of affect.
  - Schizotypal (301.22) – A pattern of acute discomfort in close relationships, cognitive or perceptual distortions, and eccentricities of behaviour.
- Cluster B
  - Antisocial (301.7) – A pattern of disregard for, and violation of, the rights of others.
  - Borderline (301.83) – A pattern of instability in interpersonal relationships, self-image, and affects, and marked impulsivity.

- Histrionic (301.50) – A pattern of excessive emotionality and attention seeking.
  - Narcissistic (301.81) – A pattern of grandiosity, need for admiration, and lack of empathy.
- Cluster C
  - Avoidant (301.82) – A pattern of social inhibition, feelings of inadequacy, and hypersensitivity to negative evaluation.
  - Dependent (301.6) – A pattern of submissive and clinging behaviour related to an excessive need to be taken care of.
  - Obsessive-Compulsive (301.4) – A preoccupation with orderliness, perfectionism, and control.

An individual's personality affects many aspects of day-to-day living, so the dysfunctional style can result in numerous other psychological disorders. As such, people rarely seek psychological treatment for a personality disorder. Rather, they would typically present for treatment of another problem, and the underlying personality disorder becomes apparent to the treating psychologist. Exceptions can be when a client has been previously diagnosed, or identified with, a personality disorder and had been referred for specific treatment (e.g., dialectical behaviour therapy [DBT] for borderline personality disorder).

From an Australasian perspective, one could speculate that the nuances of our cultures may influence how some personality disorders develop, especially given that one of the descriptors of a personality disorder is behaviour that deviates markedly from the expectations of an individual's culture. While there is no aetiological research to support this speculation (there is in fact very limited research on personality disorders in Australasia), observations from my colleagues' and my own clients does indicate potential cultural influences in the development and expression of personality pathology. For example, Australasians in general tend to be averse to *tall poppies* (people who boast about their achievements) and often set out to "cut them down to size." This tendency could influence the development and expression of disorders such as narcissistic personality disorder where the core feature is a grandiose sense of self. A leftover from colonisation is the tendency to be stoic and not show your emotions in the face of adversity. This "take a teaspoon of cement and harden up" attitude is common when dealing with hardship, especially in rural remote areas. It could influence how an individual acknowledges experiencing difficult emotions, and potentially how a borderline personality disorder (BPD) develops, with a recognised aetiological component of this disorder growing up in an invalidating environment. There also appears to be some Australasian variation in the presentation of antisocial personality disorder, with regard to what constitutes a violation of the rights of others. For example, affiliations with different types of gangs, motorcycle "clubs" and organised crime syndicates may impact on people's behaviours. Popular media examples might include the types of behaviours portrayed in the Australian television series *Underbelly* or the New Zealand (NZ) movie *Once Were Warriors*. Antisocial

Australia

There are limited statistics reporting the prevalence rates of personality disorders in Australia, with the last National Mental Health Survey in 2007 not including this category of disorders. The last survey that did assess personality disorder prevalence rates in the community was conducted in 1997. The results from this survey do not map completely onto the different types of personality disorders currently listed in *DSM-5*; however, the prevalence rate for any personality disorder was 6.62% – roughly equivalent to estimates in other countries where there are available data (Jackson & Burgess, 2000). Clearly, there is a need to conduct research on the current prevalence rates of personality disorders in the Australian community, alongside investigating potential aetiological factors in an Australian context. Most of the research about personality disorders in Australia focuses primarily on treatment outcomes for borderline personality disorder; however, even then there are only a few published studies.

Medicare Australia does not explicitly cover personality disorders in its schedule; however, they also do not explicitly exclude personality disorders (Australian Psychological Society, 2013).

Australian-specific resources and groups for treating personality disorders focus on borderline personality disorder, which anecdotally appears the most prevalent presentation at mental services, and often the most difficult to treat. The National Health and Medical Research Council (NHMRC) has produced a *Clinical Practice Guideline for the Management of Borderline Personality Disorder* (2012; 2013) (www.nhmrc. gov.au/guidelines-publications/mh25). Likewise, the Australian Psychological Society (APS) only includes treatment for BPD in their publication *Evidenced-Based Psychological Interventions in the Treatment of Mental Disorders: A Literature Review* (3rd ed.) (2010). Unfortunately, there appears to be no document on treating other personality disorders in an Australian context. Further, there are currently no personality disorder interest groups in the APS – the largest professional organisation for psychologists in Australia.

Clinicians interested in quantifying personality pathology in clients can choose between multiple personality inventories, such as the Millon Clinical Multiaxial Inventory-III (MCMI-III), the Minnesota Multiphasic Personality Inventory-II (MMPI-II), or the Personality Assessment Inventory-II (PAI-II). Australian practitioners most commonly use these three, which all use United States (US) norms. They could also use several alternative measures (see Furnham et al., 2014 for a full list and review of each measure), but none have Australian-based clinical norms.

Aside from private practitioners who specialise in this area, there are no specific services available to treat personality disorders in general in Australia. The public sector services that do offer treatment focus primarily on borderline personality disorder. These are a mixture of treatment programs funded by government and non-government organisations (NGOs), including the Westmead Psychotherapy Service (South Western Sydney Area Health Service, New South Wales), the Personality Disorder Service for Victoria, the Orygen Youth Health HYPE Program (Melbourne, Victoria), Project Air (New South Wales), and the Adelaide Health Service Dialectical Behaviour Therapy Service (Adelaide, South Australia; Statewide Mental Health Clinical Network, 2014).

New Zealand

The prevalence rates of personality disorders in NZ are also unknown. The best estimate comes from international studies, and given the similarity between Australian and NZ culture the rates across these two countries are likely to be similar. There has been some work determining the approximate prevalence rates of personality disorders in prison populations (e.g., see Wilson, 2004); however, this is not representative of the general community. In mental health settings, BPD has the most published research and available resources, albeit minimal. A contributing factor in determining accurate prevalence rates is that district health boards in NZ typically required a *DSM-4* Axis-I diagnosis to be eligible for treatment. If a client was diagnosed with an Axis-II personality disorder, they were often considered to not have a treatable pathology as it was personality based. Anecdotal observations suggest these clients were relegated to the "too hard basket" and would take away resources from those who could be more easily treated. This creates a sampling bias of prevalence rates in public outpatient settings (i.e., if they are not eligible to receive services they will not present and thus they will not be counted).

There are no recent specific treatment guidelines for personality disorders in NZ, again with the exception of borderline personality disorder. Some of the district health boards in NZ (e.g., Canterbury) have published in-house documents for managing borderline personality disorder. This treatment usually consists of either DBT or mentalisation therapy (Bateman & Fonagy, 2004) and is typically conducted by clinicians with an interest in this area. In other main centres such as Auckland, there are small groups of clinical psychologists with a specific interest in treating BPD using DBT (www.dbtnz.co.nz).

As in Australia, clinicians interested in quantifying personality pathology in clients can choose between the Millon Clinical Multiaxial Inventory-III (MCMI-III), the Minnesota Multiphasic Personality Inventory-II (MMPI-II), or the Personality Assessment Inventory-II (PAI-II). These three inventories are used most commonly in NZ, with the MCMI-III a standard measure in the Department of Corrections. All of these inventories use US norms. Several alternative measures are available (see Furnham et al., 2014 for a full review); however, none include NZ-based clinical norms.

Australian case study

The following example of BPD is a composite of real clients who presented with similar features. Given the variability of presentations for BPD, this will not reflect all possible presentations.

Anne is a woman in her early thirties currently living with her partner and her children from her previous relationship. She has been seeking help for her low mood and difficulties coping with stress, stating that she often "loses it" with her partner and children, but does not want to do this anymore. Anne often uses alcohol to help herself get to sleep at night, regularly consuming a bottle of wine per night. Anne will consume more wine on the weekends or if she has had a fight with her partner or children. She denies any current suicidal thoughts or ideation, but used to "hurt herself" (cutting her arms with a razor) if she had a fight with her boyfriend when she was younger. She reported that she no longer self-harms and prefers to have a glass of wine to "take the edge off" instead. There were no visible scars on Anne's forearms. Anne also reports a history of "comfort eating" when she feels distressed and describes fluctuating weight and some body image concerns.

Anne was the youngest of four children, having three older brothers. The family lived on a farm in a rural community where "everyone knew everyone's business." She reported that although her parents were great providers, they were not there for her emotionally. Her father worked continuously on the farm and she said she never saw him angry or upset, even when his parents passed away. If Anne or her brothers ever cried or were upset, he told them to "toughen up." Anne's mother spent her time looking after the household. Anne reported that she thought that her mother suffered from depression for a number of years and struggled living so far away from her own family of origin. Anne described her mother as often distant and in her own world.

At age 13, Anne moved to a boarding school in a large city to complete high school. Anne found her time at the boarding school difficult and she struggled to make friends. Making friends was a new experience for her and she found the girls "bitchy," preferring instead to spend her time with the boys, to whom she could better relate, having older brothers.

At age 16, Anne became pregnant to her boyfriend at the time John (17 years), who also lived at the boarding school. Neither of their families supported the pregnancy, so the two of them decided to move interstate together, dropping out of school. Towards the end of the pregnancy, Anne reported that the relationship started to become abusive. John was not coping with the stress of having to work to support two people, and having missed the opportunity to make something of himself at university. Anne reported that John would often use drugs and alcohol to cope; taking out his frustrations on her, often resulting in forced sex. Anne got pregnant again at 19. Anne left John when she was 25, after she contracted a sexually transmitted infection (STI) from John and found that he had multiple sexual relationships with other women.

Anne receives a diagnosis of borderline personality disorder. Therapy for Anne consists of developing internalised emotional regulation strategies as opposed to external (i.e., cutting, alcohol, eating) and teaching her to recognise and express her emotions, rather than suppressing and ignoring these. Anne's therapy lasts for approximately 24 months.

Australia – DBT service

In South Australia, clients diagnosed with BPD can be referred to the Adelaide Health Service Dialectical Behaviour Therapy Service, run by SA Health. Potential clients are assessed for their suitability to engage effectively in a group setting. Depending on the client's specific history and severity, they are included in either a 6-month DBT Skills Training Group or a 12-month DBT Intensive Therapy Program. Individual therapy is also provided with the latter, with clients in the former group required to source their own adjunct individual therapy in the community. While there has been no peer-reviewed published research on the outcomes of these groups, information from clients and therapists suggests positive outcomes for those clients who attend and complete these programs.

New Zealand – Balance Programme

In Auckland, people diagnosed with BPD can seek treatment through the Balance Programme, run by the Auckland District Health Board (www.adhb.govt.nz/ balanceprogramme). The Balance Programme is an intensive community-based treatment program for clients with a primary diagnosis for BPD. Balance provides DBT for clients with the diagnosis of BPD. Each of the four community mental health centres (Cornwell House, Epsom; Manaaki House, Panmure; St Luke's Community Mental Health Centre, Morningside; Taylor Centre, Ponsonby) have their own Balance Team, which specialises in providing DBT to clients within their communities.

Bibliography

Feather, N. T. (1989). Attitudes towards the high achiever: The fall of the tall poppy. *Australian Journal of Psychology, 41,* 239–267. http://dx.doi.org/10.1080/00049538908260088

Lewin, T., Slade, T., Andrews, G., Carr, V., & Hornabrook, C. (2005). Assessing personality disorders in a national mental health survey. *Social Psychiatry and Psychiatric Epidemiology, 40,* 87–98. http://dx.doi.org/10.1007/s00127-005-0878-1

References

American Psychiatric Association. (2013). *Diagnostic and statistical manual of mental disorders* (5th ed.). Arlington, VA: Author.

Australian Psychological Society. (2010). *Evidence-based psychological interventions in the treatment of mental disorders: A literature review* (3rd ed.). Melbourne: Author.

Australian Psychological Society. (2013). *APS fact sheet: Medicare rebates for mental health services provided by psychologists.* Melbourne: Author.

Bateman, A. W., & Fonagy, P. (2004). Mentalization-based treatment of BPD. *Journal of Personality Disorders, 18,* 36–51.

Furnham, A., Milner, R., Akhtar, R., & De Fruyt, F. (2014). A review of the measures designed to assess DSM-5 personality disorders. *Psychology, 5,* 1646–1686. http://dx.doi.org/10.4236/psych.2014.514175

Jackson, H. J., & Burgess, P. M. (2000). Personality disorders in the community: A report from the Australian national survey of mental health and wellbeing. *Social Psychiatry and Psychiatric Epidemiology, 35,* 531–538. http://dx.doi.org/10.1007/s001270050276

National Health and Medical Research Council. (2013). *Clinical practice guideline for the management of borderline personality disorder.* Canberra: Author. Available: www.nhmrc.gov.au/guidelines-publications/mh25

Statewide Mental Health Clinical Network. (2014). *Borderline personality disorder: An overview of current delivery of borderline personality disorder services in the public service across South Australia and proposed way forward.* SA Health.

Wilson, N. J. (2004). *New Zealand high-risk offenders: Who are they and what are the issues in their management and treatment?* Hamilton, New Zealand: Department of Corrections, Psychological Services.

Recommendations for further reading/resources

General

Relevant website:

- American Psychological Association: www.apa.org/topics/personality

Australia

Relevant websites:

- NHMRC, Clinical Practice Guideline for the Management of Borderline Personality Disorder: www.nhmrc.gov.au/guidelines-publications/mh25

- Spectrum, The Personality Disorder Service for Victoria: www.spectrumbpd.com.au
- Illawarra Health and Medical Research, Project Air Strategy for Personality Disorders: https://ihmri.uow.edu.au/projectairstrategy/index.html

New Zealand

Relevant websites:
- Auckland District Health Board, Balance Programme: www.adhb.govt.nz/balanceprogramme
- Dialectical Behaviour Therapy consultation and training in New Zealand, DBTNZ: www.dbtnz.co.nz

23

Paraphilic disorders

Michael Proeve and Peter Chamberlain

Introduction: paraphilias and paraphilic disorders

A distinctive feature of paraphilic disorders is that they are diagnosed largely in forensic settings. Indeed, paraphilic disorders are related to criminal activity to varying degrees, depending on the particular disorder. For example, acting on paedophilic sexual arousal results in criminal sexual activity with children, whereas fetishistic sexual arousal may result in sexual behaviour between consenting adults. However, fetishism may also involve criminal activity; for example, stealing feminine articles of clothing.

Atypical patterns of sexual arousal have been familiar to practitioners of psychiatry and psychology since Richard von Krafft-Ebing's landmark work *Psychopathia Sexualis* in the late 19th century. The European psychiatrist described numerous cases of fetishism, sadism, masochism, and other sexual behaviour. Atypical sexual arousal was known as sexual deviation in the second edition of the *Diagnostic and Statistical Manual of the American Psychiatric Association* (DSM-II), but the term *paraphilia* replaced it in subsequent editions. The current edition, *Diagnostic and Statistical Manual of Mental Disorders:* (5th ed.; *DSM-5*; American Psychiatric Association, 2013), retains the term "paraphilia," but introduces the additional term of "paraphilic disorder."

With the intent of reducing stigma associated with atypical sexual arousal, the *DSM-5* defines the term "paraphilia" as an intense, persistent sexual interest other than in genital stimulation or preparatory sexual fondling with physically mature, consenting human partners. In itself, this would not constitute a disorder. However, a paraphilic disorder is a paraphilia that is accompanied by clinically significant distress or impairment. Therefore, the *DSM-5*'s paraphilic disorders require two criteria to be met for a diagnosis. Criterion A is the paraphilia component, which requires an atypical focus of sexual arousal and an arousal pattern that is recurrent, intense, and persists for a minimum of 6 months. Criterion B is a harm component, which requires the presence of distress, impairment in functioning, or the involvement of non-consenting persons. Some paraphilic disorders include a third criterion which is specific to that paraphilia.

The *DSM-5* lists eight specific paraphilic disorders: voyeuristic, exhibitionistic, frotteuristic, sexual masochism, sexual sadism, paedophilic, fetishistic, and transvestic. There are two additional residual disorder categories: other specified paraphilic disorder and unspecified paraphilic disorder. Other specified paraphilic disorders include those that do not meet the criteria for specific paraphilic disorders and focus on non-human objects (e.g., zoophilia, animals), suffering or humiliation (e.g., vomiting), non-consenting persons (e.g., necrophilia, an interest in dead bodies), or involving human subjects (e.g., hypoxyphilia, the practice of choking for the effects of heightened sexual arousal and euphoria from cerebral hypoxia).

This chapter limits the focus to: exhibitionistic disorder, sexual masochism disorder, sexual sadism disorder, paedophilic disorder, and fetishistic disorder. For information about frotteuristic disorder, voyeuristic disorder, and transvestic disorder, refer to the book edited by Laws and O'Donohue (2008).

Exhibitionistic disorder

Exhibitionistic disorder (*DSM-5* and ICD-10 [WHO, 2011] codes 302.4 and F65.3, respectively) concerns the behaviour of exposing one's genitals to an unsuspecting person. The prevalence is unknown, but could range from 2% to 4% in the male population (Murphy & Page, 2008). Exhibitionistic disorder is thought to be almost exclusively a male disorder, but it may occur in women more frequently than official police statistics indicate (Murphy & Page, 2008). Public masturbation and exhibitionism should perhaps be considered as two forms of exhibitionism, as nearly two-thirds of male exhibitionists had also masturbated in a public place (Abel et al., 1988).

Exhibitionists may have varied motivations. While some wish to evoke anger or disgust in their victims, many desire mutual sexual activity including the idea that the victim may also show her genitals or desire intercourse (Freund, Watson, & Rienzo, 1988). However, actual effects on the victims of exhibitionists include fear, disgust, and anger (9%), although curiosity and amusement were also reported. In an Australian study, victims under 16 years were twice as likely to recall fear as an immediate response to the incident (Kapardis, 1984). Men diagnosed with exhibitionistic disorder are likely to have histories of additional paraphilic behaviour, including paedophilic, voyeuristic, and frotteuristic behaviour (Abel et al., 1988). According to a study based on police records, about a quarter of exhibitionists had symptoms of mental illness and a quarter have substance abuse problems, while 84% had non-sexual criminal charges, mostly traffic offences, public order offences, or failures to appear in court (Bader et al., 2008). A recent review of studies of exhibitionists showed that 5% to 10% escalated their behaviour to contact sexual offending (such as sexual assault) and 25% committed further exhibitionism offences. Escalation was associated with indicators of antisocial behaviour (McNally & Fremouw, 2014).

According to a classic study (Gebhard et al., 1965), individuals with exhibitionist disorder are more likely to have a poor relationship with their fathers than those in control, prison, and other sexual offender groups; however, an equal number got along well with their fathers. They are less likely than other sexual offenders to be sexually abused, but no different from controls. An Australian study showed that childhood emotional abuse and family dysfunction were developmental risk factors for exhibitionism, but this effect was similar for paedophilia and multiple paraphilias (Lee et al., 2002).

The courtship disorder model is a theoretical explanation specific to exhibitionism. According to this model which is drawn from ethology, normal courtship consists of phases including location of a partner, pre-tactile interactions, tactile interactions, and genital union. Exhibitionism is seen as a distortion of this courtship sequence in the pre-tactile interaction phase. This model is supported by the overlap with voyeuristic and frotteuristic behaviour, which are viewed as distortions of the location and tactile interaction phases respectively. However, the model does not easily explain overlaps with child molestation behaviour (Murphy & Page, 2008) and does not lend itself to empirical testing.

Most of the treatment literature for exhibitionism consists of case studies and clinical recommendations. Pharmacological treatments include hormonal treatments such as medroxyprogesterone acetate and cyproterone acetate, to reduce sexual drive and masturbation. However, most show a return to deviant sexual drive once medication is discontinued. Psychotropic medications including fluoxetine and clomipramine have also been used with exhibitionists, as they reduce sexual drive in most patients, and may also treat any concurrent depression (Maletzky, 1997). Behavioural treatment approaches include systematic desensitisation to reduce anxiety to females (Kilmann et al., 1982), covert sensitisation that reduces the frequency of overt exhibiting acts and aversive techniques such as shame aversion, in which an exhibitionist commits exhibitionistic acts in front of treatment professionals (Maletzky, 1980). Marshall (2006) reported the successful treatment of an exhibitionist using ammonia aversion, with concurrent effects on self-esteem and depression.

Less behavioural treatment approaches include training in emotion regulation, based on the observation that awareness and discharge of anger may be key conflicts for exhibitionists. Hackett, Saber, and Curran (1980) helped their clients to recognise anger and find socially acceptable ways of expressing anger in a series of 37 case studies. More recently, acceptance and commitment therapy and functional analytic therapy were reported in a case study, resulting in a decrease in depression, anxiety, and urges to expose (Paul, Marx, & Orsillo, 1999).

Sexual masochism disorder and sexual sadism disorder

Sexual masochism refers to sexual arousal resulting from humiliation, pain, or suffering. It often occurs in the context of role-playing fantasy, with the masochist playing the role of slave or student. Masochistic acts can be physical or psychological acts that are either self-inflicted (e.g., self-mutilation) or delivered by another acting in the role of master or teacher. Suffering behaviours can range from benign to life-threatening acts (including physical restraint such as handcuffs, cages, or chains) and punishment or pain by means of beating, burning, and rape. Autoerotic asphyxia is the most dangerous of the masochistic behaviours, involving masturbation and asphyxiation to intensify orgasm. Unfortunately, the thrill can kill, with the United States reporting an annual fatality rate exceeding 1000.

There is no consensus on the aetiology of sexual masochism disorder (302.83, F65.51), but several theories have been proposed. One is grounded in learning theory and argues that paraphilias come about because people suppress sexual fantasies considered to be socially inappropriate. Subsequently, these urges and fantasies increase so that by the time they are enacted, the person is significantly aroused or distressed. Another theory proposes that sadomasochist behaviour is simply a means of escape by acting out fantasies of being a different person.

The prevalence of sexual masochism disorder is unknown although, based on an Australian study (Richters et al., 2008), it is estimated to be around 2% for males and 1% for females. There are no practice guidelines for treating this disorder, and like most paraphilias, disclosure of relevant thoughts or behaviours is rare. Therapy is most likely around situation crises or the distress resulting from the disorder.

Sexual sadism is arguably indicative of significant psychopathy whereby an individual experiences sexual arousal from the psychological or physical suffering of their victim. Behaviours include beatings, necrophilia, rape, torture, and murder. Comorbidity with other paraphilias is common; for example, masochism, exhibitionism, and paedophilic disorder. The primary focus of the concern has been around the consequences of a false negative finding; that is, the likelihood of a person with sexual sadism disorder (302.84, F65.52) being misdiagnosed, released into the community and re-offending. Sometimes, an associated feature of the disorder is an extensive use of pornography depicting the infliction of pain and suffering.

Although this disorder is often presented as characteristic of evil protagonists in a fictional thriller, the prevalence is largely unknown and predominantly based on people who have been incarcerated for sexual offending. Little is known about the aetiology of sexual sadism, although it predominantly occurs in males with onset in puberty, and becomes evident in early adulthood. The trajectory of the behaviour may commence with fantasies, acted out in benign forms within consensual relationships (e.g., mild spanking, physical restraint, and sensory bondage), and possibly extending to non-consensual and more violent activities including death. For those individuals who engage in non-consensual sexual sadism, the violent behaviour can escalate as the perpetrator seeks to stimulate the sexual response. This increased need for stimulation could be explained by the process of neuroplasticity which refers to the adaptability of the brain. Essentially, the brain changes its structure (neural connections) to apply the brake to the overstimulation of the limbic system. This dampening response results in greater levels of stimuli required to achieve the desired level of sexual arousal.

No practice guidelines have been developed for sexual sadism disorder, although surgical and pharmacological castration and stereotactic neurosurgery have been applied with limited success. Given that most individuals experiencing the disorder are unlikely to publicly disclose their sexual interests, they may never come to the attention of the mental health or justice system.

Paedophilic disorder

Paedophilic disorder (302.2, F65.4) involves recurrent and intense sexual interest in children (generally aged 13 years or younger), in an individual who is at least 16 years of age and at least 5 years older than the child or children. It is an important diagnostic feature of the disorder that if it can be objectively demonstrated that a person has never acted on their paraphilic impulses, reports an absence of guilt, shame, or anxiety, and is not functionally limited, then they have a paedophilic sexual orientation but not paedophilic disorder. Paedophilic sexual orientation or the diagnosis of the disorder does not mean that the person will act out their desires against children. Indeed, sometimes sexual offences against children are committed by people who do not have a sustained sexual orientation towards children. For example, the perpetrator may take advantage of circumstances to achieve sexual gratification by exploiting a vulnerable young person.

The prevalence of paedophilic disorder is unknown, although estimates suggest an upper limit of 3% to 5% for males and less for females. Males become aware of a paedophilic sexual orientation around the time of puberty, and this appears to be a stable condition (Seto, 2008).

Conditioning approaches have been applied to changing paedophilic sexual preference, but with mixed results (Camilleri & Quinsey, 2008). Most treatment programs are designed to reduce sexual recidivism among those who sexually abuse children rather than to change paedophilia. They are generally cognitive behaviour therapy (CBT) programs delivered in group format. A meta-analysis of outcome studies reported a 40% relative reduction in re-offending compared to control groups (Hanson et al., 2002). Treatment programs generally concentrate on addressing factors such as emotional regulation and pro-offending thinking which are empirically associated with reducing sexual re-offending. A recent treatment framework originating in New Zealand (NZ) emphasises leading a positive life that is free of offending (Ward, Yates, & Willis, 2012). Beyond treatment programs, close community supervision is the most common approach to reducing the risk of sexual recidivism in Australia and NZ.

Fetishistic disorder

Fetishistic disorder (302.81, F65.0) concerns recurrent and intense sexual arousal from using nonliving objects, or a highly specific focus on non-genital body parts. Fetishistic disorder is nearly exclusively reported in males in clinical samples. The objects of fetishistic interest seem to cluster into specific groups, including a part of the body, an article of clothing, or a source of specific tactile stimulation, such as rubber or leather. Although a proportion of individuals with fetishistic disorder may steal their fetish objects, this disorder otherwise rarely results in contact with the law.

Explanations for fetishistic disorder include psychoanalytic, behavioural, and sociocultural perspectives. According to some psychoanalytic views, traumatic experiences in childhood determine which fetish object they select. The fetish object represents a penis, protecting the male from his fear of castration. Sociocultural factors may also influence paraphilic behaviour, giving erotic significance to particular body parts, thus promoting a fetishistic focus. From the classical conditioning perspective, the sexual response is conditioned to various stimuli which are usually physical characteristics of a sexual partner. The fetish object is the conditioned stimulus, but operant conditioning is also involved. The operant response is masturbation, which is reinforced by orgasm (Junginger, 1997). Experimental studies support this explanation of fetishism to an extent, but it does not explain why some individuals develop fetishism and others do not.

Treatment of fetishistic disorder, based on single-case studies, has included aversion therapy, using emetic drugs or aversive odours, and orgasmic reconditioning (Kilmann et al., 1982). However, results are only suggestive because of the lack of controlled research. Recently, a report of treatment of a man with a fetish related to women's feet as well as symptoms of PTSD, anxiety, and depression, included behavioural activation, a common intervention for depression. Apparently, this enhanced his marital relationship, reduced his mood symptoms, and resulted in his no longer meeting diagnostic criteria (Sarver & Gros, 2014).

Australian case study

This case is a composite example created for illustrative purposes.

Albert is an Aboriginal man of 42 years who lives in an Australian regional city. He was educated to Year 7 in school and is married and currently living with his wife. He reports that he suffers from erectile dysfunction. Albert was recently charged with exposing his penis to a girl of approximately 16 years, in his preferred age range, when she walked past him in a laneway. He was home alone on the day in question, depressed regarding his current marital situation.

Albert states that he has about 40 previous convictions for exhibitionistic behaviour. He has previously been imprisoned for non-sexual offences of unlawful use of motor vehicles and alcohol-related assaults. At interview, Albert also describes infrequent incidents of other sexual behaviour, including viewing couples having sex from outside their houses and making sexually suggestive telephone calls. He has a history of alcohol abuse over approximately 20 years. Albert reports that he, his two brothers, and three sisters experienced a family atmosphere characterised by alcoholism and domestic violence. He was taken from his parents and placed in a residential institution from the ages of 13 to 17, where he was exposed to severe physical discipline. He said that many boys in the institution were sexually abused by an older boy in his late teens. Albert himself was forced to engage in anal intercourse on a number of occasions, and was 16 when the abuse ceased. He was confused about his sexuality for many years.

Albert is diagnosed with exhibitionistic disorder, alcohol use disorder, and erectile disorder. Although he has a history of telephone scatalogia and voyeurism, he does not meet criteria for the diagnosis of voyeuristic disorder or other specified paraphilic disorder, as he does not experience recurrent and intense sexual arousal in relation to these behaviours. Treatment recommendations for Albert include covert sensitisation or olfactory aversion to address his exhibitionistic urges. In addition, he should be referred to the culturally appropriate services for treatment of alcohol abuse and to a medical practitioner in the first instance for investigation and treatment of erectile dysfunction.

Australia – Owenia House

Owenia House is a South Australian Forensic Mental Health multidisciplinary community treatment service, established originally to treat people who have sexually offended against children, or fear they may do so. It currently provides a comprehensive range of evidence-based intervention programs for sex offenders living in the community. The service has close collaborative ties with correctional services, with complementary programs that enable eligible incarcerated offenders to be released into the community without affecting their rehabilitation program. Specific risk-orientated programs are provided for sexual offences against children and adults, accessing child exploitation material (pornography) and paraphilias. A program for rural offenders and those with an intellectual disability are also delivered. The largely CBT-based programs include elements of social learning theory and address issues such as cognitive distortions and victim empathy, and promote personal values and skills that are known to reduce risk and encourage a productive life free from offending. Assessments of sexual functioning and risk of re-offending are provided for various agencies, including courts and the parole board, together with the provision of specialist education services to the community and child protection services.

New Zealand – Te Piriti Special Treatment Unit

The Te Piriti Special Treatment Unit, which is part of the NZ Department of Corrections, is designed for offenders imprisoned for sexual offences against children. The unit was designed to promote a therapeutic environment within a framework of Māori cultural practices. The treatment program integrates typical CBT and social learning interventions in sexual offender treatment with social processes that are culturally appropriate for Māori. Māori greetings, meetings, and style of debate and discussion are part of daily activities. In addition, ways of thinking and behaving and spiritual understandings consistent with Māori customs, based on individual and collective rights and responsibilities, provide a framework for viewing oneself and others. The Te Piriti program was found to be effective in reducing sexual reconviction for Māori *and* non-Māori men. In addition, Māori men who completed the Te Piriti program reoffended sexually at a lower rate than Māori men who completed a standard treatment program (Nathan, Wilson, & Hillman, 2003). For non-Māori men, the reduction in sexual recidivism was comparable to non-Māori participants in a standard treatment program, and they did not appear to be negatively affected by participating in a program which had specifically Māori values and processes.

Bibliography

First, M. B. (2014). DSM-5 and paraphilic disorders. *American Academy of Psychiatry and the Law, 42*, 191–201.

Krafft-Ebing, R. (1998). *Psychopathia sexualis (complete English edition)*. New York: Arcade Publishing.

Mason, F. (1997). Fetishism: Psychopathology and theory. In D. R. Laws & W. T. O'Donoghue (Eds.), *Sexual deviance: Theory, assessment and treatment*, (pp. 75–91). New York: Guilford Press.

Milner, J. S., & Dopke, C. A. (2008). Paraphilia not otherwise specified: Psychopathology and theory. In D. R. Laws & W. O'Donohue (Eds.), *Sexual deviance: Theory, assessment, and treatment*, (pp. 394–423). New York: Guilford Press.

Morin, J. W., & Levenson, J. S. (2008). Exhibitionism: Assessment and treatment. In D. R. Laws & W. O'Donohue (Eds.), *Sexual deviance: Theory, assessment, and treatment* (pp. 76–107). New York: Guilford Press.

References

Abel, G. G., Becker, J. V., Cunningham-Rathner, J., Mittelman, M., & Rouleau, J-. L. (1988). Multiple paraphilic diagnoses among sex offenders. *Bulletin of the American Academy of Psychiatry and the Law, 16*, 153–168.

American Psychiatric Association. (2013). *Diagnostic and statistical manual of mental disorders* (5th ed.). Arlington, VA: Author.

Bader, S. M., Schoeneman-Morris, K. A., Scalora, M. J., & Casady, T. K. (2008). Exhibitionism: findings from a Midwestern police contact sample. *Journal of Offender Therapy and Comparative Criminology, 52*, 270–279.

Camilleri, J. A., & Quinsey, V. L. (2008). Pedophilia: Assessment and treatment. In D. R. Laws & W. T. O'Donohue (Eds.), *Sexual deviance: Theory, assessment, and treatment* (2nd ed., pp. 183–212). New York: Guilford.

Freund, K., Watson, R., & Rienzo, D. (1988). The value of self-reports in the study of voyeurism and exhibitionism. *Annals of Sex Research, 1*, 243–262.

Gebhard, P. H., Gagnon, J. H., Pomeroy, W. B., & Christensen, C. V. (1965). *Sex offenders: An analysis of types*. London: Heinemann.

Hackett, T. P., Saber, F. A., & Curran, W. J. (1980). Exhibitionism. In W. J. Curran, A. L. McGarry, & C. S. Petty (Eds.), *Modern legal medicine, psychiatry, and forensic sciences* (pp. 827–838). Philadelphia: Davis.

Hanson, R. K., Gordon, A., Harris, A. J. R., Marques, J. K., Murphy, W., Quinsey, V. L., & Seto, M. C. (2002). First report of the collaborative outcome data project on the effectiveness of psychological treatment for sex offenders. *Sexual Abuse: A Journal of Research and Treatment, 14*, 169–194.

Junginger, J. (1997). Fetishism: Assessment and treatment. In D. R. Laws & W. T. O'Donoghue (Eds.), *Sexual deviance: Theory, assessment and treatment* (pp. 92–110). New York: Guilford Press.

Kapardis, A. (1984). Research note: indecent exposure: A survey of victims in Melbourne. *Australian and New Zealand Journal of Criminology, 17*, 233–238.

Kilmann, P. R., Sabalis, R. F., Gearing, M. L., Bukstel, L. H., & Scovern, A. W. (1982). The treatment of sexual paraphilias: A review of the outcome research. *Journal of Sex Research, 18*, 193–252.

Laws, D. R., & O'Donohue, W. T. (Eds.). (2008). *Sexual deviance: Theory, assessment, and treatment*. New York: Guilford Press.

Lee, J., Jackson, H. J., Pattison, P., & Ward, T. (2002). Developmental risk factors for sexual offending. *Child Abuse and Neglect, 26*, 73–92.

Maletzky, B. (1980). Assisted covert sensitization. In D. J. Cox & R. J. Daitzman (Eds.), *Exhibitionism: Description, assessment, and treatment* (pp. 187–251). New York: Garland Press.

Maletzky, B. (1997). Exhibitionism: Assessment and treatment. In D. R. Laws & W. O'Donohue (Eds.), *Sexual deviance: Theory, assessment, and treatment*, (pp. 40–74). New York: Guilford Press.

Marshall, W. L. (2006). Ammonia aversion with an exhibitionist: A case study. *Clinical Case Studies, 5*, 15–24.

McNally, M. R., & Fremouw, W. J. (2014). Examining risk of escalation: A critical review of the exhibitionistic behavior literature. *Aggression and Violent Behavior, 19*, 474–485.

Murphy, W. D., & Page, I. J. (2008). Exhibitionism: Psychopathology and theory. In D. R. Laws & W. O'Donohue (Eds.), *Sexual deviance: Theory, assessment, and treatment* (pp. 61–75). New York: Guilford Press.

Nathan, L., Wilson, N. J., & Hillman, D. (2003). *Te Whakakotahitanga: An evaluation of the Te Piriti special treatment programme for child sex offenders in New Zealand*. Wellington, NZ: Psychological Service Report, Department of Corrections.

Paul, R. H., Marx, B. P., & Orsillo, S. M. (1999). Acceptance-based psychotherapy in the treatment of an adjudicated exhibitionist: A case example. *Behavior Therapy, 30*, 149–162.

Richters, J., De Visser, R. O., Rissel, C. E., Grulich, A. E., & Smith, A. M. A. (2008). Demographic and psychosocial features of participants in bondage and discipline, "sadomasochism" or dominance and submission (BDSM): Data from a national survey. *Journal of Sexual Medicine, 5*, 1660–1668.

Sarver, N. W., & Gros, D. F. (2014). A modern behavioral treatment to address fetishism and associated functional impairment. *Clinical Case Studies, 13*, 336–351.

Seto, M. C. (2008). Pedophilia: Psychopathology and theory. In D. R. Laws & W. O'Donohue (Eds.), *Sexual deviance: Theory, assessment, and treatment* (pp. 164–182). New York: Guilford Press.

Ward, T., Yates, P. M., & Willis, G. (2012). The good lives model and the risk need responsivity model. *Criminal Justice and Behavior, 39*, 94–110.

World Health Organisation. (2011). *International statistical classification of diseases and related health problems 2010 edition (ICD-10)*. Geneva: Author.

Recommendations for further reading/resources

Chivres, M., Roy, C., Grimbos, T., Cantor, J., & Seto, M. (2014). Specificity of sexual arousal for sexual activities in men and women with conventional and masochistic sexual interests. *Archives of Sexual Behaviour, 43*, 931–940.

Fedoroff, J. (2011). Forensic and diagnostic concerns arising from the proposed DSM-5 criteria for sexual paraphilic disorder. *The Journal of the American Academy of Psychiatry and Law, 39*(2), 239–241.

Finkelhor, D. (1984). *Child sexual abuse: New theory and research*. New York: Free Press.

24

Other conditions that may be a focus of clinical attention

Susana Gavidia-Payne and Bianca Denny

Introduction

This chapter covers conditions and problems that may attract clinical attention or otherwise affect diagnosis, course, prognosis, or treatment. The conditions are *not* diagnoses or mental disorders. They are issues that may affect patient care and help explain the need for a test, procedure, or treatment. These may also be included in medical records as useful information. Including them in the *Diagnostic and Statistical Manual of Mental Disorders* (5th ed.; *DSM-5*; American Psychiatric Association, 2013) acknowledges that a broad range of additional issues can impact patient care. Documenting them systematically is useful to clinicians and beneficial to patients.

These conditions have *International Statistical Classification of Diseases and Related Health Problems* codes ICD-9-CM (V codes) and ICD-10-CM (Z codes) and include: relational problems; child abuse (physical and sexual) and neglect; partner abuse or violence (psychological, physical, and sexual); educational and occupational problems; housing and economic problems; other problems related to the social environment; problems related to crime or interaction with the legal system; other health service encounters for counselling and medical advice; problems related to other psychosocial, personal, and environmental circumstances; other circumstances of personal history; problems related to access to medical treatment; non-adherence to medical treatment; overweight or obesity; and malingering,

This chapter specifically examines various problems related to relationships, child and adult maltreatment and neglect, housing and economic difficulties, and other psychosocial, personal, and environmental circumstances.

Many of the issues to be discussed occur in addition to other presentations/ diagnoses. As such, they are likely to be addressed in the context of other presentations. Therefore, treatment should typically follow guidelines for main presentation/diagnosis. In addition to the conditions addressed here, refer to the *DSM-5* for information on various other problems that may be the focus of clinical attention.

Australia

Relational problems

Recent statistics on incidence and prevalence indicate the number of divorces decreased in 2013 by 2279 (4.6%) and the crude divorce rate decreased from 2.2 divorces per 1000 population in 2012 to 2.1 in 2013 (Australian Bureau of Statistics [ABS], 2014). About 31.6% of children aged 5–9 years who had a natural parent living elsewhere had daily/weekly frequency of face-to-face contact between parent and child, compared to 24% of less than once a year or never (ABS, 2011).

In analysing the Longitudinal Study of Australian Children data, Mullan and Higgins (2014) examined family relationships and the impact on child outcomes. Specifically, family functioning was measured as family cohesion (i.e., parental warmth and parent–child activities) in families of two cohorts of children (birth to 6/7 years, and kindergarten to 10/11 years). About 90% of families reported cohesion to be "good," "very good," or "excellent." Two to three year olds whose families were enmeshed were more likely to be underweight, whereas disengaged families were more likely to have toddlers who experienced more injuries per year. Children's perspectives have also been considered as shown in a recent report by the Australian Research Alliance for Children and Youth (ARACY, 2013), which found that 23% of 11–24 year olds were concerned about family conflict and approximately 16% of parents of 4–5 year olds using harsh parenting practices half the time or more.

Parenting interventions feature prominently among standard practices and treatments in this area. An analysis of evidence (commissioned by FaCHSIA) of parenting interventions in Australia revealed that only two programs, Triple P and Parent–Child Interaction Therapy, were supported by strong empirical evidence (Parenting Research Centre, 2012). In another review of parent early childhood education and health programs for Indigenous children and families in Australia (Bowes & Grace, 2014), it was reported that several evidence-based programs exist. While the authors argued for their implementation, they acknowledged the need for adaptations to emphasise strength-based, family-centred approaches as well as collaboration with communities in a coordinated service approach.

Speciality treatment guidelines via the Australian Psychological Society (APS) are of note. One major initiative has been KidsMatter, a national mental health promotion, prevention, and early intervention initiative being implemented in approximately 2200 Australian primary schools and 2160 early childhood services. The program (www.kidsmatter.edu.au) provides a range of resources supporting the social and emotional wellbeing of Indigenous and non-Indigenous children, their families, and communities.

Child and adult maltreatment and neglect

Child maltreatment and neglect figures are typically described in terms of child protection service usage. A report by the Australian Institute of Health and Welfare

(AIHW, 2014) indicates that 5000 children at a rate of 26.1/1000 children were receiving child protection services investigation, care and protection order and/or in out-of-home care from 2012 to 2013. Aboriginal and Torres Strait Islander children were eight times as likely as non-Indigenous children to be receiving child protection services, while most child subjects of substantiation were from low socio-economic status (SES).

In regards to adult maltreatment, one in five women had experienced sexual violence, while one in three women experienced physical violence, with 36% experiencing violence from someone they knew in 2014 (Australia's National Research Organisation for Women's Safety [ANROWS], 2014). Indigenous individuals are between two and five times more likely to experience violence as victims or offenders (Willis, 2011, as cited in ANROWS, 2014).

Research on self-reported child abuse and its relationship with clinical and other characteristics has been also conducted. In a sample of 1825 Australians with a psychotic illness aged 18–64 years and in contact with mental health services, the prevalence of child abuse was 30.6%. Women were almost three times more likely to report child abuse compared to males (Shah et al., 2014). Astbury (2013) also provides a comprehensive review of the literature about the long-term effects of child sexual abuse on mental health and the determinants of these outcomes.

A range of efforts designed to address the risks associated with child abuse and neglect has been recommended. Larger services may contain secondary preventative interventions; for example, targeted maternal and child health home visiting services, such as South Australia's Nurse Family Home Visiting program that provides home visiting to mothers with risk factors. The *Building Blocks* report from Western Australia describes a range of evidence-based program elements to improve the wellbeing of all children and young people, including those who experience vulnerability (Commissioner for Children and Young People, Western Australia, 2014). Adult-focused services that tackle specific risks and disadvantage faced by parents can also be helpful (O'Donnell et al., 2008). Generally, however, you need careful and distinctive assessment and treatment phases in working with children who have experienced child abuse (Kambouridis, 2013). The APS has developed guidelines for the mandatory reporting of suspected child abuse, and its implications for psychologists under the National Registration Scheme (2010). Specifically, a Child Sexual Abuse Issues and Psychology Interest Group has been created (Australian Psychological Society, 2013) to share psychological knowledge, skills, and information about the causes, treatment, and prevention of child sexual abuse, and research on related issues.

In one of the major federal government initiatives to date, the Council of Australian Governments delivered the National Framework for Protecting Australia's Children 2009–2020, *Protecting Children is Everyone's Business* (Commonwealth of Australia, 2009). At a state level, under the "Keep them Safe initiative," the New South Wales government has also set up the "Sustaining NSW Families" program. This provides a sustainable, coordinated, and integrated high-intensity health home visiting service that: strengthens relationships between children, parents and/or carers; builds parenting capacity; and enhances child development, wellbeing, and health in vulnerable families (see www.keepthemsafe.nsw.gov.au/initiatives/prevention_and_early_intervention/sustaining_nsw_families).

Housing and economic problems

The ABS (2011) identified one in 204 Australians (total of 105 200) who were homeless. Of these, 26 744 were Aboriginal and Torres Strait Islander peoples, although this number is generally thought to be underreported. More recently, the AIHW (2013) reported that 17% of all homeless people were aged under 12 and 25% aged over 45. Despite little empirical research in the area, the significant human, social, and economic costs of homelessness are widely recognised, yet few cohesive policies exist (Baldry et al., 2012).

Despite Australia's standing as one of the wealthiest countries in the world, the number of people in poverty is increasing. An estimated 2.55 million people (13.9% of all people) were living below the poverty line (50% of median income) of $400 per week for a single adult in 2012 (ACOSS, 2014). No published poverty estimates are available for Indigenous populations; however, ACCOS (2014) reports on data obtained from the Household Income and Labour Dynamics in Australia (HILDA) survey, which shows that the rate of poverty is higher among Aboriginal and Torres Strait Islander peoples (19.3%, compared with 12.4% of the total Australian population). With 17.1% of all children living below the poverty line (Australian Council of Social Service [ACOSS], 2014) the wellbeing of young Australians is compromised with 3700 young people indicating numerous economic problems (ARACY, 2013). This is manifested in revelations of a strong link between homelessness, child protection, and juvenile justice (AIHW, 2012).

Problems related to other psychosocial, personal, and environmental circumstances

Religion and spirituality problems

Australia has a diversity of religious affiliations, with Christian religions dominating. In the 2011 ABS census, the largest single religion reported was Western (Roman) Catholic (25.1%), Anglican (17.1%) was nominated next, followed by Uniting Church (5.0%). The psychological aspects of belonging to a religious minority have received some attention. Using a minority stress model, Every and Perry (2014) examined the relationship between self-esteem and religious discrimination in 49 Australian Muslims. Findings revealed a negative relationship between interpersonal discrimination and self-esteem, and a positive relationship between systemic discrimination and self-esteem.

Exposure to disaster, war, or other hostilities

Exposure to bushfires, floods, severe storms, earthquakes, and landslides – all of which have been associated with financial hardships for communities, social costs, and loss of life – is a large part of Australian life. As the driest continent on earth, droughts are a particular feature. The period from 2002 to 2007 ranks with the Federation Drought of 1895 to 1902 and the Forties Drought as one of the three most severe, widespread, and prolonged dry periods since 1900 (Australian Government, 2015). Bushfires have also been severe; the Ash Wednesday (1983) and the Black Saturday (2009) fires are notable, with the latter resulting in the nation's highest ever loss of life from a bushfire. There have been calls for informed, sustained, and interdisciplinary community preparedness and response programs, and promotion of community health and wellbeing and preventative mental health initiatives. Specifically, resources to deal with these events have become more readily available. Of note is *Psychological First Aid: An Australian Guide for People Affected by Disaster* (Burke, Richardson, & Whitton, 2013) developed under the auspices of the APS and Australian Red Cross.

New Zealand

Relational problems

There are approximately 10 000 divorces per year in New Zealand (NZ), a lifetime prevalence of one-third of marriages ending. However, there has been a slight decline in divorce rates in recent years (Statistics New Zealand, 2001). Relationship separation is associated with an overall higher prevalence of mental health problems, including depression and suicidal behaviour. Interestingly, separation is not associated with increased anxiety disorders, alcohol abuse/dependence, or illicit drug abuse/dependence (Gibb, Fergusson, & Horwood, 2011). This longitudinal research on a large cohort of Christchurch residents also indicated no significant gender difference in mental health problems. Further research is required to determine the causal direction of the association between relationship difficulties and mental health problems (i.e., the impact of mental health problems on relationships and vice-versa).

Child and adult maltreatment and neglect

Rates of abuse and neglect in NZ are comparatively high compared to other developed countries. NZ has the fifth highest rates of child abuse from 31 OECD countries. One in three women will experience psychological or physical abuse from partners over their lifetime. Additionally, 55% of ever-partnered women have experienced intimate partner violence (IPV); 22% and 33% have experienced one or more types of IPV, respectively (most commonly psychological/emotional violence and physical and/or sexual violence; Fanslow & Robinson, 2011). However, rates of abuse are difficult to estimate due to lack of disclosure and underreporting. For example, more than 25% of respondents to the New Zealand Violence Against Women Study reported they had not disclosed one or more incidents of IPV (Fanslow & Robinson, 2010).

Despite difficulty in assessing and quantifying abuse, research indicates the importance of early intervention. For example, research found that only 6% to 10% of abused children attained a university degree, compared with 28% of those not abused (Fanslow & Robinson, 2011).

The New Zealand Psychologists Board's Code of Ethics provides guidance for psychologists concerned about potential cases of abuse and neglect. As well as consulting relevant legislation and seeking supervision with senior colleagues before making decisions about reporting (which may involve breaching confidentiality), psychologists should consider whether non-disclosure would endanger the client or public safety.

Several speciality services provide further guidance and empirically validated treatments for children experiencing abuse and neglect. Child Matters (www.childmatters.org.nz) and the Jigsaw network of 44 organisations (www.jigsaw.org.au) focus on preventing and treating child abuse, neglect, and family violence. Developed and conducted in NZ, the Early Start program has shown significant benefits to reducing child abuse (MacMillan et al., 2009). The program includes home visitations, enhanced practitioner partnerships, and parent education and training. Further, the Incredible Years is a parenting program aimed at parents of children with conduct problems. It has been found to be culturally appropriate and effective for both Māori and non-Māori populations. This is of particular importance given the higher rates of conduct problems reported for Māori children (Sturrock et al., 2014).

Housing and economic problems

Homelessness in NZ is under-researched and often incorrectly assumed to not represent a major social problem. However, while NZ lacks consistent data on homelessness, recent statistics indicates Māori and Pacific Island peoples are disproportionately affected by housing problems (Richards, 2008). For example, Māori and Pacific Island peoples comprise 68% of homeless families in one area of NZ (Legatt-Cook, 2007).

Similar to Australia, NZ is considered a high-income society. However, Māori people continue to have poorer psychosocial and SES outcomes, and are more likely to experience economic problems (Marie, Fergusson, & Boden, 2014). Low SES is strongly associated with adverse psychosocial outcomes in adulthood with regards to educational achievement and welfare dependence, with weaker associations between low SES and mental health conditions, substance use, and criminal offending. Māori people most at risk of disadvantaged outcomes include those who identify solely as Māori, with low skills and living in communities where the Māori population is high and outcomes are, on average, poor (Chapple, 2000).

Homelessness and inadequate housing have psychological and physical impacts on families and children. Recent research indicates that controlling for SES reduced the magnitude of differences between psychosocial outcomes for Māori and non-Māori individuals, indicating that improvements among SES in Māori people may ameliorate the disparities between the groups (Marie et al., 2014).

Problems related to other psychosocial, personal, and environmental circumstances

Religious or spiritual problems

While NZ is a secular country, census statistics indicate approximately half of its inhabitants identify with a Christian belief system, including the main denominations of Anglican, Catholic, and Presbyterian. Māori adopted Christianity across NZ in the 19th century. Similar to other countries, religion and spirituality is important to many New Zealanders, particularly during specific times such as at the end of life and while experiencing mental health concerns (Egan et al., 2011). The literature recognises the role of religion and spirituality in mental healthcare. Integrating and including it in psychological treatment is encouraged where appropriate. For example, Carey and Del Medico (2013) explored the role of chaplains working in mental health in NZ, noting positive benefits in assessing and monitoring patient wellbeing, ongoing support and presence, advocacy, undertaking of religious rituals and worship activities, and guidance on cultural and spiritual issues.

Exposure to disaster, war, or other hostilities

Several major earthquakes have affected NZ, notably the Christchurch earthquakes of September 2010 and February 2011. The latter caused 185 fatalities. There are ongoing environmental difficulties and disruptions to everyday life due to widespread damage, including building demolition, re-building, and concern about future earthquakes.

Several research initiatives have investigated the psychological impact of the earthquakes. Findings have prompted calls for greater consideration of mental health and psychological trauma reactions following natural disasters such as earthquakes. For example, survey-based research of 295 50-year-olds indicated Christchurch residents scored significantly lower than population norms on social functioning, mental health, vitality, and emotional wellbeing (Spittlehouse et al., 2014). Similarly, a qualitative investigation of Christchurch residents' responses to the 2010 earthquakes also indicated the impact of natural disasters on psychological wellbeing. Reported experiences include psychological sequelae consistent with posttraumatic stress reactions, including fear, anxiety, sleep disturbance, and hypervigilance. The cumulative impact of several earthquakes and threat of further incidents also has implications for the resilience and future adaptive capacity of individuals and the community as a whole (Wilson, 2013).

Australian case study

This case is a composite example created for illustrative purposes.

Bella is a 36-year-old mother of Aboriginal background, currently living in the western suburbs of Melbourne. Most of her family lives in rural northern Victoria. She has four children under 10 years of age, one of whom (6-year-old Charlie) experiences academic and behavioural problems at school. Bella is currently 8 months pregnant from her current partner Tom. She has been attending antenatal classes, supported by the local hospital nurse and the maternal and child health nurse (MCHN), with whom she has remained in contact through one of her younger children.

Bella reports that she is finding it difficult to deal with her son's school problems and increasingly challenging behaviour at home, as well as the demands of her younger children, with virtually no support as her partner works long hours. She also does not feel confident to approach her son's school. She exhibits hostility towards her children, and does not want to spend time with them, all of which makes her feel guilty. She is also confused about not looking forward to the arrival of her new baby. She does not want to leave the house, and presents with chest pains for no apparent reason. In the past, she experienced some difficulties in parenting her children, but was supported by the local MCHN, whose assistance she seeks once again.

The MCHN conducts a preliminary assessment of Bella's concerns which reveals Bella's loss of confidence in her parenting, for which she is referred to the local community health centre's psychologist. The latter also identifies Bella's stress and generalised anxiety symptoms. The psychologist organises a meeting with Charlie's school teacher, MCHN, and partner and agrees that a key worker will be identified as the one contact person for Bella as there are a number of issues to address. Bella is diagnosed with generalised anxiety disorder with a specifier of relational problems. Bella's intervention plan includes sessions with the psychologist to address her stress and anxiety using mindfulness techniques, interventions to strengthen her parenting capacity, and access to funding to finance after school care for the older children so Bella can have some respite.

KidsMatter Aboriginal and Torres Strait Islander social and emotional wellbeing resources

The APS has created a series of 12 animated videos to communicate key messages about the day-to-day caring for Aboriginal and Torres Strait Islander children's wellbeing. Aboriginal and Torres Strait Islander people worked alongside the KidsMatter team at the APS across all stages of project development, which has resulted in these evidence-based resources. Refer to www.kidsmatter.edu.au/atsi-resources for further information.

An online resource portal has also been developed, designed to assist educators, health professionals, and families to access existing resources as well as changes to the KidsMatter online programs guide, which more specifically include programs and projects relevant to the social and emotional wellbeing of Aboriginal and Torres Strait Islander children. The resource portal contains information and links to over 200 useful reports, websites, tools, and services. Refer to www.kidsmatter.edu.au/atsi-resources/search for further information.

Christchurch Health and Development Study

The Christchurch Health and Development Study is a longitudinal study that has been following a group of 1265 individuals for more than 35 years. The cohort has now been studied from infancy to childhood, adolescence, and adulthood.

Data has been gathered related to psychiatric conditions, such as depression, anxiety, usage and dependence related to alcohol and illicit substances, and conduct disorders. Psychosocial and life course outcomes of the cohort have been extensively investigated.

Cultural consideration is made at both data collection and interpretation stages of the project. The cohort includes both Māori and non-Māori individuals. Western Science and Kaupapa Māori perspectives are reconciled using He Awa Whiria (a Braided Rivers Model).

Visit www.otago.ac.nz/christchurch/research/healthdevelopment/otago011648.html for further information.

References

American Psychiatric Association. (2013). *Diagnostic and statistical manual of mental disorders* (5th ed.). Arlington, VA: Author.

Astbury, J. (2013). Violating children's rights: The psychosexual impact of sexual abuse in childhood. *InPsych, 35,* 8–11.

Australian Bureau of Statistics. (2011). *Census of population and housing, 2011 (Usual residence data).* Canberra: Author.

Australian Bureau of Statistics. (2014). *Marriages and divorces, Australia 2013.* Canberra: Author. Available: www.abs.gov.au/AUSSTATS/abs@.nsf/allprimarymainfeatures/5938B 16BA4FF5270CA257F0700140D1B?opendocument

ACOSS. (2014). *Poverty in Australia.* NSW: Australian Council of Social Service.

Australian Government. (2015). *Natural disasters in Australia.* Available: www.australia. gov.au/about-australia/australian-story/natural-disasters/.

Australian Institute of Family Studies. (2013). *The longitudinal study of Australian children. Annual Statistical Report, 2012.* Melbourne: Commonwealth of Australia.

AIHW. (2012). *Children and young people at risk of social exclusion: Links between homelessness, child protection and juvenile justice.* Cat. no. CSI 13. Canberra; Australian Institute of Health and Welfare.

AIHW. (2013). *Australia's welfare 2013. Australia's Welfare Series No. 11.* Cat. no. AUS174. Canberra; Australian Institute of Health and Welfare.

AIHW. (2014). *Child protection Australia 2012–13. Child Welfare Series No. 58.* Cat. no. CWS 49. Canberra: Australian Institute of Health and Welfare.

ANROWS. (2014). *Indigenous family violence: Fast facts.* Sydney: Australia's National Research Organisation for Women's Safety. Available: www.anrows.org.au/ publications/fast-facts

Australian Psychological Society. (2010). Mandatory reporting of suspected child abuse: Implications under the national registration scheme. Melbourne: Author. Available: www.psychology.org.au/publications/inpsych/2010/august/jifkins/?ID=3249

Australian Psychological Society. (2013). Child sexual abuse issues and psychology. Melbourne: Author. Available: http://groups.psychology.org.au/csa/

Australian Research Alliance for Children and Youth. (2013). *Report card: The wellbeing of young Australians.* Canberra: Author. Available: www.aracy.org.au/projects/report-card-the-wellbeing-of-young-australians

Baldry, E., Dowse, L., McCausland, R., & Clarence, M. (2012). *Lifecourse institutional costs of homelessness for vulnerable groups, National Homelessness Research Agenda 2009–2013,* Canberra: Commonwealth of Australia.

Bowes, J., & Grace, R. (2014). *Review of early childhood parenting, education and health intervention programs for Indigenous children and families in Australia. Issues Paper No. 8. Produced for the Closing the Gap Clearing House.* Canberra: Australian Institute of Health and Welfare, Melbourne, and Australian Institute of Family Studies.

Burke, S., Richardson, S., & Whitton, S. (2013). *Psychological first aid: An Australian guide for people affected by disaster.* Report developed under the auspices of the APS and Australian Red Cross.

Carey, L. B., & Del Medico, L. (2013). Chaplaincy and mental health care in Aotearoa New Zealand: An exploratory study. *Journal of Religion and Health, 52,* 46–65. http://dx.doi.org/10.1007/s10943-012-9622-9

Chapple, S. (2000). Māori socio-economic disparity. *Political Science, 52*(2), 101–115.

Commissioner for Children and Young People, Western Australia. (2014). *Building blocks: Best practice programs that improve the wellbeing of children and young people – Edition 2.* WA: Author.

Commonwealth of Australia. (2009). *Protecting children is everyone's business national framework for protecting Australia's children 2009–2020: An initiative of the Council of Australian Governments.* Canberra: Author.

Egan, R., MacLeod, R., Jaye, C., McGee, R., Baxter, J., & Herbison, P. (2011). What is spirituality. Evidence from a New Zealand hospice study. *Mortality, 16*(4), 307–324.

Every, D., & Perry, R. (2014). The relationship between perceived discrimination and self-esteem for Muslim Australians. *Australian Journal of Psychology, 4,* 241–248.

Fanslow, J. L., & Robinson, E. M. (2010). Help-seeking behaviors and reasons for help seeking reported by a representative sample of women victims of intimate partner violence in New Zealand. *Journal of Interpersonal Violence, 25*(5), 929–951.

Fanslow, J. L., & Robinson, E. M. (2011). Sticks, stones, or words? Counting the prevalence of different types of intimate partner violence reported by New Zealand women. *Journal of Aggression, Maltreatment and Trauma, 20*(7), 741–759.

Gibb, S. J., Fergusson, D. M., & Horwood, L. J. (2011). Relationship separation and mental health problems: Findings from a 30-year longitudinal study. *Australian & New Zealand Journal of Psychiatry, 45*(2), 163–169. http://dx.doi.org/10.3109/00048674.2010.529603

Kambouridis, H. (2013). Using co-operative inquiry and participatory action research with therapists in the Victorian sexual assault field to better deliver services to families who have experienced sibling sexual abuse. In S. Goff (Ed.), *From theory to practice; Context in praxis; 8th Action Learning, Action Research and 12th Participatory Action Research World Congress proceedings, 2010*. Melbourne: World Congress on Action Learning.

Legatt-Cook, C. (2007). *Homelessness in New Zealand: A discussion and synthesis of research findings*. Available: www.mmn.org.nz

MacMillan, H. L., Wathen, C. N., Barlow, J., Fergusson, D. M., Leventhal, J. M., & Taussig, H. N. (2009). Interventions to prevent child maltreatment and associated impairment. *Lancet, 373*(6959), 250–266. http://dx.doi.org/10.1016/S0140-6736(08)61708-0

Marie, D., Fergusson, D. M., & Boden, J. M. (2014). Childhood socio-economic status and ethnic disparities in psychosocial outcomes in New Zealand. *Australian & New Zealand Journal of Psychiatry, 48*(7), 672–680.

Mullan, K., & Higgins, D. (2014). *A safe and supportive family environment for children: Key components and links to child outcomes, Occasional Paper No. 52*. Canberra, Australia: Commonwealth of Australia.

O'Donnell, M., Scott, D., & Stanley, F. (2008). Child abuse and neglect: Is it time for a public health approach? *Australian and New Zealand Journal of Public Health, 32*(4), 325–330.

Parenting Research Centre. (2012). *Evidence review: An analysis of the evidence for parenting interventions in Australia*. Melbourne, Australia: Author.

Richards, S. (2008). *Homelessness in Aotearao: Issues and recommendations*. Regional Public Health.

Shah, S., Mackinnon, A., Galletly, C., Carr, V., McGrath, J. J., Stain, H. J., Castle, D., Harvey, C., Sweeney, S., & Morgan, V. A. (2014). Prevalence and impact of childhood abuse in people with a psychotic illness. Data from the second Australian national survey of psychosis. *Schizophrenia Research, 159*(1), 20–26.

Spittlehouse, J. K., Joyce, P. R., Vierck, E., Schluter, P., & Pearson, J. F. (2014). Ongoing adverse mental health impact of the earthquake sequence in Christchurch, New Zealand. *Australian & New Zealand Journal of Psychiatry, 48*, 756–763. http://dx.doi.org/10.1177/0004867414527522

Statistics New Zealand. (2001). Marriage and divorce in New Zealand. *Key statistics*. March. 7–10. Available: www.stats.govt.nz/browse_for_stats/people_and_communities/marriages-civil-unions-and-divorces/marriage-and-divorce-in-nz.aspx

Sturrock, F., Gray, D., Fergusson, D., Horwood, J., & Smits, C. (2014). *Incredible years follow-up study: Long-term follow-up of the New Zealand incredible years pilot study*. Wellington, NZ: Ministry of Social Development. Available: www.msd.govt.nz/documents/about-msd-and-our-work/publications-resources/evaluation/incredible-years-follow-up-study/indredible-years-follow-up-study.pdf

Willis, M. (2011). Non-disclosure of violence in Australian Indigenous communities. *Trends & Issues in Crime and Criminal Justice. No. 405*. Canberra, Australia: Australian Institute of Criminology.

Wilson, G. A. (2013). Community resilience, social memory and the post-2010 Christchurch (New Zealand) earthquakes. *Area, 45*, 207–215. http://dx.doi.org/10.1111/area.12012

Recommendations for further reading/resources

Australia

Australian Institute of Family Studies. (2014). *The longitudinal study of Australian children annual statistical report 2013.* Melbourne: Author.

Dudgeon P., Walker R., Scrine C., Shepherd, C., Calma, T., & Ring, I. (2014). *Effective strategies to strengthen the mental health and wellbeing of Aboriginal and Torres Strait Islander people.* Issues paper no. 12. Produced for the Closing the Gap Clearinghouse. Canberra: Australian Institute of Health and Welfare & Melbourne: Australian Institute of Family Studies.

Lohoar, S., Butera, N., & Kennedy, E. (2014). *Strengths of Aboriginal cultural practices in family life and child rearing.* (CFA Paper No. 25). Melbourne: Australian Institute of Family Studies.

New Zealand

Durie, M. (2011). Indigenizing mental health services: New Zealand experience. *Transcultural Psychiatry, 48*(1–2), 24–36. http://dx.doi.org/10.1177/1363461510383182

Fergusson D. M., & Horwood L. J. (2013). The Christchurch health and development study. In P. Joyce, G. Nicholls, K. Thomas, & T. Wilkinson (Eds.), *The Christchurch experience: 40 years of research and teaching* (pp. 79–87). Christchurch: University of Otago.

Section **IV**

Special foci relevant to abnormal psychology

25

Suicide and self-harm

Kenneth Kirkby and Sunny Collings

Introduction

Suicide, intentional self-harm, and suicidal thinking form a wide spectrum of treatable thought patterns and behaviours. Together suicide and intentional self-harm are often known as "suicidal behaviours" and can be emotionally confronting. Intentional self-harm commonly presents as an event, such as taking an overdose of prescribed tablets or deliberate cutting of the skin. However, it is usually part of an ongoing story with themes that may include past abuse, relationship conflicts, employment difficulties, personal illness and especially mental illness, bereavement, and substance misuse. Intentional self-harm behaviours are usually associated with suicidal thinking or intent of varying frequency, intensity, and chronicity.

Self-harming behaviours are widely stigmatised. The national identities of both Australia and New Zealand (NZ) include notions that they are healthy and peaceful societies with fewer apparent reasons for despondency than in many other parts of the world. Yet suicidal behaviours are significant problems in both jurisdictions. The topic is a highly emotional subject for many people, reacted to on the basis of simple moral precepts regarding self-conduct and personal responsibility.

In Australia, about 2500 people die by suicide each year, around 1.7% of all deaths, with an age-standardised rate of 11/100 000 in 2012 (Australian Bureau of Statistics [ABS], 2010). It is the leading single cause of death from age 15–34 years, in 2013 accounting for over one-quarter of all deaths in that age band, and similarly for those aged 35–44 years, accounting for almost 16% of all deaths (ABS, 2015).

In NZ, each year more than 500 people die by suicide, with an age-standardised rate of 12.2/100 000 in 2012, the most recent year for which official figures are available (Statistics New Zealand, 2016). Suicide deaths in NZ peaked in 1998, with 577 deaths (age-standardised rate of 15.1/100 000; Statistics New Zealand, 2016). In 2012, young adults aged 15–24 years had the highest suicide rates, with males significantly more likely to die by suicide than females (Ministry of Health NZ, 2015a, 2015b).

Suicide is a topic of great societal concern. Often the deaths themselves are difficult to understand. Every suicide death has significant emotional impacts on friends, family, health professionals, and witnesses, often for many years. While the effects of suicide can be great, it is actually a statistically rare event. Because of the low base rate of suicide and because experimental studies cannot be conducted, it is almost impossible to prove the effectiveness of any single intervention to reduce such deaths.

Intentional self-harm presents a different picture. Up to a quarter of females and an eighth of males in their mid-20s report having harmed themselves in their lifetime. In 2012 in NZ, there were 3031 intentional self-harm hospitalisations, an age-standardised rate of 71 per 100 000 (Statistics New Zealand, 2016). Note that while methods for compiling national suicide statistics are broadly similar in reliability across Australia and NZ, intentional self-harm statistics are not readily comparable. Rates of hospitalisation for intentional self-harm for females aged 15–19 years, the most at-risk group, in Australia in 2012 were over 400 per 100 000 (ABS, 2010).

In the case of intentional self-harm, the person concerned can be interviewed to establish full details on any aspect of their history, and observed to clarify behaviour and mental state. This has helped develop a better understanding of the possibilities for prevention.

Thoughts of suicide or self-harm, whether fleeting or persistent, are relatively common in community samples. Figures from the Australian national mental health survey of 2007 are 2.3% in the previous year, comprising around 8% of those with and 0.8% of those without a mental illness during that period (ABS, 2007). This prevalence is illustrative of the realities of many peoples' private thoughts, emotions, and struggles. These are not unusual issues; they may trouble us or the people around us, often hidden from view. It is unclear why there are differences in the reported rates of suicidal ideation in the two countries. The rates are derived from individual studies, without head-to-head comparison. Explanations may include many factors ranging from response biases to rates of depression to differences in social cohesion.

Who is most at risk?

Completed suicide is around four times more frequent for males, largely because they use more lethal methods – hanging, carbon monoxide poisoning, overdose, shooting, and jumping. This pattern is the same in Australia and NZ (Blisker & White, 2011).

There are also ethnic differences, with the Indigenous/bicultural people of both countries being at greater risk. In Australia, suicide rates in the Aboriginal and Torres Strait Islander population for 2001 to 2010 were 2.6 times higher, with the Indigenous youth rate four times higher than the non-Indigenous population. Among NZ Māori youth, the age-standardised rate in 2012 was 48 suicide deaths per 100 000 Māori population, a rate 2.8 times higher than for non-Māori (Ministry of Health, 2015a; Hunter & Harvey, 2002).

Rural rates are higher than for cities, being around twice as high in rural Tasmania and the Northern Territory as in Melbourne or Sydney. In NZ, rural rates are higher, but the differences are not statistically significant. This is possibly partly due to smaller numbers involved overall. Note also that in Australia, rural areas include very remote locations that do not exist in NZ, so the definition of rurality is not directly comparable across the two countries.

The highest suicide rates for individuals are those associated with diagnosed mental illness and substance abuse. For instance, those with a diagnosis of schizophrenia or bipolar disorder are at higher risk (Hawton et al., 2005; Jamison, 2000).

Certain age groups carry higher rates, notably the elderly, and there are also age cohorts who carry a higher risk through the lifespan. The general patterns of risk noted here are found internationally in comparable developed nations such as those in the Organisation for Economic Cooperation and Development (OECD).

What drives suicidal behaviours?

There is no simple single cause of suicidal behaviours. They arise from a complex interplay of individual, family, cultural, and societal factors. Individual level factors include: the presence of mental illness; family history of suicide death; psychological resilience; and repertoire of coping strategies. Social cohesion at family, cultural, and societal levels is also highly relevant. For example, generally suicide rates reduce in wartime and increase in times of economic recession. It is also likely that social conditions prevailing over a particular period might confer a risk profile that persists among those exposed while at a certain age. This phenomenon is known as a cohort effect (Snowdon & Hunt, 2008).

As an example, in Australia the early 1990s was a time of economic recession when youth unemployment was high, particularly in rural areas. Having no structure to the day and lacking the social connectedness that school and work provide, for many meant increased substance abuse and other risk behaviours. Many were denied the major rite of passage of entering the workforce, unemployment was stigmatised, and the prevailing status symbols of a consumer society were unaffordable. Acquisition of work skills was delayed. For some, feelings of worthlessness and hopelessness were reinforced by the circumstances.

Such complex and interwoven circumstances can unbalance life's equilibrium to the extent that death seems a release or perhaps a form of revenge on an unfair world. The epidemiological profiles of those who die by suicide and engage in intentional self-harm capture the salient factors well. Key factors in death by suicide include: male gender; being in younger or older age groups; being divorced or separated; having debilitating or terminal disease; substance abuse; and depressive illness (Kessler, Borges, & Walters, 1999). Conversely, non-fatal intentional self-harm is more commonly associated with female gender, being under 25 years of age, recent relationship breakup, problems at work, being intoxicated with alcohol, and a spur of the moment decision to take tablets at hand such as paracetamol (Bilsker & White, 2011).

In cases of recurrent self-harm, a history of abuse or neglect in childhood and parental substance abuse are common antecedents. Other at-risk populations include people in prison and asylum seekers in detention centres. In rare cases, a recognised biological cause may be a primary explanatory factor. For example, Lesch-Nyan syndrome, a genetically determined disease of uric acid metabolism, is associated with repeated biting of forearms and head banging (Winchel & Stanley, 1991).

Often the interplay of factors in the mind of a person attempting suicide are well portrayed in the contents of a suicide note. The intent to end their life is evident both on questioning and in the lethality (real or believed) of the means (Eisenwort et al., 2006).

There are socially codified ways of taking one's own life and these may change over time and vary between societies. Gunshot-related deaths have declined in Australia since the gun buyback that followed the Port Arthur massacre in 1996, while hanging is more common. Carbon monoxide poisoning from car exhaust is common though more difficult to enact because catalytic convertors remove most of this gas and the car may run out of petrol before it builds to fatal levels. In much of Asia, self-poisoning with herbicides is the most common and highly lethal method but is rare in Australia, where pharmaceuticals are the poisons of choice. There are iconic locations for dying by suicide by jumping, such as The Gap in Sydney or Grafton Bridge in NZ. Publicising the means of suicide through social and older-style media may emerge as a risk factor in the case of temporal clusters of suicide with specific characteristics, such as an unusual method or in social circles including those linked by social media. Loss of friends through suicide is itself a risk factor (Large & Nielssen, 2010).

Currently society is debating the merits of assisted suicide, particularly in cases of terminal illness, though in some countries this has been extended to severely handicapped children and young adults with mental illness. Societal views can change substantially, thus suicide used to be a criminal offence in both NZ and Australia.

What can be done to reduce suicide and self-harm?

The complexity of self-harm and suicide and the persistence of these behaviours indicate that there is no simple remedy. However, there is much that can be done at both a population and individual level of intervention.

At a population level, the first obvious target is prevention by reducing access to the means. Thus pills that are dangerous in overdose, such as paracetamol, are sold in blister packs and smaller pack sizes. Gun purchases may have cooling off periods, and compulsory registration and safe storage requirements reduce access and impulsive use. Catalytic convertors have been mentioned. Fencing of jump spots reduces suicides by that method and research demonstrates this does not usually result in people jumping elsewhere, although there may be some degree of method substitution.

Destigmatisation campaigns aimed at mental illness and substance abuse are another important consideration. Reducing stigma towards variety in sexual orientation and gender identity in the gay, bisexual, lesbian, transgender, and intersex (GBLTI) population is another area that is receiving attention. It is important to reach high-risk groups such as men. Thus, beyondblue, the National Depression Initiative, has used ads on beer coasters to reach men in pubs in Australia. In NZ, a Defeat Depression initiative has involved a high-profile national sportsman over many years.

The next level of intervention involves clinical assessment and treatment. It is not helpful to regard incidents of intentional self-harm as "failed suicide attempts" or attention-seeking behaviour. Such incidents usually indicate genuine psychological distress and overwhelmed coping mechanisms. Those with a history of intentional self-harm have a greatly increased risk of eventual death by suicide. They need compassionate and non-critical clinical assessment and a sound management plan. The assessment draws on history from and observations of the client, at interview, supplemented by any written documentation, such as a suicide note or clinical file.

A main consideration is the safety of the person, in two respects. The first is whether they require immediate treatment and further assessment for any injuries sustained in the attempt. These include the effects of poisoning, notably with paracetamol which may result in potentially fatal liver damage several days later and also the possibility of brain damage following asphyxiation by hanging or carbon monoxide poisoning, which may cause memory deficits. These will generally require attention in a hospital setting. The second safety concern is whether the person has ongoing preoccupation about ending their life and intends to do so, which will require close observation. Sedation or other after-effects of a suicide attempt may make it difficult to conduct an assessment, but it is important to persist and do so when appropriate, and ensure clients are not discharged without proper assessment and follow-up arrangements.

With conditions more conducive, the interview focuses on what has happened, the history of the event, and what led up to it. Items of particular concern are to understand what has been troubling the person, how the suicidal thoughts developed in this context, what they determined to do, what plans they may have made, what actions they then took to harm themselves (the method), what they expected to happen as a result and any measures they took to settle their affairs or avoid interruption or discovery (their intent), and what has occurred subsequently. Further, in searching for explanatory factors, the interview also assesses the presence of any mental illness or substance abuse, which may be evident to the observer but not the client.

The response of others to the suicide attempt is also very important. Often the client has not fully disclosed their difficulties to others. In many cases, those near or dear to them may have been involved in the emotional conflicts that have preceded the self-harm or are key supports for their recovery.

This information will contribute to assessing risk and shaping decisions about the appropriate level of care required. Hospitalisation may be necessary initially, for medical stabilisation or to provide round-the-clock supervision where immediate risk is very high. For example, hospitalisation may be required for psychotic depression or following a catastrophic loss or bereavement.

Assessment of risk

Predicting the future is an imperfect science and while suicide is a high-stakes matter, the base rate of completed suicide is low. Hence, the risk of the client taking their life in the near future may be high (compared to normal) but the actual day-to-day risk low. Thus, for any risk assessment, sensitivity may be satisfactory but specificity will be questionable. As a consequence, assessment can often determine the risk was high, when in reality it was not.

For the clinician, it is important not to get blindsided by the assessment and thus focus all one's clinical attention to risk. The client is typically suffering considerable emotional turmoil, at a crisis point in their life, and may have a mental disorder of consequence. Care and treatment must be directed to these issues primarily.

Risk assessment aims to provide an appropriate and safe environment at the most critical time to reduce the risk of suicide, while other measures are implemented. It also alerts the clinician to the likelihood of self-harming behaviours recurring and the need to tolerate the emotions and conflicts this may engender in the clinician and the ongoing therapeutic relationship.

The Australian Psychological Society (APS) does not endorse any specific questionnaire or other document for assessing risk of suicide or self-harm but many associations present summaries of relevant issues and resources on their websites, including:

- headspace Position Paper on Suicide Prevention (https://headspace.org.au/assets/Uploads/Corporate/Suicide-Position-Paper.pdf)
- The Australian Psychological Society (www.psychology.org.au/suicideprevention)
- Ethical guidelines (www.psychology.org.au/Assets/Files/APS-Code-of-Ethics.pdf)
- Psychology Board of Australia Ethics and Guidelines (www.psychologyboard.gov.au/Standards-and-Guidelines/Codes-Guidelines-Policies.aspx)

A risk assessment form that the APS refers to in training workshops (public domain) is the: Australian Institute for Suicide Research and Prevention (AISRAP) Protocol Suicide Risk Assessment (www.psychology.org.au/practitioner/clinical/resources).

The APS website (see www.psychology.org.au/practitioner/clinical/resources) also lists a series of Clinical Practice Guidelines for the management of the suicidal person and self-harm, both acute and chronic including:

- the Royal Australian and New Zealand College of Psychiatrists (RANZCP) guidelines commissioned by the Australian Department of Health
- the National Institute for Health and Care Excellence (NICE) guidelines from the UK.

Treatment

Treatment is best when individualised and will depend on the circumstances. Thus, a client may be at risk of suicide, by virtue of a mental illness such as severe depression in bipolar disorder. Treatment in this instance may be directed at the illness episode, including medication, and safe keeping during the period of risk through increased observation in hospital or by family.

The client may have attempted suicide by overdose following upsetting circumstances and have been referred to a psychologist for follow-up as an outpatient after medical clearance. The case study that follows later in this chapter illustrates some of the issues involved. Typically, a crisis intervention approach is taken in the short term, identifying the problems that have contributed to the presentation and resolving these where possible. This helps the client to return to their status quo and use their coping skills to adjust and deal with problems.

There will often be value in assisting the client to develop more advanced problem-solving skills, enhance their social connectedness, and build their self-esteem; in particular, using techniques from cognitive behaviour therapy (CBT). Reducing substance use, particularly alcohol, is often important.

Prevention of suicide

Public health initiatives to prevent suicide in Australia and NZ are many and varied. They have solid foundations in programs shown to reduce self-harm rates. Typically, these involve engaging a whole community. They include: up-skilling general medical practitioners in enquiring about and recognising suicidal preoccupations and treating commonly associated conditions such as: depression; enlisting lay people in positions of influence in the community such as teachers and spiritual leaders (ministers, priests, and rabbis); positive broad media campaigns advising people that help is available and how to access assistance; and targeting at-risk groups with services such as help phone lines.

An overview of activity in the sector is given in Suicide Prevention Australia (2014) *Discussion paper: One World Connected: An Assessment of Australia's Progress in*

Suicide Prevention (see http://suicidepreventionaust.org). Lifeline is a well-established non-government organisation that provides volunteer-serviced phone support for persons troubled by thoughts of suicide (see www.lifeline.org.au; www.lifeline.org.nz). beyondblue, the National Depression Initiative, has been highly active in destigmatisation of depression in Australia, and provides extensive psychoeducational resources. It is also a frequently recommended resource in NZ (see www.beyondblue.org.au).

New Zealand case study

This case has been created as an example for illustrative purposes.

Luke is 20 years old and lives with his older brother and sister-in-law and their two young children in a small NZ city. He moved from his home marae in a rural area 3 years ago after he left school, having not completed the final year qualifications. Since then he has had several jobs as a kitchenhand in cafes. Initially, he struggled with the regular commitment that work requires but has held his current job for 14 months, made good relationships with his workmates, and is thinking of training as a chef.

Luke's whanau (extended family) back home have had loose connections to the Black Power gang for many years. When Luke was in mid-childhood, his father spent several years in jail after being an accessory to an armed robbery in which a police officer was injured. His mother had a volatile personality and a drinking problem. She found it difficult to care for her five children, of which Luke is the second youngest. Because the older children were leaving home and living their own lives, Luke adopted a role of responsibility for his younger sister, to whom he was close. He would frequently intervene when their mother was in a drunken rage or arguing with one of her various boyfriends. Luke's younger sister has recently disclosed that she had been sexually abused by one of their mother's boyfriends while their dad was in prison.

Luke's sister recently made a serious suicide attempt by jumping from a height and spent several weeks in hospital. Since then Luke has been plagued by increasing thoughts that he failed his sister when they were children. For the past 6 weeks, he has been experiencing initial insomnia and anxiety about leaving the house, and has had trouble focusing at work. This has now been noticed by his co-workers as he has been overlooking tasks at work. The usually placid Luke has become irritable with others and has begun using alcohol to manage his symptoms. Last week after an evening drinking with friends, Luke went home and attempted to hang himself in the garden shed. He was interrupted by his sister-in-law who saw the light on.

An ambulance was called and Luke was admitted to hospital overnight for observation. Fortunately, he suffered only some bruising to his neck. He was transferred to the care of a community mental health team. The clinical psychologist assigned to his care allowed several sessions of 1 hour per week to gain Luke's trust, as he was initially very guarded. It appeared after thorough assessment that Luke was in the early stages of depressive illness, and CBT was his preferred mode of treatment. After some 6 weeks of treatment Luke has revealed to his therapist that the man who had abused his sister had also tried to abuse him but had not persisted when Luke resisted and repeatedly threatened to report him. Luke's mood symptoms continue to reduce and he has been able to see that his sister's abuse was the responsibility of the abuser, not himself.

Luke has become able to recognise his strengths and to self-manage his distress and anxiety when it arises, although this has become less frequent. A meeting with his sister was facilitated and she has planned to move to the city to live with her older brothers and finish her final year at school.

Australian Psychological Society – stigmatising language

In 2013, the APS outlined some suicide stigmatising language and the more acceptable alternatives. For example:

- stigmatising
  - committed suicide
  - failed attempt at suicide
  - successful suicide
- acceptable
  - died by suicide
  - non-fatal attempt at suicide
  - suicided.

New Zealand – SoPop

The Social Psychiatry and Population Mental Health Research Unit (SoPop) is a multidisciplinary team of researchers and clinicians. SoPop contributes to knowledge, policy, and services by conducting high-quality research in the areas of mental health, mental illness, and suicide prevention. In the last 2 years alone, five publications from the group have focused on suicide and self-harm including the role of culture in suicide prevention and those attending emergency departments due to intentional self-harm. Interested in learning more? One of the authors of this chapter, Professor Sunny Collings, is the director of SoPop. Visit SoPop online www.otago.ac.nz/wellington/research/sopop/ for further information.

References

Australian Bureau of Statistics. (2007). *National survey of mental health and wellbeing: Summary of results.* Cat no. 4326.0. Canberra: Author. Available: www.abs.gov.au/ausstats/abs@.nsf/mf/4326.0

Australian Bureau of Statistics. (2010). *Suicides.* Cat. no. 3309.0. Canberra: Author. Available: www.abs.gov.au/ausstats/abs@.nsf/Latestproducts/8D157E15E9D912E7CA2 57A440014CE53?opendocument

Australian Bureau of Statistics. (2015). *Causes of death, Australia 2013.* Cat. no. 3303.0. Canberra: Author. Available: www.abs.gov.au/AUSSTATS/abs@.nsf/DetailsPage/3303. 02013?OpenDocument#Data

Australian Psychological Society. (2013) *Suicide and language: Why we shouldn't use the 'C' word.* Melbourne: Author. Available: www.psychology.org.au/Content.aspx?ID = 5048

Bilsker, D., & White, J. (2011). The silent epidemic of male suicide. *BC Medical Journal, 53*(10), 529–534. Available: www.bcmj.org/articles/silent-epidemic-male-suicide

Eisenwort, B., Berzlanovich, A., Willinger, U., Eisenwort, G., Lindorfer, S., & Sonneck, G. (2006). Suicide notes and their importance to suicide research. The representativeness of suicide note writers. *Zentrum Fur Public Health, 77*(11), 1355–1356.

Hawton, K., Sutton, L., Haw, C., Sinclair, J., & Deeks, J. J. (2005). Schizophrenia and suicide: Systematic review of risk factors. *British Journal of Psychiatry, 187*(1), 9–20.

Hunter, E., & Harvey, D. (2002). Indigenous suicide in Australia, New Zealand, Canada, and the United States. *Emergency Medicine (Fremantle), 14*(1), 14–23.

Jamison, K. R. (2000). Suicide and bipolar disorder. *Journal of Clinical Psychiatry, 61*(9), 47–51.

Kessler, R. C., Borges, G., & Walters, E. E. (1999). Prevalence of and risk factors for lifetime suicide attempts in the national comorbidity survey. *Archives of General Psychiatry, 56*(7), 617–626. http://dx.doi.org/10.1001/archpsyc.56.7.617

Large, M., & Nielssen, O. B. (2010). Suicide in Australia: Meta-analysis of rates and methods of suicide between 1988 and 2007. *Medical Journal of Australia, 192*(8), 432–437.

Ministry of Health New Zealand. (2015a). *Suicide and intentional self-harm.* Wellington, NZ: Author. Available: www.health.govt.nz/our-work/populations/maori-health/tatau-kahukura-maori-health-statistics/nga-mana-hauora-tutohu-health-status-indicators/suicide-and-intentional-self-harm

Ministry of Health New Zealand. (2015b). *Suicide facts: deaths and intentional self-harm hospitalisations 2012.* Wellington, NZ: Author. Available: www.health.govt.nz/publication/suicide-facts-deaths-and-intentional-self-harm-hospitalisations-2012

Snowdon, J., & Hunt, G. E. (2008). Age, period and cohort effects on suicide rates in Australia, 1919–1999. *Acta Psychiatrica Scandinavica, 105*(4), 265–270.

Statistics New Zealand. (2016). *New Zealand social indicators. Suicide.* January. Available: www.stats.govt.nz/browse_for_stats/snapshots-of-nz/nz-social-indicators/Home/Health/suicide.aspx

Winchel, R. M., & Stanley, M. (1991). Self-injurious behavior: A review of the behavior and biology of self-mutilation. *The American Journal of Psychiatry, 148*(3), 306–317.

Acknowledgements

Special thanks to Natalie Jackson, demographer, for her assistance with the statistical referencing for this chapter.

26

Compulsory treatment

Christopher Ryan, Cristina Cavezza, Gregg Shinkfield,
and Sascha Callaghan

Introduction

Self-determination is greatly valued in Australasian society. The primacy given
to an individual's autonomy is reflected both in various ethical codes (Australian
Psychological Society, 2007; New Zealand Psychological Society, 2012) and in law as it
applies to psychological treatment.

Generally, individuals should not be provided treatment unless they are adequately
informed of its risks, its benefits, and the alternatives available to them. Individuals
then freely agree to the treatment offered. If a psychologist failed to gain valid consent
in this way, and some injury to the client were to result, the psychologist could be open
to a claim of negligence (Kerridge, Lowe, & Stewart, 2013). Additionally, it is generally
unlawful to restrict the movement of, or even touch, another person without his or her
consent.

In most cases, as long as adults are able to understand the information relevant to a
treatment choice, and are able to adequately consider that information, they cannot be
forced to have treatment they refuse (Ryan, Callaghan, & Peisah, 2015). This is true even
if their refusal will result in their own serious injury or death. This is why, for example,
people of the Jehovah's Witness faith can successfully refuse certain medical procedures.

There are circumstances, however, where the law permits treatment without
consent. Some of these circumstances relate to psychological conditions. The laws and
ethical considerations that apply in these circumstances are the subject of this chapter.

Compulsory treatment of severe psychiatric illness

Each jurisdiction in Australia and New Zealand (NZ) has a mental health Act that
sets down conditions under which a person with a serious mental illness may be
detained and treated without consent. In the Acts, the definitions of mental illness are

described in terms of various symptoms (e.g., delusions, serious disturbance of mood, irrationality). The exact definitions vary between jurisdictions but all are designed to capture not only severe depression, mania, and schizophrenia, but also people temporarily overcome with emotional turmoil, such as might occur in extreme grief.

As outlined so far, general medical treatment cannot be given to an adult unless the adult has lost the ability to understand and weigh the information relevant to the decision. Up until 2014, however, the presence or absence of decision-making capacity was not relevant to whether or not a person could be forced to have psychiatric treatment under any piece of Australasian mental health legislation (Callaghan & Ryan, 2014). In 2008, both Australia and NZ ratified the United Nations *Convention of the Rights of Persons with Disabilities* (United Nations, 2006). The Convention stipulates "States Parties shall recognise that persons with disabilities enjoy legal capacity on an equal basis with others" (United Nations, 2006, Article 12 Item 2). As a result of the ratification, all Australian jurisdictions that have reviewed their mental health legislation in recent years have reformed their Acts to make the presence or absence of decision-making capacity more important.

Currently, different mental health Acts give varying levels of prominence to decision-making capacity. In Tasmania and Western Australia, recently reformed mental health Acts provide that compulsory psychiatric treatment cannot be given unless the person lacks decision-making capacity. In Victoria, New South Wales, and the Australian Capital Territory, however, although recent reforms made decision-making capacity more prominent, legislators stopped short of mandating its absence before compulsory treatment can be given. The remaining Australian jurisdictions and NZ are yet to complete reforms influenced by the Convention.

Whether or not a mental health Act includes a reference to decision-making capacity, in all jurisdictions compulsory treatment will not be able to be delivered unless it can be demonstrated that without treatment the mentally ill person, or members of the public, may come to some sort of harm (variously defined in the several Acts) and unless compulsory treatment represents the option least restrictive of the person's freedom or human rights. Since it is increasingly recognised that it is not possible to usefully identify a group of acute psychiatric patients who are at relatively higher risk of harm to themselves or others (Ryan & Large, 2013), it is this "least restrictive option" arm that is often the element that determines if compulsory treatment can be provided or not (Ryan, Callaghan, & Large, 2015).

In all jurisdictions, it is a clinician who makes the initial determination of whether or not a person can be subject to compulsory psychiatric treatment. Usually this clinician is a medical practitioner or psychiatrist, but in some jurisdictions, psychologists are empowered to order initial detention and treatment after completing special training. To better protect patient rights, most jurisdictions require that these initial clinician-based determinations are confirmed by at least one other clinician within days. The determination must then also be reviewed by a tribunal, in NZ by a court, within days or weeks. Psychologists may be called on to present at these tribunal inquiries and to provide evidence that the patient fulfils criteria for compulsory treatment. Research has demonstrated that tribunals only rarely disagree with the conclusions of the treating clinicians and this has raised some concerns as to whether these inquiries represent effective safeguards of patient rights (Carney et al., 2011; Thom, 2014).

The Code of Ethics of the Australian Psychological Society (APS) stipulates that even if a client's consent is not required under the law, a psychologist should still "as far as practically possible" properly inform the client and gain consent (2007). The Society's Guidelines for Psychological Practice in Forensic Contexts gives further detail on obtaining consent in such situations (Australian Psychological Society, 2013).

Every mental health Act in Australia and NZ also contains provisions to allow compulsory treatment in the community. These provisions often go by different names, but they are most commonly referred to as community treatment orders (CTOs). CTOs can only be ordered if the patient meets criteria that are the same or similar to the relevant criteria for compulsory hospital treatment, but it is thought that community treatment is a safe and workable alternative for the individual. In practice, CTOs tend to be applied to people with severe mental illness who have repeatedly relapsed for reasons associated with treatment non-compliance. The conditions of a CTO are tailored to an individual client and usually include the requirement that the person continue to take regular psychiatric medication. However, some form of compulsory psychological treatment is also very common and this may involve psychologists in a CTO regime.

Research in 2012 revealed that rates of CTO use in Australasia were very high by international standards, that rates were increasing, and that rates varied more than threefold between jurisdictions (Light et al., 2012). Given that there is a paucity of evidence to support any claim that CTOs are effective in deceasing re-admission or improving other outcomes these figures are concerning (Kisely & Hall, 2014). It may be that the new prominence given to decision-making capacity in mental health legislation will see a decrease in CTO use, since it is likely that many people placed on CTOs previously retained decision-making capacity and thus may not be able to be compulsorily treated under reformed legislation (Ryan, Callaghan, & Peisah, 2015).

Each jurisdiction's mental health legislation also contains provisions designed to allow careful review of the use of electroconvulsive therapy (ECT) and neurosurgical interventions for psychiatric illness (frequently referred to as psychosurgery). Typically, consent for these interventions must be given, or reviewed, by a specialist tribunal, and at times psychologists may be called to give evidence as to a patient's cognitive function or decision-making capacity.

Compulsory treatment of people with cognitive impairment

In Australia, the unconsented treatment of people with cognitive impairment that is due to causes other than a mental illness (e.g., dementia and intellectual impairment) is usually regulated by one of the variously named guardianship Acts. Each jurisdiction's Act provides authority for a relative or close friend, or in certain circumstances a tribunal, to consent to treatment on behalf of the incompetent patient. Generally speaking, substitute decision makers are bound to make decisions in the patient's best interests or decisions that promote or maintain the patient's health and wellbeing. Substitute decision makers must also make decisions least restrictive of the person's rights. These and similar legislative instruments also allow patients, while they are competent, to appoint people (variously termed as appointed health attorneys, enduring guardians, or medical agents) to consent to medical treatment after capacity is lost (Kerridge et al., 2013). In NZ, similar provisions exist under the *Protection of Personal and Property Rights Act 1988.*

In some jurisdictions, mental illness is defined by local mental health legislation sufficiently broad to allow some psychological treatment of people with dementia. However, in most circumstances the provisions of the guardianship-type legislation offer better protection of the incompetent individual's rights. For this reason, generally, the guardianship-like legislative instruments are to be preferred unless the person is suffering classic psychiatric symptoms such as delusions or hallucinations.

Compulsory treatment of substance use disorders

New South Wales, Victoria, Tasmania, Northern Territory, and NZ have legislation that facilitates the compulsory treatment of people severely affected by substance use disorders (Pritchard, Mugavin, & Swan, 2007). The provisions of these Acts vary enormously but tend to mirror those of the older mental health Acts written before the influence of the *Convention on the Rights of Persons with Disabilities.* They require that the person be dependent on a substance, although definitions of dependence vary, as do the substances covered, between jurisdictions. Each Act requires that a judgement be made that, because of the substance dependence, the welfare, health, or safety of the substance-dependent person, or the welfare, health, or safety of another is likely to be compromised. Again, the wording varies remarkably between Acts. In NZ, for example, an "alcoholic" or a "drug addict" need only cause "serious annoyance" to others to meet criteria for detention. No current Act contains a requirement that the person lack decision-making capacity with respect to a decision to refuse treatment. Those who may initiate this sort of civil compulsory substance dependence treatment also varies between jurisdictions, but in some a psychologist might be able to apply on behalf of a patient or their family. In all jurisdictions, medical practitioners are involved in the initial assessment and a tribunal or magistrate must initiate or eventually review the order, but the period of time before review is required varies enormously.

Like the older mental health Acts, these Acts may be used to force treatment on adults who are competent to refuse it, and as a result they are in violation of the *Convention.* In addition, there is very little evidence that this sort of coerced treatment is effective in substance dependence, a fact which psychologists are likely obliged to inform their clients of and one which may interfere with the application of some of the more modern laws that require that there be a reasonable prospect that the person will benefit from the compulsory treatment.

While only the five jurisdictions noted at the start of this section have laws enabling compulsory treatment of substance dependence in a civil context, all Australasian jurisdictions have legal regimes to facilitate the compulsory treatment of offenders who are alcohol or drug dependent. In some circumstances, the offender may be legally bound to comply with treatment, while in others undergoing treatment may be an option the offender is free to take up if he or she wishes to avoid significant negative consequences.

Depending on the jurisdiction, diversion measures may occur at any point along an offender's journey through the criminal justice system (Joudo, 2008). Pre-arrest, police may offer minor offenders a prescribed education or treatment program in order to avoid a charge. Pre-trial, a magistrate may refer an offender for assessment and subsequent compliance with a recommended treatment plan to avoid a conviction. Magistrates may also delay sentence of a substance-dependent offender, diverting them into treatment and potentially avoiding a criminal record. Alternatively, magistrates may impose treatment programs diverting offenders from incarceration. Lastly, a convicted prisoner may gain early release if discharged into a supervised residential or non-residential treatment program.

In Australia, there are specific diversion programs for Aboriginal and Torres Strait Islander people at both the police and court level. Likewise, in NZ, Kaupapa Māori substance treatment services have been developed which demonstrate better retention rates of Māori clients than mainstream services (New Zealand Ministry of Health, 2010). Most jurisdictions aim to modify mainstream programs and employ Indigenous workers to ensure programs are culturally appropriate.

Emergency compulsory treatment

The mental health Acts of each Australian and NZ jurisdiction contain provision for an individual to be detained and treated in a designated mental health service in an emergency situation. While the specific provisions vary across jurisdictions, typically emergency involuntary treatment can only occur if a delay in treatment could be reasonably deemed to cause a deleterious effect on the person's health. A person is initially detained and compelled into assessment or treatment via a short-term order (e.g., Inpatient Assessment Order in Victoria, Emergency Examination Order in Queensland), which typically lasts for 24 to 48 hours. Once received into care, the clinician responsible (typically a psychiatrist or other medical professional), must then follow the normal application process required in non-emergency situations to permit ongoing compulsory care, as specified in the legislation of each jurisdiction.

Compulsory treatment of "dangerous offenders"

NZ and four Australian states (New South Wales, Victoria, Queensland, and Western Australia) have legislation facilitating the treatment of a certain class of offender, most commonly sex offenders, judged to be at high risk of recidivism. These statutes function to create orders that are operative while the person is on parole, or after the period when any sort of sentence would otherwise have ended. The orders may require that the offender participate in a treatment program which may include both psychological input and pharmacological agents such as antiandrogens (McSherry, Keyzer, & Freiberg, 2006). In some states, psychologists may be involved in assessments used by the court to determine if the orders should apply. Psychologists can certainly be involved in conducting therapy aimed at reducing the likelihood of recidivism.

These provisions raise similar ethical issues about the role of a psychologist in treating a person (who in some cases has already served out the punishment for their crime) being compelled, or at least strongly coerced, to undergo psychological treatment. Again, these issues are further complicated by a paucity of evidence to support the notion that coerced treatment is effective at reducing recidivism among sex offenders (Dennis et al., 2012).

New Zealand case study

This case has been created as an example for illustrative purposes and is not based on an actual client. It demonstrates the process of coming into contact with mental health services, receiving compulsory inpatient treatment, and voluntary community follow-up care.

Paul is a 23-year-old man living with his parents in Auckland, NZ. His father is Samoan and his mother is of Irish ancestry. Paul was born in Auckland. He has one older brother and sister. Both of his siblings are married with children and live within the same community. Paul would regularly spend time with his family and attend gatherings at their local Christian church. Paul had been in an 8-year relationship with a woman, named Suzanne, whom he thought he would marry. He was a social drinker and had experimented with cannabis in his teens. Paul was employed as a mechanic.

Recently, Paul discovered that Suzanne was having an affair. To deal with his anger and sadness over the break up, Paul began drinking more frequently and consuming more alcohol on his own whereas previously he tended to drink in the company of friends. In addition to an increase in alcohol consumption, Paul began experimenting with various illicit substances, including methamphetamine. Paul's substance use quickly began affecting his familial and work responsibilities. He became erratic, often arriving at work late, and had a few verbal altercations at work. Paul accused his co-workers of purposefully sabotaging his work and came to believe that someone was trying to harm him. Around this time, he had increased to daily methamphetamine use and he was beginning to isolate himself from his family and friends. He also stopped attending church and his family was becoming quite concerned. One evening while intoxicated on methamphetamines, he was walking alone in the Auckland City Centre when he came to believe someone was following him and wanted to kill him. He approached a stranger on the street and suddenly began screaming: "What do you want from me? Why are you trying to hurt me?" At this point, Paul was scared for his own wellbeing but appeared highly agitated and verbally aggressive towards the stranger. A bystander who happened to notice what was taking place alerted police, who attended the scene and approached Paul. Paul began expressing persecutory themes that someone was trying to kill him. Paul's speech was rapid, difficult to follow, and incoherent. After questioning witnesses and trying to calm Paul down, the police decided to take Paul to the emergency department where he was assessed by the triage team.

Paul was assessed by a consultant psychiatrist who deemed it necessary for Paul to be detained in hospital on an order as set out in part 1 of the *Mental Health (Compulsory Assessment and Treatment) Act 1992*. As such, Paul was admitted into the inpatient psychiatric ward (Te Whetu Tawera) at Auckland City Hospital for compulsory psychiatric treatment. Given his recent methamphetamine intoxication and persecutory delusions that someone was trying to harm him, Paul received a provisional diagnosis of substance-induced psychotic disorder and was under careful medical observation to control his withdrawal symptoms.

Paul's mental state and intoxicated condition have been carefully monitored by hospital staff. He has also met with the clinical psychologist to discuss his previous drug use and paranoia. Fortunately, with the withdrawal from methamphetamines, Paul's mental state has improved fairly rapidly and within 2 weeks he is no longer experiencing paranoid thoughts that someone is trying to harm him.

With support from his family and hospital staff, Paul has realised that he requires ongoing drug and alcohol counselling. Paul is discharged from hospital and is receiving drug and alcohol counselling in the community to assist him in developing a relapse prevention plan and avoid further drug use. He is continuing to live with his parents and plans to resume working.

Emergency contacts for mental health services

- Australian Capital Territory: 1800 629 354
- New South Wales: 1800 011 511
- Northern Territory: 1800 682 288
- Queensland: 13 HEALTH (13 432 584)
- South Australia: 13 14 65
- Tasmania: 1800 332 288

continued ›

> **continued ›**
>
> - Victoria: Call the local mental health team as listed at www.health.vic.gov.au/mentalhealthservices
> - Western Australia: 1800 522 002
> - New Zealand: Call the local mental health team as listed at www.health.govt.nz/your-health/services-and-support/health-care-services/mental-health-services/crisis-assessment-teams

References

Australian Psychological Society. (2007). *Code of ethics*. Melbourne: Author.

Australian Psychological Society. (2013). *Guidelines for psychological practice in forensic contexts*. Melbourne: Author.

Callaghan, S., & Ryan, C. J. (2014). Is there a future for involuntary treatment in rights-based mental health law? *Psychiatry, Psychology and Law, 21*(5), 747–766. http://dx.doi.org/10.1080/13218719.2014.949606

Carney, T., Tait, D., Perry, J., Vernon, A., & Beaupert, F. (2011). *Australian mental health tribunals: Space for fairness, freedom, protection and treatment?* Sydney: Themis.

Dennis, J. A., Khan, O., Ferriter, M., Huband, N., Powney, M. J., & Duggan, C. (2012). Psychological interventions for adults who have sexually offended or are at risk of offending. *Cochrane Database of Systematic Reviews, 12*, CD007507.

Joudo, J. (2008). *Responding to substance abuse and offending in Indigenous communities: Review of diversion programs*. Research and public policy series no. 88. Canberra: Australian Institute of Criminology. Available: www.aic.gov.au/documents/1/8/0/%7b1807C117–551B-4D5A-B30C-CF07EF532F7D%7drpp88.pdf

Kerridge, I., Lowe, M., & Stewart, C. (2013). *Ethics and law for the health professions* (4th ed.). Sydney: Federation Press.

Kisely, S., & Hall, K. (2014). An updated meta-analysis of randomized controlled evidence for the effectiveness of community treatment orders. *Canadian Journal of Psychiatry, 59*(10), 561–564.

Light, E. M., Kerridge, I. H., Ryan, C. J., & Robertson, M. (2012). Community treatment orders: Rates and patterns of use. *Australasian Psychiatry, 20*, 478–482.

McSherry, B., Keyzer, P., & Freiberg, A. (2006). Preventive detention for "dangerous" offenders in Australia: A critical analysis and proposals for policy development. *Report to the Criminology Research Council*. Available: www.criminologyresearchcouncil.gov.au/reports/200405–03.pdf

New Zealand Ministry of Health. (2010). *Mental health and addiction: Service use 2009/10*. Wellington, NZ: Author. Available: www.health.govt.nz/publication/mental-health-and-addiction-service-use-2009-10

New Zealand Psychological Society. (2012). *Code of ethics for psychologists working in Aotearoa/New Zealand*. Wellington, NZ: Author. Available: www.psychologistsboard.org.nz/cms_show_download.php?id=237

Pritchard, E., Mugavin, J., & Swan, A. (2007). *Compulsory treatment in Australia. A discussion paper on the compulsory treatment of individuals dependent on alcohol and/or other drugs*. Canberra: Australian National Council on Drugs. Available: http://apo.org.au/node/8087

Ryan, C. J., Callaghan, S., & Large, M. M. (2015). The importance of least restrictive care: The clinical implications of a recent High Court decision on negligence. *Australasian Psychiatry, 23*(4), 415–417.

Ryan, C. J., Callaghan, S., & Peisah, C. (2015). The capacity to refuse psychiatric treatment – A guide to the law for clinicians and tribunal members. *Australian & New Zealand Journal of Psychiatry, 49*(4), 324–333.

Ryan, C. J., & Large, M. M. (2013). Suicide risk assessment: Where are we now? *Medical Journal of Australia, 198*(9), 462–463. http://dx.doi.org/10.5694/mja13.10437

Thom, K. (2014). New Zealand Mental Health Review Tribunal characteristics and outcomes 1993–2011. *Australasian Psychiatry, 22*(4), 341–344. http://dx.doi.org/10.1177/1039856214541300

United Nations. (2006). *Convention on the rights of persons with disabilities*. Available: www.un.org/disabilities/convention/conventionfull.shtml.

Index

abnormality, psychological, 6–7
Aboriginal and Torres Strait Islander populations
  see Indigenous population
abuse *see* adult abuse; child abuse
acceptance and commitment therapy (ACT),
  120–1, 124
acquired diversity, 10, 34
acute stress disorders (ASD), 143, 145–7, 148–9
addictions, behavioural, 229
  See *also* substance-related and addictive
  disorders
adjustment disorders, 143
adult abuse, 278
age–sex structures, of mental health
  professionals, 28, 48–50
age structures
  of Australian Indigenous population, 17–18
  birth rates and, 23, 42
  birthplace and, 39–41
  employment rates and, 28, 47
  family/household compositions and, 25, 43,
    44
  income and, 48
  of migrant populations, 20–1
  mortality rates and, 24, 43
  of New Zealand's ethnic groups, 37–8, 39
  qualification levels and, 26, 27, 46
  spatial diversity and, 15–16
  suicidal behaviours related to, 292
agoraphobia, 117, 122
alarm training, 191
Alzheimer's disease
  assessment, 246
  prevalence and mortality rates, 245, 248
  research, 252
  treatment and prevention, 247–8
  See *also* neurocognitive disorders (NCDs)
ancestry (statistics), 21
anger management, 221–2
anorexia nervosa (AN)
  clinical description, 175
  obsessive compulsive disorder and, 135
  prevalence, 176–7
  treatment and assessment, 177–9, 183

antisocial personality disorder, 224
anxiety disorders
  in Australia, 117–22
  case study, 124
  clinical description, 116–17
  comorbidity with, 118, 122
  in New Zealand, 122–3
  prevalence, 117–20, 122–3
  treatment and assessment, 119–22, 123
assisted suicide, 293
attention deficit hyperactivity disorder
    (ADHD)
  diagnosis, 65
  prevalence, 66, 69
  treatment, 68, 70
attention processes, 161–2
Australia
  diversity in, 10, 11
  socio-economic characteristics, 26–8
  See *also* demographic factors; socio-
  demographic characteristics
Australian Imaging, Biomarker and
    Lifestyle (AIBL) Flagship Studying of
    Aging, 245–6
Australian Schizophrenia Research Bank (ASRB),
    88
autistic spectrum disorder (ASD)
  case study, 71
  diagnosis, 65
  in the Māori population, 70
  prevalence, 66, 69
  research, 67
  support services, 69
  treatment and assessment, 68–9, 70
avoidant/restrictive food intake disorder
    (ARFID), 176–7

Balance NZ, 112
behavioural addictions, 229
  See *also* substance-related and addictive
  disorders
behavioural therapy *see* psychological
    treatment
binge eating disorder (BED)

clinical description, 176
consequences, 177
prevalence, 176–7
treatment and assessment, 177–9
bipolar and related disorders
in Australia, 107–9
case study, 111–12
clinical description, 106
comorbidity with, 106, 110
diagnostic criteria, 106–7
education and research on, 109
genetics and, 76
history, 76
in New Zealand, 109–11
prevalence and impact, 106, 107,
109–11
research, 108
support services, 112
treatment and assessment, 108–9, 111
in young people, 108
bipolar I disorder, 107
bipolar II disorder, 107
birth rates, 23, 42
birthplace data, 20–1, 39–44
Bleuler, Eugen, 76
body dysmorphic disorder (BDD)
aetiology, 131
clinical description, 130
treatment, 133, 136
borderline personality disorder (BPD)
case study, 262–3
treatment, 260, 261, 263
bowel program, 191
brief psychotic disorder, 78
bulimia nervosa (BN)
case study, 181
clinical description, 175
consequences, 177
obsessive compulsive disorder and, 135
prevalence, 176–7
treatment and assessment, 177–9

Cade, John, 108–9
cannabis use, psychosis and, 85
CAPS-5 (diagnostic interview), 146–7
case studies
anxiety disorders, 124
bipolar disorders, 111–12
compulsory treatment, 306–7

conversion disorder, 167
depression, 100–1
disruptive, impulse-control, and conduct
disorders, 224
elimination disorders, 196
feeding and eating disorders, 181
hoarding disorder, 137–8
neurocognitive disorders, 250–1
neurodevelopmental disorders, 71
paraphilic disorders, 271–2
personality disorders, 262–3
posttraumatic stress disorder, 149–51
schizophrenia, 87–8
sleep-wake disorders, 209–10
substance-related and addictive disorders,
235–6
suicidal behaviours, 297–8
child abuse, 277–9, 280–1
childhood-onset fluency disorder (stuttering),
65, 67
children, mental illness in, 86
Christchurch earthquakes (2010, 2011), 35–6,
148, 282
Christchurch Health and Development Study
(CHDS), 85, 148, 284
circadian rhythm sleep-wake disorder,
206–7
clozapine, 80
cognitive appraisal processes, 135
cognitive behaviour therapy (CBT)
for anxiety disorders, 120–1, 124
for bipolar disorders, 109
for depression, 97, 99
for feeding and eating disorders, 182
for obsessive compulsive disorder, 133,
138
for schizophrenia, 80–1
for somatic symptom and related disorders,
166
cognitive impairments, compulsory treatment
for, 303–4
cognitive inhibition, 161–2
cognitive remediation therapy (CRT), 81,
88–9
communication disorders, neurodevelopmental,
65, 67, 68
community treatment orders (CTOs), 303
compulsions see obsessive compulsive disorder
(OCD)

compulsory treatment
  appointed decision makers, 303–4
  case study, 306–7
  in emergency situations, 305
  for high risk offenders, 306
  legislation regarding, 301–3
  standard safeguards against, 301
  of substance-use disorders, 304–5
conduct disorder (CD)
  assessment and diagnosis, 219–20
  clinical description, 216–17, 219
  comorbidity with, 219, 220
  prevalence and impact, 219–20
  treatment, 220–2
Convention of the Rights of Persons with Disabilities, 302
conversion disorder, 167
counsellors, 7, 8
courtship disorder model, 268
cyclothymic disorder, 107

danger ideation reduction therapy (DIRT), 132
data, diversity, 10–11, 34
death rates *see* mortality rates
delusional disorder, 78
dementia *see* neurocognitive disorders (NCDs)
demographic factors
  Australia, 10, 11–18
  New Zealand, 35–6
  See also socio-demographic characteristics; socio-economic characteristics
depersonalisation/derealisation disorder (DRD), 155
depression
  aetiology, 96
  assessment, 96
  in Australia, 95–8
  case study, 100–1
  clinical description, 94–5
  genetics and, 99
  in New Zealand, 98–9
  prevalence and impacts, 95, 98–9
  support services, 95, 101, 112
  treatment, 96–8, 99, 111
depressive disorders, 94–5
  See also depression; major depressive disorder (MDD)
developmental coordination disorder, 66

Diagnostic and statistical manual of mental disorders (5th ed.) (*DSM-5*), 6–7
disordered eating, 182
'disparate impact' discrimination, 19, 45–6
disruptive, impulse-control, and conduct disorders
  case study, 224
  clinical description, 216–17
  support services for, 225
dissociative amnesia (DA), 154–5, 156–7
dissociative disorders
  in Australia, 156–62
  clinical description, 154–6
  conflicting positions on, 156–7
  in New Zealand, 162–3
  research, 159–62
  treatment, 158–9
dissociative fugue, 155, 159
dissociative identity disorder (DID)
  clinical description, 155–6
  conflicting positions on, 156–7
  research, 159–62
  treatment, 158–9
diversion measures, 305
diversity data, 10–11, 34
divorce rates, 277, 280
drug therapy *see* pharmacological treatment
DSM-5 see Diagnostic and statistical manual of mental disorders
Dunedin Multidisciplinary Health and Development Study (DMHDS), 85–6
dyscalculia, 66
dyslexia, 66, 67
dysthymia, 111

earthquakes, community impact of, 35–6, 148, 282
eating disorders *see* feeding and eating disorders
education (statistics), 26–8, 46–7
electroconvulsive therapy (ECT), 109, 303
electroencephalogram (EEG) coherence, 159–60
elimination disorders
  in Australia, 190
  case study, 196
  clinical definition, 189–90
  in New Zealand, 194–6
  prevalence, 194

support services, 193–4, 195, 197
treatment and assessment, 190–4, 195–6
emergency situations, compulsory treatment in, 305
employment rates, 27–8, 47
encopresis (faecal soiling)
case study, 196
clinical definition, 189–90
prevalence, 190, 194
support services, 193–4, 195
treatment and assessment, 190–4, 195–6
engagement, clinical, 82–3
enuresis (wetting)
clinical definition, 189–90
prevalence, 190, 194
support services, 193–4, 195
treatment and assessment, 190–4, 195–6
environmental risks, schizophrenia and, 79
ethnic groups (New Zealand)
age structures of, 37–8, 39
anxiety disorders in, 123
bipolar disorders in, 110
neurocognitive disorders in, 248, 250
obsessive compulsive disorder in, 134, 135, 136–7
resident population, 36–9
schizophrenia in, 85
socio-demographic characteristics of, 39–44
socio-economic characteristics of, 46–8, 281
spatial distribution, 35
substance-related and addictive disorders in, 233, 234
See also Māori population
excoriation (skin picking), 130, 133
exhibitionistic disorder, 267–8, 271–2
exposure and response prevention (ERP), 132, 133, 134
externalising disorders *see* disruptive, impulse-control, and conduct disorders

family/household compositions, 24–6, 43–4
feeding and eating disorders
in Australia, 176–9
case study, 181
clinical description, 175–6
disordered eating and, 182
in New Zealand, 179–81, 183
obsessive compulsive disorder and, 135

prevalence, 176–7, 179–80
risk factors and consequences, 177, 180
support services, 179, 180–1
treatment and assessment, 177–9
fertility rates *see* birth rates
fetishistic disorder, 271

gambling disorder, 229–30, 231–3, 234–5
gender differentials *see* sex differentials
generalised anxiety disorder
age of onset, 118, 122
case study, 282–3
clinical description, 117
prevalence, 117, 122
treatment, 119, 121
generations (population waves), 19, 21
genetics
bipolar disorders and, 106
depression and, 99
obsessive-compulsive and related disorders and, 131
schizophrenia and, 76, 79, 88
screening, 68
global developmental delay (GDD), 64, 68
guardianship acts, 303–4

hallucinations, 160–1
heritability *see* genetics
hoarding disorder, 130, 131, 133, 137–8
homelessness, 279, 281
household/family compositions, 24–6, 43–4
hypersomnolence disorder, 205–6
hypomanic episode, 107

illness anxiety disorder (health anxiety), 165
income (statistics), 16, 35, 47–8
Indigenous Network Suicide Intervention Skills Training (INSIST), 101
Indigenous population (Australia)
age structures in, 16, 17–18
anxiety disorders in, 119–20
clinical approaches and considerations, 57–60
conduct disorders in, 222
culture and identity, 57, 59–60
depression in, 95
disparate impact on, 19
diversion programs for, 305
feeding and eating disorders in, 176, 178
mental illness in, 107

Indigenous population (Australia) (*cont.*)
　narrative therapy and, 60, 97–8
　neurocognitive disorders in, 251–2
　neurodevelopmental disorders in, 68
　obsessive-compulsive and related disorders in,
　　133–4
　parenting intervention programs in, 277
　population composition, 17–18, 39
　posttraumatic stress disorder in, 145
　socio-demographic characteristics of, 22, 23–6
　socio-economic characteristics of, 26–7, 28,
　　279
　substance-related and addictive disorders in,
　　230, 231, 232
　suicidal behaviours in, 291
　suicide risk in, 95
　support services for, 54–5, 101, 283
　violence in, 278
　See also Māori population
inherent diversity, 10, 34
insomnia disorder, 204–5
intellectual development disorder, 64–5
intellectual disability, 64–5
intentional self-harm *see* suicidal behaviours
intermittent explosive disorder, 222–4
internet gaming disorder (IGD), 230, 233, 235,
　236

jet lag, 207

Kimberly Indigenous Cognitive Assessment
　(KICA-Cog), 251–2
Kraeplin, Emil, 76

language disorder, 65
languages, dominant, 22, 41–4
learning disorders *see* specific learning disorders
legislation, mental health, 301–3
life expectancy, 24, 43
lithium, 108–9

major depressive disorder (MDD)
　aetiology, 96
　clinical description and diagnosis, 94–5
　prevalence, 98
　treatment, 97
　See also depression
manic depression *see* bipolar and related
　disorders

manic episode, 107
Māori population
　age structure and, 41
　anxiety disorders in, 122–3
　autism spectrum disorder in, 70
　bipolar disorders in, 110
　disparate impact on, 19, 45–6
　dissociation in, 163
　diversion programs for, 305
　elimination disorders in, 195
　feeding and eating disorders in, 180
　mental health needs in, 99
　neurocognitive disorders in, 248, 250
　obsessive compulsive disorder in, 134, 135,
　　136–7, 138
　posttraumatic stress disorder in, 148
　resident population, 36–9
　schizophrenia in, 85, 87–8
　socio-demographic characteristics of, 41–4,
　　282
　socio-economic characteristics of, 46–8, 281
　spatial distribution, 35
　substance-related and addictive disorders in,
　　233, 234
　suicidal behaviours in, 291
　See also ethnic groups
marital status (statistics), 43–4
masochism, 268–9
mathematics, impairment in (dyscalculia), 66
medications *see* pharmacological treatment
memory processes, 161–2
mental health legislation, 301–3
mental health professionals, 7–8, 28, 48–50
mental illness, compulsory treatment of, 301–3
metacognitive therapy, 99, 132
migrant populations (Australia)
　depression in, 95
　socio-demographic characteristics of, 19–26
　socio-economic characteristics of, 15–16,
　　27–8
　spatial distribution, 12
migrant populations (New Zealand) *see* ethnic
　groups
mood disorders *see* bipolar and related disorders;
　depressive disorders
mortality rates, 24, 43, 77
motor disorders, neurodevelopmental, 66, 67
'multiple count' method, 36, 37
mutism, selective, 116

narrative therapy, 60, 97–8
National Disability Insurance Scheme, 69
natural disasters, psychological effects of, 148, 279–80, 282
neurocognitive disorders (NCDs)
  assessment, 246–7, 249–50
  in Australia, 245–8, 251–2
  case study, 250–1
  clinical description, 243–4
  DSM-5 coding for, 244–5
  in New Zealand, 248–50, 252
  prevalence and mortality rates, 245, 248
  research, 245–6, 252
  treatment and prevention, 247–9
neurodevelopmental disorders
  in Australia, 66–9
  case study, 71
  clinical description, 64–6
  incidence and prevalence, 66–7, 69–70
  in the Māori population, 70
  in New Zealand, 69–70
  related factors, 70
  research, 67
  support services, 69
  treatment and assessment, 67–9, 70
neurosurgical interventions (psychosurgery), 303
New Zealand
  diversity in, 10, 34, 36–9
  socio-economic characteristics, 35, 46–8, 281
  See also demographic factors; socio-demographic characteristics
nightmares, 208

obsessive-compulsive and related disorders
  in Australia, 130–4
  case study, 137–8
  clinical description, 129–30
  in New Zealand, 134–7
obsessive compulsive disorder (OCD)
  aetiology, 131–2, 135–6
  clinical description, 129–30
  comorbidity with, 135
  prevalence and impact, 130–1, 134–5
  support services, 138
  treatment and assessment, 132–4, 136–7
offenders (high risk), compulsory treatment for, 306

online therapies
  for anxiety disorders, 121
  for depression, 97
  for obsessive compulsive disorder, 132, 134, 138
oppositional defiant disorder (ODD)
  assessment and diagnosis, 218
  case study, 224
  clinical description, 216–17
  comorbidity with, 217, 218
  prevalence and impact, 218
  treatment, 218–19
oral tradition, 60
other specific dissociative disorder (OSDD), 156
other specified bipolar disorder, 107
other specified feeding or eating disorder (OSFED), 176

paedophilic disorder, 270
Pākehā populations *see* ethnic groups
panic disorder
  clinical description, 117
  prevalence, 117, 122
  treatment, 119, 121, 123
paraphilic disorders
  case study, 271–2
  clinical description and diagnosis, 266–7
  support services, 272–3
parasomnias, 207–8
partner abuse, 280–1
personality disorders
  in Australia, 260–1
  case study, 262–3
  clinical description, 258–9
  cultural perspectives on, 259–60
  in New Zealand, 261
  prevalence, 260, 261
  resembling schizophrenia, 79
  treatment and assessment, 260–1, 263
pervasive developmental disorders *see* autistic spectrum disorder (ASD)
pharmacological treatment
  for bipolar disorders, 108–9
  for exhibitionistic disorder, 268
  for neurodevelopmental disorders, 68
  for schizophrenia, 79, 80
  for somatic symptom and related disorders, 166

pica, 176–7
population share, 12
posttraumatic stress disorder (PTSD)
    in Australia, 144–7
    case study, 149–51
    clinical description and diagnosis, 143–4
    comorbidity with, 145, 146, 148
    prevalence and risk factors, 144–5, 148
    support services, 147
    treatment and assessment, 145–7,
        148–9
poverty, 279, 281
professionals *see* mental health professionals
psychiatric nurses, 49–50
psychiatrists, 7
psychological disorders, 6–7
psychological treatment
    for anxiety disorders, 119–22
    of Australian Indigenous population, 57–60
    for bipolar disorders, 109
    for dissociative disorders, 158–9
    for elimination disorders, 191–3, 196
    for exhibitionistic disorder, 268
    for neurodevelopmental disorders, 68–9
    for obsessive compulsive disorder (OCD),
        132–4
    for personality disorders, 260, 261, 263
    for posttraumatic stress disorder, 145–7
    for schizophrenia, 79, 80–1
    for somatic symptom and related disorders,
        166
    See also compulsory treatment
psychologists, 7, 8, 28, 48
psychopathology, 6–7
psychosis, 78, 81–2, 84
    See also schizophrenia
psychosurgery, 303
psychotic disorders *see* schizophrenia

qualification levels (statistics), 26–8, 46–7

reading, impairment in (dyslexia), 66, 67
regulation, of mental health professionals, 7–8
rehabilitation, vocational, 81
relational problems, 277, 280, 282–3
religious affiliations, 22–3, 42, 279, 282
residential distribution *see* spatial distribution
rumination disorder, 176–7
rural populations, 15, 119, 292

sadism, 269–70
schizoaffective disorder, 76, 78, 83–4
schizophrenia
    in Australia, 83–4
    case study, 87–8
    causes, 76, 79, 85–6
    clinical features and diagnosis, 77–8, 81–2
    history of, 76
    in New Zealand, 85–7
    obsessive compulsive disorder and, 136
    prevalence and impact, 77, 83–4, 85
    research, 84, 88
    spectrum and related disorders, 78–9
    support services, 83
    treatment and assessment, 79–83, 84, 86–7,
        88–9
schizophreniform disorders, 78, 85
selective mutism, 116
self-harm, intentional *see* suicidal behaviours
separation anxiety disorder, 116
sex differentials (statistics)
    in anxiety disorders, 118
    in disruptive, impulse-control, and conduct
        disorders, 219, 220
    in employment rates, 28
    of mental health professionals, 28, 29, 48,
        50
    in qualification levels, 26
    in substance-related and addictive disorders,
        232
    in suicidal behaviours, 291
sexual masochism disorder, 268–9
sexual sadism disorder, 269–70
sleep terrors, 208
sleep-wake disorders
    case study, 209–10
    clinical description, 202–3
    prevalence and impact, 203
    research, 210–11
sleepwalking, 207–8
social anxiety disorder (social phobia)
    case study, 124
    clinical description, 116
    prevalence, 117, 122
    treatment, 119, 121, 123
Social Cognition and Interaction Training (SCIT)
    tool, 88–9
social (pragmatic) communication disorder, 65
social phobia *see* social anxiety disorder

social workers, 7, 8
socio-demographic characteristics (Australia)
   ancestry, 21
   birth rates, 23
   birthplace data, 20–1
   dominant languages, 22
   family and household compositions, 24–6
   methodological implications, 17
   mortality rates, 24
   religious affiliations, 22–3, 279
   See also demographic factors; socio-economic
      characteristics
socio-demographic characteristics (New Zealand)
   birth rates, 42
   birthplace data, 39–44
   dominant languages, 41–4
   ethnic diversity measurement, 36–9
   family and household compositions, 43–4
   methodological implications, 45
   mortality rates, 43
   religious affiliations, 42, 282
   See also demographic factors; socio-economic
      characteristics
socio-economic characteristics
   Australia, 10, 15–16, 26–8, 279
   New Zealand, 35, 46–8, 281
somatic symptom and related disorders
   aetiology, 165
   case study, 167
   clinical description, 163–4
   management, 166
   risk factors, 165
somatic symptom disorder (somatisation
      disorder), 164–5
somatoform disorders *see* somatic symptom and
      related disorders
somatoform dissociation, 165
spatial distribution, 11–18, 20, 35–6
specific learning disorders, 66, 67
specific phobia, 116, 123
speech sound disorder, 65, 67
standardisation technique (data), 17, 45, 46
stereotypic movement disorder, 66
structural ageing (Australia), 16
stuttering (childhood-onset fluency disorder),
      65, 67
substance-induced disorders, 229
substance/medication-induced anxiety disorder,
      117

substance-related and addictive disorders
   in Australia, 230–3, 236
   case study, 235–6
   clinical description, 229–30
   in New Zealand, 233–5, 236
substance-use disorders (SUDs)
   assessment and treatment, 231, 233–4, 236,
      304–5
   case study, 235–6
   clinical description, 229
   comorbidity with, 233
   prevalence and associated risks, 230–1, 233
suicidal behaviours
   in Australian Indigenous population, 95
   in bipolar disorders, 106
   case study, 297–8
   causes and risk factors, 292–3
   depression and, 95, 98–9
   in obsessive compulsive disorder, 135
   presentation, 290
   prevalence and impact, 290–2
   reduction, 293–5
   research, 298
   risk assessment, 295–6
   in schizophrenia, 84
   services addressing, 101
   stigmatisation of, 290, 298
   treatment and prevention, 296–7

The Black Dog Institute, 112
tic disorders, 66, 68
Torres Strait Islander population *see* Indigenous
      population (Australia)
Tourette's syndrome, 67
trauma (as aetiological factor), 160–1, 165
Trauma and Dissociation Unit (TDU) (Brisbane),
      158–9
trauma- and stressor-related disorders (TSRD)
   in Australia, 144–7
   clinical description, 143
   in New Zealand, 148–9
trauma-focused psychological therapy, 145–6
treatment, psychological *see* psychological
      treatment
trichotillomania (hair pulling), 130, 133

unspecified communication disorder, 65
unspecified dissociative disorder (USDD),
      156

unspecified feeding or eating disorders (USFED), 176
urbanisation, 15, 35
urotherapy, 191

vascular dementia, 250–1
See also neurocognitive disorders (NCDs)

violence, 85–6
See also adult abuse; child abuse
vocational rehabilitation, 81
voice disorders, 67

written expression, impairment in, 66